"In Jesus' Name"
The History and Beliefs of Oneness Pentecostals

Journal of Pentecostal Theology
Supplement Series

31

Editors

John Christopher Thomas
Rickie Moore
Steven J. Land

ISSN 0966 7393

Deo Publishing

"In Jesus' Name"

The History and Beliefs of Oneness Pentecostals

David Reed

deo
PUBLISHING

BLANDFORD FORUM

In memory of my parents
Dow and *Bessie*
who led me to Jesus

and to

Carlynn my dear wife
and our sons
Kirkland and *Christopher*
with whom I have shared the journey

––––––––––––––

Journal of Pentecostal Theology Supplement Series, 31
ISSN 0966 7393

Published by Deo Publishing
P.O. Box 6284, Blandford Forum, Dorset DT11 1AQ, UK

The Odyssea Greek font used in the publication of this work is available from Linguist's Software, Inc., www.linguistsoftware.com, PO Box 580, Edmonds, WA 98020-0580 USA, tel. (425) 775-1130.

British Library Cataloguing-in-Publication data
A catalogue record for this book is available from the British Library

ISBN 978-1-905679-01-0

Contents

Preface..ix

Chapter 1
Introduction..1

PART I: THE LEGACY IN ONENESS PENTECOSTALISM

Chapter 2
A Pietist Legacy – Experiential Faith.....................................9
    1.   The Hermeneutic of Heart Religion...............................10
    2.   The Legacy of Heart Religion 14
    3.   The Contours of Heart Religion 19
    4.   Jesus-centrism and Evangelical Faith 32
    5.   Jesus-centrism and Christology 36
    6.   Summary..43

Chapter 3
An Evangelical Legacy – Theology of the Name...................44
    1.   The Revelation of God and the Name............................45
    2.   God and the Trinity..49
    3.   The Name and Person of Jesus..54
    4.   The Name and Work of Jesus..59
    5.   The Name and the Christian..61
    6.   Summary..68

EXCURSUS: The Name of God – Finding a Lost Theme?...69
    1.   A Lost Theme in a Jewish Metaphor? 69
    2.   A 19th-Century Restoration? 70
    3.   Summary..73

PART II: THE BIRTH OF ONENESS PENTECOSTALISM

Chapter 4
Pentecostal Polemics 77
1. Two Birthplaces: 1901 and 1906 79
2. Revival Wanes and Schism Is Born – The Finished Work of Calvary 83
3. Summary 105

Chapter 5
Old Themes for New Times 108
1. A Second Crisis Looms 109
2. A Theological Paradigm 111
3. The Apostolic Gospel 113
4. The Full Gospel 120
5. The Simple Gospel 128
6. Summary 135

Chapter 6
Revelation of the Name 136
1. Encounter – April 1913 136
2. Incubation and Birth – 1913-1914 141
3. The Revival Spreads – 1914-1915 144
4. Summary 146

Chapter 7
Controversy and Rejection 147
1. Trinitarian Defense by E.N. Bell – Spring 1915 147
2. Re-baptism of E.N. Bell – Summer 1915 150
3. The Truth according to Bell 151
4. Bell's Defense of His Rebaptism 155
5. Experiment in Liberality – Third General Council 158
6. Division on Doctrine – Fourth General Council 161
7. Summary 165

Chapter 8
From Issue to Doctrine – Revelation of God and the Name 167
1. Architects of the Doctrine 167
2. The "Revelation" 169
3. The Plan 174
4. The Oneness of God 176

5. Summary 183

Chapter 9
From Issue to Doctrine – One Lord and One Baptism 184
    1. One Lord Jesus Christ 184
    2. One Baptism 188
    3. Summary 205

Chapter 10
From Issue to Organization 207
    1. Organizational Beginnings 207
    2. The Issue of Race 211
    3. Segregation and Re-Organization 214
    4. Attempts to Re-Unite and Further Fragmentation 215
    5. Formation of United Pentecostal Church 218
    6. Assessment 221

PART III: THEOLOGY OF ONENESS PENTECOSTALISM

Chapter 11
Theology of the Name 227
    1. Lenses and Labels 228
    2. Constructing the Paradigm 233
    3. Contextualizing the Paradigm 235
    4. Summary 244

Chapter 12
One God and One Name 246
    1. The Name of God 246
    2. The Monarchy of God 252
    3. God as Three-in-One 256
    4. Classification of the Oneness View of God 265
    5. Summary 272

Chapter 13
The Name and Christology 274
    1. The Name of God in Jesus 274
    2. The Person of Christ 279
    3. Classification of Oneness Christology 303
    4. Summary 306

Chapter 14
The Name and the Christian Life 308
    1.   The Name in Salvation 308
    2.   The Name in Baptism 309
    3.   The Name in the Church 326
    4.   The Name in Ministry 331
    5.   Summary 335

Chapter 15
Whose Heresy? Whose Orthodoxy? 338
    1.   Why Take Oneness Pentecostalism Seriously? 339
    2.   Whose Heresy? 341
    3.   A Theological Method 345
    4.   The Method Applied 349
    5.   Summary 360

Chapter 16
Conclusion 361

Bibliography 364

Index of Names and Subjects 384
Index of Biblical References 392

Preface

My earliest experience of church was located on the front "bench" in Full Gospel Assembly, a small mission in rural New Brunswick, Canada. Occupying the converted living room of my aunt's former home, this small gathering was born during the first wave of the Pentecostal Revival in the early 1920s along the Saint John River Valley. One of my most vivid memories – and probably my first reading experience – was staring at the large wall poster behind the pulpit with the words of Acts 2:38 emblazoned on it: "Repent, and be baptized every one of you in the name of Jesus Christ for the remission of sins, and ye shall receive the gift of the Holy Ghost" (KJV).

For many years this was the only kind of Pentecostalism I knew. But as a teenager my curiosity was piqued. I recall my pastor, Earl Jacques (one of the first convert-preachers this Revival produced), reminisce about the "precious truth of Jesus' name" brought to our area by evangelist John Dearing. I remember asking my mother where "we Pentecostals" came from – she murmured something about a revival in Los Angeles. A few years later I had the privilege of personally meeting Howard A. Goss, one of the very earliest Pentecostal pioneers. I listened with immense curiosity as he recounted the events of the early days of the Revival, but I could not have imagined that within a decade I would be studying the history he had lived.

That moment of transition occurred for me at Harvard University where I was introduced to then Pentecostal doctoral student, Russell Spittler. Far more aware than I that scholarship on the Pentecostal movement was about to explode on the international scene, he urged me to consider the Oneness movement for my doctoral research. The catalyst came during my doctoral studies when another emerging Pentecostal scholar, Vinson Synan, contacted me to read a paper at the third annual meeting of the Society for Pentecostal Studies in 1973. I am grateful for the counsel and opportunity provided me by these two leaders of a new generation of Pentecostal pioneers. I am indebted also to my mentors at Boston University who patiently guided me to the completion of my thesis, especially the late J. Robert Nelson (1920-

2004) whose theological conviction of the centrality of Christ as norm and method contributed much to my own thinking, and E. Kent Brown who introduced me to the Methodist roots of Pentecostalism.

More than thirty years have passed since this study began. During the period of my graduate studies there were details of the early Pentecostal movement I did not know, and primary material yet to be unearthed. My attention was then redirected for more than a decade into pastoral ministry. Present opportunities in an academic institution have afforded me with both opportunity and time to complete a revision and expansion of the original work.

Institutions and individuals from the beginning until now have been generous in providing resources, counsel and hospitality. I am grateful for those persons (some now deceased) during my initial research who assisted me in so many ways by taking time for interviews, making archives available, and welcoming a researching sojourner: Arthur Clanton, Robert Cunningham, Morris Golder, W.E. Kidson, Gordon Magee, William Menzies, S.G. Norris, L.R. Ooton, Juanita Raudzsus, Kenneth Reeves, William G. Rowe, Robert Sabin, Philip Stairs, Ken Taylor, Nathaniel Urshan, Smallwood E. Williams, the leadership of St. Paul's Episcopal Church, Huntington, CT, that granted me time to write, and Collins Dawson who offered seclusion in North Carolina to complete my dissertation.

Scholarly friends have provided resources, insight and encouragement: David Bundy, Donald Dayton, Ralph Del Colle, William Faupel, Kenneth Gill, Bernie Gillespie, Harold Hunter, Charles Jones, James W. Jones, Manuel Gaxiola-Gaxiola, Roswith Gerloff, Jeffrey Gill, Geir Lie, Frank Macchia, Patricia Pickard, Mark Roberts, the late James Tinney, Grant Wacker, and Amos Yong.

I am grateful for the invitations afforded me over the years to reflect further on Oneness Pentecostalism, occasions that are woven into this study: the First Occasional Symposium on Oneness Pentecostalism at Harvard Divinity School in 1984, the 1985 Conference on The Nature of God in the American Religious Tradition, the Mexican *Iglesia Apostólica de la Fe en Cristo Jesús* whose ministers listened to my lectures on Oneness Pentecostalism in 1986, the Theology Track of the 1995 NARSC Congress on the Holy Spirit and World Evangelization in Orlando, and Asia Pacific Theological Seminary whose dean, Wonsuk Ma, graciously invited me to deliver the 2002 Occasional Pentecostal Lecture Series.

The following churches, denominational headquarters, and libraries made their material available to me: Apostolic Bible Institute, Apostolic World Christian Fellowship, Assemblies of God Archives, Duke University, Evangel College, Nyack College, Oral Roberts University,

Pentecostal Assemblies of Canada Archives, Pentecostal Assemblies of the World Archives, Princeton Seminary, United Pentecostal Church Archives. My special thanks to Wycliffe College and its Board of Trustees for the support and sabbatical time needed to complete this project.

I am pleased that this volume is finding its place in the *Journal of Pentecostal Theology Supplement* Series. The JPTS is a recent and excellent contribution to the field of Pentecostal scholarship. I am grateful to Chris Thomas for encouraging me in the completion of the project, and his keen editorial eye in preparing it for publication. I thank Mark Bowald for his diligence and patience in attending to the tedious details of manuscript editing.

I reserve my deepest gratitude for my family that has had to endure my occasional long absences and chronic diverted attention; most especially my wife, Carlynn, whose support, encouragement and sacrifice for this study can only be accounted for by love that never gives up.

1

Introduction

Robert E. McAlister mounted a makeshift platform to deliver a baptismal sermon at the 1913 "worldwide" Pentecostal camp meeting on the outskirts of Los Angeles. The turning point in the message came when the preacher made what appeared to some as a surprising exegetical move: an effort to explain why the Apostles used some variation of "Lord Jesus Christ" in the baptisms recorded in the Acts of the Apostles when the Lord's command in Matthew 28:19 was a clear commission to baptize in the name of the Trinity.

This momentary flourish of exegetical creativity earned McAlister a swift but fleeting gasp from the crowd, as it echoed the teaching of a local Dr. Sykes who was regarded by many as a heretic.

A second more memorable ripple occurred during the early hours of the following morning when a relatively unknown man, John G. Schaepe, ran through the camp proclaiming that he had received a "revelation" of baptism in the name of Jesus Christ. Short on details, the burst of insight was clearly related to McAlister's baptismal sermon. This event survives as an important part of the narrative of origins for Oneness Pentecostals, largely due to Schaepe's appeal to revelation, but it plays no significant role in the formation of Oneness theology.[1] The third ripple did not occur until a year later, when Frank Ewart, McAlister's friend and fellow evangelist who also heard the sermon, launched a new movement from a tent and a baptismal tank in the town of Belvedere on April 15, 1914.

This surprising turn of events precipitated a second schism and launched the third stream of the modern Pentecostal movement. The

---

[1] Brumback, *Suddenly from Heaven*, p. 191; Arthur L. Clanton, *United We Stand – A History of Oneness Organizations* (St. Louis, MO: Pentecostal Publishing House, 1970), p. 15; Fred J. Foster, *"Think It Not Strange" – A History of the Oneness Movement* (St. Louis, MO: Pentecostal Publishing House, 1965), p. 52.

initial rhetoric burned with accusations of heresy, dissent, and betrayal. But as decades passed and organizational distance turned old partners into strangers, feelings of animosity were transmuted into questions of curiosity: where did such a puzzling heterodox teaching come from? A crisis over a fourth-century heresy and water baptism seemed worlds removed from the intense preoccupation of a Revival invested in the eschatological outpouring of the Holy Spirit.

And for the leaders of the schismatic movement, an appeal to special revelation only intensified the sense of discontinuity with anything historical.

For the first wave of Pentecostal scholars who were emerging in mid-century, however, the contours of a Pentecostal phenomenon began to take shape. The reasoned conclusion was that the "New Issue" was a thoroughly Pentecostal moment in the early Revival, though slightly gone off the rails.[2] It was at this point that I began my own research. Though it later became clear that William Durham's ministry provided the immediate backdrop – especially his teaching on the Finished Work of Calvary and the centrality of Acts 2:38 as its paradigm in practice – I realized that the roots lay far deeper in history.

I made two initial observations. One is that Ewart and others were drawing much of their new teaching on the name of Jesus from pre- and non-Pentecostal evangelical sources.[3] This meant that, while the New Issue was well within the Pentecostal trajectory, there were identifiable influences from the wider evangelical tradition. Second, I noted in the New Issue writings, as well as from personal experience, that piety and theology mutually invigorate each other, a symbiotic dance of doctrine and doxology. This led me to take the long route home by way of Pietism and its various expressions in the late 19th century Wesleyan and Keswick Holiness movements. The Jesus-centric devotion that included praise to the name of Jesus became a spiritual cradle with theological *leitmotifs* that provided raw material for the later New Issue doctrine. This rather extended prologue to One-

---

[2] This conclusion appears to have become a consensus among such scholars as William Menzies, Russell Spittler and Vinson Synan, who shared these thoughts with me as I was beginning my research in 1973.

[3] Ewart acknowledged the influence of William Phillips Hall on his understanding of the name of God, and reports that he personally corresponded with him. Though Ewart cites from a later edition, Hall's first publication of his study was in 1913; see William Phillips Hall, *What is "The Name"? Or "The Mystery of God" Revealed* (Greenwich, CT: By the Author, 1913).

ness Pentecostalism comprises Part I of the study. The works of Donald Dayton and William Faupel have been helpful at various stages of my own study in enlarging my understanding of the theological relationship between the Holiness movement and Pentecostal beginnings.[4]

Part II traces the immediate Pentecostal context within which the New Issue emerged, attending primarily to the various theological themes that are woven into the fabric of the early movement. The key figure in this stage is William Durham, whose Finished Work ideas held a particularly strong appeal for four other early pioneers who were closely following his lead – Frank Ewart, Garfield T. Haywood, R.E. McAlister, and Franklin Small. All except McAlister became primary architects of the New Issue doctrine, with Andrew Urshan contributing his considerable influence after departing the Assemblies of God in 1919. Since this study focuses primarily on the doctrinal development of the Oneness movement, I give little attention to its organizational history. My limited task is to trace the bodily expression of the movement through the early years to a period of institutional stability in mid-century.

In Part III I review and analyze the three doctrines that constitute foundational Oneness theology: the oneness of God, the centrality of Christ and name of Jesus, and the paradigmatic praxis of Acts 2:38. The study is limited to a critical reflection on the various claims made in Oneness theology rather than an exhaustive exegetical and theological analysis. In the conclusion, I assess the movement's core teaching in light of the church's historic doctrines of God and Christ, as well as the familiar charge that Oneness Pentecostalism is a heresy at best, and a cult at worst.

This study is limited in scope by two important factors. First, it concentrates on the history and development of Oneness Pentecostalism in North America. The present growth of the movement in the Global South means that a study of the Oneness movement in another part of the world will likely reveal a portrait quite different in important details from the one described here. The second factor is the lack of in-depth analysis of the African-American presence in the movement, a constituency that comprises nearly half of all Oneness Pente-

---

[4] Note especially Donald Dayton, *Theological Roots of Pentecostalism* (Grand Rapids, MI: Zondervan, 1987); William D. Faupel, *The Everlasting Gospel: The Significance of Eschatology in the Development of Pentecostal Thought* (Sheffield: Sheffield Academic Press, 1996; repr. Blandford: Deo, 2007).

costals in the United States. On the face of it, Haywood's core doctrinal beliefs are consistent with influences in the wider movement,
including William Durham's Finished Work teaching. But I am convinced that in theological vision and ministry, Haywood exemplifies a
holistic breadth of perspective and spirit that is likely formed and informed by his black heritage. One has only to be reminded of his leadership of an interracial congregation and the fight to build racial unity
in the first Oneness organization, the Pentecostal Assemblies of the
World.

Finally, a number of recent publications examine various sub-
themes in the Oneness movement and theology. One study is
Roswith Gerloff's extensive treatment of black Oneness churches in
Britain. In it she maps out common African elements that resonate
closely with Oneness themes and spirituality, such as the immediacy of
spiritual experience, theological narrativity, empowerment through the
Spirit, and healing. She emphasizes the considerable influence of the
black experience on the overall Oneness movement, and the cultural
reappropriation of commonly held Oneness doctrines in significantly
different ways within the black community.[5] Another contextual study
is Kenneth Gill's irenic treatment of the indigenous Mexican Oneness
denomination, *Iglesia Apostólica de la Fe en Christo Jesús.*[6] Applying a
missiological paradigm, Gill exposes the inability of western theologians to grasp the significance of concepts and practices that operate
within a different religio-cultural setting – specifically, a Mexican
Oneness Pentecostal denomination – and provides canons of interpretation to assist in the process of deeper understanding.

Three studies more directly challenge the teachings of the United
Pentecostal Church International. The first major study of Oneness
theology is a 1956 doctoral dissertation. In it James D. Rider examines
and judges Oneness teaching to be defective in light of the orthodox
doctrines of the Trinity and Christ, and weak in its doctrine of grace
with the emphasis that many of its proponents place upon obedience.[7]

---

[5] Roswith I.H. Gerloff, *A Plea for British Black Theologies: The Black Church Movement in Britain in Its Transatlantic Cultural and Theological Interaction with Special Reference to the
Pentecostal Oneness (Apostolic) and Sabbatarian Movements* (New York: Peter Lang, 1992).

[6] Kenneth D. Gill, *Toward a Contextualized Theology for the Third World: The Emergence and Development of Jesus' Name Pentecostalism in Mexico,* Studies in the Intercultural
History of Christianity 90 (New York: Peter Lang, 1994).

[7] James Donald Rider, "The Theology of the 'Jesus Only' Movement" (Th.D.
diss., Dallas Theological Seminary, 1956).

The second and more recent study is a theological critique by Gregory Boyd of the Oneness doctrine of God, attempting to show how Oneness theology misunderstands the doctrine of the Trinity and makes misguided claims for itself to apostolic doctrine. The strength of this study is its clarification of the differences between a Oneness view of God and the classical doctrine of the Trinity. It is largely analytical, however, and gives little attention to historical and contextual detail.[8] The third project is a major study by Thomas Fudge on the two doctrines of salvation (hence, two interpretations of Acts 2:38) that have coexisted from the early years, but which produced a struggle for ascendancy by one of those views in the UPCI.[9] Fudge's attention to oral sources in retrieving a fading tradition is an important contribution.

Finally, two brief studies have been published from a historical perspective. One is a sympathetic treatment by Douglas Jacobsen of the teachings of Haywood and Andrew Urshan in a volume on the theologies of early Pentecostal leaders. Jacobsen is the first scholar to examine the overall writings of these pioneers with an eye to their broader theological interests.[10] The second is an essay by David Bundy on the urban character of Haywood's life and ministry; especially his courage in overstepping the restrictive "holiness" boundaries of fellow Pentecostals and the racial boundaries of the Klan dominated Indiana of his time.[11]

---

[8] Gregory Boyd, *Oneness Pentecostalism and the Trinity* (Grand Rapids, MI: Baker Book House, 1992. Boyd's study, it seems to me, does not take sufficient account of either the historical context or the Oneness genre as popular theology. The result is unfortunately a more polemical rendering than need be, and example of an evangelical hermeneutic for assessing doctrine that is sometimes more interested in the words alone than in exploring their various historical and cultural meanings.

[9] Thomas A. Fudge, *Christianity without the Cross: A History of Salvation in Oneness Pentecostalism* (Parkland, FL: Universal Publishers, 2003).

[10] Douglas Jacobsen, *Thinking in the Spirit: Theologies of the Early Pentecostal Movement* (Indianapolis: Indiana University Press, 2003). Jacobsen describes Haywood and Urshan as "speculative theologian" and "spiritual theologian" respectively.

[11] David Bundy, "G.T. Haywood: Religion for Urban Realities," in James R. Goff, Jr. & Grant Wacker, eds., *Portraits of a Generation: Early Pentecostal Leaders* (Fayetteville, AR: The University of Arkansas Press, 2002), pp. 237-53. See also Bundy's essay on the challenges of conducting research globally on the Oneness movement, "Documenting 'Oneness' Pentecostalism: A Case Study in the Ethical Dilemmas Posed by the Creation of Documentation," *Summary of Proceedings – Fifty-Third Annual Conference of the American Theological Library Association, June 9-12, 1999*, ed. Margaret Tacke Collins (Evanston, IL: American Theological Library Association, 1999), pp. 155-75.

The common thread throughout this study is the Name. It appears in strands of evangelical literature as a biblical defense of the deity of Christ. It is the revelation of the Name that drives New Issue advocates to re-baptize other Pentecostals and get themselves driven out of churches. It is the cohering theme that holds together the foundational doctrines of God, Christ and Soteriology. At least, this is what I will argue here.

Though generally disfellowshipped by Trinitarian Pentecostals, except when calculating numerical strength, it can be argued that this third stream within the Pentecostal family represents the most indigenous theology – or what Charles E. Jones calls its "nonderivative character" – the modern Pentecostal movement produced.[12] Jacobsen makes a more specific claim for the unique contribution of Oneness theology to the early Pentecostal movement:

> The Oneness theologies of Urshan and Haywood gave the early pentecostal movement a new breadth and depth of vision…. In a certain sense, the Oneness theologies of Haywood and Urshan were also more distinctively pentecostal than anything that preceded them; at the very least, they were less dependent on previous forms of Christian theology.[13]

As I began this study asking where Oneness Pentecostals came from, at the end I must ask where they are going. Unlike radical separatist sects, they have an evangelical and Pentecostal legacy that continues to elicit engagement with other Christians. Such ecumenical intersections are the fragile threads of respect that, if nurtured, grow strong bonds of fellowship.

[12] Cited in Gerloff, *Plea for British Black Theologies*, part 1, p. 93.
[13] Jacobsen, *Thinking in the Spirit*, p. 259.

Part I

The Legacy in Oneness Pentecostalism

2

A Pietist Legacy – Experiential Faith

> One thing you lack and with it everything,
> the inward knowledge of Christ.[1]

The appearance of movements and sects upon the religious scene frequently leaves the observer speechless at the apparent newness of their
teaching.[2] Their distinctiveness, however, is seldom in the creation of a
religious system *ex nihilo* but in the innovative way through which
ideological and cultural factors present in the context coalesce. As British sociologist Bryan Wilson notes, a sect is "a unique combination of
variations, few of which in themselves are wholly distinctive of that
sect alone."[3]

Such a description belongs to Oneness Pentecostalism. Unlike traditions that chart their lineage through institutions, movements or
leaders, the Oneness movement has given us little *direct* theological
ancestry for its distinctive doctrines. Rather, it claims to be the bearer

---

[1] These words appear in a cemetery in Jyväskylä, Finland, on the stone monument
memorializing the words of a local blacksmith, Jaeko Hogman, in 1799 to Paavo
Ruotsalainen, who became the father of the Pietist movement in that country. See C.
John Weborg, "Pietism: Theology in Service of Living toward God," Donald W.
Dayton & Robert K. Johnston, eds., *The Variety of American Evangelicalism* (Downers
Grove, IL: InterVarsity Press, 1991), p. 179.

[2] The approach taken in this study is that Oneness Pentecostalism is a sectarian
movement within the wider parameters of the Church rather than a cult, as popular
anti-cult groups and writers contend. It will be argued that theologically it is a heterodox rather than a heretical movement. Sociologically it follows the conceptual
framework of Rodney Stark and William Sims Bainbridge in, "Of Churches, Sects,
and Cults: Preliminary Concepts for a Theory of Religious Movements," *Journal for the
Scientific Study of Religion* 18/2 (1979): 117-131. See also Irving Hexham & Karla
Poewe, *New Religions as Global Cultures: Making the Human Sacred* (Boulder, CO:
Westview, 1997), pp. 27-40.

[3] Bryan R. Wilson, *Sects and Society, A Sociological Study of the Elim Tabernacle, Christian Science, and Christadelphianism* (Berkeley, CA: University of California Press, 1961),
p. 7.

of a latter-day revelation of apostolic truth and practice hitherto lost in
the acculturation of institutional Christianity. Like most Pentecostals
and other popular leaders of their day, the architects of the new teaching offered few clues to the human sources of inspiration for their
ideas. To discover these connections, attention must be directed to the
cultural, religious and theological forces that pressed upon them in the
formation of their teaching.

As part of the early Pentecostal Revival, the immediate roots of
Oneness Pentecostalism lay in the Holiness and Keswick Higher
Christian Life movements of the late-19th century. But both Pentecostalism and the Holiness movement are products of the formative
influences of John Wesley and the Pietistic tradition before him. The
latter generated both theological ideas and practices that were embraced, though modified, by their heirs.

1. The Hermeneutic of Heart Religion

Pietism was one expression of a larger cultural movement of "heart"
religion that spanned the 17th and 18th centuries.[4] It emerged first in
17th-century German Lutheranism as a "protest of living faith against a
lifeless and unbending orthodoxy."[5] Its primary burden, like that of the
English Puritans, was to continue the reformation of the Church. As a
religiously optimistic movement – or what the Pietist scholar, F.
Ernest Stoeffler, calls a form of "religious idealism"[6] – Pietism in turn
spawned much of the Protestant perfectionist and Holiness movements
of later generations.

Pietism began as a reaction to increasing formalism within the
church and rationalism without, all of which had created a stifling
environment of spiritual dearth. Dissatisfied with faith that appeared to
be mere intellectual assent to the evangelical doctrines of the church,

---

[4] Dale Brown points out that this larger movement included Roman Catholics,
Protestants, mystics, Puritans and Jansenists; the influence of Spanish Quietism, a form
of mysticism, can be traced in Wesley and the Holiness movement of the late 19th
century; see Brown, "The Wesleyan Revival from a Pietist Perspective," *Wesleyan
Theological Journal* 24/1 (Spring 1989): 6-16.

[5] Gerald R. Cragg, *The Church and the Age of Reason, 1648-1789* (Pelican History of
the Church, 4; Baltimore, MD: Penguin, 1960), p. 100.

[6] F. Ernest Stoeffler, *The Rise of Evangelical Pietism* (Studies in the History of Religions 9; Leiden: E.J. Brill, 1965), p. 16.

these second generation reformers asserted that "there can be no faith apart from an experience of the heart."[7]

By "heart" Pietists meant *experiential* faith. Recent scholarship has done much to correct the long-standing bias that Pietism represented passive inwardness in religion.[8] Scholars such as Stoeffler and Dale Brown have demonstrated that experiential faith, not subjective inwardness, was at the heart of Pietism.[9] Fundamentally it called for a personal and subjective appropriation of the objective events of the Gospel that touched both affections and moral living; in other words, a *theologia practicia*.[10] For example, the written word of God is believed but must be "inwardly appropriated through the Spirit in the fellowship of the Church."[11] Or, in Stoeffler's words, Pietism was a form of "*praxis pietatis*."[12]

Drawing upon Luther's personal *pro me*, Pietists interpreted this spiritual experience in terms of personal *regeneration*.[13] Without nullifying the necessity for the external action of justification, they were convinced of the need to give a personal account of that event. Great

---

[7] Donald G. Bloesch, *The Evangelical Renaissance* (Grand Rapids, MI: Eerdmans, 1973), p. 106.

[8] This bias has persisted primarily through the influence of the major 19th century work by Albrecht Ritschl, *Geschichte des Pietismus*, 3 vols. (Bonn: A. Marcus, 1880-86). Kenneth Collins comments that Ritschl "maintained that Pietism was not, after all, a progressive movement; ... rather, it was a backward movement in more than one respect," in "John Wesley's Critical Appropriation of Early German Pietism," *Wesleyan Theological Journal* 27/1 & 2 (Spring-Fall 1997): 57. See also C. John Weborg, "Pietism: Theology in Service of Living toward God," pp. 161-83. For a favorable examination of the social conscience and activism in 19th-century American Revivalism, see Timothy Smith, *Revivalism and Social Reform in Mid-Nineteenth-Century America* (New York: Abingdon, 1957), and Donald W. Dayton, *Discovering an Evangelical Heritage* (New York: Harper & Row, 1976).

[9] See Dale Brown, *Understanding Pietism* (Grand Rapids, MI: Eerdmans, 1978). David Bundy has provided an excellent review of Pietism and its influence on Pentecostalism in "European Pietist Roots of Pentecostalism," *Dictionary of Pentecostal and Charismatic Movements*, eds. Stanley M. Burgess and Gary McGee (Grand Rapids, MI: Zondervan, 1988), pp. 279-81. The important distinction is that experiential faith does not instinctively lead to inwardness and passivity but frequently motivates the believer to action, often in a radical form.

[10] Weborg, "Pietism," p. 163.

[11] Stoeffler, *Evangelical Pietism*, p. 10.

[12] *Ibid.*, p. 9.

[13] Dale Brown points out that one of the favorite passages of Pietists to counter the charge of works righteousness by their orthodox opponents was "Luther's preface to his commentary on Romans, in which he defined faith as a 'living, creative, active, powerful thing,'" in "The Wesleyan Revival from a Pietistic Perspective," *Wesleyan Theological Journal* 24 (1989): 9.

emphasis, therefore, was placed upon the "personally meaningful relationship of the individual to God."[14] The result was the distinctively
Pietistic doctrine of the "new birth," which has continued to be the
hallmark of evangelical religion.[15] Over the span of two centuries one
can trace within Pietism the tension between the Reformers' doctrine
of external justification and the emphasis on personal conversion: a
shift from justification being "one element in the conversion process
that then became the entire *ordo salutis.*"[16]

The first two generations of Pietists in Germany were guided by the
leadership of Philip Jacob Spener (1635-1705; considered the founder
of Halle Pietism), August Hermann Francke (1663-1727), and later,
Nicholaus Ludwig Zinzendorf (1700-1760). Although the 19th-
century Pietists developed new directions in the areas of Eschatology
and "kingdom spirituality," the existential emphasis on repentance and
conversion continued.[17]

In Pietism all theology was fundamentally practical theology, concerned to nurture the presence of God in every aspect of the believer's
life. For Spener, only those doctrines were given prominence that
"played a direct part in personal religious experience." He viewed all
the external aspects of the faith such as the Scriptures, doctrine, and
sacraments, as inadequate until they became a personal reality in the
soul. It was not enough to hear the Word of God preached. One must
"let it penetrate inwardly into your heart and allow the heavenly food
to be digested there." Although Spener encouraged careful attention
to sermons, he found this method insufficient to meet the needs of the
individual. For this reason he pressed for diligent personal Bible reading and small group Bible discussion.[18]

Spener also clashed with the Lutheran orthodoxy of his day in the
priority he gave to moral living over correct doctrine. For him the
Christian life "consists rather of practice." Spener believed that Chris-

---

[14] Stoeffler, *Evangelical Pietism*, p. 13.

[15] We shall see later that this spiritual "experience" is always an experience of something. In early Pietism it was primarily the experience of conversion or new birth. In a
later generation it was extended to the experience of sanctification or "perfection". By
the end of the 19th century, it was described as an experience of "power". It is in this
last period that the spiritual power attending the "Name of Jesus" appears.

[16] Frank Macchia, *Spirituality and Social Liberation: The Message of the Blumhardts in the
Light of Wuerttemberg Pietism* (Metuchen, NJ: Scarecrow, 1993), p. 30.

[17] *Ibid.* Macchia traces these continuities and new directions, especially in the period directly preceding the emergence of Johann and Christoph Blumhardt.

[18] Phillip Jakob Spener, *Pia Desideria*, trans. and ed. by Theodore G. Tappert (Philadelphia: Fortress, 1964), pp. 26, 66, 87-89.

tian ethical action is the direct fruit of an awakening of "a fervent love among our Christians, first toward one another and then toward all men." All external means must be put to the service of the inner person. It is the heart that must be receptive "so that we may hear the Holy Spirit speak there, that is, with vibrant emotion and comfort feel the sealing of the Spirit and the power of the Word."[19] From the inward work of the Spirit issues the fruit of righteous living.

August Francke likewise laid great stress upon the personal and subjective benefits of salvation in the life of the individual believer. While holding firmly to the necessity of the objective work of Christ, he placed increasing emphasis upon "what God does now for a sinner in need." The benefits of Christ were extended to a practical piety marked by "devotional use of Scripture and the need for daily prayer."[20] Francke's own personal conversion became the inspiration for his theological direction. He later recorded that experience:

> Even as one turns his hand, so all my doubts were gone. In my heart I was assured of the grace of God in Jesus Christ.... All the sadness and restlessness of heart was taken away at once. On the other hand, I was suddenly overwhelmed by a flood of joy, so that audibly I praised and magnified God, who had manifested such great grace to me.[21]

In this brief narrative one can discern a shift in the individual's assurance of divine acceptance from the external promises of God and the sacramental signs of grace to the inner experience of joy and peace.

Much of this experiential faith was bound up with the Pietist doctrine of the new birth, though there was a marked difference in its expression between Spener and later Pietists. Spener considered the new birth an appropriate existentializing of the Reformers' focus on the personal nature of faith. But a later development recast that experience in the form of a protracted and agonizing struggle leading up to repentance.[22]

---

[19] *Ibid.*, pp. 95, 96, 117.

[20] Stoeffler, *German Pietism during the Eighteenth Century* (Leiden: E.J. Brill, 1973), p. 10.

[21] Cited in *ibid.*, p. 12.

[22] See Kenneth Collins, "John Wesley's Critical Appropriation," p. 69. Collins points out that Brown and Stoeffler differ on the origin of the protracted struggle that leads to the new birth: Brown credits Francke and his disciples, while Stoeffler locates it in Halle Pietism. Weborg cautions of the danger of reading Pietism through the lens of 19th-century Revivalism. Unlike the latter which tended to emphasize the crisis moment of conversion ("When were you saved?") and the human initiative in producing a revival, Pietism focused more on spiritual process and growth ("Are you

The next generation of heart religion was shaped by the ministry of Nicholaus Ludwig Count von Zinzendorf, a German layman in the first half of the 18th century. His preoccupation with piety and conversion was intense. His christocentric piety was focused almost exclusively on the suffering and bleeding Savior. Often criticized for excessive emotion and sentimentality in his religious fervor, his contribution is noteworthy for the way in which he employed romantic and sensual imagery to describe the love relationship between the believer and Christ. Love is not simply right action toward God and neighbor. This Zinzendorf called the "dry way which will in the end make the Saviour into a Confucius."[23]

Rather, to know Christ is to love him in a deeply intimate way: "We begin to know Him only when we have loved Him very tenderly." This love of Christ was depicted in erotic language: "May He kiss you with the kiss of His mouth; may He let you experience His grace; may He let you share in His bloody atonement." When one experiences the love of Christ, Zinzendorf believed that the change would be similar to that of one having fallen in love, "as a consort, as a playmate for the marriage-bed of the blessed Creator and eternal Husband of the human soul." This deeply intimate spiritual experience could also include tears and weeping: "My heart wept for joy when His nail prints, His wounds, His bloody side stood before my heart." When the Holy Spirit penetrates the inner person, "he melts the heart; then the eyes fill with tears, then the body and soul rejoice."[24]

The mission of German Pietism was to revitalize the spiritual and moral life of the church in its own day. Whatever its success or failure, this experiential faith did not die with the movement but guaranteed for itself a future in spiritual movements of another generation known by other names.

2. The Legacy of Heart Religion

Pietism spread into the English-speaking world influencing both Puritanism and the Wesleyan Revival. Indeed, the evangelical revivals of

---

living yet in Jesus?) and viewed any human action as a *response* to the inner working of the Spirit; see Weborg, "Pietism," pp. 178-79.

[23] Nicholaus Ludwig Count von Zinzendorf, *Nine Public Lectures on Important Subjects in Religion*, trans. and ed. George W. Forell (Iowa City, IA: University of Iowa Press, 1973), p. 50.

[24] *Ibid.*, pp. 48, 53, 64, 84, 86.

the eighteenth century became interwoven with Pietism that one could speak with justification of "a single evangelical revival."[25]

In the matter of experiential religion, the Puritan divines of the seventeenth century believed essentially the same as the Continental Pietists. For leaders like William Perkins (1558-1602), personal piety was directed toward the Divine Law in which "godliness" was expressed through practical rules for daily living.[26] For Richard Sibbes (1577-1635), God's law was now to be experienced as God's nature made available in Christ. The Pietistic ideal of inward assurance of salvation was crucial. Salvation cannot be merely reasoned; it must be experienced in the heart. Sibbes reflected the religious idealism of Pietism in the reliability he placed in inward desires to convey divine truth and reality. In *A Breathing after God* he wrote:

> Words and actions may be counterfeit, but the desires and affections cannot, because they are the immediate issues and productions of the soul; they are that that comes immediately from the soul, as fire cannot be counterfeit.[27]

Richard Baxter (1615-91) likewise gave priority to practical piety, emphasizing the twin Pietist pillars of conversion and Holiness of life. These themes were kept alive for generations through the popular writings of John Bunyan (1628-88). Stoeffler points out that his classic work, *The Pilgrim's Progress*, was "a major achievement of the Pietistic tradition." Like others, Bunyan had experienced a dramatic conversion that became for him the paradigm of the Christian life.[28]

John Wesley came under the influence of the Pietistic tradition through his contact with the Moravians, and in the eighteenth century carried its message throughout the English-speaking world. Its influence can be seen in the two-fold emphasis on conversion and Holiness of life or "perfection."[29] American Methodist scholar, Albert Outler, states that the Pietistic foundation for Wesley's whole theological system can be seen "in the notion of the believer's immediate awareness

---

[25] Claude Welch, *Protestant Thought in the 19th Century, 1799-1870* (New Haven, CT: Yale University Press, 1972), p. 27.

[26] Stoeffler, *Evangelical Pietism*, pp. 29, 58-68.

[27] Cited in *ibid.*, p. 83.

[28] *Ibid.*, pp. 91, 96.

[29] A.M. Allchin and H.A. Hodges, *A Rapture of Praise – Hymns of John and Charles Wesley* (London: Hodder & Stoughton, 1966), p. 11.

of the reality of God's gracious presence in the inmost self ('the heart')."[30]

Wesley's doctrine of the "assurance of salvation" or the inward "witness of the Spirit" echoes the Pietistic concern for heart religion. He shared with Pietists the skepticism toward a faith that had been reduced to doctrinal propositions. Such faith is a "speculative, rational thing, a cold, lifeless assent, a train of ideas in the head." Rather, a full response to the gospel calls for "a disposition of the heart." [31] It is "a divine evidence or conviction in my heart that God is reconciled to *me* through his Son."[32] This is "saving faith." Consequently, Wesley was determined to devote his energies to promote "vital practical religion; and by the grace of God to beget, preserve and increase the life of God in the souls of men."[33]

The immense hymnology that was produced by John and Charles Wesley reflects the influence of Pietism. Through his hymns, Charles showed that Jesus Christ "was never old, remote or distant to their writer."[34] For example,

> Safe in Thy arms / lay me down,
> Thy everlasting arms of love
>
> While Thou art intimately nigh,
> Who, who shall violate my rest?

The love of Jesus displayed on the cross likewise drew from Charles deep emotion:

> O let me kiss Thy bleeding feet
> And bathe and wash them with my tears.
>
> The closeness of Jesus could be expressed as gentleness with a child:
> Gentle Jesus, meek and mild,
> Look upon a little child.

Even hymns of strength and vigor bore the constant mark of that intensely personal relationship with God or Christ. To the unconverted, the appeal was intense and direct:

[30] Albert Outler, ed., *John Wesley* (New York: Oxford University Press, 1964), p. 209.

[31] Philip S. Watson, ed., *The Message of the Wesleys – A Reader of Instruction and Devotion* (New York: Macmillan, 1964), p. 135.

[32] Outler, *Wesley*, p. 189.

[33] Watson, *Message*, p. 29.

[34] J. Ernest Rattenbury, *The Evangelical Doctrines of Charles Wesley's Hymns* (London: Epworth, 1942), p. 155.

Why will you your Lord deny?
Why will you resolve to die?

But the appeal always carried with it the deep personal sense of God's universal love for humankind:

Amazing mystery of love!
While posting to eternal pain,
God saw His rebels from above,
And stoop'd into a mortal man. [35]

The spirit of Pietism, therefore, was carried on as much in the hymnody of the Wesleys as in their sermons and writings. [36]

The legacy of Pietism's "heart" religion continued on American soil through the impact of the Great Awakenings. Here in particular it blended with the distinctive North American culture. Individualism, independence, pragmatism, concern for the common person – all were characteristic of frontier America: "Baptists, Methodists and other popular denominations helped to infuse society in the American West with certain traits now regarded as typically Western, if not characteristically American." [37]

This grassroots culture, however, did not emerge immediately but resulted from a major cultural shift between the First and Second Great Awakenings. The First Awakening occurred during the colonial period in which the social institutions had been transplanted from Europe and were serving the colonies well. Under the leadership of a learned clergy such as Jonathan Edwards, the appeal was directed primarily to the conversion of persons within a somewhat stable communal environment. By the Second Awakening, however, there was an urgency to "Americanize" the social fabric of the new nation. The strategy was to build from the bottom up, creating new institutions at every level of society. The new Revivalists were populists who "sought to affect every aspect of political, social, and economic life.

---

[35] *Ibid.*, pp. 155, 156, 159, 195, 192.

[36] Attention to Wesley's experiential, or what he called "experimental," religion is not intended to ignore the differences with Pietism or the ways in which he drew upon the British empirical philosophical tradition to articulate the role of experience and reason in confirming the truth of Scripture. An excellent introduction to the roots and development of the "Wesleyan Quadrilateral" is provided in the *Wesleyan Theological Journal* 20/1 (Spring 1985), and Donald A.D. Thorsen, *The Wesleyan Quadrilateral: Scripture, Tradition, Reason and Experience as a Model of Evangelical Theology* (Grand Rapids, MI: Zondervan, 1990).

[37] T. Scott Miyakawa, *Protestants and Pioneers – Individualism and Conformity on the American Frontier* (Chicago: The University of Chicago Press, 1964), p. 5.

every aspect of political, social, and economic life. They spoke in the language of the laity, giving shape and voice to their hopes."[38]

The populism of the Revivalists suited well this new spirit of individualism and the pragmatic, non-speculative outlook on life and religion that came to characterize nineteenth-century frontier America. As William Warren Sweet observes, the American spirit of individualism was decisive in communicating effectively with the "common man."[39] In the new religious culture, the Pietist simplicity of faith and the impatience with intellectual speculation became intensified, and sometimes distorted. In fact, the individualism and biblicism that finally defined 20th-century Fundamentalism "came directly from the pietistic and revivalist heritage."[40]

Pietism's experiential faith is exemplified in Charles G. Finney (1792-1875), leading Revivalist and theologian who became identified with what was known as Oberlin Perfectionism.[41] Impatient with speculation apart from personal experience, he insisted upon the sequential priority of conversion as the means whereby one could come to understand with the mind the meaning of the gospel. In a sermon, "On Believing with the Heart," he emphasized that "the atonement is accepted by the heart unto salvation, before its philosophy is understood." To his credit he rejected "groundless credulity" as the basis for a sound faith, but he warned his students that "it never can be well to put your intellectual philosophy in the place of the simplicity of gospel faith."[42] Such error would surely lead to a loss of piety, even faith. Objective truth, in other words, was of little value unless it produced a transforming personal experience. H. Richard Niebuhr summed up

---

[38] Faupel, *Everlasting Gospel*, p. 52.

[39] William W. Sweet, *Revivalism in America: Its Origin, Growth and Decline* (New York: Scribner's, 1944), p. 25.

[40] George M. Marsden, *Fundamentalism and American Culture – The Shaping of Twentieth-Century Evangelicalism: 1870-1925* (New York: Oxford University Press, 1980), p. 7.

[41] For a summary of the influence of Finney on the Holiness movement, see Dayton, "Asa Mahan and the Development of American Holiness Theology," *Wesleyan Theological Journal* 9/1 (Spring 1974): 60-69; see also Melvin Dieter, *Holiness Revival*, pp. 18-20. Weborg's distinction between Pietism and Finney's Revival method is important to remember: the former was less interested in spiritual crisis moments than in the process of living more deeply in the life of Christ; "Pietism," p. 178.

[42] Charles G. Finney, *Sermons on the Way to Salvation* (Oberlin, OH: Edward J. Goodrich, 1891), pp. 323, 329.

this revivalist axiom well: "Gospel experience alone could convince of gospel truth."[43]

Experiential faith anticipates transformation of soul or society. Not surprisingly then, the idealism of the Pietistic vision cultivated in the revivalist culture a receptivity to perfectionist themes. Melvin Dieter states:

> [Pietism] symbolized religious emphases which favored experience over theology and the call to individual commitment to a Christian life of witness and charity. It was not enough to be a "formal" Christian. Individuals had to know for themselves that they were "born again" Christian. The logical goal of such a life was individual Christian perfection.[44]

By the Second Great Awakening the Pietist legacy of experiential faith (received most directly through Wesley and the growth of Methodism in America) was a powerful populist movement on American soil. It produced evangelists who were effective communicators with the "common folk," who spoke to issues of persons and society, and whose idealism raised high the expectation of great things to come, even the kingdom of God.

3. The Contours of Heart Religion

Pietism and Wesleyanism were twin reactions to what they considered an excessive allegiance to intellectual religion by the church of their day. For the former, Lutheran scholasticism had so elevated doctrinal correctness that it was strangling the spiritual vitality of the church and dividing it over confessional differences.

a. Creedal Orthodoxy and Heart Religion

Pietists were doctrinally orthodox, but their emphasis on spiritual and ethical praxis displaced the imperial control of doctrinal hair-splitting. Though this shift had benefits for practical Christian living, it produced at the same time an anti-creedal culture. This was in part due to Pietism's biblicism that had the effect of losing the benefits of the intellectual task which only doctrinal reflection can provide. Furthermore, being praxis-oriented meant that the Bible was treated

---

[43] H. Richard Niebuhr, *The Kingdom of God in America* (New York: Harper & Row, 1959), p. 108.

[44] Melvin E. Dieter, *The Holiness Revival of the Nineteenth Century* (2nd ed.; Lanham, MD: Scarecrow, 1996), p. 17.

less as a fundamental doctrinal text than as a devotional resource and guide for daily Christian living.[45] Intellectual effort was expended by Pietists; but, as illustrated by Spener and later, John Albert Bengal (1687-1752), it was directed primarily toward the work of biblical exegesis rather than theology.[46]

Likewise, Wesley reacted against the church's romance with rationalism, although he maintained what he considered to be the proper role of reason in the hierarchy of theological authorities.[47] Doctrinal formulations were of value but "secondary to the knowledge of God; they are dependent upon traditionally normative readings of Scripture and they are of no value apart from the practice of Christian virtues."[48]

Once on the American soil of pragmatism and popular religion, impatience with doctrinal precision encouraged a more than occasional anti-intellectualism that was to manifest itself in anti-creedal rhetoric.[49] This was particularly evident in certain strands of Revivalism. The opinion of Sam P. Jones – the popular southern revival preacher at the end of the last century (dubbed the "southern Billy Sunday") – was undoubtedly representative of many: "If I had a creed I would sell it to

---

[45] See Brown, *Understanding Pietism*, ch. 3, pp. 64-82.

[46] Theological discourse of course did occur within the Pietistic tradition and its heirs. The difference is that the ground shifted from confessional theology to that of spiritual and ethical praxis. Indeed, historian Grant Wacker points out that many observers of Pentecostalism miss (in their preoccupation with the "emotionalism" of Pentecostal worship) the fact that for early Pentecostals as much as for any fundamentalist, "the definition and defense of correct belief was a matter of eternal importance," in "The Functions of Faith in Primitive Pentecostalism," *Harvard Theological Review* 77/3-4 (1984): 166. But it must be acknowledged that biblicism and the reaction to confessionalism produced a suspicion of certain kinds of theological thinking, especially within the context of popular religion.

[47] Brown observes that, like many protest movements, "Pietists, especially Moravians, retained more of the *sole fide* stance of Luther than their negative critiques would seem to allow, while Wesley maintained a greater place for reason than his criticisms would seem to concede," in "Wesleyan Revival," p. 9.

[48] David Bundy, "Christian Virtue: John Wesley and the Alexandrian Tradition," *Wesleyan Theological Journal* 26/1 (Spring 1991): 146.

[49] Although anti-intellectualism has been present in much of American evangelicalism, there are significant strengths within the Wesleyan and Holiness traditions which have contributed a sense of proportion in doctrinal matters and refused to allow those intellectual pursuits to hinder the Christian moral mandate of holy living, especially in the Church's ministry to the poor. See Donald Dayton, *Discovering an Evangelical Heritage,* and "Presidential Address: The Wesleyan Option for the Poor," *Wesleyan Theological Journal* 26/1 (Spring 1991): 7-16.

a museum…. It was over creed that men fought, and not over Christ. Orthodexes [sic] are what has ruined this world."[50]

Indeed, what counted was "truth" as experienced, not merely believed with the mind. Phoebe Palmer (1807-1874), leading Methodist lay evangelist during and after the Revival of 1857-58, recorded one minister's testimony that, before being touched by the Holy Spirit, truth for him "was a creed, not a life."[51] In another testimony, it is clear that creeds were perceived to be a barrier to the full gospel life: "I came to the word of God with a determination to lay aside my former creed; … and understand for myself what the salvation of the gospel was."[52]

Anti-creedal sentiment and its effects are particularly noticeable in the writings of Essek W. Kenyon (1867-1948), a prominent evangelist and radio preacher whose ministry stretched from the northeast United States to the Pacific Northwest and California. There are a number of reasons for Kenyon's anti-creedal attitude. First, he shared with other evangelical leaders of his day the view inherited from Pietism that the traditional church was spiritually dead, due largely to its "cold creed-bound orthodoxy."[53] He stated bluntly that creedalism was the source of confusion and disunity in the church:

> Thinking men and women of this age have been rebelling against the orthodox interpretation of the Bible as presented in denominational creeds…. The Faith of millions has been shattered… There is almost no coherence of doctrine in any of our great denominational bodies.[54]

Second, the blend of Restorationism and millenarian eschatology fueled the attack on creeds. The drive to restore the doctrine and life of the apostolic church "disposed them to avoid association with the historic creeds of Christendom."[55] After all, the traditional Church

[50] Cited in Mrs. Sam P. Jones, *The Life and Sayings of Sam P. Jones* (Atlanta, GA: Franklin-Turner, 1907), p. 461.

[51] Phoebe Palmer, *Promise of the Father, or, A Neglected Specialty of the Last Days* (Boston: Henry V. Degen, 1859), p. 402.

[52] Palmer, *Promise of the Father*, p. 371.

[53] Dale H. Simmons, *E.W. Kenyon and the Postbellum Pursuit of Peace, Power, and Plenty* (Studies in Evangelicalism, 13; Lanham, MD: Scarecrow, 1997), p. xii. Simmons points out that Kenyon shared this anti-creedal and anti-institutional spirit with both the metaphysical sect New Thought and the Higher Christian Life movement.

[54] Essek W. Kenyon, *The Father and His Family: A Restatement of the Plan of Redemption* (7th ed.; Lynnwood, WA: Kenyon's Gospel Publishing Society, 1937), p. 9.

[55] Grant Wacker, "The Functions of Faith in Primitive Pentecostalism," *Harvard Theological Review* 77:3-4 (1984): 367.

with its creeds was perceived to be the culprit in suppressing the apostolic golden age. Pre-millennial teaching on the soon return of Christ heightened the expectation that the "last days" would witness a restoration of apostolic truths buried by centuries of traditional Christianity. Kenyon was not hesitant to claim that his own teachings were such a rediscovery. He made the rather immodest remark that his teaching "is not a New Philosophy. It is an unveiling of a lost truth, the most vital of all that God gave to us in Christ."[56]

At the same time, this Restorationist-eschatological coalition produced a culture of innovation, as exemplified in Kenyon. Instead of a conservative entrenchment, it encouraged novel interpretations of scripture that were presented them as "lost apostolic truths." Simmons states that, "in thrashing out his own teaching, Kenyon displayed an independent streak and an overwhelming need to come up with teachings that no one else had ever discovered."[57]

This anti-creedal and anti-institutional bias continued in Pentecostalism. Pentecostal pioneer, Charles Parham (1873-1929), used characteristically colorful language to denigrate creeds and the institutional church:

> The best of creeds are but the sawdust of men's opinions, stuffed in skins and feathers of truth to give them a pleasing and attractive appearance; to draw people into the support of an organized ecclesiasticism, or an individualistic propaganda.[58]

He was not averse to charging the Pentecostal movement itself with the sin of creedalism when he encountered ideas that clashed with his own. In 1910 he decried the new "Finished Work of Calvary" teaching as "remnants of dead creeds and worn out doctrines of men. . . . Eminent men who have been converted from their creed bound, earth-born religious organizations have been instrumental in this."[59]

Anti-creedalism also produced in the early Pentecostal Revival a cry for "creedless unity." In so doing it was carrying forward the Pietist conviction that doctrine divides, but the Spirit unites. William J. Seymour (1870-1922), leader of the Azusa Street Revival of 1906-09, witnessed a unity that at least initially transcended doctrinal, denomi-

---

[56] Kenyon, *The Two Kinds of Life: The Biological Miracle of the Age* (Seattle, WA: Kenyon's Gospel Publishing House, 1943), p. 1.

[57] Simmons, *Kenyon*, p. xii.

[58] Charles F. Parham, *A Voice Crying in the Wilderness*, p. 66, reprinted in *The Sermons of Charles F. Parham*, ed. Donald Dayton (New York: Garland, 1985).

[59] See Parham, "Preface to 2nd Edition," *Voice Crying*.

national and racial boundaries. In the first issue of his magazine, *The Apostolic Faith*, he could claim that God "recognizes no man-made creeds, doctrines nor classes of people."[60] Ironically, Frank Ewart (1876-1947), a leader in the first two schisms within Pentecostalism (the "Finished Work of Calvary" and the Oneness teaching), would make the same appeal, that when God's love is truly experienced it will transcend the human barriers to unity created by doctrines and creeds:

> Since God is love, … you are obliged to yield your whole being as a vehicle of the Divine Nature. This kind of a ministry will not divide the people into many diverse creeds, but will consolidate them into a many membered body – the Creedless Christ, ever and essentially One.[61]

Ewart's early restorationist appeal to unity within the fledgling Pentecostal movement revealed its inherent bias against creeds. To be authentic, unity must be consistent with biblical truth, which for him was reflected in the "platform" of the Pentecostal movement, including the most recent teaching of the "Finished Work of Calvary." Creeds, on the other hand, produced the divisive proliferation of denominations. Teachings that countered this platform he labeled heresies. In the Revival, "creeds have been slaughtered, doctrines have been rejected and others have been added…. One after another of the tenets that we have tenaciously clung to have been given up because unscriptural." Rejection of restored truth, not the "new" teaching itself, divided Christians: "Many seceded from the unity of the faith, and schism and confusion are the result."[62]

For pragmatic Revivalists and radical Restorationists, creeds were human constructions. Christ, getting saved and "right with God" – these were of God. Consequently, the subtleties of speculative theology were forced into the background. And the only doctrines worthy of being embraced would be those set forth by their proponents as restored apostolic truths. This meant for some that the doctrine of the

---

[60] William J. Seymour, "Fire Falling at Hermon," *The Apostolic Faith* 1/1 (September 1906): 3.

[61] Ewart, *The Name and the Book* (Chicago, IL: Daniel Ryerson, Inc., 1936), p. 103. As late as 1930 Franklin Small, a Oneness Pentecostal pioneer from Winnipeg, cautioned against strong centralized authority when he was forming the Apostolic Church of Pentecost, Inc.; see Robert A. Larden, *Our Apostolic Heritage: An Official History of the Apostolic Church of Pentecost, Incorporated* (Calgary: Kyle Printing and Stationery, 1971), p. 96.

[62] Frank J. Ewart, "Defending Heresies," *The Good Report* 1/3 (1912): 12.

Trinity with its paradoxical conundrums was an eligible candidate for sidelining.

b. Revelation and Heart Religion

One of the most searing criticisms that would be laid against Oneness Pentecostals from their beginning was the appeal to "revelation" as a defense for the new teaching. Though both sides were certain what they themselves meant by the claim, neither took pains to explain it nor to understand the other.

But the appeal was not as novel as it first appeared. At the turn of the century, American culture was undergoing psychological fatigue from the effects of industrialization, urbanization and immigration. To treat their ailments, many turned to the "spiritual" realm. One response came from the metaphysical cults represented in such movements as Mind-Cure, New Thought and Christian Science. Special "knowledge" and spiritual insight could wield power over the physical and emotional world of humans.

The other response came from highly "spiritual" evangelical movements such as Wesleyan Holiness and Keswick Higher Christian Life, movements that preached spiritual power for daily living. While the evangelicals roundly denounced the "cults," the traffic between them moved in both directions. So while the content may have been different, in language and methodologies there was resemblance.[63] An indication of the popularity of spiritual topics at the turn of the century is evident in the apparent proliferation of books on the subject of the Holy Spirit. At least it was C.I. Scofield's observation, though hyperbolic, that,

> we are in the midst of a marked revival of interest in the person and work of the Holy Spirit.... Within the last twenty years more has been written and said upon the doctrine of the Holy Spirit than in the preceding eighteen hundred years.[64]

---

[63] In his study of Essek W. Kenyon, Simmons reveals the interrelatedness of these movements through a comparison of Kenyon's thought with those of New Thought and Keswick Higher Life. It is Simmons' observation that "although the two groups differed in their definitions of the nature of the individual's power source, the methods employed in tapping into this power and the promised results of its proper exercise were strikingly similar," *Kenyon*, p. xiii.

[64] Cited in Donald Dayton, "The Doctrine of the Baptism of the Holy Spirit: Its Emergence and Significance, *Wesleyan Theological Journal* 13 (Spring 1978): 119-20.

We have already observed that the spiritual and theological fountainhead of the Holiness and Higher Life movements can be traced to their Pietist heritage. It was in Pietism that the focus of theological enquiry shifted from scholastic doctrinal debates to experiential theology of spiritual and ethical praxis. Moving beyond Calvin's doctrine of the Holy Spirit as "inner witness" to Scripture, Pietism existentialized the Spirit's enlivening work by insisting that "it was when the Scripture was in use that its power came to be known."[65]

This openness to personal revelation can also be traced to another stream of influence on both Pietism and Wesley – a strain of mysticism called Quietism found in the teachings of Madame Guyon and François Fénelon. Emphasis on the "inner Word" legitimated personal intuitions and illuminations of divine grace so long as they were rigorously tested. Wesley's doctrines of prevenient grace and inner assurance in particular gave scope for such experiences. But Dale Brown makes the astute observation that, in contrast to classical expressions of mysticism that appealed to direct personal illumination in favor of Scripture, for Pietism and Wesley "experience was emphasized as a receptive medium rather than the productive source of revelation."[66]

Charles Finney reflects the same approach to revelation. He believed that rational proof of the Gospel is insufficient for the soul. It is divine truth revealed to the heart that creates an unshakable certainty: "The faith of the heart is proof against all forms of infidelity. Without this, nothing is proof." But, like others before him, Finney was careful to clarify that this "revelation" of truth is not a special revelation beyond biblical truth, but a personal appropriation and witness to the soul: "I do not mean to imply here that we are not certain of the facts of observation. But this is a stronger assurance and certainty. The mind becomes personally acquainted with God, and is conscious of this direct and positive knowledge."[67]

[65] C. John Weborg, "Pietism: Theology in Service of Living toward God," *The Variety of American Evangelicalism,* ch. 10, p. 170. See also Brown, *Understanding Pietism,* p. 68.

[66] Brown, "Wesleyan Revival," p. 10. It has also been argued persuasively that, in the appropriative aspects (i.e. the "sufficiency") of Scripture in particular, Wesley was equally influenced by the Thirty-Nine Articles of his own Anglican Church; see Paul Merritt Bassett, "The Theological Identity of the North American Holiness Movement: Its Understanding of the Nature and Role of the Bible," in: Dayton & Johnston, *American Evangelicalism,* ch. 6, p. 78.

[67] Finney, *Sermons on the Way to Salvation,* pp. 321, 319.

Early Pentecostals demonstrated the same dynamic understanding of revelation. Pentecostal scholar, Harold Hunter, observes that, "to the degree that contemporary evangelicalism extracts its formulation of inerrancy from Scottish Common Sense Realism, Pentecostals clearly stand closer to the Pietistic preoccupation with the inspiration of persons rather than texts."[68] As will be discussed later, Oneness Pentecostals – with their distinctive appeal to "revelation" – must first be understood, not as a heretical or metaphysical sect, but as inheritors of a family of orthodox-believing Protestants for whom divine revelation is not satisfied until it has done its work within the human heart, mind, affections and will.

c. Heart Religion and the Christian Life:
New Birth and Baptism with the Spirit

Pietism believed that heart religion was most clearly expressed in the personal experience they called the new birth. John Wesley and the Methodist movement that followed him drew on the spiritual and theological resources of this teaching. The theme of Spirit-baptism became associated with it, and was later to exert an influence in ways that paved the way for the Pentecostal movement.

Wesley's View of the New Birth and Baptism with the Spirit. Wesley struggled, not always successfully, to bring together elements of the Christian life that he considered neglected in the Church of England. Nominalism had produced little evidence of vital experience of the gospel in people's lives. In a bold sermon at the height of the Evangelical Revival, "The Almost Christian" (1741), Wesley attacked this spiritual disease by contrasting what he called the "almost" Christian and the "altogether" Christian. While the former looked uncannily like the average churchgoer, the latter was a "born again" Christian; that is, one through whom issues a deep love for God and neighbor, and a faith that yields the fruit of repentance, purity of heart, and works of love.[69]

The new birth or regeneration was central to Wesley's theology: "If any doctrines within the whole compass of Christianity may be properly termed fundamental they are doubtless these two – the doctrine of

---

[68] Harold D. Hunter, "The Resurgence of Spirit Christology," *EPTA Bulletin: The Journal of the European Pentecostal Theological Association* 11/1 & 2 (1992): 53.

[69] John Wesley, "The Almost Christian," *The Works of John Wesley* (Bicentennial ed.), ed. Albert Outler (Nashville: Abingdon, 1984), I, pp. 131-41.

justification, and that of the new birth."[70] In addition to what God does *for us* (justification proper), God renews our nature (new birth). To this he added that sanctification begins at the moment of regeneration, not subsequent to it. For Wesley these great actions of God could not be conveniently separated as had been done in Protestant scholastic theology. While he permitted a *theological* distinction for purposes of discussion, he insisted that they remain an existential unity in the life of the believer. To be truly justified, one would experience the regenerating power of the new birth and the first stirrings of sanctification in the soul.

The coalescence of these realities into one event had two important implications. First, it located sanctification at the very beginning of the Christian life. Wesley made a distinction between new birth and sanctification, but they appeared together at the moment of regeneration when "our sanctification, our inward and outward Holiness, begins." Here Wesley used the analogy of human birth. Although growth occurs, there is nothing qualitatively added to the reality of being human. In his sermon, "The New Birth," he stated:

> A child is born of a woman in a moment ... afterward he gradually and slowly grows till he attains the stature of a man. In like manner a child is born of God in a short time, if not in a moment. But it is by slow degrees that he afterward grows up to the measure of the full stature of Christ.[71]

Elsewhere he reiterated the same conviction: "At the same time that we are justified, yea, in that very moment, sanctification begins."[72]

Wesley's concern was to reverse the blight of Nominalism and antinomianism in the church. These weaknesses were often represented by those who insisted they were born again when they were baptized. His answer was that outward sign and inward sacramental grace must be sharply distinguished from each other and not to be conflated:

> For what can be more plain than that the one is an external, the other an internal work? That the one is a visible, the other an invisible thing, and therefore wholly different from each other: the one being an act of man, purifying the body, the other a change wrought by God in the soul... As

---

[70] John Wesley, "The New Birth," *Works* (Bicentennial ed.), II, p. 187. For an examination of Wesley's understanding of the new birth, see Kenneth Collins, "John Wesley's Doctrine of the New Birth," *Wesleyan Theological Journal* 32/1 (Spring 1997): 53–68.

[71] Wesley, "New Birth," p. 198.

[72] Wesley, "The Scripture Way of Salvation," *Works* (Bicentennial ed.), 2: 157.

the new birth is not the same thing with baptism, so it does not always accompany baptism; they do not constantly go together.[73]

This distinction, however, was not generally shared by the Anglican divines of this period. But for Wesley, it was necessitated by the evangelical need to preserve the integrity and centrality of conversion.

Antinomianism was in Wesley's thinking the result of the defective teaching that misplaced sanctification *after* justification. To this he responded: "If all your past sins were now to be forgiven, you would immediately sin again; that is, unless your heart were cleansed; unless it were created anew."[74] By shifting sanctification to the beginning of the Christian life, Wesley thereby created a climate of both optimism and high expectation of "holy living," themes that would be repeated and intensified generations later.

The second implication is that, for Wesley, being born again was synonymous with being baptized in the Spirit. In an essay in which he was explaining the proper role of repentance, he stated: "Not repentance alone – for then you know only the baptism of John – but believe and be 'baptized with the Holy Ghost and with fire.'"[75] By this he meant the new birth. Wesley consistently taught the importance of water baptism to initiate one into the life of the church, but insisted that alone it did not guarantee regeneration. But, as Victor Reasoner observes, it was the biblical imagery of Spirit-baptism as a "pouring out" of the Spirit that led Wesley and subsequent Methodists to prefer affusion to sprinkling in water baptism. This connection between water and Spirit-baptism was based on his belief that Spirit-baptism and the new birth indeed are the same experience. But the Holiness movement of the next century shifted Spirit-baptism to an event subsequent to the new birth, resulting, as some argued, in an anemic faith

---

[73] Wesley, "New Birth," p. 197.

[74] Cited in Collins, "Wesley's Doctrine of the New Birth," p. 55. Collins states that the new birth is sometimes called "initial sanctification", which "marks the beginning not simply of an incremental change, not merely one of degree, but of a qualitative change which issues in a distinct kind of life," p. 60. Elsewhere Wesley reiterated his criticism of those who relied on their baptism but lacked the experience of the new birth as a *present* reality in, "The Marks of the New Birth," *Works* (Bicentennial ed.), 1. This aspect of Wesley's doctrine of sanctification as integral to the new birth will be significant later for understanding the teachings of E.W. Kenyon and William Durham.

[75] Wesley, *Works. The Appeals to Men of Reason and Religion and Certain Related Open Letters*, ed. Gerald R. Cragg (Bicentennial ed.), XI, 253.

devoid of holiness.[76] Finally, it bequeathed to the Pentecostal and Oneness movements of the 20th century paradigms in conflict.

From Piety of Purity to Piety of Power. Prior to the Civil War in America, Revivalism was deeply influenced by the Pietistic spirit, especially its emphasis on personal conversion as the *sine qua non* of the new birth. But other Pietistic themes emerged in the developing theology of Charles Finney, which came to be known as Oberlin Perfectionism. Here greater attention was given to personal holiness and purity in the Christian life. The Wesleyan Holiness movement that emerged on the American scene in the latter half of the 19th century was a blend of Pietism, American Revivalism and Wesleyan Perfectionism.[77]

After the Civil War a shift in theological focus emerged in some circles. Gradually more attention was being given to the theme of spiritual "power" and the "Baptism of the Holy Spirit."[78] Combined with a growing restorationist impulse to replicate the life of the New Testament church, there was more concern to restore apostolic power than apostolic purity. The combined emphasis on "salvation" and "baptism in the Holy Spirit" was bound together by a pietistic hermeneutic that "internalizes and subjectivizes the events of the *Heilsgeschichte*, requiring that each be replicated in the life of the individual believer."[79]

As early as Wesley's time, his contemporary John Fletcher had suggested that the Pentecostal power of the Holy Spirit be distinguished from the experience of salvation.[80] And in 1845 John Morgan of Oberlin taught that this Pentecostal experience of the "Baptism of the Holy Ghost" was not only for the New Testament Church but available to all believers.[81]

Donald Dayton marks the shift from a Holiness theology with its emphasis on perfection to a Pentecostal theology centering on power in the "Baptism of the Holy Spirit" with Finney's successor, Asa

---

[76] Victor Paul Reasoner, "The American Holiness Movement's Paradigm Shift Concerning Pentecost," *Wesleyan Theological Journal* 31/2 (Fall 1996): 132-33, 141.

[77] Dieter, *The Holiness Revival of the Nineteenth Century*, p. 3.

[78] For a discussion of this development, see Melvin Dieter, "Wesleyan-Holiness Aspects of Pentecostal Origins," ed. Vinson Synan (Plainfield, NJ: Logos International, 1975), pp. 57-80, and Donald Dayton, *Theological Roots of Pentecostalism*, pp.87-113.

[79] Donald Dayton, "Theological Roots of Pentecostalism," paper read at the annual meeting of the American Academy of Religion, Washington, DC, 26 October 1974, p. 2.

[80] Dayton, "Theological Roots," p. 4.

[81] Dayton, "The Evolution of Pentecostalism," *The Covenant Quarterly* 32 (August 1974), p. 31.

Mahan (1800-1889).[82] This change in focus occurred over a thirty-one year span between the writing of Mahan's two most popular books, *The Scripture Doctrine of Christian Perfection* (1839) and *The Baptism of the Holy Spirit* (1870). In his later years, Mahan was active in the more Reformed stream of the Holiness movement, centered in the Keswick Conventions in Britain.[83] This in turn provided a link with the late-19th century evangelicals, D.L. Moody and R.A. Torrey, who also taught this second experience of power. By 1900 the new Pentecostal theology "had become widely accepted not only in Holiness circles but to a certain extent beyond them."[84]

This emphasis on spiritual power is evident in the writings of Albert B. Simpson (1844-1919), founder of the Christian and Missionary Alliance and representative of Keswick theology. The subtitle of his extensive two-volume work on the Holy Spirit is, *Power from on High*.[85] Elsewhere he states that Christ "has for us the power of the Holy Spirit, the power of prayer, the power that will conquer circumstances and control all events for His will."[86] The reason why we cannot comprehend and experience Christ more fully in our life is "because we cannot understand or stand the fullness of His power."[87]

The same link between power and the Spirit-baptism is present in R.A. Torrey's popular booklet, *The Baptism with the Holy Spirit*. In it he stated that, "the baptism of the Holy Spirit is not for the purpose of cleansing from sin, but for the purpose of empowering for service."[88] Pentecostalism built upon this earlier "Pentecostal theology," adding to it the teaching that the baptism of the Holy Spirit is, in the words of the Assemblies of God historian, William Menzies, "believed to be evidenced by the accompanying sign of 'speaking with other tongues as the Spirit gives utterance.'" According to Menzies, Pentecostals interpreted the experience of Spirit-baptism as an "enduement of

---

[82] Dayton, "Asa Mahan and the Development of American Holiness Theology," *Wesleyan Theological Journal* 9 (Spring 1974): 60-69.

[83] Dayton, "Evolution," p. 32.

[84] Dayton, "Asa Mahan," p. 61.

[85] A.B. Simpson, *The Holy Spirit or Power from on High* (2 vols.; Harrisburg, PA: Christian Publications, n.d.).

[86] Simpson, *The Christ of the Forty Days* (New York: Christian Alliance, n.d.), p. 20.

[87] Simpson, *Christ of Forty Days*, p. 18.

[88] R.A. Torrey, *The Baptism With the Holy Spirit* (Minneapolis, MN: Bethany Fellowship, n.d.), p. 4.

power."[89] In this way the "power" theme was carried into the early Pentecostal Revival.

d. Heart Religion and Spirituality

Another distinguishing mark of Pietism throughout this era was the personal and affective quality of its spirituality, which was evident in prayers, poems and gospel songs. An intimate relationship was sought between Jesus and the believer. At its best Pietistic spirituality promoted a vital personal faith, but there was an inherent tendency to an individualistic and sentimental piety. Zinzendorf, for example, in earlier years had carried this subjective aspect of piety to excess.

The evangelical spirituality of Revivalism, the Keswick movement and the Wesleyan Holiness movement all expressed their devotion in the highly personal terms inherited from Pietism, as is illustrated in this poem by A.B. Simpson:

> When Jesus died on Calvary,
> I too was there;
> When Jesus rose with life divine,
> I too was there;
> When Jesus comes some day for me,
> I shall be there;
> O blessed life, so deep, so high,
> Lord, keep me there.[90]

Other songs written by Simpson reflected the same personal character: "The Saviour's Charm," "I Have Seen Jesus," "The Everlasting Arms," "Jesus is Mine." The first stanza of "The Saviour's Charm" spoke of the warmth of Jesus' friendship:

> There are faces here that are strangely fair,
> There are hearts that glow with love,
> But I know a face that is fairer far,
> And a friend all friend above.[91]

This deeply personal, intimate, sometimes sentimental, devotion to Jesus was a hallmark of Pietism.

---

[89] William W. Menzies, *Anointed to Serve – The Story of the Assemblies of God* (Springfield, MO: Gospel Publishing House, 1971), p. 9.

[90] Simpson, "Crucified, Resurrected and Glorified with Christ," in *Echoes of the New Creation* (New York: Christian Alliance, 1903), n.p.

[91] Simpson, *Songs of the Spirit* (New York: Christian Alliance, 1920), p. 102.

e. Prologue to Oneness Pentecostalism

Pietism was a stream of spirituality that emphasized the affective and practical aspects of faith. In two important ways it contributed to the working out of the distinctive doctrine of Oneness Pentecostalism.

First, it offered a personal and experiential piety that would later be applied by Oneness believers to the name of Jesus. The earliest Oneness leaders received the "revelation" of the name of Jesus in baptism in the heat of revival, not the cold logic of church councils. The heartfelt devotion to Jesus and the Bible that was a hallmark of Pietism became one of the primary appeals to the authenticity of the new message. As one architect of the Oneness doctrine, Frank J. Ewart, would later write: "Mere intellect cannot open the treasury of the Name of God. God speaks to the heart. If the heart is dead, the Name is sealed."[92]

The second contribution was a hermeneutic for expressing the existential and personal aspects of biblical or doctrinal truth. Objective truth was confirmed by the subjective experience of the believer. Indeed, the whole story of salvation history became the story of the believer. Experience was certainly not the foundation of one's salvation. But, as in the case of John Wesley, "it was rather established on Scripture and confirmed by experience, that is, by the inner and direct testimony of the Holy Spirit."[93]

Dayton contends that this hermeneutical pattern was kept alive in the Pentecostal teaching on the baptism in the Holy Spirit.[94] The believer does not appropriate Spirit -baptism by a mere act of faith alone but receives the experiential confirmation in the sign of speaking with other tongues.

Oneness Pentecostals extended this Pietistic hermeneutic beyond Spirit-baptism to the name of Jesus. The truth of their doctrine would be confirmed by the devotion generated at the exaltation of the name of Jesus and the power that attended the Name. As was later claimed by a leading Fundamentalist: "The Book of Acts is largely our Text Book, it is a series of stories of the triumphs of the Name of Jesus . . . . that NAME has power in it."[95]

---

[92] Frank J. Ewart, *The Name and the Book*, p. 85.

[93] Welch, *Protestant Thought*, p. 25.

[94] Dayton, "Evolution," p. 29.

[95] Essek W. Kenyon, *The Father and His Family* (Spencer, MA: Reality Press, 1916), p. 256.

4. Jesus-centrism and Evangelical Faith

The evangelical Protestant tradition has been characteristically christo-centric. The reality of Jesus Christ is consciously taken as the fundamental hermeneutic for interpreting the full scope of the theo-logical spectrum. All theological subject matter in some way relates to Christology. Theology begins and ends with Christ. Christocentric theology is not a rejection of Trinitarian faith. But, in the words of Swedish Lutheran theologian, Gustaf Aulén, "Where Christ is, there is God; and where Christ works, there God effectively realizes his will."[96]

Within this christocentric tradition there is a discernible strand that can be best described as Jesus-centrism. It is not different in kind from christocentrism, since it does not deny other doctrines or disapprove of orthodox teaching. The difference is in emphasis and scope: Jesus-centrism tends to be almost exclusively *practical* theology. There is no comprehensive theological system or systematic effort to relate the wide range of theological topics to the christocentric center. Instead, it is concerned almost exclusively with Jesus in his relationship with the believer. Though Christ's deity is resolutely defended, there is little reflection upon his eternal existence or cosmic mission. His identity within the Trinity is believed but is obscured or neglected. Rather, the historic Jesus becomes the object of attention, with particular attention to his deity, his atoning work and his second coming. The result is a truncated view of God and the world. Even where attention is given to other doctrines, they are not treated as a systematic whole. In other words, a truly systematic theology is lacking.

Jesus-centrism is also primarily *devotional* and inspirational rather than theologically speculative. The unbeliever is encouraged to turn to Jesus, and the believer finds in Jesus the source of salvation and object of devotion. While God the Father is never denied, God's role as Creator is not accorded the same priority as Jesus the Redeemer. This may be due in part to the fact that for much of popular piety God is remote, whereas Jesus is immanent and approachable.[97]

---

[96] Gustaf Aulén, *The Faith of the Christian Church,* trans. Eric H. Wahlstrom (Phila-delphia: Fortress, 1960), p. 54.

[97] Theologian Ray Anderson believes the weakness of Jesus-centric piety is demon-strated in even the choice of address to "Jesus" only, rather than to "Christ Jesus." The latter phrase is theologically important in order to connect Jesus with the mission of the Father and the Holy Spirit. The single name shifts the focus from this full divine action to the experience of the worshipper, which thereby results in a "loss of conti-nuity between the present experience of the Spirit (Jesus) and the messianic Spirit of Jahweh manifested through Israel and united with Christ Jesus in a full trinitarian

Jesus-centric faith emerges from the Pietist stream of evangelical tradition that in North America helped shape Revivalism and the Holiness movement. Though its beliefs were historically and theologically orthodox, Pietism was a protest against a faith that accorded primacy to doctrine. It was practical and affective. The combination of doctrinal and practical interests was well suited to the emerging middle class Victorian culture that, in the words of historian George Marsden, "placed great value on both rationality and sentiment."[98]

In Revivalism, the evangelical doctrines of the deity and atonement of Christ blended with Pietism's emphasis on the new birth in the conversion experience. Conversion or "evangelical repentance" was the result of the personal appropriation of Christ's atoning work on the cross.[99] This work of "shedding his blood" was made effective by his being divine. With this as the primary experience and message, the Revivalists expended their intellectual energies in proclaiming the centrality of Jesus. This is well illustrated in a sermon by Henry Ward Beecher in the 1850's, attacking the Unitarianism of his day:

> Could Theodore Parker worship my God? Christ Jesus is his Name. All there is of God to me is bound up in that Name. A dim and shadowy effluence rises from Christ, and that I am taught to call Father. A yet more tenuous and invisible film of thought arises, and that is the Holy Spirit. But neither are to me aught tangible, restful, accessible… But Christ stands my *manifest* God. All I know is of him and in him.[100]

In his Oneness appeal decades later, Frank Ewart claimed that Beecher's christocentric declaration was in effect more congruent with the new Pentecostal teaching than with the traditional doctrine of Christ as the second Person in the Godhead: "Nothing could be plainer than Mr. Beecher's meaning… He held that Jesus, the Christ, was very God, and that the entire Godhead was incarnated in him."[101]

---

experience." Though Anderson criticizes Pentecostal piety in particular for this form of christocentric reductionism, the tendency can be traced in varying degrees through evangelical piety over the past two centuries. See Ray S. Anderson, *Ministry on the Fireline: A Practical Theology for an Empowered Church* (Downer's Grove, IL: InterVarsity Press, 1993), p. 155.

[98] George M. Marsden, *Fundamentalism and American Culture: The Shaping of Twentieth-Century Evangelicalism: 1870-1925* (New York: Oxford University Press, 1980), p. 21.

[99] Sweet's phrase; see *Revivalism*, p. 68.

[100] As quoted in Thomas J. Sawyer, *Who Is Our God? The Son or the Father? A Review of Rev. Henry Ward Beecher* (New York: Thatcher & Hutchinson, 1859), p. 3. The attack by Sawyer suggests that Beecher's bold christocentric preaching drew criticism.

[101] Frank J. Ewart, *The Name and the Book*, p. xv.

Jesus-centric spirituality, with its priority on the conversion experience, remained strong in the Revivalist tradition. Historian William McLoughlin points to this singular theme in the flamboyant Revivalist preacher and evangelist, Billy Sunday (1863-1935):

> Sunday succeeded in reducing the systematic theology which Finney had taken five hundred pages to elaborate, into a single sentence of ten words: "With Christ you are saved; without him you are lost."[102]

The doctrine of the Trinity may have been formally believed, but the consuming passion was Christ and salvation through the cross.

Revivalist piety was equally Jesus-centric. Prayers were freely directed to Jesus. Billy Sunday would frequently open his prayers with, "'Now Jesus, you know … or 'Well, Jesus, isn't this a fine bunch here tonight?'" Gospel songs frequently lacked broader doctrinal content or any concern to develop a trinitarian hymnody.[103] Composers were content to exalt Jesus and sing of the benefits of his salvation.

The gospel songs of the camp meetings were predominantly Jesus-centric. In his study of camp-meeting religion, Dickson D. Bruce discovers a paucity of songs ascribed to God: "Out of one hundred-and-eighty-six distinct choruses in the tune books, only six placed a major emphasis on God." The choruses lacked a single reference to God the Creator. Instead, Jesus was the central figure. In the meetings "the power of God was manifested, but only Jesus could be directly invoked."[104]

In reflecting on this tension, H. Richard Niebuhr observes that a full Trinitarian faith is endangered in two ways – by inordinate attention given to any one Person of the Godhead, and by allowing one's operative theology to function independently of the formal doctrine. Specifically, one can formally hold to the doctrine of the Trinity but in effect operate with a *practical* unitarianism of any one of the Persons in the Godhead.

In Jesus-centric faith, attention is limited almost exclusively to the historical Jesus and his atoning work, thereby producing a "practical monotheism of the Son." This particular strand appears within various forms of practical piety, especially when the focus is upon personal salvation. There is a proclivity in much of Revivalism, as Niebuhr

---

[102] William G. McLoughlin, Jr., *Billy Sunday Was His Real Name* (Chicago: University of Chicago Press, 1955), p. 123.

[103] McLoughlin, *Billy Sunday*, pp. 177, 85.

[104] Dickson D. Bruce, Jr., "And They All Sang Hallelujah: Plain-Folk Camp-Meeting Religion, 1800-1845" (Ph.D. diss., University of Pennsylvania, 1971), pp. 129-33.

illustrates in the preaching of Henry Ward Beecher, to reduce a full Trinitarian theology to a Jesus-centric faith: "Practically the whole thought about God is concentrated here in the thought about the Son; he is the sole object of worship and all the functions of deity are ascribed to him."[105] Even when the Trinity is affirmed as a fundamental doctrine, its function is concentrated in Jesus.

5. Jesus-centrism and Christology

Concerns over the doctrine of Christ were not absent in Jesus-centric faith. Although its priorities were practical, affective and evangelistic, efforts were made to defend doctrinal foundations that appeared to be under threat.

The All-encompassing Christ. The doctrinal focus on the deity of Christ and his atoning work continued and intensified in the second half of the 19th century. Suffering from external erosion by the new science and internal sterility by skepticism, evangelical religion responded by defending its most cherished doctrine of Christ and his saving work. The literature of this period was filled with devotional writings and polemics that expounded and defended the uniqueness of Christ. It would be a legacy passed on to Pentecostals. As Pentecostal scholar, Walter J. Hollenweger, points out, "only two articles of orthodox Christology are of real importance in Pentecostal religion, the virgin birth of Jesus and the atonement through his blood."[106]

Oneness pioneers likewise discovered in these writings ample resources for articulating their own distinctive rendering of Jesus-centric faith. Canadian Oneness leaders, Franklin Small and John Paterson, read and quoted favorably the appeals made by early evangelicals for a strong christocentric theology.[107] One prominent author was the English Presbyterian progressive theologian, J. Monro Gibson:

> We are learning to make our theology more and more central in Christ, and we believe that as the combat thickens, our apologetics will follow in

---

[105] H. Richard Niebuhr, "The Doctrine of the Trinity and the Unity of the Church," *Theology Today* 3 (October 1946): 371-84.

[106] Walter J. Hollenweger, *The Pentecostals – The Charismatic Movement in the Churches*, trans. R.A. Wilson (Minneapolis, MN: Augsburg, 1972), p. 312.

[107] Franklin Small, *Living Waters – A Sure Guide for Your Faith* (Winnipeg: Columbia, n.d.), p. 85; John Paterson, *The Real Truth about Baptism in Jesus' Name* (Hazelwood, MO: Pentecostal Publishing House, 1953), p. 19.

the same path, and in every department of Christian thought, Christ will be acknowledged as Himself the Truth.[108]

Another citation by Small was a classic sermon by Elijah Hedding addressing the New England Conference of the Methodist Episcopal Church in 1822.[109] Though Hedding was an orthodox Trinitarian, his purpose is clear from the sermon title, "Jesus Christ is the Supreme God."[110] Undoubtedly to counter attacks on the deity of Christ, Hedding proceeded to demonstrate from scripture that Jesus was frequently called God, that he was given prerogatives accorded Yahweh (therefore, he must be one with God), and that he was an eternal, immutable, omniscient, omnipresent, omnipotent being worthy of worship.

Concern for the centrality of Christ in Jesus-centric faith extended to the increasing preoccupation with eschatology in the second half of the 19th century. Adventist groups that grew out of the Millerite movement of the 1840's and the later stream of evangelical religion that embraced Dispensationalism directed their attention primarily to the second coming of Christ. The Great Tribulation, Rapture, Millennium and Final Judgment all focused on Jesus.[111]

The theme of holiness that dominated much of 19th-century evangelical religion through Wesley's influence in Methodism developed in two directions. One was the Wesleyan Holiness movement that emerged from the ministry and writings of Phoebe Palmer from 1840 until her death in 1874. The other was the more Reformed Holiness movement that grew out of the Keswick Conventions beginning in 1875 in the Lake District of England.[112] New formulations of the Holy Spirit were being forged in both movements that would prepare the way for the later Pentecostal Revival, especially the non-Wesleyan Assemblies of God.[113] However, in piety and doctrine, even with its distinctive teaching on life in the Spirit, Keswick spirituality remained strongly Jesus-centric.

---

[108] John Monro Gibson, *Christianity according to Christ* (2nd ed.; Nisbet's Theological Library; London: James Nisbet, 1889), p. 52.

[109] Small, *Living Waters*, p. 86.

[110] Elijah Hedding, *The Substance of a Sermon Delivered in Bath, (Maine), July 4, 1822* (Boston: Lincoln & Edmands, n.d.), p. 4.

[111] Ernest R. Sandeen, *The Roots of Fundamentalism – British and American Millenarianism – 1800-1930* (Chicago: University of Chicago Press, 1970), pp. 95-96.

[112] See Marsden, *Fundamentalism*, ch. 8, pp. 72-80.

[113] William W. Menzies, "The Non-Wesleyan Origins of the Pentecostal Movement," in *Aspects of Pentecostal-Charismatic Origins*, ed. Vinson Synan (Plainfield, NJ: Logos International, 1975), pp. 85f.

When one participant was asked the meaning of the Keswick teaching on perfection, he replied: "I want you just to say: 'Well, I will enter into the secret of Keswick, for to-day Christ shall be my Alpha, and He shall be my Omega. Nothing before Him!'"[114] A similar response is given by an Anglican cleric, Canon Harford-Battersby, after listening to the preaching of Evan Hopkins: "I got a revelation of Christ to my soul ... I found *He* was *all* I wanted, I shall never forget it; the day and hour are present with me."[115] Such personal narratives fall into a Jesus-centric pattern of progression characteristic of Keswick piety:

> Beginning with the exceeding sinfulness of sin, especially sin in the believer; consequent defeat and powerlessness in life and witness; God's provision for the rehabilitation of the sinner, in Christ's sanctification, consecration, and the Spirit-filled life.[116]

Thus, even in the renewed interest in the Holy Spirit and sanctification for which Keswick was noted, Jesus Christ was still the central figure for devotion and doctrine.

A prominent American leader within the Keswick stream of Holiness whose Jesus-centric spirituality probably influenced more than any other the early Reformed branch of Pentecostalism – and subsequently the Oneness movement – was A.B. Simpson.[117] A former Presbyterian minister, he eventually founded the Christian and Missionary Alliance organization. Simpson's teaching is basically outlined in what he called the "four-fold gospel."[118] The work of Jesus Christ is summed up in his role as Savior, Sanctifier, Healer and Coming King. This teaching was so thoroughly taken over by later Pentecostals that, as Dayton observes, "one has only to shift the emphasis from Christ to the Holy Spirit and substitute the 'Baptism of the Holy Spirit' for 'sanctification' and one has the complex of ideas that are 'Pentecostal.'"[119]

This four-point doctrinal system became the foundation for another organization formed by the Pentecostal evangelist, Aimee Semple McPherson (1890-1944). At one time affiliated with the Assemblies of

---

[114] George Wilson, "The Alpha and the Omega of the Blessed Life," *The Keswick Week*, 1898, ed. Evan H. Hopkins (London: Marshall, 1898), p. 122.

[115] Cited in Herbert F. Stevenson, *Keswick's Authentic Voices – Sixty-Five Dynamic Addressed Delivered at the Keswick Convention, 1875-1975* (Grand Rapids, MI: Zondervan, 1959), p. 16.

[116] Stevenson, *Keswick's Authentic Voices*, p. 17.

[117] Menzies, "Non-Wesleyan Origins," p. 87.

[118] A.B. Simpson, *The Four-Fold Gospel* (New York: Christian Alliance, 1890).

[119] Dayton, "Evolution," p. 33.

God, she is known primarily as evangelist and founding pastor of Angelus Temple in Los Angeles. McPherson adopted Simpson's doctrine of Jesus as Savior, Baptizer, Healer and Soon Coming King, and memorialized it in the name of her organization, the International Church of the Foursquare Gospel.[120]

Jesus-centric faith was initially a product of the Pietist legacy and later the stimulus for defending the deity of Christ against the human and Arian Christ of the Unitarians. Eventually it led to a christological understanding of Jesus more as the central figure in the Godhead than as the second Person of the Trinity.

Jesus-centrism and the name "Jesus." The name "Jesus" holds special prominence in the Christian spiritual tradition as a focus of devotion. The name carries more than historical significance because the person who bears it is confessed to be the divine Son of God. One of the richest resources for the use of the name of Jesus in piety is the ancient "Jesus Prayer" in the Orthodox tradition. As a form of prayer, its origins are in fourth-century Desert spirituality. But the actual prayer itself is the cry of blind Bartimaeus, "Lord Jesus Christ, Son of God, have mercy on me, a sinner" (Luke 18:38). In Orthodox spirituality it is highly valued because, as Metropolitan Anthony Bloom states, "the Jesus Prayer sums up the whole of the gospel." It can be used by anyone as a simple act of prayer or as an ascetical form of meditation.

The only doctrine attached to the name is that the person, Jesus, is also God incarnate, and calling on his name brings the believer "to stand in God's presence with no other thought but the miracle of our standing there and God with us."[121] In the past quarter century, The Jesus Prayer has enjoyed surprising popularity in many Christian traditions, including Protestant, which demonstrates the power of a piety that finds in Jesus a rich and full access to the heart of God.

The strong devotion to Jesus in Pietism not surprisingly included the name of Jesus. This is particularly evident in the hymns of the 18th century German Pietist, Gerhard Tersteegen (1697-1769). His piety was inward but directed to the transcendent love of Jesus. The inward spiritual sanctuary was the place where the worshipper encountered the risen Christ through adoration of the name of Jesus: "Our spirits thus become the temple in which the glory of God, as in the Holy of

---

[120] John T. Nichols, *The Pentecostals – The Story of the Growth and Development of a Vital New Force Appearing in the Christian Church* (rev. ed.; Plainfield, NJ: Logos International, 1971), p. 120; also Synan, *The Holiness-Pentecostal Tradition: Charismatic Movements in the Twentieth Century* (Grand Rapids, MI: Eerdmans, 1997), pp. 200-202.

[121] Anthony Bloom, *Living Prayer* (Springfield, IL: Templegate, 1966), pp. 84-88.

Holies, is near to us. The altar is the Name of Jesus; the sacrifice is our heart, our will, our all."[122]

For Tersteegen, the name of Jesus expressed more than spiritual affections. It was a strong christological statement to distinguish his devotion from that of the Rhineland Catholic mystics for whom, as J. Steven O'Malley states, "God is inherently present in the depths of every soul, only waiting to be discovered and obeyed through a program of asceticism."[123] For Tersteegen, the God encountered within the soul is none other than the incarnate One who is also Savior, the one who bears the name of Jesus. The influence of this piety of Jesus and his name on John Wesley was significant, due in so small part to the hymns of Tersteegen for which he had admiration spiritually and theologically.

The name of Jesus continued to appear in the devotional literature, hymnody and teaching of the spiritual descendents of Pietism, who mined its resources for their own purposes. Though it was common to intermingle the name "Jesus" with the larger constellation of titles familiar in New Testament usage, such as "Lord Jesus," "Jesus Christ," or "Lord Jesus Christ," one can detect a distinctive use of the name of "Jesus" alone.

The phrase "Jesus" and "Jesus only" became commonplace among Keswick and Holiness writers. Hannah Whitall Smith (1832-1911), lay evangelist for the National Association for the Promotion of Holiness during the latter period of the 19th century, used expressions such as, "acquainted with the Lord Jesus," "Jesus came to save you," "the truth in Jesus," "the salvation of Jesus," "Jesus saves me now," and "the fullness there is in Jesus."[124] Many of the narrative accounts recorded in Robert Sandall's *History of the Salvation Army* reveal the use of the name "Jesus" alone in popular usage: "died in Jesus," "sake of Jesus," "singing praises to Jesus," and "seeking Jesus."[125] At one Keswick Convention, a motto was recommended by Miss Wilson Carmichael of the Keswick Mission in Japan: "Nothing too precious for Jesus."[126]

---

[122] Cited in J. Steven O'Malley, "Pietistic Influence on John Wesley: Wesley and Gerhard Tersteegen," *Wesleyan Theological Journal* 31/2 (Fall 1996): 69.

[123] O'Malley, "Pietistic Influence," p. 60.

[124] Hannah Whitall Smith, *The Christian's Secret of a Happy Life*, new and enlarged (New York: Fleming H. Revell, 1888), pp. 16-69.

[125] Robert Sandall, *The History of the Salvation Army* (2 vols.; London: Thomas Nelson, 1947), I, pp. 118-26.

[126] "The Missionary Meeting," *The Keswick Week*, 1895, ed. Evan H. Hopkins (London: Marshall, 1895) p. 110.

While Simpson used many titles interchangeably, he frequently used the name of "Jesus" only, especially in his songs and poems. In his *Songs of the Spirit*, the following titles used "Jesus" only or referred to his name: "Look to Jesus," "Jesus Only," "Jesus Is Mine," "Glory to the Name of Jesus," "The Power of His Name," "I Have Seen Jesus."[127]

Other writers likewise used the singular name of Jesus. Arno C. Gaebelein (1861-1945), Methodist preacher, Bible teacher, writer and champion of the popular pre-millennial teaching, called the name of Jesus "that worthy Name, the Name above all other names."[128] The name "Jesus" appears frequently throughout his writings. Essek W. Kenyon, an evangelist and Bible teacher at the turn of the 20th century, regularly used the language of "Jesus," including the title of his popular book, *The Wonderful Name of Jesus*.[129]

The phrase "Jesus Only" was not uncommon during this period. It appears as a chapter title in Simpson's book, *In Heavenly Places*,[130] and in the book title by a Holiness preacher, M.W. Knapp, *Jesus Only – A Full Salvation Year Book*.[131] A chapter in *Mother Whittemore's Records of Modern Miracles* (Holiness) was entitled, "The 'Jesus Only' Girl."[132] The caption, "Jesus Only," hung over the door of a Salvation Army Chapel in London.[133] It was not uncommon for devotional poems to be entitled, "Jesus Only."[134]

Beyond the legacy of Pietism, there are two other possible explanations for the rise of "Jesus" language in the evangelical writings of the late 19th century. First, there are clues in the books of the Bible that were being given the most attention. Except for the Gospels, there are three books in the New Testament that frequently use the distinctive language of "Jesus" only – the Acts of the Apostles, Hebrews and

---

[127] Simpson, *Songs of the Spirit*, pp. 22-103.

[128] Arno C. Gaebelein, *Listen – God Speaks* (New York: "Our Hope," 1936), p. 131.

[129] Essek W. Kenyon, *The Wonderful Name of Jesus* (Los Angeles: West Coast, 1927).

[130] Simpson, *In Heavenly Places* (New York: Christian Alliance, 1892), p. 227.

[131] M.W. Knapp, ed., *Jesus Only – A Full Salvation Year Book* (Cincinnati, OH: M.W. Knapp, n.d.).

[132] F.A. Robinson, ed., *Mother Whittemore's Records of Modern Miracles* (Toronto: Missions of Biblical Education, n.d.).

[133] Robert Sandall, *The History of the Salvation Army*, vol. I: *1865-1878* (London: Thomas Nelson, 1947), p 137.

[134] Harriette B. Bainbridge, "Jesus Only," *Christian Alliance and Foreign Missionary Weekly* 14 (1 May 1895): 275; M.E. Lewis, "Jesus Only," *Christian and Missionary Alliance* 20 (19 January 1898): 63.

Revelation.[135] There was a renewed interest in a study of the Book of Acts that occurred as a result of the shift from "perfectionism" to "Baptism of the Holy Ghost."[136] Luke frequently refers "to the proclamation of the Christian message as 'preaching Jesus' (Acts 8:35, 9:20, 17:18)."[137] Even the expression, "Lord Jesus," appears many more times in Acts than in any other book in the New Testament.[138]

The Epistle to the Hebrews gained attention in the 19th century through the rise of Dispensationalism, a covenantal teaching originating with J. Nelson Darby (1800-1882), founder of the Plymouth Brethren. "Dispensational Premillennialism," as it was called, was popularized throughout segments of the evangelical church in America, especially Fundamentalism and Pentecostalism, by means of the teaching of C.I. Scofield and the publication of his Reference Bible in 1909.[139] The Epistle to the Hebrews was the key for interpreting the New Testament in light of the "types and shadows" of the Old Testament.[140]

The interests of Dispensationalists were not primarily historical but eschatological and evangelistic as millenarian expectations motivated preachers and Bible teachers. Advocates such as Arno C. Gaebelein (who followed Scofield), A.J. Gordon (1836-1895), and A.B. Simpson, were all looking for the second coming of Christ in the "Rapture" of the Church followed by a period of persecution and a literal millennial reign of peace by Christ. The apocalyptic books of Ezekiel, Daniel and Revelation were studied intensely, because therein lay the source for interpreting the events of the last days prior to the return of Christ. It is significant that in Revelation, "the Name of Jesus appears several times, especially in the phrase, 'the witness of Jesus' (1:9; 12:17; 19:10, 20:4)."[141] It is not surprising then, that "Jesus only" language would emerge as a result of intense study of these popular sections of the Bible. Frequent attention to and quoting of key passages would help shape vocabulary and expression.

---

[135] Everett F. Harrison, "Jesus," in *Baker's Dictionary of Theology*, ed. Everett F. Harrison (3rd ed.; Grand Rapids, MI: Baker Book House, 1966), pp. 297-98.

[136] See Dayton, "Asa Mahan," and "'Christian Perfection' to 'Baptism of the Holy Ghost.'"

[137] Harrison, "Jesus," p. 298.

[138] The name, "Lord Jesus," is used 15 times in Acts, in contrast to the next highest, five in 1 Corinthians.

[139] Menzies, "Non-Wesleyan Origins," p. 84.

[140] Ernest F. Kevan, "Dispensation," *Baker's Dictionary of Theology*, p. 167.

[141] Harrison, "Jesus," p. 298.

The second reason for the rise of "Jesus" language may be found in the distinctive Jesus-centric thrust of the late 19th century; namely, a focus on the human Jesus. Not only in Protestant liberalism and Unitarianism but also among orthodox Christians who sought to speak to the issue, "the characteristic focus of this concern for the humanity of Jesus was again typical."[142]

Although evangelical religion strongly reacted to liberalism, it engaged with the same issues and often with the same mindset. In its effort to defend the deity of Christ, it concentrated on the christological themes of incarnation and atonement. But it tended to reduce these doctrines to the historical moments of the virgin birth and the efficacy of the shed blood of Christ as a substitutionary atonement. Remarking on the atonement, Simpson wrote that, "it stands for the cross of Calvary, the blood of cleansing and the gospel of salvation."[143]

Evangelicals' central claim was that this human Jesus is really the "Supreme God." They attempted to demonstrate by historical and textual argumentation that redemption is possible only through the virgin birth of Jesus and the substitutionary atonement by this "sinless lamb." While the doctrinal intent was surely orthodox, the language and apologetic interests were historical. It is not implausible that such attention given to the life of Jesus should lead to "Jesus" only language, even while they sang and prayed to him.

6. Summary

Much of American evangelical faith with its roots in Pietism was Jesus-centric in doctrine and devotion. The two most prominent doctrines centered on the deity of Christ and the atonement. From this piety emerged the popular appellation of "Jesus" only when writing about or addressing him. This practice was eventually extended to the *name* of Jesus itself. Through leaders like A.B. Simpson, Jesus-centric spirituality exerted a strong influence upon early Pentecostalism, including the Oneness movement.

We now turn our attention to the theological influence of this interest in the "Name" to the doctrine of God.

---

[142] Welch, *Protestant Thought*, p. 233.

[143] Simpson, *The Gospel of Matthew* (Christ in the Bible, 13; Harrisburg, PA: Christian Publications, n.d.), p. 21.

3

An Evangelical Legacy – Theology of the Name

> The name of Jesus is the name,
> The name in which I gladly trust;
> For written it will be in gold
> When others turn to dust.
>
> There is a name that shall abide
> When others fade and die;
> Tho' great of earth be all forgot,
> This shall endure on high.
>
> When kings of earth have lost their charms,
> And all their jewels fade,
> The Saviour will be king of kings;
> To him be honors paid!
>
> Though mountains from their seats depart,
> And seas shall empty be,
> Yet shall the name of Jesus stand
> Thro' all eternity.
>
> His name is an eternal name,
> It cannot pass away;
> For God himself has sure decreed
> That it shall live for aye.[1]

A rudimentary theology of the name of Jesus eventually emerged from a stream of Jesus-centric piety in evangelical Christianity and all the forces that made such teaching possible. Preachers, teachers and hymn writers were motivated not only by practical and devotional considerations but also the apologetic urgency to counter what they perceived

---

[1] "The Abiding Name," *New Songs of the Gospel, No. 2 – For Use in Religious Meetings*, ed. Herbert J. Lacey, C. Austin Miles, & Maurice A. Clifton (New York: Hall-Mack, n.d.), no. 3.

as a threat to their christological foundations from Unitarianism and liberal Protestantism. They turned their attention to the person and work of Jesus, which included an extensive biblical study of the Name. Their theological conclusions of that study became the basis upon which the cardinal evangelical doctrines of incarnation and atonement would be vindicated.

To the first doctrine, a biblical analysis of the name of the Lord Jesus Christ yielded a cogent argument for his deity. William Phillips Hall, an evangelical who wrote on the theme of the "Name of God" in the early 20th century, concluded that had the Church not lost the truth of the name of God in the Lord Jesus Christ in the post-apostolic era, "it appears that there never would have been any doubt whatever among Christians of the Deity of the Lord Jesus Christ."[2]

Second, a study of the name of Jesus revealed the power made available through his atoning work on the cross. Just as there was "power in the blood," the cross also brought power through the Name. This theme was particularly emphasized by Essek Kenyon, who argued that in the atonement Christ made his Name available as the legal power of attorney which the Christian can appropriate in prayer.[3]

1. The Revelation of God and the Name

Many of the early evangelicals who embarked on a study of the Name were representatives of the Keswick movement and the emerging pre-millennial eschatology. As we shall see, occasionally other authors from this period with christocentric concerns appeared in the writings of early Oneness leaders. In various ways, they discovered in the nature and name of God evidence of the centrality of Jesus for revelation and salvation.

a. The Name of God in Jesus
The starting point for a theology of the Name was an examination of the christological names or titles in the New Testament. This in turn led to a comparative study of the Old Testament names of God, especially "Elohim" and "Jehovah." Here they discovered the same promises hidden in the Name that were embodied in the name, "Lord-Jesus-Christ."

---

[2] William Phillips Hall, *Remarkable Biblical Discovery, Or "The Name" of God according to the Scriptures* (3rd ed.; New York: American Tract Society, 1931), p. 16.
[3] See especially Kenyon, *Wonderful Name of Jesus.*

One example is Frederick L. Chappell, a disciple of the prominent premillennial leader, A.J. Gordon, and teacher at Gordon Bible College in Boston. He devoted a series of lectures to the names of God in which he gave special attention to "Elohim" and "Jehovah."[4] Arno C. Gaebelein, in a study on the name "Jesus," observed that "the Greek *Jesus* is the same as the Hebrew *Joshua* – *Jehovah* saves .... Jehovah Himself is the great Hope."[5] J. Monro Gibson likewise traced the meaning of the name of Jesus to Joshua and Jehovah-our-salvation.[6] He was read and quoted favorably by early Oneness writers, including Andrew D. Urshan.[7] A.B. Simpson, in *The Names of Jesus*, made the same point that "the Christ of the Gospels is the Jehovah of the Old Testament."[8] Prominent Keswick figures published articles in the Keswick magazine on the Name in Scripture, especially linking the Old Testament meanings of the name, "Lord Jesus Christ."[9]

The study of the name of God by William Phillips Hall, originally published in 1910, included an extensive analysis of the Name in the Old Testament.[10] His purpose was to "identify the true God the Father," and to "ascertain the relationship of Christ to Him according to the Scriptures."[11] His "remarkable discovery" was that the Name revealed Jesus in his deity to be none other than the God of the Old Covenant.

---

[4] Reprinted in the magazine published by Oneness pioneer, Andrew Urshan, "Hear Ye! Hear Ye!" *Witness of God* (n.d.): 206.

[5] Gaebelein, The Hope of the Ages – The Messianic Hope in Revelation, in History and in Realization (New York: "Our Hope," 1938), p. 34.

[6] John Monro Gibson, The Gospel of Matthew (The Expositor's Bible, 15; New York: A.C. Armstrong, 1902-08), p. 10.

[7] Andrew D. Urshan, *The Almighty God in the Lord Jesus Christ* (Los Angeles: By the Author; reprint ed., Portland, OR: Apostolic Book Corner, n.d.), pp. 79-81.

[8] Simpson, *The Names of Jesus* (New York: Christian Alliance, 1892), p. 18.

[9] See A.T. Pierson, "Jesus-Christ-Lord," *The Keswick Week, 1909*, ed. Evan H. Hopkins (London: Marshall, 1909): 16-21; Prebendary Webb-Peploe, "Jesus Christ, Lord," *The Keswick Week, 1910*: 125-31; Evan H. Hopkins, "Our Lord's Names and Their Message," *The Keswick Week, 1911*: 157-61.

[10] Hall, *Remarkable Biblical Discovery*. Hall was part of the premillennial tradition represented by the prominent leader, Arno C. Gaebelein, who had requested that he undertake a study of the subject of the name of God; see "Prefatory Note," *Biblical Discovery*, p. 13. Hall was also President of the American Tract Society of New York; see A.D. Urshan, "The Name of God," *Pentecostal Outlook* 9 (January 1940): 4. Hall's work was a more thorough treatment of the name of God than is present in writers like A.B. Simpson, A.J. Gordon, A.C. Gaebelein, J.M. Gibson, E.W. Kenyon, and others.

[11] Hall, Biblical Discovery, p. 28.

John Miller, a Presbyterian minister from Princeton, wrote *Is God a Trinity?* (1876), in which he made similar arguments about the significance of the name of God as did later Oneness writers, though his name does not appear in their literature. Like the premillennial evangelicals, he concluded that, "Jehovah was the proper Name of God"[12] (based in Exod. 3:14), and that Jesus himself "is called Jehovah."[13]

b. The Fullness of God in Jesus

In their study of the names of God in Scripture, these evangelical teachers were attempting to defend what they called the "full" or "supreme" deity of Jesus. The focus of their interest was the *oneness* of the Son and Father, not the eternal distinctions between them. The following phrases about the person and dignity of Jesus reflect this concern: "the Supreme God,"[14] his "full deity,"[15] the "I AM,"[16] and "all in all,"[17] the "fulness of the Godhead,"[18] the manifestation of the "WHOLE GODHEAD,"[19] and the phrase "Jesus only."[20]

J.M. Gibson was more explicit in his displeasure with the classical formulations of the Trinity that in effect diminish the centrality of Jesus and his name. "In their zeal for personal distinctions in the Holy Trinity," theologians have lost the close relationship between the Divine Being and the particularity of His Name, thereby crushing the sweetness "out of the rich and precious Old Testament Name." They have attempted to "unfold a knowledge of God apart from His Son Christ Jesus ... apart from that Name by which He has made Himself known to us."[21]

These representative writers were orthodox Trinitarians (with the exception of Miller and Weeks) whose purpose was to defend the deity of Christ. Their distinctive method concentrated on the oneness of Christ with the Father in a way that supported a christocentric

---

[12] John Miller, *Is God a Trinity?* (3rd ed.; Princeton, NJ: By the Author, 1922), p. 122.

[13] Miller, *God a Trinity?* p. 80.

[14] The central point of the sermon preached by Elijah Hedding was, "Jesus Christ is the Supreme God," in *A Sermon*, p. 4.

[15] The phrase used by J.D. Davis and Clarence MacKinnon in referring to the deity of Christ, "Bible Scholarship and the Deity of Christ," *Sunday School Times* 52 (25 December 1910): 635.

[16] Gaebelein, The Lord of Glory – Meditations on the Person, the Work and Glory of Our Lord Jesus Christ (New York: "Our Hope," 1910), p. 8.

[17] Gibson, Christianity According to Christ, p. 102.

[18] A phrase from Col. 2:8-9, by Gibson, *Christianity,* p. 80.

[19] Miller, *Trinity?* p. 16.

[20] See Chapter 2 above.

[21] Gibson, *Christianity*, p. 8.

Trinitarian theology. Jesus is hermeneutically the revelational source of the knowledge and experience of the Trinity. A study of the distinctions between the divine Persons would not serve the purpose of these evangelicals. They continued to think and express themselves in terms of the three persons in the Trinity. But their passion and vision of God became centered in Jesus Christ and, in some cases, his Name.

Gibson is an example of this direction. He expressed concern that there was insufficient attention given to Christ in most orthodox teaching on the Trinity. Without denying the truth of the creeds, he was content to ground ecumenical Christian fellowship in the one faith that, "Christ is all and in all." Undoubtedly in criticism of some form of liberalism of his day, he stated that we are not called to seek the "absolute essence of Deity," but rather to seek the Father in the Son: "The whole knowledge of the Father is provided in Christ. We are 'complete in him.'"[22] He made much of Paul's statement, "In Him [Christ] dwelleth all the fulness of the Godhead bodily" (Col. 2:9). This passage led him to conclude that we will see the Trinity of God by "sitting at the feet of Jesus and looking into His face." All that God as Father, Son and Holy Spirit, has revealed of Himself for us "is manifest in Christ."[23]

Gaebelein likewise was passionate to retain a strong christocentric focus. His goal was to exalt and "give preeminence to Jesus Christ," because "Christ is worthy of all honor and glory," and people need "to have Christ lifted before them constantly."[24]

Simpson never tired of speaking of the "preeminence" of Christ and his being the "brightness of the Father's glory ... the King of Kings and Lord of Lords." Christians were bound to "give Jesus the supreme glory." In the end, "Christ shall be all, and in all," a state of bliss with "everything in Jesus, and Jesus in everything."[25]

For John Miller this christocentric direction "puts the WHOLE GODHEAD in Christ." Anticipating, as it were, the later Oneness polemic, he posed a rhetorical question, "Is the Deity in Christ the Second Person of the Trinity, or the One Personal Jehovah?" His answer, "We believe in the Sole Person of the Almighty as present in our Great Redeemer."[26]

---

[22] Gibson, *Christianity*, pp. 73-74, 102.

[23] Gibson, reprinted as "The Mystery of the Father, Son, and Holy Spirit," *Pentecostal Herald* 28 (December 1953): 5.

[24] Gaebelein, The Christ We Know – Meditations on the Person and Glory of our Lord Jesus Christ (New York: "Our Hope," 1927), p. 3.

[25] Simpson, *Names of Jesus*, pp. 49-58.

[26] Miller, *Trinity?* pp. 16, 72.

It is clear that in this period Jesus-centric and otherwise evangelical piety was producing a doctrinal defense for the deity of Christ. One aspect of that apologetic was to set forth a strongly christocentric understanding of the Trinity, one that would foreclose on any approach to God other than through Christ. Their language and approach were biblical: Jesus is the "manifestation" of God, the "fulness of the Godhead," the "Alpha and Omega."

The christology that emerged reflects the spiritual optimism of the perfectionist and Revivalist traditions. It reveals the glory, majesty and power of God in contrast to a kenotic christology that veils Christ's glory in suffering. Here we do not worship the Father *through* Christ, but we worship the God *in* Christ. Following Gibson's impatience with speculation on the Trinity apart from Christ, there is hardly a trace of theological reflection on the distinction between the eternal Son and Father so familiar in the historic fourth-century debates. The overriding passion was to acclaim that the deity who indwelt the human Jesus was fully, absolutely and completely God.

2. God and the Trinity

The doctrine of the Trinity in its historical development is the product of a complex and philosophically dense process that developed during the first four centuries of the church's history. When inherited by relatively uneducated preachers and evangelists, the effect has often been either indifference or distortion.

a. "Tri-Personality" Trinitarianism

The doctrine of the Trinity among the Holiness and Revivalist leaders of this period was often obscured by the intensity with which Jesus was proclaimed and worshipped. It appeared to be in large part borrowed baggage, but believed and defended primarily against Unitarians and others who denied both the Trinity and the deity of Christ. Even among otherwise christocentric writers were some who described the Trinity in ways that bordered on tritheism. Reuben A. Torrey, prominent Fundamentalist at the turn of the century and a learned man, described the unity of God as a "compound unity" in which "the Father, the Son and Holy Spirit are all clearly designated as Divine

Beings and as clearly distinguished from one another." They are, he stated, "separate personalities."[27]

Simpson's approach was similar in that it lacked awareness of the historical and theological complexities and perhaps served foremost a homiletical purpose. Referring to God's preparation for the creation of the world, Simpson states that, "[God] called a solemn council of the Trinity, and with the most majestic deliberation He decreed, 'Let us make man in our image after our likeness.'"[28] Simpson said of Jesus after the descent of the Spirit at Jordan that, "from that moment there were two persons in the life of Jesus, the Son of God and the Spirit of God."[29]

Equally crude was the opinion of Essek Kenyon who wrote that "person" in the Godhead is "an individual personality who has intellect, sensibilities and will." In this case Kenyon was attempting to establish the Holy Spirit as a person and not simply "an emanation from the Spirit of God." The effect, however, was to assert three distinct centers of consciousness: "The Holy Spirit is a distinct being, a personality distinct from God the Father, and God the Son."[30]

These rather literalistic interpretations of the Trinity are within the range of the traditional social analogy theory. But the language is imprecise and the authors show little grasp of the theological implications of terms inherited from another language and culture. These leaders after all were schooled in the Bible, not speculative metaphysics. They inherited a doctrine worked out in a Greek philosophical milieu, but were compelled to make it work within a popular Christian culture in which the one and only goal was "to know Christ and to make him known." Furthermore, they inherited terminology susceptible to distortion in its English translation – "God in three persons." Such a phrase is obviously open to a variety of interpretations as well as serious misunderstanding of the meaning of "person."

b. Christocentric Trinitarianism
We have already observed one leading figure who proposed a christocentric approach to the doctrine of the Trinity, J. Monro Gibson.[31]

---

[27] Reuben A. Torrey, *What the Bible Teaches* (New York: Fleming H. Revell, 1898), pp. 18–20.

[28] Simpson, *Wholly Sanctified* (Harrisburg, PA: Christian Publications, 1925), p. 73.

[29] Simpson, *The Gospel of Mark* (Christ in the Bible, 14; Harrisburg, PA: Christian Publications, n.d.), p. 33.

[30] Kenyon, *Father and Family*, p. 210.

[31] See also C.G. Finney, *Skeletons of a Course of Theological Lectures*, vol. I (Oberlin, OH.: James Steele, 1840), pp. 101–103; Asa Mahan, *Out of Darkness into Light; Or, The Hidden Life Made Manifest* (new ed.; London: Charles H. Kelly, 1874), p. 161.

Defensively, he claimed that the doctrine is "the only thoroughly rational basis for an intelligent Theism."[32] And though the term "Trinity" was not a Scriptural one, it "seems justified by this threefold representation."[33] However, its importance lies in its relationship to the revelation of Christ. The Christian is not to "seek a separate knowledge of the Father, Son and Holy Spirit," for they are "all in Jesus Christ," in the manifestation or "face of Christ."[34] Gibson's contribution was to bring the Trinity into harmony with a fully-orbed christocentrism without altering the traditional doctrine.

c. Some Non-Trinitarian Evangelical Alternatives

The Unitarian tradition has historically been far from uniform in its beliefs, other than a common rejection of the orthodox doctrine of the Trinity. At times efforts were made to reconcile a Unitarian view of God with an orthodox christology. Historian Timothy Smith describes this stream as Evangelical Unitarianism. He even records a revival that broke out among New England Unitarians in the mid-19th century, a detailed account of which was given by Frederic Dan Huntington, pastor of South Church in Boston:

> A large group of Unitarians believed the essence of Christianity to be a "special, supernatural redemption from sin, in Christ Jesus" the "eternally begotten Son of God," the "ever-living present head of the Church and personal intercessor for his disciples."[35]

Similar in spirit to this was what historian Robert Handy called the "Christocentric liberal tradition," represented by theologians such as William Newton Clarke, George A. Gordon and William Adams Brown whose ideas flourished around the turn of the 20th century. Historian Robert Handy states that they "not only believed in the unique divinity of Jesus Christ, but they seriously endeavored to ground that divinity in the ontological being of God."[36]

Both movements, however, were short-lived. An alternative proposal appeared with the publication of a book (mentioned above) by

---

[32] Gibson, *The Inspiration and Authority of Holy Scripture* (New York: Fleming H. Revell, n.d.), p. 99.

[33] Gibson, *Christianity*, p. 120.

[34] Gibson, "Mystery," p. 5.

[35] Cited in Timothy Smith, *Revivalism and Social Reform in Mid-Nineteenth-Century America* (New York: Abingdon, 1957), p. 95.

[36] H. Sheldon Smith, Robert T. Handy, Lefferts A. Loetscher, *American Christianity: An Historical Interpretation with Representative Documents*, vol. II: *1820-1960* (New York: Charles Scribner's Sons, 1963), p. 263.

John Miller, *Is God a Trinity?* In it he maintains a high Christology and resembles an approach similar in many ways to Oneness theology. A Presbyterian minister in Princeton, New Jersey, Miller confessed to be a "high Calvinist in all the realities of my creed." He refused the traditional appellations of heterodoxy such as Socinian, Arian, Pelagian, or Arminian. In place of what he called the "Platonic Trinity," he proposed a radically christocentric view that "puts the WHOLE GODHEAD in Christ."[37]

For Miller, God in his being is one without distinctions: "No hypostatic difference separates the Father from the Son."[38] Similar to Oneness theologians, he worked out a Unitarian view of God by means of the name of God in revelation, in Christ, and in baptism. To the charge of modalism, he declared, "no objection." God holds three "offices," but these do not imply "any intended threeness."[39] Although I have found no reference to Miller in early Oneness literature, the complex of ideas relating to the nature of God, the person of Christ, the revealed name of God, and baptism are nearly identical to the theology of Oneness Pentecostals.[40]

Miller represents an alternative to the substance theology of the creeds in favor of a more Jewish view of the monarchy of God and a christocentric substitute for the hypostatic distinctions within the Godhead. He attempts to hold together a Unitarian view of God and the deity of Christ. He further reaffirms his belief in the "evangelical doctrines" of incarnation, redemption, mediation, intercession, regeneration, justification, adoption, sanctification, the final judgment, and the glorification of the redeemed.[41]

A second non-trinitarian view from an evangelical perspective comes from Robert D. Weeks, an orthodox, Calvinistic Presbyterian from Newark, New Jersey.[42] Although he published the same year as fellow Presbyterian, John Miller (1876), there is no indication of mutual influence, and their views differ substantially. While Weeks's book does not appear to be known by early Oneness writers, it was discov-

---

[37] Miller, *Trinity?* pp. 13-16.

[38] Miller, *Trinity?* p. 39.

[39] Miller, *Is God a Trinity?,* reprint in *Questions Awakened by the Bible* (2nd ed.; Philadelphia: J.B. Lippincott, 1877), p. 12.

[40] Later Oneness teachers discovered Miller's book. His work on the Trinity was being studied as early as 1974 at Apostolic Bible Institute, a Oneness Bible school in St. Paul, MN. Interview with Robert Sabin, Apostolic Bible Institute, St. Paul, MN, 20 May 1974.

[41] Miller, *Trinity?* p. 132.

[42] Robert D. Weeks, *Jehovah-Jesus: The Oneness of God; The True Trinity* (New York: Dodd, Mead & Co., 1876), p. 7.

ered and edited by Oneness leader and longtime presbyter with the United Pentecostal Church, C. Haskell Yadon (1908-1997), in 1952.[43] Weeks considered himself to be orthodox, holding to "the great essential truths of the Gospel." Nor did he desire to dissociate himself from this fellowship. His concern was to expose what he considered to be the error of a "PLURALITY OF DIVINE PERSONS" in the Godhead. He also claimed no heterodox influences but credited his views to a "careful study of the Word of God."[44]

The goal of Weeks's book was to defend the monarchy of God, the "unqualified absolute unity of the Godhead,"[45] against any form of pluralism – which is suggested by the term, "Oneness", in the book's title. But his christology is semi-Arian; he gave little attention to the name of God, and none to baptism. Consequently, this alternative garnered little support, if any, among other Oneness Pentecostals. Yadon's interest seems to have been primarily Weeks's monarchical view of God.

d. The Trinity and Early Pentecostals

The early Pentecostals inherited, like other evangelicals, the doctrine of the Trinity as part of their Christian heritage. It would be more accurate to say that they *experienced* the Trinity rather than reflected upon it. They were Jesus-centered and claimed an experience of baptism with the Holy Spirit. It is Hollenweger's conclusion that the Oneness doctrine is more commensurate "with the religious feeling and practice of Pentecostalism than a doctrine of the Trinity taken over without understanding from the traditional churches."[46] While most Pentecostals held to a "trinity of experience," they formulated it in the borrowed terminology of traditional trinitarian theology. It can be argued that Oneness Pentecostals, in contrast, developed a theology *sui generis* that was more compatible with their Pentecostal experience of God.

The Jesus-centric evangelicals of the late 19th century concentrated their efforts on defending the full deity of Jesus and his *oneness* with

---

[43] Yadon discovered the book at random in a used book store, edited and republished under the title, *Jehovah-Jesus: The Supreme God – Son of God, Son of Man* (Twin Falls, ID: By the Editor, 1952). Because of Yadon's executive position in the Oneness organization, United Pentecostal Church, he was asked to discontinue promoting the book, as its heterodox Christology diverged significantly from the "orthodox" Oneness position (interview with Nathaniel A. Urshan, Calvary Tabernacle, Indianapolis, IN, 23 May 1973).

[44] Weeks, *Jehovah-Jesus*, pp. 5, 8, 13.

[45] Weeks, *Jehovah-Jesus*, p. 62; see also pp. 72 and 76.

[46] Hollenweger, *Pentecostals*, pp. 311-12.

God. Part of their hermeneutical strategy was a study of the titles and names of God in Scripture, thereby building a rudimentary theology of the Name – one that would express the unity of Jesus with God. They gave little serious attention to the doctrine of the Trinity. Some resorted to crude explanations that bordered on tritheism. Gibson proposes a form of christocentric Trinitarianism. Miller presents us with a full Christo-unitarian theology, and Weeks follows the route of a weak semi-Arian Christology. We know the spiritual ancestors of Oneness Pentecostals. But we are told little of who were direct influences from this period.

3. The Name and Person of Jesus

Many evangelicals at the turn of the century engaged in the apologetic task of defending the deity of Christ against what they perceived to be a lethal attack on the heart of the Christian faith by Unitarians and liberal Protestants. The evangelistic task would be utterly undermined should Jesus' identity be reduced to that of a mere human being, one whom we cannot claim as "God-with-us" or Savior. While his humanity was essential to their Christology, they viewed their mission to be to mount a vigorous defense of his deity.

The legacy of Jesus-centric piety, evangelical biblical authority and revivalistic evangelism were the forces that helped shape a distinctive christocentric faith. The result of this coalescing tendency was demonstrated in both language and doctrine. Writers would refer not simply to the "deity" of Christ, but to his "full" or "supreme" deity. It was not sufficient to affirm Christ as the Second Person of the Trinity, a doctrine that in fact seemed for some to diminish his centrality. Instead, the unity or oneness of Christ with the Father was stressed in a way that produced a christocentric doctrine of the Trinity. Many of these evangelicals represented the Reformed Keswick Holiness tradition and the emerging premillennial movement. Unlike the next generation that concentrated much of its argument for the deity of Christ on the virgin birth, these proto-Fundamentalists turned to a study of the name and titles of God in Scripture.

The name of God is transferred to Jesus in the writings of a number of evangelical writers of this period. While there is no consensus on precisely what that Name is, *that* there is a Name to which Christians can look for salvation is clear.

a. The Many Names of God
– John Monro Gibson and Arno C. Gaebelein

It was doctrinally imperative for all evangelicals that the saving benefits of Christ be grounded in his personhood, in *who* he is. As they launched upon a study of the Name, they drew conclusions regarding both his person and work. But there was no consistency among them in the choice or number of names.

For J. Monro Gibson, there was no singular name by which God is revealed. The purpose of the "Name" of God in the Old and New Covenants is primarily to affirm the *particularity* of divine revelation in Jesus, which is expressed in two ways. The whole Trinity is manifested in the "face of Jesus," who is also revealed to us as God by means of his Name.[47] Gibson referred to "Immanuel" (Matt. 1:23) as a name by which God is revealed in Jesus. But he pointed to the name "Jehovah" as the "great name" that links God with Jesus:

The Name of God was that by which He has made Himself known to us ...above all, the two great names of "Jehovah" in the Old Testament and "Jesus" in the New.[48] "Immanuel" provides a strong New Covenant interpretation that confirms Jesus to be the God of Israel: "Full and clear at last of that great Name of the old covenant, the name Jehovah: 'I AM,' 'I AM THAT I AM.'"[49] Though Gibson showed preference for the name "Jehovah" as the definitive name that ties God to the identity of Jesus, he did not limit the revelation of the name of God to only one name. His purpose was to show that the identity of Jesus and the names or titles attributed to him preserved the *personal* and *particular* dimensions of the revelation of the Trinity.

Arno C. Gaebelein's approach is similar. His conviction was that "our Lord Jesus Christ is no less person, than the I AM." He wrote frequently of the name, "that worthy name," "that blessed name," "the full worth and glory of that name,"[50] the "matchless name."[51] Yet he did not identify any one name as the only name. He could write that one day "we shall begin to learn the full worth and glory of that Name, the name of the Lord Jesus Christ,"[52] that one day "every knee

---

[47] Gibson, "Mystery," p. 5.
[48] Gibson, *Christianity*, pp. 7, 75.
[49] Gibson, "Gospel of Matthew," p. 450.
[50] Gaebelein, *Lord of Glory*, pp. 8–13.
[51] Gaebelein, *Christ We Know*, p. 45.
[52] Gaebelein, *Lord of Glory*, p. 13.

shall bow at the name of Jesus," and again that "He is to be born of *the* Virgin and His Name would be Immanuel – God with us."[53]

At times he spoke of the Name as if it had an independent status from the person of Christ and itself worthy of adoration. He would occasionally exclaim, "Glory to His Name!" "All Glory and Praise to His Holy Name,"[54] or "Oh! That worthy and matchless name!"[55] At one point he asked, "Is your heart increasingly attracted to that worthy name?"[56] The fluidity and imprecision with which Gaebelein used the Name is due in large part to his doxological and homiletical purposes, which reflect to some degree the piety that is interwoven with popular teaching.

Gaebelein seems to have held an unusual view that the Name is hidden in the present age and will be revealed only at the Second Coming of Christ. He states that Jesus now "bears many names," but there is a Name that only he himself knows (see Rev. 9:12). "The full revelation of that name awaits His future manifestation, when He comes the second time." [57] Like Gibson, Gaebelein did not draw a sharp distinction between names and titles. They were sometimes objects of devotion, at other times indicators of the divine status of Jesus. Gaebelein was less concerned to discover *the* name of God than to demonstrate that the various names and titles that Jesus bears signify the incarnational presence of God.

b. The Name as "Jesus" – A.B. Simpson

Simpson was equally hesitant to propose any particular name as the name of God. He called the triune baptismal formula in Matt. 28:19 the name (singular) of God.[58] He examined the names "Emmanuel," "Jesus," "Christ," and "King," to show the presence and work of God in Jesus.[59] Referring to the "chief cornerstone" of Isa. 28:16, he stated that "the name is upon the stone, and so we should hear the name of Jesus, and no name be seen but His,"[60] and that in the end all will "bow at the Name of Jesus."[61]

---

[53] Gaebelein, *God Speaks*, pp. 131, 101.

[54] Gaebelein, *Lord of Glory*, pp. 43, 130.

[55] Gaebelein, *Christ We Know*, p. 45.

[56] Gaebelein, *The Lord of Glory*, p. 14.

[57] Gaebelein, *The Church in the House* (New York: "Our Hope," n.d.), p. 84.

[58] Simpson, *Christ of Forty Days*, p. 217.

[59] Simpson, *Matthew*, pp. 20-21.

[60] Simpson, *Names of Jesus*, p. 211.

[61] Simpson, *In Heavenly Places* (New York: Christian Alliance, 1892), p. 54.

In his songs and hymns, Simpson shows a preference for the name "Jesus,"[62] though there is no systematic doctrinal treatment of it. His point was simply that the name of Jesus signifies "His very personality, taking the very same place as He Himself."[63] Christians are to carry out their ministry in the name of the Lord Jesus "as representatives, and in His very person."[64] In other words, the Name carries the personality of the bearer, who in Jesus is no less that God himself.

c. "Jesus" as the New Covenant Name – Essek W. Kenyon

Kenyon took a further step in the study of the name of God by identifying the name "Jesus" as the singular name in the New Covenant. The name of Jesus was given to him at birth with the purpose that it was to be as redemptive and effective as the person Jesus was in his work on the cross. In fact, the Name is inseparably bound up with Christ's atoning work, and its availability to the believer is one of the benefits of the atonement. One can realize the redemptive benefits of Christ by calling upon the name of Jesus: "All that Jesus was, that Name will be during this dispensation. That Name has lost none of the power of the Man who bore it."[65] The name of Jesus is the means by which God makes effective in the present the benefits secured for humanity by the historical Jesus.

For Kenyon, this relationship between Jesus and his Name is a legal one. He asserted that, "Jesus is great because He inherited a great Name," and because "a great Name was conferred upon Him." This conferral of God's family name at his birth seems to be for Kenyon more than merely a pointer to Jesus' deity, but is itself the means of incarnating deity in him. The identification between the Name and the person was complete: "All He [Jesus] was, all He did, all He is and all that He will be is in that Name now."[66]

d. "Lord" as the New Covenant Name – William Phillips Hall

While the substance of Kenyon's teaching was reflected in early Oneness Theology – and undoubtedly there was considerable influence – Frank Ewart credits Hall with much of the groundbreaking study on

---

[62] See Chapter 2 above.

[63] Simpson, *Heavenly Places,* p. 24.

[64] Simpson, *Heavenly Places*, p. 48.

[65] Kenyon, *Wonderful Name*, p. 14.

[66] Kenyon, *Wonderful Name*, pp. 7, 42.

the importance of the name of God in Scripture.[67] Hall claimed that his "discovery" of the Name was identical with "the original apostolic interpretation of the Deity of the Lord Jesus Christ." Specifically, he concluded that when God disclosed Himself to Moses (Exod. 3:14), He revealed his name – not a title – as "I AM." This "ineffable" Name later became the unutterable Sacred Name that was translated in the Septuagint as "Lord." It was significant for Hall that the early Christians, all Jewish converts, "never used any other word than that of Lord as the Name of God." He observed that the name "Lord" or kyrios was the only consistent Name applied to Jesus by the early church, thereby leading him to conclude that the person of Jesus and the God of Abraham, Isaac and Jacob are one and the same.[68]

Echoing Gibson's views, Hall approached the doctrine of the Trinity christocentrically. The master text was Paul's acclamation that "in him [Christ] dwelleth all the fullness of the Godhead bodily" (Col. 2:9). Hall's hermeneutic was to transfer the trinitarian phrase, "Father, Son, Holy Spirit," to the compound name, Lord Jesus Christ. "Lord" is the name of the Father, "Jesus" the name of the Son, and "Christ" the name of the Holy Spirit. As the triune revelation is in the one "incarnate triune God," so also does the triune reality have only one name, "Lord Jesus Christ."[69]

It is surprising that Ewart seems not to have observed, or at least pointed out, that Hall's choice of "Lord" as the revealed name of God differs from his own conclusion that the name is "Jesus." Nevertheless, the significance of Hall's study for Oneness theology lays in its contribution to the development of a biblical Christology of the Name, including a christocentric approach to the doctrine of the Trinity and the concept that one Name spiritually and theologically unites Jesus with the God of Israel.

4. The Name and Work of Jesus

Early evangelical writers embarked on a study of the name of God in part to reaffirm the divine nature of Christ and to identify him fully with the God of the Old Testament. But they were also interested in

---

[67] The United Pentecostal Church International, the largest Oneness denomination, publishes an abridged version of Hall's *Remarkable Biblical Discovery*.

[68] Hall, *Biblical Discovery*, pp. 26, 34-35, 44.

[69] Hall, *What Is "The Name"? Or, "The Mystery of God" Revealed* (Greenwich, CT: By the Author, 1913), pp. 80, 118, 126. See Hall's analysis in *What Is "The Name"*, pp. 86-115.

how the Name functioned in the work of Christ, particularly in the atonement.

a. A Nestorian Atonement?

The traditional Reformed evangelical understanding of the atonement was primarily that of the substitutionary theory. It was committed to a Christology in which the efficacy of Christ's death depended upon Jesus being divine. But it also required him to be human, to be the sinless Lamb without blemish. Evangelical Christology, however, tended to differentiate strongly between the two natures, probably in part to preserve the traditional Reformed emphasis on the transcendence and sovereignty of God and the untarnished deity of Christ. While in his incarnate state, he never ceased to be fully God – omnipresent, omniscient, and omnipotent – though he voluntarily chose not to exercise these powers most of the time. His miracles were customarily credited to his divine nature.[70]

At the same time, the emphasis on Jesus' perfect sacrifice focused on his sinless humanity, since it was believed that a holy God cannot look on sin. The human flesh of Jesus became the curtain that shielded the sin of the world from the holy eyes of God. In the words of Evan Hopkins of Keswick, "Jesus the Son of God, in His perfect humanity, dies a sacrifice for sin."[71] Gaebelein elaborated on this popular notion of God-in-a-body. In Mary, Yahweh was pleased "to take on the prepared body" (Heb. 10:5).[72] For Gaebelein, the two natures were so independent of each other that "He who is Immanuel ...was forsaken of God, in the sufferings of the cross."[73] Simpson, likewise, regarded Christ's body as the sacrifice: "That flesh stood between us and God, therefore it had to die in place of the guilty race, and when Christ's flesh was crucified on Calvary, it was the same as if the guilty race had been judged and slain."[74]

In an exposition on the virgin birth, Kenyon taught a peculiar kind of "supernatural biology." To protect Christ from having a sinful nature like ours, "the seed must be of divine origin instead of human."[75] God, therefore, prepared a special body by means of virgin birth to be uniquely the Son of God. It was only through this body that God was

---

[70] For example, see Gaebelein, *God Speaks*, pp. 108-109.
[71] Evan Hopkins, "Our Lord's Names and Their Message," p. 158.
[72] Gaebelein, *God Speaks*, p. 125.
[73] Gaebelein, *Hope of Ages*, p. 44.
[74] Simpson, *Names of Jesus*, p. 67.
[75] Kenyon, *Father and Family*, p. 123.

able to suffer for the sins of humankind. Like Gaebelein, Kenyon declared that God abandoned Jesus at the point of his death in which "God turns His back upon Him."[76]

Aspects of teaching on the atonement presented here have their origin in the Anselmic tradition. But the peculiarities are shaped by a popular evangelical faith that was more concerned to preserve the dignity of divine transcendence and the deity of Christ than to speculate on the unity of the two natures in Christ. Most of the teaching is echoed later in Oneness literature, especially the notion of the divine abandonment of Christ on the cross.

b. The Atonement as Legal Transaction

The illustrations presented here of a substitutionary theory of the atonement also carry Anselm's metaphor of a legal transaction.[77] Atonement and salvation language is full of legal metaphors, such as A.J. Gordon's statements that, "our sins had merited for us eternal death," and the shedding of Christ's blood had worked to "cancel our sins."[78]

Simpson used the language of Christ's "redemptive rights." Through his death Christ secured for us certain rights. It was as if a friend selected goods for us and paid for them himself, requiring only that we pick them up. In the same way Christ purchased our salvation "and paid for it to the full."[79]

Since the Name was regarded by some as an aspect of the atonement, how then did the believer appropriate it? The answer is that the Name was given as part of the legal transaction on the cross. Simpson stated that, because of the purchase, "in His name we may come and buy ...without price."[80] In a spiritually literal sense, we now have legal rights to use the Name. The name of God that became identified with the person of Jesus became a legal right to salvation's benefits with the

---

[76] Kenyon, *Father and Family*, p. 158.

[77] This view is also indebted in part to the covenant theology of Puritanism two centuries earlier, known as the Federal School. Historian Perry Miller points out that the term "covenant" came to mean "a bargain, a contract, a mutual agreement, a document binding upon both signatories, drawn up in the presence of witnesses and sealed by a notary public." Soteriologically speaking, it means that God communicates with humanity "as between two partners in a business enterprise," *Errand in the Wilderness* (New York: Harper & Row, 1956), pp. 60-61.

[78] A.J. Gordon, "Finding Her Title-Deed," *The Watchword* 1 (August 1879): 204. See also Gordon, "The Cancelled Check," *The Watchword* 2 (January 1880): 66-67.

[79] Simpson, *Heavenly Places*, pp. 13-14.

[80] Simpson, *Heavenly Places*, p. 14.

purchase of those rights on the cross. At that moment God signed the covenant with His Name and sealed it with His blood.

5. The Name and the Christian

The attention given to the Name in Christology and soteriology was extended to the life of the believer. The Name was secured in the atonement, and its benefits available to those who received the salvation offered by Christ. But the spiritual significance of the Name also extended to other aspects of the Christian life.

a. The Glory of the Name
As the name of Yahweh was the object of worship and adoration for the Jews, so also the name of Jesus Christ was exalted and worshipped among Jesus-centric evangelicals.[81] The Name is a means of grace by which the presence of God is revealed and experienced in joy, praise and intimate fellowship with the risen Christ.

For some, invoking of the name "Jesus" itself brought closeness to Christ because "it stands for the deepest, most intimate identity or personality of the one of whom it is used."[82] One writer extolled the name of Jesus as "the peerless name," even the enunciation of which "should thrill our souls with holy delight, and fill our hearts with unspeakable gladness."[83] Gaebelein once introduced a prophetic conference with the admonition "to exalt and glorify one Person and one Name, the Name which is above every other name."[84] A Keswick speaker teaching on the Name spoke passionately of the believer's response to the name of Jesus: to those who love Jesus "His name is precious, sweeter than honey and the honeycomb. It brings sometimes tears to the eyes, always joy to the heart."[85]

In the view of these evangelicals, the first response of a believer to the name of Jesus was doxological, praising it as one would praise the

---

[81] See John Pedersen, *Israel – Its Life and Culture* (2 vols.; London: Oxford University Press for Geoffrey Cumberlege, 1926), p. 249.

[82] *The Sunday School Times* 52 (5 March 1910): 118.

[83] George C. Needham, "The Name Jesus – A Bible Reading," *The Watchword* 4 (January 1882): 92.

[84] Gaebelein, ed., *Christ and Glory – Addresses Delivered at the New York Prophetic Conference, Carnegie Hall, November 25-28, 1918* (New York: "Our Hope," 1919), p. 7.

[85] Taylor Smith, "The Name above Every Name," *The Keswick Week*, 1920, ed. Evan H. Hopkins (London: Marshall, 1920): 23; see Gibson, *Christianity according to Christ*, pp. 9-10.

person. Expressions of a Jesus-centric piety that centered on the Name soon became ready vehicles for giving "glory to the Name."

b. The Power of the Name

Due in part to an increased interest in the book of Acts, evangelical teachers began to give more attention to the promise of spiritual power in the life of the believer. As teaching on the Name became popular, leaders would speak of the "power of the Name." This power usually took one of two forms – either the *effective* power that worked inwardly or in miracles, or the *legal* power of attorney that came with the use of the Name.

Evangelical and Revivalist faith was concerned with spiritual power – conversion, transformed lives, Holiness, and, in the Keswick tradition, living the victorious higher life in Christ. Many responded to what they perceived to be near apostasy in the established churches of their day, by calling on God for divine power to revitalize the church. Some believed that a rediscovery of the meaning of the name of Jesus in the New Testament would bring with it this power. Charles Haddon Spurgeon (1834-1892), the leading British Baptist preacher and writer during the latter half of the 19th century, commented that "to enter into the meaning of the Name of Jesus and give it practical effect would re-create the basis of both the power and persecution of the apostolic Age." Hall likewise was convinced that through the truth of the name of God that he had discovered, "the pure faith and power of the early Church may be restored to us in this end time."[86]

To the familiar question, "Why are prayers not answered?" Keswick speaker, Bishop Taylor Smith, responded, "because you have neglected the Power of the Name." The name of Jesus "stands for answered prayer, and it stands for assured power." He summed up the Keswick experience and what it stood for, as "claiming blessing through the Name, that we may be filled to overflowing."[87]

Simpson considered the clue to the power of the apostolic church to be in the Name: "'In my Name' was the watchword of all this power." The present church was handicapped because it "cannot understand or stand the fullness of His power."[88] Simpson's belief in the power of the name of Jesus was for him more than speculation. It came to him with force in 1907 when the issue of tongues as evidence of Spirit-baptism was causing severe tension within the Christian and

---

[86] Cited in Ewart, *Name and Book*, pp. 1, 138.
[87] Taylor Smith, "Name above Every Name," p. 23.
[88] Simpson, *Christ of Forty Days*, pp. 137, 18.

Missionary Alliance fellowship. In a journal entry dated August 22, Simpson recorded the following:

> While waiting on God on my lawn at night as I have often done this summer, I had a special season of mighty prayer, in which God revealed to me the NAME of JESUS in special power and enabled me to plead it within the veil for an hour or more until it seemed to break down every barrier and to command all that I could ask.... Now I fully take all that is promised in HIS NAME.[89]

The Name was a compelling spiritual power to break through struggles in prayer.

Healing was also regarded by some as a manifestation of power in the name of Jesus.[90] Since Jesus was the great Healer and his Name was the "intended equivalent for His personal presence," the Christian should expect the same results as those to whom Jesus was present in the body.[91]

When Frank Ewart removed himself from the Trinitarian ranks and began baptizing in the name of Jesus, he reported a new release of spiritual power in his ministry: "At the end of the Apostolic age and subsequently until 1914, the Name was missing, and consequently the miracles performed in that Name, or by virtue of that Name, never took place." The traditional powerless church had become "the laughing stock of the enemy." [92] In a similar vein, Franklin Small wrote on February 16, 1916, that since his baptism in the name of Jesus, "I have never felt more of His power and presence in my life, than since I obeyed His Word (Acts 2:38)."[93]

Like many other evangelicals, Ewart felt that the church was in a "rugged and awful crisis." The only way out of it was through spiritual power, for "the fundamental of any system of religion is that power, inherent in the system, to demonstrate its message to the world by miracles of mercy to mankind."[94] The early Oneness movement then

---

[89] Recorded in "Simpson's Nyack Diary"; cited in Charles W. Nienkirchen, *A.B. Simpson and the Pentecostal Movement: A Study in Continuity, Crisis, and Change* (Peabody, MA: Hendrickson, 1992), pp. 143-44.

[90] See Gaebelein, *God Speaks*, p. 143; George B. Peck, "In His Name," *The Christian Alliance and Foreign Missionary Weekly* 15 (14 August 1895): 102-103; "Wonderful Miracles wrought in Jesus' Name," *The Latter Rain Evangel* (July 1913): 2-4.

[91] George Peck, "In His Name," p. 102.

[92] Ewart, *Name and Book*, pp. 79, 24.

[93] Cited in Robert A. Larden, *Our Apostolic Heritage – An Official History of the Apostolic Church of Pentecost, Incorporated* (Calgary: Kyle Printing and Stationery, 1971), p. 34.

[94] Ewart, *Name and Book*, pp. 127, 128.

fell in line with the message of the others, namely, that the name of Jesus released a new power to the church in their day.

The second function of the Name was granting Christians the power of attorney, a legal right, to use the name of Jesus in prayer. Some traced the source of answered prayer and assured power to the legal right given to the Christian. In teaching on prayer, Finney had instructed that it must be offered in the name of Christ. He illustrated it in the language of a business transaction:

> If you should go to a bank with a draft or note, endorsed by John Jacob Astor, that would be giving you his name, and you know you could get the money from the bank just as well as he could himself. Now, Jesus Christ gives you the use of his name.[95]

Because of the atonement, "the value of Christ's merits are all at your disposal. If Jesus Christ could obtain any blessing at the court of heaven, you may obtain the same by asking in his name."[96]

This connection between the legal authority of the Name in prayer and the meritorious work of Christ was common after Finney's time. One evangelist's description of the privileges in prayer was nearly identical to Finney's. Christ paid for what we could not, and made it available to us: "When and where Christ expressly and specifically authorizes us to ask in His Name, he puts us in full possession of a power of attorney by which we may obtain at a throne of grace all that He could." Evangelist Wigle, a Keswick Holiness evangelist, made it clear that "we must present His sacrificial, atoning merit, as though it were our own, as the *ground* of our *right* of petition, acceptance, and salvation."[97]

A.J. Gordon, arguing that Christ's name stood for the person himself, stated that "the Christian is permitted to use the credit of that 'name which is above every name' in making his request to God."[98] R.A. Torrey, likewise, used the illustration of a bank transaction to describe prayer in the name of Jesus Christ.[99] Another writer described the relationship like that of "ownership of that name" which was

---

[95] Finney, *Lectures on Revivals of Religion* (Boston: John P. Jewett, 1856), p. 55.

[96] Finney, *Sermons on the Way to Salvation* (Oberlin, OH: Edward J. Goodrich, 1891), p. 406.

[97] E. Wigle, *Prevailing Prayer Or the Secret of Soul Winning* (Grand Rapids, MI: Stanton, 1891), p. 109; see also the teaching of Andrew Murray, cited in Wigle, *Prevailing Prayer*, pp. 107, 110.

[98] A.J. Gordon, *In Christ* (Boston: Howard Gannett, 1883), p. 135; see statement by Gordon in Peck, "In His Name," p. 20.

[99] Torrey, *Bible Teaches*, p. 445.

given to us to use in our ministry, e.g., using the Name in prayer for healing.[100] Simpson gave the illustration of the purchase of goods with another's money, concluding that we could now come and purchase "in His name."[101]

Kenyon gives the most thorough presentation of a legal model in relation to the name of Jesus. Having established the legal, transactional view of the atonement, he concluded that Jesus gave us his Name to use in prayer. As Jesus himself was the mediator or advocate, he gave us his Name as power of attorney: "This puts prayer on a purely legal basis "and even "makes it a business proposition." We are "saved by the name," "baptized into the name,"[102] pray in the name,[103] heal and exorcise demons using the name,[104] and "herald this Name among the nations."[105] In sum, Kenyon systematically developed a theology of the name of Jesus for Christian praxis by popularizing the traditional substitutionary theory of the atonement.

c. The Name in Baptism

It is not surprising that an intense biblical study of the Name would eventually lead to an examination of baptism with its precise formula for the invocation of the name of God. There were sufficient elements in the Jesus–centric evangelical tradition to create at least the conditions for what emerged in 1913 as the Oneness "revelation of the name of Jesus," an event ignited by a baptismal sermon. As ministers studied the book of Acts and preached the power of the Name, they were intuitively led to the apostolic formula of baptism in the name of the Lord Jesus or Jesus Christ.

The practice of baptism in the name of Jesus Christ is not a new phenomenon in the history of the church. Martin Luther is reported to have encountered a dispute over the use of the baptismal formula in his day.[106] Apparently certain members of the Plymouth Brethren in England were at one time using exclusively the christocentric formula of Acts 2:38.[107] And there continues to be disparate groups that are

---

[100] Peck, "In His Name," p. 21.

[101] Simpson, *Heavenly Places*, p. 14.

[102] Kenyon, *Wonderful Name*, pp. 2–22.

[103] Kenyon, *Father and Family*, p. 247.

[104] See Kenyon, *Wonderful Name*, chs. 5, 6.

[105] Kenyon, *Wonderful Name*, p. 39.

[106] John Dillenberger, ed., *Martin Luther – Selections from His Writings* (Garden City, NY: Doubleday, 1961), p. 297.

[107] G.T. Stokes, *The Acts of the Apostles* (The Expositor's Bible, 17; New York: A.C. Armstrong, 1908), p. 140.

Trinitarian in doctrine but practice baptism in the name of Jesus Christ.[108]

The logic used by Kenyon was that if the name of Jesus is a legal benefit achieved on the cross and available to the Christian, the first step would be to appropriate that Name in baptism. He explored the Trinitarian formula and its meaning, but concluded that "baptizing into the Name of the Lord Jesus Christ is even richer and fuller than either of these ('Father' and 'Holy Spirit') – it comprehends all that is in them with additions."[109]

Miller became convinced of the validity of the Acts formula through a theological reflection upon his strongly christocentric approach to the triune revelation, as well as an exegetical effort to harmonize Matt. 28:19 and Acts 2:38. Commenting on the former he stated: "If it says, Baptizing them in the name of the Father, the Son and the Holy Ghost, it means in the One Glorious Name (*sing.*), enthroned as Father, enshrined as the Son, and engrafted as the Holy Ghost." That Name is the "LORD JESUS CHRIST."[110] Miller's starting point was the radical unity of God, from which he deduced the christocentric baptismal formula. The Oneness movement, in contrast, began with a challenge to the baptismal formula, which eventually led to a rejection of the traditional doctrine of the Trinity. Hall began with a study of the Name, which led him to conclude that baptism should be administered in the "Name of the Lord Jesus Christ."[111] Like Miller, he resolved the apparent inconsistency between the formulas of Matt. 28:19 and Acts 2:38 by harmonizing the titles "Father," "Son" and "Holy Spirit" with the threefold Name, "Lord Jesus Christ."[112] Hall and Ewart were in communication following the publication of Hall's book, *Remarkable Biblical Discovery or "The Name" of God According to the Scriptures*. Though probably exaggerating, Ewart reported that "it is a matter of fact that thousands of people, after reading Mr. Hall's

---

[108] An example is the late Dr. William Aberhart, former Premier of Alberta, Canada, and Fundamentalist preacher whose radio ministry and Prophetic Bible Institute were well known during the 1930's and 1940's; personal letter from Cyril Hutchinson, President of Berean College, 8 January 1974. Baptism in the name of Jesus was also practiced in some segments of the Jesus Movement of the 1960's (interview with J. Rodman Williams, Episcopal Charismatic Clergy Conference, Dallas, TX, February 2, 1973).

[109] Kenyon, *Wonderful Name*, pp. 89, 93.

[110] Miller, *God a Trinity?* pp. 128-29.

[111] Hall, *Biblical Discovery*, pp. 62-63, 76-91, 109-13, 115-21; *What Is the "Name"?* pp. 70-71; *Calling Upon the Name of the Lord* (Cos Cob, CT: Christ Witness, 1920), p. 22.

[112] Hall, *What Is the "Name?"*, pp. 86-115.

book ... were baptized into the Name of Jesus, the Christ, and not a few ministers among them."[113]

During the first decade of the Pentecostal Revival, the "apostolic" formula was apparently used in baptisms without being challenged. Assemblies of God historian, Carl Brumback, recorded that "some had used the shorter formula for years, so its use was no drastic innovation."[114]

Charles Parham, the Holiness minister regarded by many as the father of the modern Pentecostal movement, reportedly became concerned over the right baptismal formula as early as 1902 and temporarily changed to the christocentric pattern. Employing a discernment strategy that he had used the previous year to decide whether or not speaking in tongues was the biblical "initial evidence," he claimed to have received divine confirmation of the right words to invoke in baptism when he and his students were "waiting upon God that we might know the scriptural teaching on water Baptism." Howard Goss, Pentecostal and Oneness pioneer, was converted in 1903 under Parham's ministry, and acknowledged that Parham had baptized him in Jesus' name.[115]

Andrew Urshan, another Oneness pioneer, claimed to have been convinced of the apostolic formula as early as 1910 and reportedly began straightaway to baptize his converts in Jesus' name.[116] But it was not until 1919 that he officially affiliated with the Oneness movement.

Perhaps unwittingly, the study of the Name led a number of leaders and writers to attempt to resolve the apparent inconsistency in the baptismal formulae as set forth in Christ's commission in Matt. 28:19 and the practice of the Apostles. Some approved of the christocentric formula in Acts, and a few practiced it. For those adhering to the orthodox doctrine of the Trinity, it was of no apparent concern. What was different after 1914 was the insistence upon *re-baptism* and a theology of God that challenged the cardinal doctrine of the Trinity.

---

[113] Ewart, *Name and Book*, p. 139. Since Ewart is reporting on this correspondence in 1936, it is likely that he is referring to the 1929 or 1931 edition of Hall's *Remarkable Discovery*.

[114] Brumback, *Suddenly from Heaven – A History of the Assemblies of God* (Springfield, MO: Gospel Publishing House, 1961), p. 192.

[115] Account in Fred Foster, *"Think It Not Strange" – A History of the Oneness Movement* (St. Louis, MO: Pentecostal Publishing House, 1965), pp. 70-71.

[116] Andrew D. Urshan, *The Life Story of Andrew Bar David Urshan: An Autobiography* (Stockton, CA: WABC Press, 1967), p. 141.

6. Summary

In this chapter we have traced the development of a rudimentary theology of the Name among some Jesus-centric evangelicals in the late
19th century. Their particular concern was to defend the deity of
Christ against the Unitarian and liberal threat, and to build a theology
of spiritual power upon the Revivalist and Holiness optimism that
regarded transformation as the *sine qua non* of authentic faith. A study
of the name of God confirmed for them that Jesus is indeed no other
and nothing less than Yahweh Himself. The Name that was given to
Jesus at his birth was a sign of his full deity. Kenyon taught that as
Jesus' flesh provided the purchase price for salvation on the cross, so
also was his Name made available as the power of attorney in order
that believers might have access to the benefits of Christ's atoning
work.

The name of Jesus Christ was to be an object of worship equally as
was the person, and to be invoked in prayer as a legal transaction with
God. Some concluded that the "Lord Jesus Christ" was the proper
Name to invoke in baptism.

There was growing interest in the late 19th century society with
power, a cultural effect of the Industrial Revolution and its fascination
with the strength of the machine and optimism for progress and transformation. The transformative faith of the Revivalist and Perfectionist
traditions was well suited to it, leading to the promise of "spiritual"
power as a dominant motif. The power theme can be traced in the
emerging teaching on the baptism of the Holy Spirit, with its shift in
emphasis from spiritual perfection to spiritual power.[117] The same dynamic is evident in the spiritual application of the name of Jesus.
While the Name continued to be an object of devotion, it was also
proclaimed as a God-given means of spiritual power to live the victorious Christian life and evangelize the nations. There could be no
higher appeal for the justification of a doctrine than this. Oneness Pentecostals would agree.

---

[117] See Dayton, "From 'Perfection' to 'Baptism of the Holy Ghost.'"

Excursus
The Name of God – Finding a Lost Theme?

Themes rich in biblical imagery recur throughout history in Christian spiritual traditions. In some, Old Testament themes play a more forceful role than in others. Evangelical religion of the late-19th century is one of those traditions, and the name of God one of the themes.

1. A Lost Theme in a Jewish Metaphor?

"Jewish Christianity" refers primarily to the earliest Christian community. The first Christians were Jews who interpreted the encounter with Jesus in light of their experience as Jews in the first century and the Jewish scriptures. French theologian, Jean Daniélou, identifies three categories of Jewish Christians during this period. There were those who "acknowledged Christ as a prophet or Messiah, but not as the Son of God." The dominant representative group, the Ebionites, shared this view. The second group was the Jewish Christian community in Jerusalem led by James, the brother of Jesus. Though strict monotheists, they adhered to the divinity of Jesus as well as his messianic role.[118]

The third group was not necessarily related ethnically to the Jewish community but expressed itself "in forms borrowed from Judaism."[119] Daniélou cites St. Paul as an example. Though Daniélou restricts his study to early Christianity, throughout history certain ideas borrowed from Christianity's origins, including the Old Testament, recur in renewal movements. Following the Gentilization of Christianity, the church's memory of its Jewish roots has been weak. But reformationist and restorationist movements intrinsically carry the potential for reviving distinctly Jewish categories of Christian expression, especially those biblical themes that appear to hold the promise for revitalizing a wayward and anemic church.

---

[118] Jean Daniélou, *The Development of Christian Doctrine Before the Council of Nicaea*, vol. I: *The Theology of Jewish Christianity*, ed. and trans. John A. Baker (London: Darton, Longman & Todd, 1964), pp. 7-8. This theme of the recurrence of "Jewish Christian" metaphors is taken up in more detail in Chapter 14.

[119] Daniélou, Jewish Christianity, p. 9.

2. A Nineteenth-Century Restoration?

The Protestant legacy of *sola scriptura* on American soil gave the Old Testament an authority and profile that was worked out both culturally and doctrinally. Cultural markers ranged from choosing Old Testament names (even obscure names) to practicing Sunday as the Sabbath, occasionally with legal enforcement.

a. A Reformation Influence

The dominant religious shape of America is a legacy of the Protestant Reformation, in particular its English Puritan and Methodist traditions. There were spiritual and theological forces at work that contributed to the strong influence of the Old Testament on faith and daily life. Only three are suggested here.

First, tracing the spirit of the Reformation through Puritanism, Evangelical Pietism, and the Wesleyan Revival, the Bible was not only the authority for doctrinal beliefs but also the sole guide for daily life. Scripture was often set against the alien authorities of philosophy, Romanticism, the new science, and various forms of liberal Protestantism.

With the belief that the Bible is the Word of God came the pressure to prove its supernatural origin by demonstrating its unity and internal consistency. Combined with a high view of the inspiration of the whole body of Scripture – sometimes known as the "plenary" inspiration of Scripture – according the Old Testament its proper place in light of the New was not an easy task. As a result, some appropriated particular beliefs and practices from the Old Testament as being authoritative for Christians. In some cases, only the thought forms were taken over; in others, practices and customs were brought into the Christian experience relatively unreconstructed.

A second influence may have come by way of the covenant theology of the Puritans. It created a kind of unity that would make most of the Old Testament equally authoritative as the New for Christians. The covenant of grace began with Abraham and continued through the New Testament. But as Perry Miller notes, the Puritans did away with the idea of God as promising and replaced it with "a legal theory of God's delivering to man a signed and sealed bond."[120] Such a covenant theology may have influenced the way in which the Old Testament was preached and taught.

---

[120] Perry Miller, Errand into the Wilderness, p. 62.

Third, for all the evangelical emphasis on salvation apart from works, there has been a strong moralistic strain throughout this perfectionist stream of Pietism. While there were surely other reasons, one may be found in the changing direction of the Puritan mind of the previous century. Miller points out that Calvinism was under attack for its a-moral doctrine of divine election. Its struggle to assert the need for a human moral response became "the supreme triumph of the school," namely, "the establishment of a code of ethics and of moral obligation." This was both incorporated into the covenant of grace, which began with Abraham, and extended to all humanity and society outside the covenant.[121] Everything from personal morality, family discipline, sexual taboos, and social reform could find much support from a covenant of grace rooted so deeply in the Old Testament.[122]

b. A Millenarian Influence

The Christian millenarian movement has a distinctly Jewish character. It shares with religious Jews the hope of a "time of restored national prosperity for Israel. It regards Israel as the center of the divine government of the world and Jerusalem as its glorious capital."[123] The various forms of Premillennialism that emerged in the late 19th century, which still characterize the majority of Fundamentalists today, held to this view of a literal thousand-year reign (see Rev. 20:1-10). Dispensationalism, a particular form of Premillennialism and hallmark of American Fundamentalism, further accented the Jewish hope for a restored Israel by distinguishing prophecies that referred to the New Testament church from those that were intended for Israel apart from Christ.[124]

The Restoration movement in the 19th century, initiated by Alexander Campbell, was an attempt "to reflect upon the ways and means to restore primitive Christianity."[125] The Campbellite movement in itself may not have carried from the Old Testament any peculiar teachings, but the prophetic movement in Millenarianism combined this interest in a return to biblical Christianity with a sense of eschatological

---

[121] Miller, *Errand*, p. 74.

[122] H.R. Niebuhr points to this moralistic trend in later Revivalism, but without identifying the biblical motifs involved, in *Kingdom of God in America*, pp. 181-82.

[123] E.F. Kevan, "Millennium," in *Baker's Dictionary of the Bible*, p. 353.

[124] See "Dispensationalism," in Bernard Ramm, *A Handbook of Contemporary Theology* (Grand Rapids, MI: Eerdmans, 1966), pp. 36-37.

[125] Alexander Campbell, The Christian System in Reference to the Union of Christians, and a Restoration of Primitive Christianity, As Plead in the Current Reformation (Nashville, TN: Gospel Advocate, 1956).

fulfillment in its own day. The Old Testament provided many of the categories of thought. Millenarianism depended heavily upon the prophetic books of Ezekiel and Daniel to provide the chronology for Revelation. Dispensationalism applied its hermeneutic of "types and shadows" as a way of harmonizing the two Testaments. This was frequently done by studying the Tabernacle in the Old Testament in light of the Epistle to the Hebrews.

c. A Sectarian Influence

The distinctly Jewish elements, however, were sometimes most conspicuous in the heretical sects whose *raison d'etre* was "a Judaistic perversion of Christian faith," and who tended to "circumscribe salvation by limiting it to their own communion." Horton Davies described this extreme tendency as "the retention of the scaffolding even when the headstone of the corner has been placed in position."[126]

The Jehovah's Witnesses with their teaching on the name of Jehovah and the Kingdom are Judaistic as are the Mormons with their "patriarchal ethics and ... apocalypticism."[127] There are a good many Sabbatarian groups that honor the seventh day, the largest and most prominent being the Seventh-Day Adventists.[128] There are also numerous "Sacred Name" groups generally called Yahwists.[129] Their mission is to restore the Sacred Name by hebraicizing the original names of God and Jesus to "Yahvah" and "Yahvahshua" respectively.[130]

The more sectarian groups tend to be legalistic and moralistic. Many practice the strict dietary practices of Judaism as well as observe the Seventh Day or Jewish Sabbath. It is not surprising that some do not believe in the doctrine of the Trinity, since it offends their strict monotheism.[131] The Seventh-Day Adventists believe in the earlier Old Testament belief in the "sleep of the dead," and reject the more common traditional teaching of continued existence after death as a pagan influence. Some groups baptize in the Name of "Yahshua the Messiah" instead of the name of the Trinity. The Sacred Name groups in particular have revived the Jewish belief in the revealed Sacred Name of God.

---

[126] Horton Davies, *The Challenge of the Sects* (Philadelphia, PA: Westminster, 1961), pp. 160-62.

[127] Davies, Challenge of the Sects, p. 162.

[128] See extensive listing of Sabbath-keeping groups in *Directory of Sabbath-Observing Groups* (9th ed.; Fairview, OK: Bible Sabbath Association, 2001).

[129] Sacred Name groups are also listed in *Sabbath-Observing Groups*.

[130] See the Yahwist version of the New Testament, *Restoration of Original Name New Testament* (Junction City, OR: Missionary Dispensary Bible Research, 1968).

[131] See the doctrinal statements of the various groups in *Sabbath-Observing Groups*.

3. Summary

Since the Christian Scriptures include the Old Testament, it is a perennial hermeneutical challenge to interpret the relationship of one to the other. Concepts and themes from the Old Testament shape and inform the Christian mind. Particularly when the church perceives itself to be threatened or weakened, it returns to its past for guidance and strength. This movement to origins, however, seldom emerges from the center of the institution but from the margins or below.

Some segments of American evangelical faith represent just such a movement, as popular Bible teachers struggled to defend the deity of Christ by the most familiar means at their disposal – the Old and New Testaments. Among other things, this led them to an intensive study of the name of God, a distinctly Jewish notion that is more prominent in the Old Testament than in the New. It is significant that leaders such as Arno C. Gaebelein, A.B. Simpson, A.J. Gordon, William Phillips Hall and others were strong millenarians who shared the Jewish hope for the restoration of Israel. Some were recognizing the Jewish character of their emphasis on the Name. Hall remarked that he was given an unusual enlightenment "of a distinctly Semitic or Jewish character" of the Name in Scripture.[132] John Miller was convinced that he could develop an evangelical theology without the aid of "the Platonic trinity,"[133] simply by returning to Scripture as "our whole appeal."[134] Weeks was suspicious that the doctrine of the Trinity "was the result in part of attempts to reconcile Christianity with heathen philosophy, of opposition to Judaism."[135]

Oneness Pentecostalism was a child of this evangelical Holiness movement. Familiarity with, and even attraction to, the distinctly Jewish elements in this tradition was part of the legacy.

---

[132] Hall, Remarkable Biblical Discovery, pp. 13-14.
[133] Miller, *Is God a Trinity?* p. 13.
[134] Miller, "Are Souls Immortal?" in *Questions Awakened by Bible*, p. 28.
[135] Robert D. Weeks, *Jehovah-Jesus – The Supreme God: Son of God, Son of Man*, ed. C. Haskell Yadon (Twin Falls, ID: By the Editor, 1952), p. 107.

Part II

The Birth of Oneness Pentecostalism

4

Pentecostal Polemics

> William Durham …
>
> as near being a 'damnable heresy' as anything we know[1]
> — J.H. King
> the highest and most scriptural type I have met so far, among the leaders[2]
> — E.W. Kenyon

The Pentecostal story as Pentecostals lived it and told it in pulpit and print was of a supernatural intrusion by God. It had no immediate spiritual or theological parentage.

God was doing a new thing. But recent scholarship of the modern Pentecostal movement has traced the deep roots of the Revival to late 19th-century evangelical faith. While the startling religious phenomenon of the 20th century has its own story to tell, its origins and birth owe much to the influences and ideas of a previous generation. Oneness Pentecostalism is no exception.

Interpretations of the Pentecostal Revival that have spanned the century range from eyewitness accounts to organizational histories and studies in social history. A number of recent studies, however, explore the theological ideas that influenced and shaped Pentecostal thought in its earliest years.[3] To this category is added our study of Oneness Pen-

---

[1] J.H. King, *From Passover to Pentecost* (Senath, MO: F.E. Short, 1914), cited in Jacobsen, *Thinking in the Spirit*, p. 173.

[2] Kenyon, "The Gift of Tongues," *Reality* (May 1907), p. 10; cited in Simmons, *E.W. Kenyon*, pp. 57, 292.

[3] The most significant studies that give attention to the ideas and beliefs of early Pentecostalism are: Robert Mapes Anderson, *Vision of the Disinherited: The Making of American Pentecostalism* (New York: Oxford University Press, 1979); Edith Blumhofer, *Restoring the Faith: The Assemblies of God, Pentecostalism, and American Culture* (Urbana, IL: University of Illinois Press, 1993); Donald Dayton, *Theological Roots of Pentecostalism*; D. William Faupel, *The Everlasting Gospel: The Significance of Eschatology in the Development of Pentecostal Thought* (Sheffield: Sheffield Academic Press, 1996; repr. Blandford: Deo Publishing, 2007); Douglas Jacobsen, *Thinking in the Spirit: Theologies*

tecostalism, in both its historical and systematic dimensions. While social and economic forces are necessary to understand the emergence and development of movements, including religious ones, we believe that ideas and convictions are a potent force in giving birth and life to movements and institutions.

Theological ideas appear in sweeping trends and paradigmatic patterns of thought. Grant Wacker and Edith Blumhofer argue that the primitivist or restorationist impulse is the dominant idea that motivated early Pentecostals – the belief that the church in its historical existence has been largely abandoned by God because of its apostasy but is now being restored to apostolic doctrine and practice. Robert Mapes Anderson and William Faupel interpret the Pentecostal movement primarily in terms of the millenarian vision. Faupel in particular builds his understanding on the "Latter Rain" motif popularized by the early Pentecostal leader, D. Wesley Myland, in his book, *The Latter Rain Covenant and Pentecostal Power*. In this view, apostolic life is being restored precisely to prepare the followers of Jesus for the imminent return of Christ. Donald Dayton, on the other hand, understands early Pentecostalism in terms of the theological paradigm of Jesus as Savior, Sanctifier, Baptizer in the Spirit, Healer, and Soon Coming King.[4] He argues that this theological paradigm was fully present in the teaching and practice of the late 19th-century Holiness movement in both Wesleyan and Keswick forms. The only contribution to this paradigm by the early Pentecostal movement is the doctrine that glossolalia is the necessary and exclusive evidence of the experience of the baptism of the Holy Spirit. Among these various interpretations there is considerable overlap and difference in emphasis, views than can complement rather than contradict each other.

Oneness Pentecostalism emerged in the second decade of the Pentecostal Revival with a distinctive theological paradigm. The soteriological core is the three-fold pattern of Christian initiation set forth in Acts 2:38: repentance, water baptism in the name of Jesus Christ, and the experience of Spirit-baptism with speaking in other tongues. The christological framework is the belief that Jesus Christ is the revelation

---

of the Early Pentecostal Movement (Bloomington, IN: Indiana University Press, 2003); Vinson Synan, *The Holiness-Pentecostal Tradition: Charismatic Movements in the Twentieth Century* (Grand Rapids, MI: Eerdmans, 1971, 1997); Grant Wacker, *Heaven Below: Early Pentecostals and American Culture* (Cambridge, MA: Harvard University Press, 2001).

[4] For a brief review of these interpretations, including his own, see Faupel, *Everlasting Gospel*, pp. 16-18.

of the one God (not the Second Person of the Trinity) and the name "Jesus" is the New Covenant name of God to be invoked and appropriated in water baptism.

While it initially appeared to be a radical innovation within the Pentecostal fellowship, a closer examination reveals remarkable continuity with ideas already propagated in certain circles. The immediate precursor was William Durham and his teaching of the Finished Work of Calvary. But the 1857-58 Holiness Revival and influence of Phoebe Palmer, as well as other evangelicals who were strengthening their christocentric doctrine through a study of the names of God in Scripture, contributed much to the shape of the paradigms being used. This chapter will trace briefly the birth of the Pentecostal movement and the events that led to the Finished Work schism – a crisis that set the stage for what was first called the "New Issue."

1. Two Birthplaces: 1901 and 1906

The modern Pentecostal movement has two birthplaces: Topeka and Azusa Street. Charles F. Parham, head of Bethel Bible School in Topeka, Kansas, was responsible for establishing the distinctively Pentecostal doctrinal plank that glossolalia is the evidence of Spirit-baptism, a view that clearly separated the new movement from all predecessors.[5] But it was William J. Seymour and the Azusa Street Revival in Los Angeles that turned a regional movement into a global phenomenon. Its beginnings in a small black congregation also burst the racial barriers that opened the Pentecostal door to becoming in less than a century one of the most racially diverse traditions within the Christian family.

Charles Parham was a Holiness preacher from Kansas who had been influenced by the radical "Three Blessing" stream of the Holiness movement, which taught believers to seek a crisis experience called baptism of the Holy Spirit after conversion and entire sanctification. He also embraced the new healing movement taught by A.B. Simpson and Alexander Dowie (1847-1907) from Zion City, Chicago. In 1900

---

[5] Parham taught that the baptized person supernaturally receives an actual human language, xenolalia, for the purpose of evangelizing the world in a short period of time. Many early Pentecostals accepted this teaching until missionaries who had sailed to foreign countries linguistically unprepared were faced with failures and painful disappointments. What was retained in Parham's teaching was the teaching that tongues or glossolalia is evidence of Spirit-baptism.

he founded Bethel Bible School in Topeka, Kansas, and inaugurated the *Apostolic Faith* magazine.

Parham had been studying the topic of the Spirit-baptism and was seeking the biblical teaching on the evidence that one has received that experience. Prior to leaving for a speaking engagement, he instructed his students to study the book of Acts and pray for guidance on this doctrinal matter. Upon his return, the students reported their unanimous conclusion that speaking in tongues was indeed the evidence. It is probable that Parham had already come to this decision.[6] But it was shortly after midnight during a watch night service on the first day of the new century that, as Parham laid hands on one of his students, Agnez N. Ozman, she spoke in what he claimed was the Chinese language. That moment marked the beginning of the modern Pentecostal movement.

In 1905 Parham moved his operation to Houston, Texas, where he opened The Bible Training School. It was here that he met and became theological mentor to William Seymour.[7] Seymour had been reared a Baptist in Louisiana but later accepted Holiness teaching while living in Indianapolis. He studied for two years, from 1900 to 1902, at God's Bible School in Cincinnati, founded and operated by Martin Wells Knapp, a "Third Blessing" Holiness teacher. In 1903 Seymour moved to Houston and two years later enrolled in Parham's Bible school. It was there that he was introduced to and accepted Parham's new teaching on Spirit-baptism.

During his time in Houston Seymour met Neely Terry, a Holiness woman from Los Angeles who was visiting a friend by the name of Lucy Farrow. Terry was a member of a small Holiness mission that was at this point seeking a pastor. Upon her recommendation, the church extended an invitation to Seymour. He accepted and arrived in Los Angeles early in 1906. He immediately ran afoul of the Holiness authorities with his first sermon in which he preached that glossolalia is the biblical evidence of Spirit-baptism. He was straightway locked out of the church, but found shelter in the home of a parishioner on Bon-

---

[6] See Vinson Synan, *Holiness-Pentecostal Tradition*, p. 91; Robert Mapes Anderson, *Vision of the Disinherited*, pp. 52-57. For a thorough treatment of Parham's life and ministry, see James R. Goff, *Fields White unto Harvest: Charles Fox Parham and the Missionary Origins of Pentecostalism* (Fayetteville, AR: University of Arkansas Press, 1988).

[7] For a succinct summary of Seymour's journey that led to Azusa Street, Los Angeles, see Synan, *Holiness-Pentecostal Tradition*, pp. 92-106. For a more thorough treatment of Seymour's life and teaching, see Douglas Nelson, "For Such a Time as This: The Story of Bishop William J. Seymour and the Azusa Street Revival" (PhD diss., University of Birmingham, U.K., 1981).

nie Brae Street where he began cottage prayer meetings. The turning point came on "the night of April 9, 1906, when Seymour and seven others fell to the floor in a religious ecstasy, speaking in tongues."[8] The numbers increased as the curious came and the services spilled on to the front porch. This led Seymour and his growing band of followers to seek larger quarters. They finally procured an abandoned African Methodist Episcopal Church building that most recently had been a livery stable. It was in this humble setting that a three-year revival was ignited which spread around the world. The names of those who visited and whose ministry was changed by Azusa Street represent most of the early Pentecostal leaders, including the Norwegian Methodist pastor, T.B. Barrett. Parham also visited Azusa Street but, unlike most, rendered a scathing criticism of what he witnessed – fanaticism and repulsive emotional excesses. This censure ended a friendship that was never restored. Here the story of two leaders of one movement divides. While Parham irreversibly established the signature doctrine for the movement, it was Seymour's Azusa Street Revival that marks the beginning of the Pentecostal movement as a global reality. Pentecostalism owes much to its Holiness parentage but also to two men who shaped its distinctive character for the new century. As Synan sums it up: "In historical perspective the Pentecostal movement was the child of the Holiness movement, which in turn was the child of Methodism.... Yet the movement that Parham and Seymour unleashed in Topeka and Los Angeles was destined to begin a new and important chapter in the history of Christianity."[9]

While scholars give credence to both birthplaces, preference has often been shown for one or the other. White Pentecostals, especially those in the Assemblies of God, have pinned their Pentecostal identity on Parham's doctrine of glossolalia. Black Pentecostals, on the other hand, have identified with the Azusa Street Revival and its witness to racial harmony, temporary though it was. For Seymour, the unity of the races was a greater sign of the Spirit's baptism than glossolalia. One European Pentecostal theologian, Jean-Jacques Suurmond, agrees with Seymour and decries the loss to white Pentecostals when they were cut off from their black roots: "Cut off from its black, 'Third World' roots, the Assemblies of God, like the greater part of the Western Pentecostal movement, has become a typically white, evangelical, middle-class church, politically conservative."[10]

---

[8] Synan, *Holiness-Pentecostal Tradition*, p. 96.

[9] Synan, *Holiness-Pentecostal Tradition*, p. 106.

[10] Jean-Jacques Suurmond, *Word and Spirit at Play: Towards a Charismatic Theology*

Of particular interest for our study is Suurmond's claim that it is particularly the black Oneness churches a century later whose worship most closely resembles that of the Azusa Street Revival.[11] For him, the similarity is confirmation that quintessential Pentecostalism is to be found in Azusa, not Topeka – black Pentecostals decades later emulate their origins while white Pentecostals have drifted from these roots into Fundamentalism. Joseph Howell, writing on the history of Oneness Pentecostalism, draws similar conclusions. He argues that the New Issue was a reactive move to regain the primitive Pentecostal fervor at a time when the revival fires of Azusa Street were waning. He states, "Oneness development should be viewed as a 'counter-reformation' of the Azusa revival," an attempt to recapture the early Revival's vitality, to thwart the theologizing of the Pentecostal experience, to reaffirm the eschatological zeal of the early Pentecostals, and to revive interracial fellowship within the movement."[12] That is, both Suurmond and Howell trace the Oneness impulse to Azusa Street.[13]

It is difficult, however, to substantiate this claim in terms of the origins and development of Oneness doctrine. But we concur with the observation that Oneness worshippers are more characteristically Pentecostal than most Trinitarian Pentecostal bodies. Among other reasons, Oneness doctrine and practice may be more compatible in its core with an Afro-centric worldview than with that of non-Pentecostal white evangelicals. Whether or not the reasons are persuasive, it is a curious fact that a movement that was theologically shaped by the ideas that caused the first schism in the Pentecostal movement and gave birth to the Assemblies of God, could at the same time embody the spirituality and worldview of the quintessential Pentecostal moment.

(Grand Rapids, MI: Eerdmans, 1994), p. 6.

[11] Suurmond, *Word and Spirit*, pp. 7-8.

[12] Joseph H. Howell, "The People of the Name: Oneness Pentecostalism in the United States" (PhD diss., Florida State University, 1985), p. 5.

[13] Two other scholars emphasize the black origins of Oneness Pentecostalism and its corresponding worldview: Roswith I.H. Gerloff, *A Plea for British Black Theologies: The Black Church Movement in Britain in Its Transatlantic Cultural and Theological Interaction with Special Reference to the Pentecostal Oneness (Apostolic) and Sabbatarian Movements* (2 vols.; New York: Peter Lang, 1992); and the late James S. Tinney, "The Significance of Race in the Rise and Development of the Apostolic Pentecostal Movement," paper delivered at the First Pentecostal Symposium on Aspects of the Oneness Pentecostal Movement, Harvard Divinity School (July 1994).

2. Revival Wanes and Schism Is Born – The Finished Work of Calvary

By 1909 the fires of the Azusa Street Revival were burning low. Contentious issues had been submerged beneath the energy and enthusiasm of the Revival. As unresolved matters of race, organization and doctrine began to surface, efforts were made to define what it meant to be Pentecostal, and to seek unity within an increasingly diverse constituency.[14] Ewart captured the mood of a revival movement that was becoming aware of itself as a social and spiritual force, but without a clear identity:

> A great company had received "like precious faith" in most parts of Christendom. The fire was spreading. Was a new church about to be formed, with distinctive doctrinal tenets? What would it be called? Would it be organized as all other new bodies in the history of Christianity had been?[15]

A further indication that adherents were feeling the disunity and fragmentation within the movement is evident in the frequent appeals made to a slogan adapted from Ephesians 4:3, 13: to "maintain the unity of the Spirit until we all come into the unity of the faith."[16] What followed would introduce a new doctrine that challenged the identity of the Pentecostal Revival as a Holiness movement, and create the first schism within the young movement.

a. The Author – William H. Durham

It was a young pastor in Chicago, William H. Durham, who moved into this arena of instability to capture the allegiance of the Pentecostal movement. Durham was born in Kentucky in 1873, reared in a Baptist home, but by his own testimony was not truly converted until 1898,

---

[14] For a helpful analysis of the aftermath of the Azusa Street Revival see Anderson, *Vision of the Disinherited*, pp. 137-52; and Faupel, *Everlasting Gospel*, pp. 228-306.

[15] Ewart, *Phenomenon*, p. 71.

[16] Examples abound within the "Finished Work" camp following Durham's death in 1912; see Ewart, "Union of Two Largest Pentecostal Missions in Los Angeles," *Good Report* 1/6 (1 November 1913): 4; Ewart, "The Unity of the Faith," *Good Report* 1/10 (1 March 1914): 2; D.W. Kerr, "The Oneness of Believers," *Good Report* 1/7 (1 December 1913): 4; Andrew Urshan, "A Call for Prayer and Intercession for Chicago," *Good Report* 2/1 (1 June 1913): 2. The text is printed on the masthead of *The Christian Evangel* in 1913; see James A. Tyson, *The Early Pentecostal Revival* (Hazelwood, MO: Word Aflame Press, 1992), p. 165. This appeal was still being made by Ewart as late as 1947, shortly after the organizational merger which formed the United Pentecostal Church; see *Phenomenon*, p. 35.

after having moved via Chicago to Tracy, Minnesota.[17] There he came in contact with the World's Faith Missionary Association (WFMA) – an evangelistic ministry that had grown out of Scandinavian pietistic, immigrant stock in that region – and one of its leaders, G.L. Morgan. Durham was not only awakened in faith through this ministry but also felt called to preach. In 1902 he was ordained by the WFMA.

Pentecostal scholar Edith Blumhofer has described the brand of Holiness taught by WFMA as something of a mixture of American Holiness and the more traditional Protestant focus on the finality of the work of Christ. The latter was particularly emphasized in a message published in a 1901 issue of its paper, the *Firebrand*: "Everything was fully done long, long ago.... If it were necessary for something else to be done, it would not have been a perfect sacrifice. Every soul that sees that perfect, precious offering of the Lamb of God must see that it is sufficient."[18] Blumhofer shows that through WFMA Durham was exposed early on to a version of the "Finished Work of Calvary" teaching that would eventually become the platform of his own doctrine.

Durham soon began an itinerant preaching ministry, but by 1903 he was concentrating his efforts in Chicago among the Scandinavian immigrants. He returned briefly to Minnesota in 1905 to marry an earlier acquaintance, Bessie Mae Whitmore. Until 1907, he continued to minister through his association with the World's Faith Missionary Association.[19]

Durham's first contact with the Azusa Street Revival occurred in August 1906, when a band of evangelists from Los Angeles, led by Miss Mabel Smith, toured the Chicago area witnessing to the Revival and its accompanying phenomenon of glossolalia.[20] Durham was impressed by the spiritual display of tongues and prophecy and finally decided to make his own pilgrimage to Los Angeles in February 1907.

[17] William H. Durham, "Personal Testimony of Pastor Durham," *Pentecostal Testimony* II/3 (July 1912): 3.

[18] The article entitled, "It Is Finished," is cited in Edith Blumhofer, "William H. Durham: Years of Creativity, Years of Dissent," in James R. Goff, Jr. & Grant Wacker, eds., *Portraits of a Generation: Early Pentecostal Leaders* (Fayetteville, AR: The University of Arkansas Press, 2002), p. 127.

[19] Personal interview with Dale Simmons, May 5, 1998.

[20] For the most extensive treatment of the history and teaching of William Durham, see Thomas G. Farkas, "William H. Durham and the Sanctification Controversy in Early American Pentecostalism, 1906-1916" (Ph.D. diss., The Southern Baptist Theological Seminary, 1993). A briefer but important critical analysis of Durham's teaching is provided by Faupel, *Everlasting Gospel*, pp. 228-70.

He later penned a detailed account of the event and the struggle that transpired within him over a five-day period from February 27 to March 2. From the moment he arrived he was receptive to the spiritual atmosphere of the services and was apparently hungry to receive firsthand the Pentecostal experience. He reported: "I saw clearly, for the first time, the difference between having the influence and presence of the Spirit with us, and having Him dwell within us in person." Though he records two powerful experiences that convulsed his physical body, he did not feel satisfied, indicating he had already concluded the evidential sign of the Spirit's work would be glossolalia. That moment came following an evening service when Durham was seeking the Pentecostal baptism. Seymour entered the prayer room to find Durham prostrate on the floor under the Spirit's power. Within a few moments the seeker experienced what he had come to receive: "I felt my tongue to begin to move and my lips begin to produce strange sounds.... In a few moments He was speaking clearly through me in other tongues, and then I heard Brother Seymour, the Pastor say, 'He is through now.'" At that point Seymour raised his hands over Durham and prophesied that wherever he preached, "the Holy Spirit would fall upon the people."[21]

Confirmation of Seymour's prophecy appeared to be fulfilled as soon as Durham returned to Chicago. He began a series of nightly meetings that drew increasingly larger crowds. News of the Chicago Revival and the powerful preacher at North Avenue Mission spread far beyond the city. Over the next three years, 1907-1910, many who made their spiritual pilgrimage to Chicago would become the next generation of Pentecostal leaders – E.N. Bell, A.H. Argue, Aimee Semple McPherson, Andrew D. Urshan, to name a few.[22] Faupel assesses the impact of the Chicago Revival: "Soon Chicago began to rival Los Angeles as the movement's center and North Avenue Mission became the 'Mecca' for the Pentecostal faithful."[23]

Durham's meteoric rise to fame was in part a result of a weakening among the constituencies of the Pentecostal movement, in particular its two acknowledged patriarchs. In 1907 the influence and credibility of Charles Parham crumbled in the wake of a failed takeover of Alexander Dowie's establishment in Zion City, Illinois, and a charge of

---

[21] Durham, *Personal Testimony*, p. 4.

[22] For a more thorough list of Pentecostal notables who came into the Pentecostal experience under Durham's ministry, see Farkas, "William H. Durham," pp. 123-28.

[23] Faupel, *Everlasting Gospel*, p. 232.

sexual impropriety in Texas.[24] By 1910 Seymour had lost much of his influence through racial fragmentation. Instead of supporting Azusa Street as the inter-racial center of the new movement, most whites left to form their own congregations and missions throughout the city, leaving Seymour with a small, predominantly black, congregation.[25] Furthermore, immediately following his marriage to Jennie Evans Moore in 1908, Clara Lum, the Mission Secretary responsible for publishing *The Apostolic Faith,* abruptly left Azusa Street to join the ministry of Florence Crawford (1872-1936) in Portland, Oregon – and took the mailing lists with her. Attempts to retrieve them were unsuccessful, leaving Seymour without the means to distribute his paper. The result was a slow decline into obscurity for both the man and the mission that ignited the worldwide Pentecostal movement.[26] As Farkas observes, "Durham became the prime beneficiary of all this."[27]

The earliest American Pentecostal movement prior to 1910 was Holiness in doctrine and practice. Synan points out that most of the Holiness Church of God groups became Pentecostal, and concludes: "Practically all of them were Holiness groups of the more radical type and identified themselves with the Pentecostal movement after 1906."[28] The "radical type" referred to those leaders and groups that taught a three-fold experience for all Christians: regeneration, sanctification and Spirit-baptism.

Durham himself acknowledged his prior commitment to Holiness teaching: "For years, in my preaching, I referred to sanctification as a second work of grace, bringing several things in my attempt to prove it."[29] But his Pentecostal experience at Azusa Street created an internal crisis. He clearly understood that event as a second experience called the baptism of the Holy Spirit accompanied by glossolalia. This made sense from his reading of Acts. But he could no longer find any scriptural justification for sanctification as a second work of grace. He

---

[24] Goff traces the events that eventually led to "the fall" of Parham, *Fields White unto Harvest,* pp. 128-46.

[25] Ian MacRobert, *The Black Roots and White Racism of Early Pentecostalism in the USA* (London: Macmillan, 1988), pp. 58-62.

[26] Douglas J. Nelson, "For Such a Time as This: The Story of Bishop William J. Seymour and the Azusa Street Revival" (Ph.D. diss., University of Birmingham, 1981), pp. 216-18.

[27] Farkas, "William H. Durham," p. 127.

[28] Synan, *Holiness-Pentecostal Tradition,* p. 80.

[29] William Durham, "Sanctification – Is It a Definite, Second, Instantaneous Work of Grace?" *Articles Written by Pastor W.H. Durham, Taken From Pentecostal Testimony* (Springfield, MO: Assemblies of God Archives, n.d.), p. 15.

confessed, "From the day the Holy Spirit fell on me and filled me I could never preach the second work theory again." But he refrained from teaching against it until he was certain "that there was no possibility of my being mistaken on the subject from a Scriptural standpoint."[30]

The time for public declaration of his new position was May 10, 1910, and the venue was the large annual Pentecostal convention at the prominent Stone Church in Chicago. Many leaders from the Midwest were present to hear the address that he entitled, "The Finished Work of Calvary." One observer later described it as "a shot heard round the world."[31] The title of the address immediately became the name that would identify a teaching, a controversy, a movement, and eventually a new stream within the Pentecostal Revival.

b. The Teaching

Durham's new message of the Finished Work of Calvary was a frontal attack on the prevailing pattern of "full" salvation. In particular, Durham challenged the accepted Holiness teaching of entire sanctification as a second work of grace by removing its sequential element and integrating it with justification in the atoning work of Christ on the cross. He understood that acts of grace bear salvific weight, thereby implying that both conversion and sanctification were being taught as necessary for salvation. This two-step approach was repugnant to Durham for two reasons. First, it appeared to be based not on Scripture but the testimony of an experience of entire sanctification. He declared,

> To my mind the second work theory is one of the weakest, and most unscriptural doctrines that is being taught in the Pentecostal movement.... Many seem to expect that we will accept their personal testimony instead of the plain teaching of the Word of God.[32]

Second, it implied that one could experience conversion and still be only partially saved, leaving the believer's eternal destiny in limbo until the reception of sanctification. Durham stated it bluntly:

> It has come to thousands of truly saved people declaring that they are not saved, and that, instead of men coming into Christ and receiving eternal life in conversion, all they get is pardon of their outward transgressions. They are told that when God pardoned them He left them full of sin and

---

[30] Durham, "Sanctification – Work of Grace," p. 16.

[31] Cited in Faupel, *Everlasting Gospel*, p. 237.

[32] Durham, "Sanctification – The Bible Does Not Teach That It Is a Second Definite Work of Grace," *Articles by Pastor Durham,* p. 1.

corruption, and that it requires a second work of grace to save them from hell.[33]

Elsewhere he stated that it is not possible "for a man to be justified before God, and at the same time be full of sin."[34]

Durham's solution was "identification with Christ," a theological concept that crystallizes his teaching of the Finished Work of Calvary. He described it as "Identification with Jesus Christ Saves and Sanctifies – No Second Work of Grace Taught Or Necessary."[35] From the beginning of his new teaching, Durham embraced a high doctrine of sanctification. In 1910 he declared that "we believe that God's standard is entire sanctification."[36] At one point he chided his perfectionist opponents for not holding a higher standard, given their emphasis on the doctrine:

> I was convinced of two things, namely, that the Word of God not only teaches Holiness of heart and life, but that it teaches a much higher standard of it than has been generally taught among any people that I know of.[37]

But the thrust of his teaching was that sanctification is not an experience either gradual or subsequent to Christ's justifying work, but is simultaneous with it at the beginning of the Christian life. At the moment of regeneration or conversion, the believer receives the full resources of salvation made possible on the Cross. One receives both the imputed or "external" righteousness of God and the "internal" cleansing from sin. Durham understood sanctification to be a status as well as an internal change that the believer accepts. And in Finished Work theology Christ, not the Holy Spirit, carries out the work of sanctification:

> Sanctification is a state, and an experience or life as well. In conversion we come into Christ, our Sanctifier, and are made holy, as well as righteous. When one really comes into Christ he is as much in Christ as he

---

[33] Durham, "The Finished Work of Calvary – It Makes Plain the Great Work of Redemption," *Pentecostal Testimony* II/3 (June 1912), p. 6.

[34] Durham, "Identification with Christ," *Articles by Pastor Durham*, p. 27.

[35] Durham, "The Finished Work of Calvary – Identification with Jesus Christ Saves and Sanctifies," *Pentecostal Testimony* II/1 (January 1912), p. 1.

[36] Durham, "Identification with Christ," p. 27. Writing in 1912, he reminds his readers of "our statement two years ago that God's one standard is entire sanctification," in "Some Other Phases of Sanctification, *Pentecostal Testimony* II/3 (July 1912), p. 10.

[37] Durham, "The Great Battle of Nineteen Eleven," *Pentecostal Testimony* II/1 (January 1912), p.7.

will ever be. He is in a state of Holiness and righteousness. He is under the precious blood of Jesus Christ and is clean. Every sin has been washed away. This is the state one enters at conversion.[38]

Durham's objection to the second work theory was its teaching that in conversion only "external" or committed sins were removed or forgiven, but that the "inbred" sin in human nature remained, to be eradicated only by the second work of sanctification. In an article in 1912, "Some Other Phases of Sanctification," Durham confirmed his earlier stand on the issue and extended his understanding of sanctification. He reiterated his position that, "when Jesus Christ died, He paid the whole penalty for sin, committed and original."[39] By this he was not implying a form of eradication, but simply declaring that in conversion there was no vestige of sin to be removed by a second and subsequent experience. To state that all sin was removed was not to suggest that there was no longer a "bent to sinning," but only that at the moment of conversion the new Christian was beginning with a clean record and a clean heart.

He then shifted attention to another meaning of sanctification – which he suggested was the one most common in Scripture – that of consecration or being set apart for God's service. In this form of sanctification, one is made holy "by being brought into a certain relationship with God." As with the earlier meaning, there is no hint of eradication but a call to the life of faith that trusts in the saving work of Christ. He readily acknowledged that Christians fail and sin. The solution was not a second work of grace but repentance and turning back to God. His favorite metaphor to describe this process was taken from human development. A baby is fully human at the moment of birth but will eventually grow into adulthood. Yet it is no less a human being at birth than as an adult. Any change that occurs is in human maturing, not in status as a person.

Similarly in conversion, one is truly born again. All that is required to be fully Christian is present in conversion. Yet all Christians are called to grow into maturity. The change that occurs only creates degrees of maturity, not a different class of Christian. Durham stated it this way:

> When God saves a man, He fully saves him. We believe He cleanses him from all sin. We believe, however, that this only brings one into a state

---

[38] Durham, "Sanctification – The Bible Does Not Teach," p. 2.
[39] Durham, "Some Other Phases of Sanctification," p. 10.

of spiritual babyhood and that the whole Christian life with its variety of experiences lies before him.[40]

Elsewhere he used the same analogy to show that at conversion one is completely saved and sanctified but is expected to mature in faith: "Our salvation is complete in Christ the moment we receive it, but in stature, or so far as maturity is concerned, we are simply little, innocent, helpless babes, perfectly clean, but with the whole Christian life and experience before us."[41]

Both justification and sanctification were for Durham to be received by faith, rather than relying on experiences. In conversion one "is to reckon himself dead."[42] The pastoral significance was what he considered to be faulty guidance perpetrated by the Holiness teaching for those who in weakness had failed to follow Christ fully, or, in other words, had "backslid." He believed that they were promised an experience in the second work of grace that could not deliver the power to resist the temptations of life: "Instead of telling folks that there is an experience that removes the necessity for bearing the daily cross, they should have been taught that the Christian life is a battle from conversion to glorification." His advice was to "get back under the Blood and reckon themselves dead, and live the overcoming life." The solution was not to seek a perfecting experience that would render them immune to temptation, but to appropriate God's provision by faith: "We come into Christ by faith, and by faith we keep saved."[43]

How is "identification with Christ" achieved? Following the logic that salvation is full and complete in the Finished Work of Christ, identification with Christ is accomplished by identifying with his death, burial and resurrection. The classical text to which Durham turned is Romans 6:4, which states that by faith and baptism the person dies to a former sinful existence and receives new life through the resurrection of Christ. As Durham declared, "Identification is the plain teaching of Scripture. We are dead with Christ, buried with Him, and raised up to walk in newness of life with Him."[44] Following Paul's language, we are to "reckon" ourselves dead to sin and alive to Christ.

Durham's focus on Rom. 6:4-6 as the classic text for identification with Christ is particularly noteworthy because of the prominence of

---

[40] *Ibid.*

[41] Durham, "The Great Need of the Hour," *Pentecostal Testimony* II/1 (January 1912), p. 10.

[42] Durham, "Sanctification – The Bible Does Not Teach," p. 2.

[43] *Ibid.*, p. 3.

[44] Durham, "Finished Work of Calvary," p. 3.

water baptism – a priority somewhat uncharacteristic of evangelical revivalism at the time. But Durham concluded from this text that baptism was a necessary element in the process of identification with Christ, and therefore must be integrated theologically with the act of believing faith. When a penitent sinner confesses and receives Christ in faith, Durham declared that person dead to sin. Though baptism of itself was not construed in terms of baptismal regeneration, Durham perceived it to be inseparable from faith and an essential part of God's plan. He could now state that baptism is "the dividing line between the old life and the new." He then turned to the story of Israel's exodus from Egypt as an Old Testament type of salvation. Using the symbols of the blood of the slain lamb and the crossing of the Red Sea, he concluded that "just as Christ came forth from the grave to die no more, the believer in Christ comes up from his burial in water to die no more, but rather to be identified with Jesus Christ in his new life." Elsewhere he clarified the relationship between the experience of conversion and the act of baptism: conversion was so real to the believer that one was compelled to "act it out before the world."[45]

More importantly, Durham insisted that baptism was part of the biblical pattern for receiving Spirit-baptism. He stated that one's believing faith "makes him a candidate for water baptism, which is the only thing required of him between conversion and the baptism in the Spirit."[46] He criticized over-spiritualized Pentecostal zealots who were teaching that water baptism is no longer necessary now that the baptism of the Spirit has been poured out. But for Durham that broke the biblical pattern: "Had they obeyed the Scriptures, been baptized in water and tarried for the gift of the Holy Ghost, God would certainly have met them."[47] He made the same observation regarding his own journey into the Pentecostal experience, claiming that after conversion

> I had no one to tell me that the next step was to be buried with Him, in whom I had died and been made alive. Had I been taught the truth, as the Apostles taught it, had I been baptized and had hands laid on me, I would have at once received the Holy Spirit.[48]

Romans 6 and Paul's teaching on faith and baptism was not the theological *terminus* of Durham's doctrine of identification, but became an essential element in a larger pattern of God's order. He discovered

---

[45] Durham, "Sanctification – Work of Grace," pp. 17-18.
[46] Durham, "The Two Great Experiences or Gifts," *Articles by Pastor Durham,* p. 4.
[47] Durham, "Identification with Christ," p. 30.
[48] Durham, "False Doctrines," *Articles by Pastor Durham,* p.43.

this more complete but compatible pattern in Acts 2:38. The three-fold pattern set forth in Peter's Pentecost sermon (repentance, baptism in the name of Jesus Christ, and the gift of the Holy Spirit) was, in Durham's words, "in exact harmony with the teachings of Paul on the same subject."[49] In his Finished Work teaching, Durham had replaced the two works of grace in Holiness teaching with two crisis experiences, conversion and baptism in the Spirit. But he was adamant that only in conversion did a person receive the one act of grace by which salvation is accomplished. Having incorporated water baptism as an essential element in his doctrine of identification, based on Rom. 6:4, he set forth Acts 2:38 as the pattern that incorporates the two experiences of conversion and Spirit-baptism with the added element of water baptism. Durham believed the three elements were so interrelated that, while Spirit-baptism was subsequent to conversion, there was no reason for a delay in receiving it so long as one repented, was baptized in water and sincerely sought the Spirit's blessing. Durham concluded that the Apostles followed the same pattern throughout the book of Acts, but he found in v. 38 the paradigm that embodied the essence of the Finished Work of Calvary teaching and God's order for salvation and divine empowerment.[50]

Durham drew a number of theological conclusions from the three-fold pattern in Acts 2:38. One is that repentance is the normal means by which a failing Christian is to be restored and sustained. Instead of seeking an experience of sanctification that promises to remove struggle from the Christian life, the penitent is to be "reclaimed" by returning in repentance to the cross of Christ. Since the one act of grace in the experience of conversion is sufficient and unrepeatable, repentance is the appropriate means of restoration that preserves the doctrinal integrity of the Finished Work as the sole source and ground of salvation. When a person or church in the apostolic era "backslid" and needed reclaiming, they were "exhorted to return to their first state of grace."[51]

Durham's second conclusion relates to water baptism. He chose to retain the traditional Trinitarian invocation of the divine name in water baptism, following the pattern of Matt. 28:19. He reported that there were those listening to his message who pressed him to use the christocentric name recorded in Acts. He did not identify them, though we know that Parham had begun to baptize in the name of

---

[49] Durham, "Identification with Christ," p. 27.
[50] See especially Durham, "Two Great Experiences."
[51] Durham, "Sanctification – The Bible Does Not Teach," p. 3.

Jesus Christ as early as 1902 and probably had generated a following that held to this practice. It is surprising that Durham's pivotal doctrine of identification with Christ, which had led him to give such prominence to baptism, did not also lead him to adopt the christocentric baptismal name, a practice which he labeled a "false doctrine." On another front, he regarded the practice of triune immersion as "extreme," and favored a single immersion because "baptism represents a burial."[52] Ironically, he was unwilling to extend this symbolic identification with Christ to the invocation of the name of Christ.

Finally, Durham drew a sharp distinction between Christ and the Holy Spirit in the life of the believer. The theological categories were what he called the "two great experiences" of the Christian life; namely, "eternal life in Christ and the gift of the Holy Spirit." Though he represents the usual Pentecostal interpretation that the "gift" of the Spirit in v. 38 refers to Pentecostal "baptism," he believed that the Spirit does not come to abide in the believer until that moment. One receives Christ in conversion and the Spirit with the baptism in the Spirit. Durham stated, "In the Christian life we possess what we receive. When we receive Christ we have Christ, but we have not the Holy Spirit till we receive him." His theological reasoning appears to be based upon the premise of his Finished Work doctrine; namely, that Christ is both Savior and Sanctifier.

These two ministries of Christ constitute but one act of grace. The work of the Spirit, on the other hand, is one of sealing the faithful "unto the day of redemption" and empowering the believer. It is, therefore, a great experience but not a work of saving grace. People can be truly saved by the indwelling Christ prior to the advent of the Spirit, which explains his comment that "they [the Apostles] had two definite experiences, but not two works of grace."[53]

A corollary of this view regarding the baptism in the Spirit is Durham's belief that it is not the same experience as the new birth. He reported that such a teaching had circulated a few years earlier, but he rejected it by appealing to the traditional Holiness argument that the Spirit "would never come into the temple till it was thoroughly cleansed." Therefore, the Spirit's coming must be subsequent to the saving and sanctifying work of Christ in conversion. His detractors apparently charged him with dividing the Trinity by categorically separating the works of Christ and the Spirit. His rejoinder was that

---

[52] Durham, "False Doctrines," p. 40.
[53] Durham, "Two Great Experiences," pp. 7-8.

These conclusions are important for this study, since they define the theological categories that would be used by those of Durham's followers who drafted the New Issue doctrine, and they permit us to trace the development of ideas that Durham was unable to mature owing to his untimely death.

c. The Effect

Durham's inaugural address on "The Finished Work of Calvary" at Stone Church, Chicago, in May 1910 stunned the hearers.[55] Though he was aware that his views would be controversial, it is not clear that he had initially judged the full extent of the reaction.[56] During the following months he took the opportunity to preach his message throughout the country.

Howard Goss had attended the Chicago convention and preached for three weeks at the North Avenue Mission. Though not entirely convinced, he invited Durham to present his views at the upcoming summer camp of the Midwest Apostolic Faith Movement in Malvern, Arkansas. Many listened and accepted the new teaching.[57]

Durham also reported that his teaching was well received among the Scandinavian Pentecostals in the Minneapolis area during a preaching tour in January 1911. His influence among the Canadian Pentecostals was significant, in part due to the geographical proximity to Chicago and Durham's revival. In November 1911, Durham conducted a convention in Winnipeg at the invitation of A.H. Argue, a leading Pentecostal evangelist and pastor, resulting in his capturing much of the western Canadian Prairies for the Finished Work teaching.[58] From this foothold in Winnipeg came another Finished Work leader, Franklin Small, who would eventually align himself with the New Issue and form his own Oneness organization. Another Canadian leader who attended the Chicago convention and accepted the new teaching was Robert E. McAlister (1880-1953) from Ottawa. Both Argue and

---

[54] Durham, "False Doctrines," pp. 38-39.

[55] Allen Clayton, "Jesus Paid It All" (unpublished paper, Dallas, TX, May 8, 1978), p. 13; cited in Faupel, *Everlasting Gospel*, p. 240.

[56] Farkas, "William H. Durham," pp. 144-45.

[57] Ethel E. Goss, *The Winds of God: The Story of the Early Pentecostal Days (1901-1914) In the Life of Howard A. Goss* (New York: Comet, 1958), pp. 25-26.

[58] Durham, "The Winnipeg Convention," *Pentecostal Testimony* II/1 (January 1912), pp. 11-12.

McAlister were pivotal in disseminating the Finished Work teaching throughout Canada through their respective periodicals, The Apostolic Messenger and The Good Report.[59]

By 1912 Durham's message was being accepted throughout much of the Midwest into Texas, the Southwest, Canada and worldwide. In two years 382,000 copies of Pentecostal Testimony and 250,000 of his tracts had been distributed.[60] Faupel reports that he exerted a major influence on three existing constituencies: the Apostolic Faith Movement in the Midwest, the Christian and Missionary Alliance, and Dowie's Christian Catholic Apostolic Church in Zion City, Illinois. Many from these groups responded to a call in 1914 by two leading proponents of the Finished Work teaching, Howard Goss and E.N. Bell, for an organizational meeting to consolidate the Pentecostal movement in the Midwest. The meeting was held April 2-12 in Hot Springs, Arkansas. The title of the keynote address by M.M. Pinson revealed the fruit of Durham's labor: "The Finished work of Calvary."[61] The result was the formation of the Assemblies of God, a century later to be the largest Pentecostal denomination worldwide.

Of course Durham's message was not unanimously accepted. The reaction from many Holiness leaders was swift and resolute. In characteristically colorful fashion, Parham slammed "Durhamism" as "the diabolical end and purpose of his Satanic majesty."[62] In January of 1912, he charged Durham with committing "the sin unto death," and predicted divine judgment within six months. When Durham suddenly died on July 7, Parham coldly responded, "How signally God has answered."[63]

When Durham traveled to Los Angeles with his new message, he was refused entrance to Elmer Fisher's Upper Room Mission, by that time the largest Pentecostal work on the West Coast. But Durham's message eventually drew so many that Fisher's work dwindled into near obscurity. Seymour, at the time on a preaching tour, permitted Durham to preach at the Azusa Street Mission. When he returned to discover that Durham had been attacking the second work doctrine,

[59] Faupel, *Everlasting Gospel*, p. 241.

[60] *Pentecostal Testimony* II/1 (January 1912), p. 15; and II/3 (July 1912), p. 16.

[61] J. Roswell Flower, "History of the Assemblies of God" (mimeograph, Springfield, MO: Central Bible Institute, 1949), pp. 20-21; cited in Faupel, *Everlasting Gospel*, p. 243.

[62] Charles F. Parham, *The Everlasting Gospel* (Baxter Springs, KS: The Author, 1911), p. 118; cited in Faupel, *Everlasting Gospel*, p. 249.

[63] Parham, "Supplement," *The Apostolic Faith* (July 1912), cited in Edith L. Blumhofer, "The Finished Work of Calvary: William H. Durham and a Doctrinal Controversy," *Assemblies of God Heritage* 3 (Fall 1983), p. 10; see also Faupel, *Everlasting Gospel*, p. 249.

he locked him out of the church. Seymour resisted the new teaching
and exerted his still considerable influence among the black groups,
which "helped keep them in the Holiness camp."[64] One of the more
colorful episodes occurred in Los Angeles following a service where
Durham was expounding his teaching. A converted prostitute apparently took offense at his attack on the Holiness doctrine and, following
the service, assaulted him with her hatpin. Like many others, however,
before long she too became a follower of the Finished Work.[65]

Durham then left Los Angeles for Portland, Oregon, to present his
message in the territory where Holiness leader, Florence Crawford,
had established her headquarters. Though her constituency did not
immediately receive his message, Faupel suggests that Durham laid the
groundwork for the formation of a Finished Work organization the
following year, the Pentecostal Assemblies of the World. This organization, however, had an earlier history in Los Angeles. According to
the Minute Book, the PAofW first met in 1907 as a loose association
of ministers to promote the Pentecostal movement. At its second
meeting in 1908, J.J. Frazee of Portland, Oregon, was elected permanent Secretary.[66] The name, Pentecostal Assemblies of the World,
appears in an article by E.N. Bell, just prior to the scheduled organizational meeting of the Assemblies of God in 1914. He reported that an
organization had recently received its charter in Portland, with Frazee
as Superintendent. Frazee had previously been a member of Crawford's ministry, and was likely converted to the Finished Work
teaching as a result of Durham's campaign.[67] Other Finished Work
leaders were present, confirming that the new organization was indeed
a legacy of Durham's ministry – Frank Ewart, R.E. McAlister and
G.T. Haywood.[68] The reasons for meeting in Portland are speculative.
Faupel's hunch may be correct that it was a strategy "to make a substantial inroad into Florence Crawford's territory."[69]

The region of the country that was least influenced by Durham's
message was the deep South. Some of the Holiness groups had little
direct contact with it and made little effort to understand the teaching.

---

[64] Faupel, *Everlasting Gospel*, p. 251.
[65] Carl Brumback, *Suddenly ...From Heaven: A History of the Assemblies of God*
(Springfield, MO: Gospel Publishing House, 1961), pp. 103-104.
[66] "Brief Record of Minutes, 1907-1917," in *Minute Book 1919 (1907-1919) – Pentecostal Assemblies of the World* (By the Organization, n.d.).
[67] Tyson, *Early Pentecostal Revival*, p. 189.
[68] E.N. Bell, "Bible Order Versus Fanaticism," *Word and Witness* (March 20, 1914): 3.
[69] Faupel, *Everlasting Gospel*, p. 251.

C.H. Mason (1862-1961), leader of the Church of God in Christ, on the other hand, was well exposed to it through his friend, Howard Goss, and his attendance at the first meeting of the Assemblies of God. He seems not to have been particularly threatened by the Finished Work teaching and indicated that he would not break fellowship over it. However, he was able to keep his churches solidly in the Holiness camp.[70]

Durham's journey had led him from Chicago to set up his evangelistic headquarters in Los Angeles in February 1911. A division within the North Avenue Mission over his teaching apparently triggered the decision. He severed all ties with the church and moved to the West Coast.[71] From there he traveled up the coast to Portland, then back to Chicago in February of 1912, to set up a second headquarters. But in late June his health failed. He promptly returned to Los Angeles to be with his family, where he died on July 7th at the age of 39 of pulmonary tuberculosis.[72] Frank Ewart, his associate and successor in Los Angeles, preached the funeral sermon.[73]

Durham's legacy to the Pentecostal movement was monumental. By 1930 three of every five Pentecostals had embraced the Finished Work teaching. The deep South, mostly rural, had largely resisted the new movement. But in the West, Midwest and Canada, Durham's teaching had swept in a fully eighty percent of the Pentecostal movement. The new stream would be urban and mostly white.[74] But within two years of Durham's death it would itself spawn another doctrinal controversy that would shake and divide the newly formed Assemblies of God.

d. Assessment

Durham lived only two years from the beginning of his Finished Work ministry. Time did not permit him to develop or otherwise amend his ideas. While primary sources are scant, Blumhofer has meticulously reconstructed his early years in Tracy, Minnesota, and the influence of an evangelistic organization, the World's Faith Mission Association. This gives some indication of the intellectual and theological sources that shaped his thinking. We are still left, however, with questions relating to influences upon his developing views and

---

[70] Faupel, *Everlasting Gospel*, pp. 252-56.

[71] Durham, "A Word to Correspondents," *Pentecostal Testimony* II/1 (January 1912): 15-16.

[72] "In Memoriam," *Pentecostal Testimony* II/3 (July 1912): 2.

[73] Ewart, *The Phenomenon of Pentecost: "A History of the Latter Rain"* (St. Louis, MO: Pentecostal Publishing House, 1947), p. 75.

[74] Robert Mapes Anderson, *Vision of the Disinherited*, p. 169.

the future direction that his teaching might have taken. Chief among the questions has been how to locate and classify Durham's particular understanding of sanctification and its place in the Finished Work scheme.

Faupel provides an excellent review and assessment of the various attempts to explain Durham's bold move away from Pentecostalism's Holiness identity.[75] They include Douglas Nelson's psychological profile of a power-hungry leader who was bent on taking control of the whole Pentecostal movement.[76] Robert Mapes Anderson charts a sociological profile that involves the dynamics of race, regional influences and religious affiliations.[77] Faupel acknowledges elements of truth in each, but asserts that one cannot understand the Finished Work teaching "without coming to terms with the theological significance of Durham's message."[78]

Besides his own theological analysis, Faupel reviews two others. Allen Clayton's essay in 1979 was the first such attempt at a theological analysis. Clayton argues that, among other things, Durham gave a theological articulation to an emerging christocentrism within the Pentecostal movement.[79] The most extensive treatment of

Durham's thought, however, is a dissertation by Thomas Farkas in which he attempts to locate Durham's view of sanctification within the typology of four traditional Protestant views (Lutheran, Reformed, Keswick and Wesleyan).[80] Farkas finally labels Durham's view as a "radicalized Wesleyanism."

Faupel's view is that Durham's Finished Work doctrine emerged from within the crucible of a deeply spiritual struggle that culminated in his experience of Spirit-baptism at the Azusa Street Mission. Faupel argues that by this time Durham had theologically embraced the "Pentecostal" worldview that by 1900 had come to dominate the Holiness movement in both its Wesleyan and Keswick forms.[81] The Acts of the Apostles provided the only model that could make sense of his experience. He could no longer study the Bible from the lens of perfec-

---

[75] Faupel, *Everlasting Gospel*, pp. 256-70.

[76] Nelson, "For Such a Time as This."

[77] Anderson, *Vision of the Disinherited*.

[78] Faupel, *Everlasting Gospel*, p. 261.

[79] Allen Clayton, "The Significance of William H. Durham for Pentecostal Historiography," *Pneuma* 1 (Fall 1979).

[80] Farkas, "Durham and the Sanctification Controversy."

[81] For the definitive treatment of this shift from a perfectionist to a Pentecostal worldview in the late 19th century, see Dayton, "The Doctrine of the Baptism of the Holy Spirit."

tionism (in terms of sanctification as a second work of grace). In Faupel's words, "Durham experienced within his own person the same dilemma which the Holiness movement had faced in the last half of the 19th century at the time they equated Spirit-baptism with entire sanctification."[82] Hence, Durham would later report that, "from that day to this, I could never preach another sermon on the second work of grace theory."[83]

In his personal testimony, Durham expressed the problem of his having believed and taught that he already had the Holy Spirit but soon became convinced that he did not have the same experience as the Azusa Street Pentecostals: "If this teaching were true, I had not the baptism.... So I said, 'no man can ever convince me, that I have not received the Holy Ghost.' No man ever could have done it; but God did it."[84] As Faupel points out, this change of mind led Durham to abandon his former understanding of sanctification; in particular, the matter of subsequence and eradication. Sanctification became an integral part of the one act of grace in conversion, not a crisis experience subsequent to it. And, as we noted earlier, Durham rejected the Wesleyan notion that in sanctification the "root of sin" is removed. While all sin, original and committed, is removed in conversion, the root that produces sin is still present.[85]

Farkas is correct that the language of perfectionism was absent in Durham's doctrine of the Finished Work, and that he did not hold to some form of complete eradication. But as Faupel points out, Farkas's description of Durham's view as a "single work perfectionism" identifies him too closely with the Holiness tradition and obscures the influences of "Keswickian self-understanding of sanctification as an 'abiding in Christ.'"[86] Durham's remedy for sinning was not to seek an experience that would remove the desire to sin, but to "reckon ourselves to be 'dead indeed' and to abide in Christ." God's order for restoration to communion with Him was through the act of repentance, which was a means of getting "back under the Blood."[87]

---

[82] Faupel, *Everlasting Gospel*, p. 266.

[83] Durham, "An Open Letter to My Brother Ministers," *Pentecostal Testimony* II/3 (July 1912): 14; cited in Faupel, *Everlasting Gospel*, p, 266.

[84] Durham, "Personal Testimony," p. 3.

[85] Durham, "Some Other Phases of Sanctification."

[86] Farkas, "Durham's 'Finished Work of Calvary,'" p. 262; Faupel, *Everlasting Gospel*, p. 263 n. 145.

[87] Durham, "Sanctification – The Bible Does Not Teach," p. 3.

We agree with Faupel that Durham's Pentecostal experience at Azusa Street seems to be the catalyst that reconstituted him both spiritually and theologically. But it is important to recall that Durham was engaged in careful study and reflection on the subject between that experience in 1907 and his first public address of the "Finished Work" in 1910:

> From the first, the Spirit dealt with me and revealed clearly in my heart the plain Bible truth of the Finished Work of the Cross of Calvary; but it took months for me to get it clear enough in my mind to be willing to entirely discard the old theory, and take my stand on the simple living truth of God. I moved with great care out of respect for many recognized great men, including Wesley, who had taught sanctification as a second work of grace. I waited until I was sure that there was no possibility of my being mistaken on the subject from a Scriptural standpoint.[88]

Blumhofer looks in another direction: the World's Faith Missionary Association with which Durham had been associated and which taught some form of the "Finished Work." She acknowledges that it was similar to the Keswick Holiness movement (which emphasized holiness and the "higher life" but rejected the Wesleyan teaching of sanctification as a second definite work of grace), and that Durham was likely familiar with the teaching of Essek W. Kenyon. But she concludes that there is no need to look further than the WFMA for the source of Durham's own teaching: "If there is a single formative source, G.L. Morgan and the Hanleys (of the WFMA) seem more likely than others." She hastens to add that the period of Durham's writing on sanctification and the Finished Work came during a personally intense time following the death of his young wife, Bessie Mae, in 1909:

> It was ... a period of grief, stress, and exhaustion. His personal turmoil, exacerbated by problems in his congregation that may in turn have been aggravated by Durham's personal situation, functioned as the lens through which he viewed his spiritual journey and the challenge of the moment.[89]

While the personal crisis in Durham's life undoubtedly affected his ministry and may explain his inflexible and aggressive manner of campaigning for his Finished Work teaching, it is insufficient to account fully for the doctrinal shift. Further, the early influence of the WFMA

---

[88] Durham, "Sanctification – Work of Grace," p. 16.
[89] Blumhofer, "William H. Durham," p. 136.

Finished Work teaching is undeniable but does not fully explain Durham's own reporting of the struggle. It seems that he had formerly believed and taught some version of the Holiness view. Referring to his Asuza Street encounter, he declared that, "from that day to this, I could never preach another sermon on the second work of grace theory."[90] He did report in his 1910 inaugural address on the Finished Work that he had believed in the Finished Work "from the first," but that he had had to study the issue for months "to get it clear enough in my mind to be willing to entirely discard the old theory, and take my stand on the simple living truth of God." Depriving future generations of knowing who and what else he read, one is left to speculate on the contents of his resources, if any, beyond the Bible itself. The question still remains: did anyone else contribute to Durham's formulation of the Finished Work of Calvary during this period?

e. The Kenyon Connection?

It is already clear that so far there is no theological smoking gun – a leader or writer who furthered Durham's Finished Work doctrine. But a viable possibility is Essek W. Kenyon, who was at least someone Durham knew during this period. In his extensive study of Kenyon, Dale Simmons concludes that Kenyon's doctrine and ministry lie behind Durham's own work. He traces the similarities between Kenyon's views and those of Durham, as well as the personal connection between the two leaders.[91]

Kenyon was not a Pentecostal but befriended Pentecostal leaders and left a legacy of influence, especially among Oneness Pentecostals and the Positive Confession movement.[92] Kenyon's own spiritual journey began in earnest in a small Methodist Episcopal Church in Amsterdam, New York, where he attended as a teenager and was ordained a deacon at age 19. His commitment waned but was renewed in 1893 during a service at Clarendon Street Baptist Church in Boston. He eventually aligned himself with the Free Will Baptists and began to minister in their churches. Geir Lie, Norwegian scholar on Kenyon, argues that he was immersed in the New England evangelical sub-culture, where he was deeply influenced by leading representatives

---

[90] Durham, "An Open Letter to My Brother Ministers."

[91] Dale H. Simmons, *E.W. Kenyon and the Post-Bellum Pursuit of Peace, Power and Plenty* (Metuchen, NJ: Scarecrow, 1996).

[92] Though he was never a Pentecostal, Kenyon applied for ordination credentials with the Assemblies of God while pastoring in Oakland, CA, in 1925 (Geir Lie, Personal correspondence, 15 September 15, 2002).

of the Keswickian Higher Life/Faith-Cure movement, the Premillennial Dispensationalism of John Nelson Darby, and Quietism.[93] In 1898 he founded Bethel Bible Institute, which throughout the years reflected the evangelistic spirit and teachings of the Keswick movement.[94] Kenyon's influence was primarily as a radio evangelist, Bible teacher and author. Though Kenyon was fully recognized as a Higher Life evangelical throughout his life, Simmons points out that he was highly eclectic in borrowing ideas, and "displayed an independent streak and an overwhelming need to come up with teachings that no one else had ever discovered." Though he would rail against "creedalism," he saved most of his attacks for the popular cult of his day, New Thought.[95]

The heart of Kenyon's teaching was the "Finished Work of Christ," a theme that closely parallels Durham's Finished Work of Calvary. While the emphasis can be traced to the christocentric and atonement-centered spirituality of the Keswick movement, Kenyon developed his own radical version of the substitutionary atonement. The alternate expression for the Finished Work, and which in later years he preferred, was "Identification with Christ," another central theme in Durham's teaching.[96] And, like Durham, Kenyon taught that one becomes completely identified with Christ in conversion. That means not only a change in status with God, but an inward cleansing as well.

---

[93] See Geir Lie, "E.W. Kenyon: Sektstifter eller kristen lederskikkelse? En historisk undersøkelse av Kentons teologi med særlig henblikk på dens historiske røtter og innflytelsen på samtid og ettertid" (M.A. thesis, Free Faculty of Theology, Oslo, Norway, 1994), ch. 1; English translation: "Cult Founder or Evangelical Minister?" See also R.M. Riss, "Kenyon, Essek William," in Stanley M. Burgess, ed., *The New International Dictionary of Pentecostal and Charismatic Movements* (rev. ed.; Grand Rapids, MI: Zondervan, 2002), pp. 819-20; David A. Reed, "Aspects of the Origins of Oneness Pentecostalism," in Vinson Synan, ed., *Aspects of Pentecostal-Charismatic Origins* (Plainfield, NJ: Logos International, 1975).

[94] After a number of changes in name and location, Bethel eventually became Barrington College in East Providence, RI, which is now amalgamated with Gordon College in Massachusetts.

[95] Simmons, *E.W. Kenyon*, pp. xii-xiii. Kenyon's interest in challenging New Thought ideas, combined with his lack of intellectual precision, has resulted in recent charges of heterodoxy. For example, see Daniel Ray McConnell, *A Different Gospel: A Historical and Biblical Analysis of the Modern Faith Movement* (Peabody, MA: Hendrickson, 1988). Both Lie and Simmons effectively demonstrate that Kenyon's ideas are shaped more by evangelical influences than the teachings of the metaphysical cults.

[96] See Kenyon, *Identification: A Romance in Redemption* (5th ed.; Lynnwood, WA: Kenyon's Gospel Publishing Society, 1941).

Both leaders initialized sanctification in conversion, setting them apart from the Holiness doctrine. Though Kenyon seems not to have embraced an eradicationist position, at one point he only criticized the Wesleyans for teaching that the old nature is removed subsequent to the new birth. Full salvation is provided and received in the Finished Work at the moment of conversion (though Kenyon preferred the Reformed language of "union" with Christ to sanctification language of perfection or eradication). Like Durham, Kenyon illustrated his point with the analogy of a baby: "You are just like a new-born babe without a single thing that condemns, utterly justified, and utterly declared righteous by God."[97] Thus, a comparison of their respective writings reveals that, while they diverged in details, they shared the central message of the Finished Work and identification with Christ.

The question is, would Durham have heard or met Kenyon in order for there to be a direct influence? Simmons answers with an emphatic affirmative, though evidence based on tracing Kenyon's ministry in Chicago is scanty. Simmons points out that Chicago was one of Kenyon's centers of ministry, and that he and Durham had actually spent time together. Kenyon's connection with the North Avenue Mission dates to 1901, when he conducted a series of meetings for the previous pastor, Emil L. Iverson. Kenyon had the opportunity to meet Durham personally during an extended evangelistic campaign in Chicago in 1907. He later described his impression of the young pastor in his periodical, *Reality*, as representing "the highest and most scriptural type I have met so far, among the leaders."[98] In 1908 Kenyon returned to Chicago for a campaign that lasted nearly a year. It may be worth noting that Kenyon's visits to Chicago coincided with the first two years following Durham's Pentecostal experience, the period when he was personally working through his understanding of the Finished Work. But while Simmons's conclusion is plausible – that "he undoubtedly renewed his acquaintance with Durham during this period" – there is no evidence for such a friendship or the more crucial claim that Kenyon's teaching was a formative influence on Durham.[99]

---

[97] Kenyon, *The Two Kinds of Knowledge* (18th ed.; Lynnwood, WA: Kenyon's Gospel Publishing Society, 1966; originally published in 1938), p. 68; cited in Simmons, *E.W. Kenyon*, p. 99.

[98] Kenyon, "The Gift of Tongues," *Reality* (May 1907), p. 10; cited in Simmons, *E.W. Kenyon*, pp. 57, 292. Simmons points out that this meeting occurred a brief two months after Durham's coming into his Pentecostal experience.

[99] Simmons, *E.W. Kenyon*, pp. 26, 310. Douglas Jacobsen expresses a similar hesitation that Simmons's conclusion is too definitive: "While this is an interesting thesis and may well have merit, the evidence for this influence is not incontestable.... It is

Kenyon continued to follow Durham's ministry.[100] He particularly
showed interest in his Finished Work teaching, and reprinted several
articles from the *Pentecostal Testimony*. Simmons notes that Kenyon's
reference to "Brother Durham" or "Pastor Durham" in his magazine
reveals a personal familiarity with the man, and assumes that his read-
ership likewise knew who he was. In the April 1912 issue of *Reality*,
Kenyon wrote with enthusiasm about the impact of Durham's Finished Work message in Los Angeles:

> These brethren have always held to the Wesleyan second work of grace
> theory, but recently they have seen the Finished Work of Christ. It has
> revolutionized their ministry. The writer cannot tell how happy he is to
> see the new light that is breaking in upon them.[101]

Kenyon continued in the same article to praise Durham, and express
the hope that he and his followers "will go on, and not only accept
these principles, but come to understand the deeper nature of the sufferings of Christ (i.e. Jesus' spiritual death on Calvary), the teachings of
the Blood Covenant, and a clear conception of the Family teaching of
the Scriptures, giving the Father His rightful place." As Simmons
points out, these congratulatory comments mean that at least Kenyon
regarded Durham's teaching on the Finished Work as his own, and
that his wish was for Durham to go on to accept his other distinctive
doctrines as well.[102] That the interest was mutual is a matter of speculation, since Durham makes no reference to Kenyon or his teaching.

Either Keswickian theology or more specifically Kenyon is likely
behind the unreferenced comments by two of Durham's close friends
and coworkers – McAlister in Ottawa and Ewart in Los Angeles. Each
one writing articles in *The Good Report* during the fall of 1913 refers to
the "legal" and "vital" aspects of redemption or the new birth. These
are precisely the terms that Kenyon utilized to describe the new birth:

---

difficult to know exactly what friendship the two men had or precisely what influence
Kenyon exerted on the younger Durham.... Simmons's hunch in this matter may be
correct, but I find it unnecessary either to make Kenyon's influence on Pentecostalism
as direct and explicit ... or as narrow ... as Simmons does." Like Jacobsen, I am more
inclined to follow Riss's assessment that the influence was "broader and more diffuse";
see Jacobsen, *Thinking in the Spirit*, p. 398.

[100] It is noteworthy that the initiatives and primary references to the relationship between Durham and Kenyon come from Kenyon. The latter apparently followed
Durham's ministry with interest, largely due to his Finished Work teaching and growing popularity.

[101] Kenyon, *Reality* 7 (April 1912), p. 128; cited in Simmons, *E.W. Kenyon*, p. 293.

[102] Simmons, *E.W. Kenyon*, p. 293.

"Much confusion has been occasioned, because we have not differen-tiated between the Legal and the Vital sides of the New Birth."[103] He then proceeded to lay out his teaching on these two aspects of salva-tion. Elsewhere he used the same terms to describe the work of redemption.[104] Simmons points out that this approach is nearly identi-cal to the Keswick formulation: "In this aspect, Kenyon's emphasis on the legal and vital sides of redemption parallels Keswick's stress on the legal and *experiential* sides of salvation."[105]

In 1913 Ewart wrote an article on the new birth in which he de-scribed its "legal" and "vital" aspects. He further explained fallen humanity as our "Satanic nature," and stated that the new birth brings us into "the Family of God" – all central themes in Kenyon's teach-ing.[106] Likewise, three months later McAlister published an article on redemption, using the same language of "legal" and "vital" to distin-guish its two dimensions.[107]

While there is no direct evidence of Kenyon's influence on Dur-ham, the Keswickian influence on both is clear. We shall see later that Kenyon's teaching on the Name, rather than the Finished Work, had more influence on Oneness Pentecostals.

3. Summary

New movements are characteristically born in the crucible of contro-versy. The modern Pentecostal movement is no exception. Many of its earliest leaders, beginning with Charles Parham, were anti-institutional and anti-creedal. Their chief enemy was the cold religiosity of main-stream denominationalism. Their sometimes fiercely independent streak created an unlikely amalgam of crude displays for territorial conquest and virtuous appeals for unity. It took decades of organiza-tional consolidation to create a movement with some semblance of stability. But a century later Pentecostalism is still a moving target, held

---

[103] Kenyon, *The Father and the Family* (7th ed.; Lynnwood, WA: Kenyon's Gospel Publishing Society, 1937), p.149.

[104] Kenyon, "The Holy Spirit," Lesson 33, *The Bible in the Light of Our Redemption* (Lynnwood, WA: Kenyon's Gospel Publishing Society, n.d.), pp.7-8.

[105] Simmons, *E.W. Kenyon*, p. 170.

[106] Ewart, "The New Birth," *Good Report* 2/4 (1 September 1913): 2.

[107] McAlister, "Redemption – Its Legal and Vital Aspects," *Good Report* 1/7 (1 De-cember 1913): 3. Geir Lie traces Kenyon's teaching on the legal and vital aspects of redemption to the Keswickian emphasis on the legal and experiential dimensions of salvation, and more specifically to a tract produced by the Plymouth Brethren; see Lie, Personal Correspondence, 15 September 2002.

together by the force of a transforming spiritual experience and an aptitude for cultural adaptation as it expands rapidly around the world.

The Finished Work controversy heralded by Durham marked the first schism in the infant movement. Surprisingly, the teaching that severed the majority of early Pentecostals from their Holiness origins would itself eventually become largely irrelevant. Durham's plan to write a book on the subject was aborted by his untimely death.[108] Consequently, the Finished Work doctrine remained undeveloped. Clayton's assessment is that it was sufficiently embryonic or misunderstood that, for many of his disciples, it functioned less as a doctrinal foundation than a means for uniting them "in their rejection of sanctification as a second definite experience of grace."[109]

One of the few who sustained an interest in and commitment to the doctrine was Franklin Small of Winnipeg, an early Finished Work advocate and later Oneness leader. Over the years he published articles in which he acknowledged Durham's spiritual paternity and attempted to locate the doctrine theologically in its relation to the Holiness position, the emerging "so-called fundamentalists" who were unsympathetic to the Pentecostal or "experimental aspect of the Gospel," and the modernists of the mainline denominations.[110] Looking back in 1930, Small acknowledged the fragmentary nature of Durham's teaching and the need for development: "This new message of course was not full and complete in itself. It was subject to a fuller clarification, as is nearly always the case in the introduction of a thing."[111] Undoubtedly, Small understood that he was taking up the challenge. But it was a surprise to many fellow Pentecostals that he developed the Finished Work teaching along the lines of the Reformed doctrine of "eternal security," a position that Small appears to have embraced as the logical consequence of Durham's theology.[112] The organization he founded in 1921, the Apostolic Church of Pentecost, still holds to the doctrine of eternal security, a theological rarity in the Pentecostal world.

---

[108] Durham, *Pentecostal Testimony* II/3 (July 1912): 16.

[109] Clayton, "Significance of William Durham," p. 39.

[110] Franklin Small, "The Finished Work of Calvary versus Modern Interpretations – Their Origin Exposed," *Living Waters,* pp. 25-26; cited in Faupel, *Everlasting Gospel,* p. 270.

[111] Small, "Theories and Traditions of Men Exploded, Work of the Holy Spirit – The Finished Work of Calvary," *Living Waters* (January 1930), pp. 21-24; reprinted in *Living Waters* 1/8 (March 1945).

[112] See Small, "The Finished Work of Calvary – Original Sin and Sins of Omission Contrasted," *Living Waters* 1/10 (September 1946), pp. 1-3.

The instability created during Durham's last two years bequeathed to his followers a host of other problems and possibilities. Many redirected their energies organizationally to consolidate the increasing numbers that had embraced the new doctrine. A few extended Durham's trajectory into what would shortly become the second great crisis in the Pentecostal movement. Like the shock that greeted his first address on the Finished Work in 1910, the New Issue appeared to many observers as a startling innovation. Like Durham's ideas, the continuities with the past are diffuse but discernible. We now turn to the themes that became the theological material for the construction of a less than thoroughly "New" Issue.

5

Old Themes for New Times

> [Lewi] Pethrus stepped over the theological line from being a Baptist to being a Pentecostal fairly easily, but many others would find that transition difficult. Most holiness Christians in particular determinedly resisted any kind of Pentecostal reformulation of their theology.... Differences of raw experience may well have contributed to this fight.... But the war itself was largely about words and how they were theologically used.... Words have social consequences.[1]
>
> – Douglas Jacobsen

Movements never appear *de novo*, but emerge within a particular history, with its cluster of ideas and social factors that eventually produce a tension between the movement and its surrounding environment. New movements are the social manifestation of an *angst* that seeks to make sense of a situation in which there is an increasingly perceived sense of social or ideological incoherence. Movements function as an organizing force for ordering this tension, especially in their own relationship to the surrounding environment.

In an illuminating essay on social theories of religious movements, Albert Miller argues that the deprivation theories of social change are inadequate both to explain the phenomena and give credence to the religious impulse as a determining factor in the explanation. Applied to Pentecostal historiography, he concludes that such theories are reductionistic in that they disregard "religious beliefs as a means to explain religious movements." Spiritual yearning is perceived as a human weakness – a form of deprivation – rather than a valid *datum* to be incorporated in the interpretation. Following the work of sociologists Benton Johnson, Rodney Stark and William Bainbridge, and anthropologists Gerlach and Hine, Miller reframes Pentecostalism's history of

---

[1] Jacobsen, *Thinking in the Spirit*, pp. 3-4.

"controversy, opposition and schisms" as a form of movement organization that is necessary to movement growth.[2]

A cursory review of Pentecostal history to the present reveals a movement in a state of tension with its wider social and ecclesiastical environment as well as intra-Pentecostal sub-cultures. The Finished Work controversy was not its only tensive moment, but it was the first to precipitate a new stream within the movement. And it would not be the last.

1. A Second Crisis Looms

The Finished Work crisis did not immediately settle the unrest and fragmentation that the early Pentecostal movement had been experiencing with the waning of the Azusa Street Revival. Durham's untimely death in 1912 only exacerbated the feeling of instability and division, especially in the regions that embraced his teaching (the Midwest and Southwest States, Canada, and parts of the deep South). Lines had been drawn, allegiances were being declared, but resolution was still elusive. Controversy would continue until 1916.

There are several reasons for the prolonged unrest. First, Durham's death had deprived the early Revival of one of the most popular and persuasive leaders it had produced to that time. Frank Bartleman remarked, "his word was coming to be almost law in the Pentecostal missions, even as far as the Atlantic Coast."[3] Also, the intensity of the controversy over the new teaching, and the vigor with which Durham proclaimed it, left many fresh wounds within the ranks, further fracturing much of the movement's fragile unity.[4] Fortunately, the unforeseen timing of a major revival in Dallas that summer with Maria Woodworth-Etter provided a focus for healing and unity. Her burden throughout the five-month revival was "to bring healing to the division that Durham's ministry had brought."[5]

Finally, the Finished Work theology was still too fresh and undeveloped to provide a stable center for the movement. Durham's death had produced a serious theological vacuum within the ranks. Many of the implications for the Pentecostal experience were still uncharted.

---

[2] Albert G. Miller, "Pentecostalism as a Social Movement: Beyond the Theory of Deprivation," *Journal of Pentecostal Theology* 9 (October 1996), pp. 97-114.

[3] Frank Bartleman, *How Pentecost Came to Los Angeles*, p. 150; cited in Faupel, *Everlasting Gospel*, p. 256.

[4] Faupel, *Everlasting Gospel*, pp. 257, 272.

[5] Faupel, *Everlasting Gospel*, p. 274.

Consequently, leaders who had come under the influence of Durham's teaching must have felt both the burden and the Elijah-mantle cast upon them to carry forth the mission already begun.

Prominent among them were ministers who had been part of Durham's inner circle: Frank Ewart (who had been Durham's associate at Seventh Street Mission in Los Angeles at the time of his death and had preached his funeral sermon[6]), R.E. McAlister from Canada (who became Ewart's associate following Durham's death, and was co-editor with Ewart of *The Good Report* during 1913-14), Glenn A. Cook (1867-1948; another associate, originally from Indiana, who joined Ewart when he broke rank to inaugurate the New Issue), Garfield T. Haywood (influential black pastor from Indianapolis who had worked with Cook). As mentioned earlier, these were also among the founding members of the Pentecostal Assemblies of the World, a fledgling organization formed in Portland, Oregon, in 1913 to promote the Finished Work message on the west coast.[7]

The picture that emerges in the writings of these leaders following Durham's death is one of spiritual entropy, doctrinal confusion, and struggle to work out the implications of the Finished Work teaching for unity among Pentecostals, the nature of the church, and the meaning of full salvation within the context of the Pentecostal experience.[8] Ewart despaired that "the Pentecostal movement at this time is practically littered with castaways [due to] false teaching, spiritual pride, hypocrisy and sin."[9] That the revival momentum was slowing down is suggested by his criticism of ministers whose work was not producing results in converts and healings. By 1915 William Booth-Clibborn was painting a dismal picture of the direction of the mainstream of Pentecostal converts as "the general contentment and all too-evident backsliding of the mass of the people from the former red-hot, Spirit-filled days ... enormous number of backslidden young people everywhere."[10]

Doctrinal confusion equally marked this period. Haywood described the situation:

---

[6] Ewart, *Phenomenon*, p. 75.

[7] Faupel, *Everlasting Gospel*, p. 251.

[8] This picture is consistent with the conditions prevailing in the wider Pentecostal movement at that time; see Anderson, *Vision of the Disinherited*, pp. 137-52.

[9] Ewart, "Compromise," *The Good Report* 2/4 (September 1, 1913): 3.

[10] William E. Booth-Clibborn, "The Little Rock Switch," *Meat in Due Season* 1/9 (December 1915): 1.

There have been many things written and spoken in these last few months upon this subject, and it has of late become a great topic of discussion among pentecostal brethren. Theory upon theory has been advanced, but there is but one way in which to form a conclusion and that is by the word of God only.[11]

Similarly, D.W. Kerr, a strong Finished Work proponent and later champion of the Trinitarian faction within the Assemblies of God, expressed his dismay at the disunity within the fellowship. He described a disheartening scene of congregational instability and doctrinal confusion:

At this present moment we are facing religious anarchy, and every faithful pastor is living in suspense of a stampede of his flock.... [Satan] is secretly working to keep us occupied in formulating correct doctrinal statements of the latest discovery of truth, in order to divert our attention from the Lord.[12]

He then named the key issues being debated at the time: the Finished Work teaching, one or two works of grace, and the Bride of Christ. He closed with an appeal for unity on the basis that was by now a familiar maxim: keep the unity of the spirit until they arrive at the unity of the faith.[13]

Neither unity of spirit nor a doctrine that could unify them in faith was forthcoming. They needed a cohering belief system and were ready for another Durham. So the key questions that faced them were: what will be the new orthodoxy, and who will be its spokesperson? Both questions were soon to be answered – to the jubilation of some and the consternation of many. But the answer would in large measure be woven from themes already in circulation and widely debated.

2. A Theological Paradigm

Ideas are like loose threads until there is a pattern or paradigm to draw them into a unified whole. A paradigm is the overarching structure

---

[11] G.T. Haywood, "Baptism into the Body," *The Good Report* 1/7 (1 December 1913): 3.

[12] D.W. Kerr, "The Oneness of Believers," *The Good Report* 1/7 (December 1913): 4.

[13] It is an irony of history that Kerr, who here so strongly denounced doctrinal agreements as an ineffective "old church method" for maintaining unity, only three years later drafted the rich and lengthy trinitarian statement, "The Adorable Godhead," to defend the fledging Assemblies of God fellowship against the New Issue challenge.

that helps us make sense of our world. It is the interpretive schema that makes possible the inner logic by which we order and prioritize the raw data of life. Theologically, it is the way in which we assess the importance and implication of a given belief or doctrine. When a paradigm changes, usually over a period of time, the same experience will be interpreted differently. Identifying operative paradigms has been important in interpreting modern Pentecostalism. Recent studies by Dayton and Faupel have been particularly illuminating in identifying the theological paradigms that informed early Holiness and Pentecostal leaders, especially in tracing the paradigm shift that occurred during the late 19th century.

Dayton identifies the theme of "full gospel" as the paradigm that dominates early Pentecostal consciousness and provides the language for the Pentecostal doctrine of the baptism of the Holy Spirit.[14] The four constitutive elements, all ministries of Christ, are: salvation, Spirit-baptism, healing and the second coming of Christ (a variant in Holiness circles added sanctification as a fifth element). Names by which the early movement was known are: "Pentecostal," "Apostolic Faith," and "Latter Rain" (Faupel adds "Full Gospel"[15]).[16] Faupel builds on Dayton's thesis, but argues that the underlying message of the movement is found in the Latter Rain motif, and that the other elements fill out that meaning. That is, early Pentecostalism was basically a millenarian movement, known primarily by two names, "The Everlasting Gospel" and "This Gospel of the Kingdom."[17]

All these themes are part of the theological fabric in the emergent Oneness Movement – the third stream after the Wesleyan Holiness and Finished Work traditions. The Oneness rejection of the doctrine of the Trinity and insistence on baptism in the name of Jesus sets it so apart theologically from the other streams that it appears to its more orthodox counterparts as virtually unrecognizable. Yet the many common Pentecostal elements are so visibly present that the usual response is one of cognitive dissonance.

A thesis of this study is that the relative lack of family resemblance is in some measure a function of paradigm change. Within its first two years, the New Issue developed an innovative threefold paradigm within which it would incorporate the many inherited themes from its

---

[14] In particular, see Dayton, "Doctrine of the Baptism of the Holy Spirit," and *Theological Roots of Pentecostalism*, chs. 1 and 4.

[15] Faupel, *Everlasting Gospel*, p. 28.

[16] Dayton, *Theological Roots*, p. 22.

[17] Faupel, *Everlasting Gospel*, p. 42.

pre-Pentecostal and Pentecostal forebears. The "Jesus' Name" or "Oneness" paradigm is a radical soteriology constituted by: a non-trinitarian modalistic view of God, the name of Jesus as the revealed name of God, and the threefold pattern for full salvation set forth in Acts 2:38. The Oneness paradigm is uniquely its own, though earlier paradigms and themes become theological resources for developing its doctrine and defining its relationship to other Christians. As we shall see, though the paradigm has remained consistent for nearly a century, the themes within it provide for a variety of interpretations in terms of self-identity and the degree of fellowship it permits with those outside its boundaries. We now turn to three themes that made their way into the Oneness paradigm: restorationist millenarianism, the "Full Gospel," and the Finished Work soteriology.

3. The Apostolic Gospel

Early Pentecostals were inheritors of the restorationist movement of the late 19th century that hoped to restore the unblemished apostolic life and doctrine to the church of its day.[18] It tended to ahistoricism, with even an anti-historical bias, resulting in a reaction to historical church creeds (even when they believed most of the tenets), ecclesiastical institutions and their traditional structures of authority. It allowed Pentecostals to claim that the movement was born without any human leader, and that its beliefs were absolute, supernatural truths revealed by God through the scriptures, untainted by the course of human history.

This restorationist strain became the "logical and emotional foundation" for the millenarian thrust in early Pentecostalism called the "Latter Rain."[19] Using an eschatological timeline, it spiritualized the rhythm of two annual rainfall seasons in ancient Palestine to announce that a worldwide revival, the Latter Rain "would fall at the end of the Church Age to ripen the harvest before Christ's return."[20]

---

[18] See Grant Wacker, "The Functions of Faith in Primitive Pentecostalism, *Harvard Theological Review* 77/3-4 (1984), p. 166, and "Playing for Keeps: The Restorationist Impulse in Early Pentecostalism," in *The American Quest for the Primitive Church*, ed. Richard T. Hughes (Chicago: University of Illinois Press, 1988).

[19] Anderson, *Vision of the Disinherited*, and Faupel, *The Everlasting Gospel*, emphasize the millenarian core of early Pentecostalism, while Wacker argues that the "Latter Rain" teaching rests upon the earlier restorationist foundation.

[20] Faupel, *Everlasting Gospel*, p. 35.

This adapted version of dispensational premillennialism resulted in a self-identity that positioned the Pentecostal band to be a special company of believers on the razor's edge between the close of this age and the Return of Christ. As someone at the beginning of the Azusa Street Revival remarked: "This is a world-wide revival, the last Pentecostal revival to bring our Jesus. The church is taking her last march to meet her beloved."[21]

a. The Bride of Christ: A Church for the Last Days

The doctrine of the Bride of Christ – a variant of the Church to appear in the "last days" before Christ's return – was born in the Dispensational Premillennialism of the previous century. It developed from the belief in the "inevitable decline of the church."[22] Its leaders did not share the confidence of the postmillennialists that the world was being won to Christ or that it would improve, but anticipated the future as a period of great persecution (the "Great Tribulation"). Faupel points out that the early Pentecostals adapted the Bride of Christ metaphor, their favorite, to describe themselves as the faithful eschatological remnant that would be received into heaven in the "Secret Rapture" prior to the Great Persecution.[23]

From the beginning, Parham had been drawing a distinction between the church and a more elite group called the Bride of Christ, in order to accommodate in a special category those who had experienced Spirit-baptism. As Faupel describes:

> The message to the church was the announcement that the Bride (i.e., the Pentecostal movement) was putting on her garments in preparation for the marriage supper of the Lamb. If other Christians wished to join, they must receive the wedding ring, the seal of the Holy Spirit which was speaking in unknown tongues.[24]

Charles Parham illustrates this pattern well. His innovative teaching on the Church, Bride and Man-Child gave plenty of grist for the theological mill. He was particularly concerned with the place of those who had and had not received Spirit-baptism.[25] In his view, the

---

[21] Printed in *The Apostolic Faith* 1/1 (September 1906): 4.

[22] Marsden, *Fundamentalism and American Culture*, p. 70.

[23] Faupel, *Everlasting Gospel*, pp. 24, 107-09.

[24] *Ibid.*, p. 28.

[25] For a detailed treatment of Parham's views on this subject, see Roland Wessels, "Parham's Exegetical Journey to the Biblical Evidence of the Spirit Baptism," paper presented to the meeting of the Society for Pentecostal Studies, Guadalajara, Mexico, November 11-13, 1993.

Church in the widest sense consisted of those who have been converted. Even then, they were on probation and "do not come into full
membership until you are sanctified."[26] They included many "saints"
who, like the ten foolish virgins, will be excluded from the first resurrection because they will have rejected the Pentecostal experience.[27]
Yet these were not bereft of the Holy Spirit, the "anointing that abi-
deth." The Spirit was present in conviction, witnessing to conversion
and sanctification.[28]

Those who had received Spirit-baptism constituted a special group
called the Bride of Christ. Parham came to believe that the "seal"
mentioned in the Scripture referred to Spirit-baptism that marked
those who will participate in the First Resurrection, and endowed
them with spiritual power to evangelize the world in the last days,
using the gift of speaking in other languages without learning them.[29]
He appears to have added another sub-set of Spirit-baptized believers
called the Man-Child – "overcomers" who will receive incorruptible
bodies and will be rulers with Jesus during the thousand-year reign
after the Tribulation.[30]

Such segregating of Christians had the effect of excluding many
from eternal salvation or at least its primary benefits. To this dilemma
Parham contributed his share. Surprisingly, he held to a much more
liberal view of the final demographics of heaven than most Fundamentalists. Convinced that God will save those who "walked in all the
light they had," he anticipated the eternal company to include "all the
babes, and all those from the formalistic churches, or wretched publi-
cans and harlots, or darkened heathen, whom the Christ of God deems
worthy of life."[31]

Thus an earlier millenarian framework provided a hermeneutic for
Pentecostals to understand themselves within the context of the "last
days" and the hostile world of wider Christendom. The doctrine of

[26] Parham, "The Everlasting Gospel," p. 104, in *Sermons of Charles F. Parham*, ed.
Donald Dayton (New York: Garland, 1985). It is only after sanctification that one can
in truth be considered born again; see p. 11.

[27] Parham, *Voice Crying in the Wilderness*, p. 124.

[28] Parham, "Everlasting Gospel," p. 16.

[29] Faupel claims that most early Pentecostals follow Parham in identifying the "seal"
with the baptism in the Holy Spirit; see *Everlasting Gospel*, p. 28. Phoebe Palmer appears to have associated the sealing with the divine sanction of one's total consecration
to God; see Palmer, *Promise of the Father*, p. 419; and *Way of Holiness*, p. 97, in *The
Devotional Writings of Phoebe Palmer*, ed. Donald Dayton (New York: Garland, 1985).

[30] Parham, *Voice Crying in the Wilderness*, p. 90.

[31] Parham, *Everlasting Gospel*, p. 51.

the Bride of Christ would be used to exclude or to persuade as they saw fit. For those who did not meet the standards of "full salvation" or experience all the stages in God's plan, the solution was to grant Pentecostals special status in the Kingdom and provide a hermeneutic for excluding or diminishing the status of those with whom they disagreed. To the list of criteria, Oneness Pentecostals would soon add their own.

b. Restored Revelation: Doctrinal Truth for the Last Days

Millenarian ecclesiology was matched by a millenarian theory of doctrine, which illuminates the contentious appeal made by New Issue leaders to "revelation." According to the theory, apostolic truth, as well as apostolic power, had been lost in the church. In this time of the Latter Rain, Pentecostals could expect to be the special recipients of God's progressive and complete revelation of His "Plan of the Ages," now being restored to the church: "Each age foreshadows and anticipates the next, disclosing more of God's plan for the ages."[32] Although Howard Goss's observation must be trusted that many ministers in that milieu were seeking "to dig up some new slant on a Scripture, or get some new revelation to his own heart,"[33] it is more accurate to set the revelational impulse within its millenarian context of restored apostolic and biblical truth. For our purposes it is significant that this practice of appealing to revelation became a means to validate doctrine. Promoters of innovative teachings in particular often claimed the *imprimatur* of revelation for their views.

The millenarian appeal is already discernible in Parham. As he made plans to visit a number of centers of revival in 1900, he wrote that his purpose was "to know more fully the latest truths restored by the later [sic] day movements."[34] He, in fact, spent that summer with one who claimed to receive immediate spiritual guidance, Frank W. Sandford, at his Holy Ghost and Us Bible School near Durham, Maine.

Durham, undoubtedly alluding to his Finished Work teaching, regarded the Revival as God's "first step toward restoring to His people, the church, the portions of truth and gifts of power which they had

---

[32] Faupel, *Everlasting Gospel*, p. 105.

[33] Ethel E. Goss, *The Winds of God*, p. 155.

[34] In Mrs. Charles Fox Parham, *The Life of Charles F. Parham* (Baxter Springs, KS: Printed by the author, 1930), p. 48; cited in Roland Wessels, "Charles Parham's Exegetical Journey to the Biblical Evidence of the Spirit Baptism," Paper presented to the 23rd Annual Meeting of the Society for Pentecostal Studies, Guadalajara, Mexico, 11-13 November 1993.

not come into possession of heretofore.... God will have just such a church in these last days."[35] In 1913 Ewart was using the language of revelation to dismiss the second work teaching: "God graciously sent the revelation of the 'Finished Work of Calvary' and liberated most of His people from these errors."[36] His view of revelation was in effect a form of faith seeking understanding, in that he clarified that one cannot grasp biblical doctrine without being born again, since it is in the realm of "experimental knowledge."[37]

While the perils of such an approach are obvious, the appeal was apparently intensified in the wake of Durham's death. As late as 1914, A.G. Garr, an early leader, lamented that there were those who vainly attempt to fill the shoes of their fallen leader by seeking doctrinal innovations:

> These seducing spirits work on the pride of men and women, telling them that they can be the one through whom will come a "new doctrine" that has been long hidden in the Scriptures, and by their bringing it out they will be equal to some who in reality GOD has sent forth to lead people into the whole truth. All who are posted in any way in the movement of God in these latter days know that God is opening up new truth which has increased more or less since the power of the Holy Spirit fell in this city of Los Angeles nearly eight years ago.... Not a few have tried to imitate Pastor William Durham by claiming to have something new for the people; but alas, unless God is behind the message, it is nothing more than a cloud without rain ...and is good for nothing but to halt the progress of God's people.[38]

Only a month before the New Issue broke into public view, Glenn Cook was applying the Latter Rain hermeneutic to the Finished Work teaching, with probable allusions to something greater:

> The evening light has come. The Lion of the Tribe of Judah has prevailed to open the Book, and as the light shines forth the fogs of theology and man-made creeds and dogmas disappear and the simple plan of redemption stands forth.[39]

---

[35] Durham, "Restoration," *Articles by Pastor Durham*, p. 47.

[36] Ewart, "False Teaching Regarding the Baptism in the Holy Ghost," *Good Report* 2/3 (1 August 1913): 4.

[37] Ewart, "The New Birth," *Good Report* 2/4 (1 September 1913): 2.

[38] A.G. Garr, "That 'Yellow Book,'" *Good Report* 1/8 (1 January 1914): 3.

[39] Glenn Cook, "Paul's Gospel of Free Grace," *Good Report* 1/10 (1 March 1914): 3.

In the same issue Ewart used the phrase, "the evening light has come," a fresh application of this early millenarian slogan to a new stage in the Revival.[40]

It is no surprise then that the New Issue leaders perceived their new doctrine to be a restoration of apostolic truth. One evangelist, Winifred Westfield, in 1915 made a direct link with the new revelation: "The GREAT MYSTERY of God, hid for ages, is now being revealed as he hath declared to his servants the prophets."[41] Glenn Cook openly claimed that, "the Son hath revealed to us the mystery of the Father and the Son," and that, for those who still do not understand, the truth will be revealed to those who "obey Him and keep His commandments."[42] Ewart made a similar appeal to the Spirit as the revealer of Jesus without whom the seeker would only be confused. The key was that this mystery was now being revealed to all who desired to know and obey the truth.[43] More than thirty years later, Ewart still held to the Latter Rain hope for a full apostolic restoration, even though he was considerably less confident that it was imminent: "How the Apostolic fellowship and unity is to be restored we do not know. But we read in the scriptures that it will be in the end time."[44]

The language of revelation is sprinkled through Holiness and Pentecostal literature. Its roots most likely trace back to Wesley's emphasis on the experiential faith and the "inner testimony" of the Spirit. As Wesleyan scholar, Paul Bassett, points out, Wesley doubted that the Scripture was effectual "apart from the operations of the Spirit."[45] By the time Pentecostalism appears on the scene, Wesley's inner witness was being reinterpreted within the restorationist-millenarian hermeneutic and applied to doctrinal ideas – views that were being elevated to the status of restored apostolic truth in the Last Days. Faupel records the story of an early Methodist, George D. Watson, whose struggle with accepting the premillennial view illustrates this appeal to divine revelation as justification for a particular doctrine:

[40] Ewart, "A Beautiful Type of Redemption," *Good Report* 1/10 (1 March 1914): 3. For example, the phrase was part of the name of an earlier periodical called *Evening Light and Church of God Evangel*; see Anderson, *Vision*, p. 314.

[41] Westfield, "What Is Truth?"

[42] Glenn Cook, "A Revelation," *Meat in Due Season* 1/13 (June 1916): 3.

[43] Ewart, "The Quickening Spirit," *Meat in Due Season* 1/13 (June 1916): 3.

[44] Ewart, *Phenomenon*, p. 35.

[45] Paul Merritt Bassett, "The Theological Identity of the North American Holiness Movement: Its Understanding of the Nature and Role of the Bible," in *Variety of American Evangelicalism*, p. 82.

> Early in 1896 I began to pray very earnestly for the Holy Spirit to open
> the Scriptures to me clearly on that subject. In two or three weeks after-
> wards the Spirit began unfolding in my mind in a remarkable way ... the
> premillennial coming of Christ.[46]

Kenyon, likewise, used the language of revelation. Probably with
New Thought in mind, he wrote that the truth of the Christian's life
in Christ "is not a New Philosophy. It is an unveiling of a lost truth,
the most vital of all that God gave us in Christ."[47] He contrasted
"revelation" knowledge with "sense" knowledge, claiming that only
the Spirit directs the former. According to Simmons, he followed the
restorationist-millenarian view that God was gradually restoring apostolic truth to the church: "He became more and more convinced that
God was challenging the church 'in these last days to get the light and
the knowledge that will fit us for the closing of this dispensation.'"[48]
D. Wesley Myland, early Pentecostal leader who developed the doctrine of the Latter Rain Covenant, claimed that his teaching came by
revelation:

> I am proceeding to analyze the Word of God relative to this great Cove-
> nant as God gave it to me. As far as I know, God has given this to no
> other man, and I have communicated with many bible students upon this
> subject. God revealed it to me when He baptized me in the Holy Ghost
> and fire, the third of November, 1906.[49]

When Haywood later made the Oneness claim that "the mystery of
God [is] only known by revelation," he directed the reader to the
Scriptural teaching, and then turned the tables on Trinitarians who, in
their worldly wisdom, do not see: "Is Jesus revealing this mystery to
them contrary to His own words that these things are hidden from the
'wise and prudent,' but are revealed unto babes?"[50] Wacker correctly
observes that Oneness Pentecostals were only applying the same hermeneutic of revelation as other Pentecostals: both expected people to
follow in the new light, and failure to do was to "defy God's commandments to guarantee abandonment in the Great Rapture."[51]

---

[46] Cited in Faupel, *Everlasting Gospel*, pp. 185–86.

[47] Kenyon, *Two Kinds of Life*, p. 1.

[48] Simmons, *Essek W. Kenyon*, pp. 104–105.

[49] D. Wesley Myland, *The Latter Rain Covenant and Pentecostal Power* (Chicago: Evangel, 1910), p. 32.

[50] Haywood, *The Victim of the Flaming Sword* (Indianapolis: Christ Temple, n.d.), p. 46.

[51] Wacker, "Functions of Faith," p. 165.

Douglas Jacobsen comes to a similar conclusion; namely, that for all early Pentecostals it was the immediacy of the Spirit's revelatory work that distinguished them from the Fundamentalists: "For fundamentalists, the relationship between God and the world was constant and unchanging; for pentecostals, that relationship was dynamic and progressive." The Bible was not a hermetically sealed repository of unchanging truths but "the touchstone for evaluating the veracity of new claims of revelation." Both then and now, Jacobsen rightly observes: "Pentecostals, for all their openness to new revelation, remain solidly committed to the Bible as the word of God."[52]

In the early period of the Revival, the new claims were welcomed as part of the Spirit's Last Days restoration of apostolic truth and practice, a conviction that did not permit them to stray far from Scripture. The New Issue, though radically sectarian for even other Pentecostals, nonetheless situated itself within the millenarian expectations of the Pentecostal movement. Its millenarian ecclesiology, which created a special classification for its own adherents, had been in the Revival since Parham. While its appeal to revelation was sometimes blatant and theologically naïve, it was only applying a hermeneutic that had already been well established and by some well used.

4. The Full Gospel

The Gospel may never have been as simple as many evangelists presented it. But the Holiness tradition, with its emphasis upon sanctification subsequent to conversion, was the antecedent by which a more complex understanding of the Christian life occurred. The "full gospel" or "full salvation" was viewed as multifaceted, with stages and acts of grace beyond the initial event of justification and conversion. By the eve of the Pentecostal Revival, five major themes could be identified: salvation, sanctification, baptism in the Holy Spirit, healing and the Return of Christ.[53]

The fundamental message of full salvation was that there is more for the believer after conversion, and this apostolic reality is to be received if one is to expect apostolic blessing. Indeed, the Christian life cannot be lived fully unless the "more" is appropriated. In exhorting his followers to seek perfection, Wesley wrote that, "unless you press

---

[52] Jacobsen, *Thinking in the Spirit*, pp. 357, 363.

[53] For a study of the development of the four- and fivefold gospel schemes in Holiness and Pentecostal theology, see Donald Dayton, *Theological Roots of Pentecostalism*.

believers to expect full salvation now, you must not look for any re-vival."[54] William Boardman, a Presbyterian leader who embraced the Oberlin version of holiness, taught that justification alone was not enough to live victoriously and that "a second crisis experience was necessary to experience 'full trust' by which to enter 'full salvation.'"[55]

The *gestalt* of full salvation became the hermeneutic by which early Pentecostals, like Holiness teachers before them, were able to define and refine spiritual crisis experiences, stages in the Christian life, and classification of Christians. We will now explore specifically the role played by Acts 2:38, and the three elements of repentance, water bap-tism, and baptism in the Holy Spirit, in the emerging Pentecostal and subsequent New Issue theologies.

a. The Pattern for Full Salvation – Acts 2:38

Before Charles Parham's arrival, the book of Acts was being studied with great interest in Holiness circles. This attention accompanied the shift in Holiness theology from a focus on sanctification to that of baptism of the Spirit, a move that prepared the way for a Pentecostal understanding of Christian experience. Charles E. White, in tracing the roots of the Pentecostal pattern, argues that, as early as the 1850's Phoebe Palmer was teaching a tripartite approach to living the full Christian life.

Palmer proposed a three-stage process for securing the experience of entire sanctification. While the content differed, White claims that Pentecostals appropriated the pattern. Though Palmer's three steps were entire consecration, faith and testimony, White suggests that these themes were adapted in Pentecostalism for seekers of Spirit-baptism: "(1) be converted, (2) obey God fully, and (3) believe."[56] One can discern the contours of the three-stage pattern in Acts 2:38: (1) repent (be converted), (2) be baptized in the name of Jesus Christ (obey God fully), and (3) receive the gift of the Holy Spirit (believe).

Parham's restorationist passion was to replicate the experience of the early church, especially its fountainhead, the Day of Pentecost. This led to an intensive study of the second chapter of Acts, the text that Parham assigned his Bethel College students to examine during his

---

[54] John Wesley, *Works, VI*, p. 761; cited in Paul G. Chappell, "The Divine Healing Movement in America" (Ph.D. diss., Drew University, 1983), p. 60.

[55] Cited in Faupel, *The Everlasting Gospel*, p. 71.

[56] Charles E. White, "Phoebe Palmer and the Development of Pentecostal Pneu-matology," *Wesleyan Theological Journal* 22/1-2 (Spring-Fall 1988): 207.

absence on the eve of 1901.[57] Later, in his attempt to sort out the respective roles of water and Spirit-baptism, his attention was directed to Peter's Pentecost sermon.[58]

In 1902 Parham wrote that God spoke to him: "Have you obeyed every command you believe to be in the Word?"[59] At that point his mind was directed to the "convincing evidence of the necessity of obedience," in which the words of Peter came rushing into his mind, "Repent and be baptized every one of you in the name of Jesus Christ" (Acts 2:38).

It was Durham, however, who elevated Acts 2:38 to normative pattern for Pentecostal belief and practice. Following Peter's command in Acts 2:38 to "repent and be baptized," Durham wrote, "This is the continual order of things in the Acts of the Apostles." Instead of seeking a second work of grace, once a person is saved, "this makes him a candidate for water baptism, which is the only thing required of him between conversion and the baptism in the Holy Spirit."[60] He concluded that the standard practice in the apostolic Church was "as soon as a man was saved they baptized him and laid hands on him that he might receive the Holy Spirit."[61]

Palmer had provided a triple paradigm for entering into the full salvation of entire sanctification. Parham adapted it through the lens of Acts 2:38 and the conviction that water baptism was to be administered in the name of Jesus Christ. Durham further modified it to refute the second work of grace teaching and establish it as the norm for Pentecostal experience within the framework of his teaching on the Finished Work.

It is little surprise that the proto-Oneness disciples of Durham were already committed to Acts 2:38 as the apostolic pattern of the full gospel and standard for Pentecostal experience.

Before publicly declaring himself on the New Issue, Ewart had been teaching that the Church was to be formed on the Acts 2:38 pattern, consisting of those "who are called out of the world, made new creatures in Christ Jesus, buried with him by baptism unto death, and filled with the Holy Spirit."[62] He identified Acts 2:38 as the "normal plan"

---

[57] Anderson, *Vision*, p. 53.
[58] Wessels, "Parham's Exegetical Journey," p. 6.
[59] Parham, *A Voice Crying in the Wilderness*, p. 21.
[60] Durham, "Two Great Experiences," p. 5.
[61] *Ibid.*, p. 7.
[62] Ewart, "The Church – What Is It?" *Good Report* 2/1 (1 June 1913): 3.

of salvation.[63] In one exposition on the significance of water baptism, his exposition closely parallels Palmer's second stage of obeying God fully, or full consecration of one's life on the altar. On the eve of his public declaration, Ewart wrote that, on the Day of Pentecost, converts "came forth from the water with the sentence of death passed upon themselves. There could not have possibly been a deeper consecration.... No wonder God sealed their devotion and faith in His Son with the gift of the Holy Ghost."[64] He proceeded to connect this consecration with possible martyrdom, drawing upon Parham's application of Palmer's teaching on consecration; namely, that for those who have resisted the Pentecostal experience, "martyrdom ...takes the place of consecration."[65] Similarly, Glenn Cook recognized that the "one salvation" emphasized in the Finished Work teaching still left room for "steps in the plan of salvation." These steps were laid out in Acts 2:38 as "the Gospel plan then, and it has not changed."[66]

This focus on Acts 2:38 did not change for New Issue leaders when they emerged publicly in 1914. It has consistently remained *the* plan of salvation, a plan inherited from its Holiness roots, adapted to reject those roots, and employed to set apart the New Issue movement from its Pentecostal companions.

b. The Dance of Full Salvation – Blood, Water and Spirit

While the pattern of Acts 2:38 remained foundational, the interpretation and significance of the pattern and its constituent elements were more fluid, beginning with Parham. While he was creating a special status for those who were "sealed" by the Spirit, Parham was also exploring the role of water baptism. If the latter was not the seal, as some had taught, then what place did it have in the salvation plan? His search for the correct practice was rooted in his desire to achieve unity among believers on the basis of pure biblical doctrine, rather than the restrictive creeds and dogmas of a dead church and the skeptical eye of the higher critic.

The shift in Parham's thinking came during a session at the Bible School after he and the students had been studying in earnest the subject of water baptism. He had taught and practiced triple immersion in the name of the Father, Son and Holy Spirit. But this day the Spirit showed him that water baptism was identification with Jesus Christ in

---

[63] Ewart, "Beautiful Type of Redemption."

[64] Ewart, "The Gospel of the Kingdom," *Good Report* 1/10 (1 March 1914): 4.

[65] Parham, *Voice Crying in the Wilderness*, p. 126.

[66] Glenn Cook, "Standards of Justification," *Good Report* 2/4 (1 September 1913): 2.

his death, and that, "God the Father, and God the Holy Ghost never died."[67]

The theological implications for Parham are threefold. First, he realized that the biblical precedent was inconsistent with the church's practice. His antagonism toward institutional religion led him to appeal for the reader to "lay your teachings, creeds and doctrines at His feet."[68] Second, he came to understand that baptism in the name of Jesus Christ was an act of confessing his deity, a doctrine under attack by the liberal church of his day. Parham's logic was as follows: Jesus instructed that the sign of his divine origin was Jonah; with Jesus' death and resurrection he had "proved his divinity"; by identifying with Jesus, after the pattern of Rom. 6:4, the believer is confessing faith in the true identity of Jesus at a time when it is being attacked by higher critics who dismissed the Jonah story as myth. Third, Parham abandoned his practice of triple immersion for a single act in order to harmonize baptism in the name of one person in the Godhead with the act itself. He offered this as his theological rationale:

> So if you desire to witness a public confession of a clear conscience toward God and man, faith in the divinity of Jesus Christ, you will be baptized by single immersion, signifying the death, burial and resurrection; being baptized in the name of Jesus, into the name of the Father, Son and Holy Ghost; they are one when in Christ you become one with all.[69]

The result was to give greater prominence to water baptism, to locate it more centrally within the context of early Pentecostal thought and practice, and to lay the foundation for exercising more fully the believer's identification with Christ.[70]

Parham attempted to integrate his understanding of the Pentecostal Revival with Dispensational eschatology. He secured a special place for those baptized in the Spirit, and opened the door wide for even the unchristianized "heathen." He established the practice of baptism in the name of Jesus that would eventually secure a place in New Issue practice.

---

[67] Parham, *Voice Crying in the Wilderness*, p. 23.

[68] *Ibid.*, p. 22.

[69] Parham, *Voice Crying in the Wilderness*, p. 23.

[70] See Wessels, "Parham's Exegetical Journey," p. 6. Water baptism in some early Pentecostal circles seems to have been a combination of frequent practice and low theology. For instance, A.J. Tomlinson is reported to have advocated baptism with every spiritual crisis experience; see Anderson, *Vision of the Disinherited*, pp. 176-77.

William Durham's Finished Work of Calvary teaching in 1910 was the first major challenge to Pentecostalism's Holiness identity. Though he collapsed the prevailing theology of two works of grace into conversion, his "simple Gospel" was still obliged to deal with the Pentecostal reality of Spirit-baptism.

Durham agreed with Parham on a number of points. First, he recognized that the Christian life begins with the new birth, an experience in advance of Spirit-baptism. In conversion one is truly and completely saved: "When [one] receives Christ, he receives a full salvation in Him." He agreed that Spirit-baptism is an experience subsequent to conversion, through which one "is sealed unto the day of redemption."[71] This phrase without explanation suggests that Durham believed that Spirit-baptism is the guarantee of participation in the First Resurrection. Durham followed Parham's baptismal theology that water baptism is primarily identification with Christ. It was so central in his own teaching that he could say, "The plain teaching of the Word of God is identification with Christ."[72]

Unlike Parham, however, Durham was adamant that sanctification is not a second work of grace but integral to the initial work of Christ in the new birth. There are "two great experiences" for the Christian, the new birth and Spirit-baptism. The first experience is the one and only work of grace, incorporating both justification and sanctification. Without resorting to a form of baptismal regeneration, he incorporated the act of water baptism as a forceful demonstration of the sanctifying power granted to the new convert, which is the death of the "old man," "to be buried there, never to rise again."[73]

But Durham also taught that not only is Spirit-baptism subsequent to conversion but so is the coming of the Spirit. Unlike Parham, he insisted that the Spirit delays coming to abide in the believer until Spirit-baptism. In conversion one receives Christ, and receives the Spirit later in Spirit-baptism. As he stated, "Christ and the Holy Spirit are not in the Scripture one and the same."[74] For Durham, to equate the two would be either to weaken the necessity for the Pentecostal Spirit-baptism or to conclude that only those who have received

---

[71] Durham, "Two Great Experiences," p. 7.

[72] Durham, "Sanctification – Work of Grace," p. 16

[73] *Ibid.*, p. 18. He elaborates on the theme by using the typology of the Passover and Red Sea crossing of the Israelites. The Passover symbolizes salvation by the shed blood of a lamb. But it is in the Red Sea that the "old man" is drowned and the redeemed are "forever free from [his] bondage."

[74] Durham, "False Doctrines," p. 38.

Spirit-baptism are saved. Neither was acceptable to him, but his position was sufficiently untenable that the theological dilemma was left to his disciples to resolve.

Durham built his baptismal theology upon Parham's view of identification with Christ, but made it even more central to his Finished Work teaching. If identification with Christ was his operative principle, then baptism is the one act of obedience that brings the believer into conformity with it: "The thought of God concerning our salvation is expressed in a death, burial and a resurrection. Our faith in God's plan is clearly expressed in the ordinance of baptism." Unlike Parham, baptism was not primarily an act to confess the deity of Christ, but the visible accompaniment by which one enters into the death and resurrection of Jesus. It was important enough for Durham to call it the "dividing line between the old life and the new."[75]

Durham reworked the elements in the full salvation plan laid out by Parham in hopes of grounding Christian experience solely in Christ. But in doing so, he made the division harder between conversion and Spirit-baptism by separating the works of Christ and the Spirit. Furthermore, he made water baptism even more prominent than it was in Parham, by linking the believer's identification with Christ with his three-fold Pentecostal hermeneutic of Acts 2:38.

The disciples of Durham who initiated the New Issue continued to adapt the Pentecostal themes. They eventually embraced Parham's practice of baptism in the name of Jesus Christ against Durham's warning.[76] But they carried the torch for his Finished Work teaching, the choice of Acts 2:38 as normative pattern, and the central role he gave to water baptism.[77] And like Durham, they defined the church as, in his words, "composed of Pentecostal people," by which they meant those who had obeyed Acts 2:38.[78] The true church was synonymous with the Bride of Christ and Body of Christ.[79]

---

[75] Durham, "Sanctification – Work of Grace," p. 16; see "Identification with Christ," p. 27.

[76] Durham, "False Doctrines," p. 40.

[77] For example, see Glenn Cook, "Standards of Justification"; Garr, "'Yellow Book'"; R.E. McAlister, "Salvation through Grace," *Good Report* 2/1 (1 June 1913): 3; Ernest A. Paul, "Believer's Baptism," 1/8 (1 January 1914): 4.

[78] Durham, "The Church."

[79] Ewart, "False Teaching Regarding the Baptism in the Holy Ghost"; also, "The Church – What Is It?" *Good Report* 2/1 (1 June 1913): 3; G.T. Haywood, "Baptised into One Body," *Good Report* 1/7 (December 1, 1913): 3; Harvey McAlister, "The Church – Spiritual Gifts – Other Tongues," *Good Report* 2/3 (1 August 1913): 3.

They still retained the distinction between being "saved" and being baptized with the Spirit. Believers must be first saved *before* they can be sealed with Spirit-baptism and become members of the church. As Ewart exclaimed, "What could be plainer than the statement here that God took of both Jews and Gentiles and after saving them through the precious blood of His Son, baptized them into one body, the church." Apparently, there were those who were already radicalizing the doctrine of salvation by collapsing initial salvation into the experience of Spirit-baptism. Ewart assailed some in the Finished Work camp who "are preaching the very thing that this great truth destroys, namely, that one is not saved until they are baptized in the Spirit. No one can have the revelation of the Pauline gospel in their souls who hold to this theory."[80] Already the distinction between "being saved" as Durham had taught it was being confused with the fourfold gospel of *full* salvation.

But what about those who had not come into the full experience of Acts 2:38? What Parham and others called old Christendom, Durham described as "abnormal" Christianity.[81] He complained, "We have an abnormal Christianity in the world today (that is, those we must recognize as Christians, but who are not filled with the Holy Spirit) for which it is impossible to find any scriptural provision."[82] There was so little resemblance of apostolic Christianity in the denominations that he refused to look for any. He acknowledged the presence of true Christians in those churches, but had no tolerance for the institutions themselves.

Durham's attitude and his choice of description only served to encourage many of his followers to further rigor.[83] Ewart displayed a shift in attitude when he drew upon the familiar "unity of the Spirit" slogan by shifting the emphasis to the unity of the faith. Shortly before he made his public break in 1914, he criticized those who, to achieve

---

[80] Ewart, "False Teaching."

[81] It is very possible that Durham borrowed the image of abnormal Christianity from a comment by R.A. Torrey in *What the Bible Teaches*: "If we had the normal state of the Apostles we would baptize repentant sinners in the name of our Lord Jesus Christ, and lay hands on them and they would receive the Holy Spirit baptism; but, unfortunately, we have not got the normal," cited in Ewart, *Name and Book*, p. 51.

[82] Cited in Ewart, "False Teaching."

[83] For instance, Haywood made reference to an article in which the author attempted to locate within the Body of Christ "a place to justify this abnormal state of the present-day Christianity," in "Baptized into One Body." See also Frank Bartleman, "Why I Was Re-Baptized in the Name of Jesus Christ," *Meat in Due Season* 1/9 (December 1915): 1; Sister King, "Abnormality," *Good Report* 1/10 (1 March 1914): 2.

unity, felt compelled to "recognize an abnormal experience." Challenging his readers to walk in the new light as God was revealing it, he expressed the hope that, as the full faith of the Apostles finally burst on the scene, true unity would be restored and all forms of abnormal Christianity evaporate. In other words, the time had come to stand for the faith, and the unity of the faith would bring a spiritual unity.[84]

In summary, the concept of the "full gospel" spawned a number of themes that made their way into Pentecostal experience and terminology. The strength of the fourfold paradigm lay in its capacity to bring into focus such dimensions of the Christian life as justification, sanctification, water baptism and Spirit-baptism. But, when combined with other less defined themes in the early Pentecostal movement (e.g. millenarianism), and the constant struggle to work out a consistent theological position, the result was less than unifying. From within the Finished Work camp the New Issue leaders constructed their doctrine from existing Pentecostal and pre-Pentecostal ideas. This task would prove to be neither easy nor consensual. By initializing all the elements of Acts 2:38 in the Finished Work structure, they were faced with competing interpretations: is Acts 2:38 the Pentecostal paradigm for full identification with Christ, as Durham had taught, or is it synonymous with the new birth itself? Furthermore, is it the familiar "full salvation" plan, or is it the exclusive salvation plan, offered without salvific remainder? These would be crucial issues for the New Issue.

5. The Simple Gospel

The Finished Work theology, in which the New Issue was born, attempted to consolidate the Pentecostal experience in the atoning work of Christ. Durham and his followers were fond of calling it the "simple Gospel."[85] The move was an attempt to simplify the prevailing multiplicity of experiences expected and sought in the Holiness pattern. But the process was itself anything but simple. It would involve a shift in at least three directions: (1) to redirect the believer's confidence from feeling to faith, from subjective experiences to trust in the objective promises of Christ, (2) to collapse all stages of Christian experience

---

[84] Ewart, "Unity of the Faith."
[85] The phrase is sprinkled throughout Finished Work literature. See especially Haywood, "The Simple Gospel," *Good Report* 1/10 (1 March 1914): 2; and "Be Strong in the Lord," *Good Report* 2/3 (1 August 1913): 1. See also W.E. Moody, "Preach the Word," *The Good Report* 1/3 (1912): 7-8.

into one instantaneous event, and (3) to move this event to the beginning of the Christian life.

There are clues that this process began with Phoebe Palmer in the mid-19th century. The historical trail from her to the New Issue is murky at best. But the theological scent is stronger.

a. From Feeling to Faith

Reading Phoebe Palmer following the Revival of 1857-58 leaves one with the impression that she was witnessing experience fatigue. Believers were becoming highly introspective. Some were not sure if their experience was in fact the much desired sanctification. Others were tarrying for months without success. Still others were devoid of spiritual affections, which only increased their anxiety.[86]

In response, Palmer counseled seekers to secure their sanctification, not in Wesley's nebulous doctrine of the "inner witness," but in "the objective word of Scripture."[87] They were to measure their spiritual life by neither their own inner feeling states nor the feelings of others. Scripture itself did not provide a standard for feelings. They were simply a gift of which God "will give you just the amount and kind of emotion that will best fit you to glorify his exalted name."[88]

One was to lay hold of sanctification by an *act of faith* that appropriates the atoning benefits of Christ.[89] Palmer made her point by use of the legal or juridical theory of the atonement: one could claim full salvation on the grounds that God had made provision in the atonement. Since the atonement was God's objective work on our behalf, one was to seek no other sign than the promise in Scripture itself.[90]

The effects of this shift in focus were numerous. It reversed the revivalist preoccupation with feeling by calling on the believer to make an act of will in faith.[91] It redirected attention to the Scripture as the

---

[86] See Palmer's counsel to a woman who was brooding over her lack of religious emotions, *Faith and Its Effects*, in *The Devotional Writings of Phoebe Palmer*, p. 27.

[87] White, "Phoebe Palmer," p. 206. She seems to have come by this conviction as much by the struggles in her own spiritual journey as by reasoning. She stated that she regarded her penchant for intellectual answers as a spiritual detriment until she realized that it motivated her to submit every aspect of her spiritual life to "the requirement of his written word," *The Way of Holiness – Is There Not a Shorter Way?* in *Devotional Writings*, p. 82.

[88] Palmer, *Faith and Its Effects*, pp. 15, 67, 105.

[89] *Ibid.*, p. 35; see also *Promise of the Father*, p. 398.

[90] Palmer, *Faith and Its Effects*, pp. 242, 342.

[91] Palmer contributed to reversing the trend in Revivalism which stresses "emotionalism at the expense of reason," Faupel, *Everlasting Gospel*, p. 60.

appropriate authority for interpreting Christian experience. It established Christian experience on outward evidence rather than inward experience. And it secured a christocentric foundation for its theology of sanctification.[92] On the last point, it seems that the christology-pneumatology tension in the Holiness movement was not so much that it minimized the doctrine of the atonement than that it promoted a subsequent means, the sanctification experience, to appropriate the work of atonement – a direction that, for some, diminished the all-sufficiency of Christ.

The reaction to dependence upon subjective feelings or experience for assurance of Spirit-baptism is discernible in early Pentecostalism. Wacker points out that the early Pentecostal canon of tongues as evidence of Spirit-baptism is rooted in the ahistorical spirit of the Restorationist movement. This allowed Pentecostals to ignore the relativities of history and personal subjectivity in favour of an objective, absolute authority in Scripture.[93]

Palmer and Parham agreed in their suspicion that subjective experience is reliable proof of divine blessing. Parham rejected as evidence the revivalist gestulations of "shouting, leaping, jumping, and falling in trances or unctions and divine revelations."[94] But, unlike Palmer who was satisfied that a simple act of faith in the objective authority of the Bible was sufficient, Parham led off the Pentecostal parade with his teaching that tongues was the normative biblical evidence of Spirit-baptism. Likewise, William Seymour tried to keep the Azusa Street Revival on the evidential track by criticizing those who were "running off with blessings and anointings with God's power, instead of tarrying until Bible evidence of Pentecost come."[95]

Durham's Finished Work teaching further challenged prevailing Pentecostal subjectivities, this time in the universally accepted second work of grace doctrine. As committed as any other Pentecostal to the supernatural experiences of conversion and Spirit-baptism, he attacked the Holiness teaching for what seemed to him to be doctrine based upon personal experience "instead of the plain teaching of the Word

---

[92] Palmer's increased use of Pentecostal language that looked back to Christian foundations, and her Christ-centered "altar theology" strengthened the christocentric emphasis in the Holiness movement; see Dayton, *Roots of Pentecostalism*, pp. 90-94; White, "Phoebe Palmer," p. 206.

[93] Wacker, "Functions of Faith," p. 160.

[94] Cited in Wessels, "Parham's Exegetical Journey," p. 15.

[95] William Seymour, "Tongues as a Sign," *The Apostolic Faith* 1/1 (September 1906): 2.

of God."[96] His antidote for the shifting sands of experience was for believers to "reckon" themselves dead to sin, because in the cross Christ had imputed to them his righteousness. Like Parham and Seymour, Durham maintained a theological distance between spiritual experiences and Spirit-baptism in order to maintain the distinctiveness of the latter, since "one can have wonderful experiences and yet not receive the personal Holy Ghost."[97]

Durham pressed for obedient action over experience from another direction as well. His central theme of identification with Christ and the Acts 2:38 plan of salvation led him to emphasize the necessity of being baptized in water without which one would be hindered in receiving the promised Holy Spirit: "I had no one to tell me that the next step was to be buried with Him.... Had I been taught the truth ...I would have at once received the Spirit."[98]

Ewart and others followed Durham's emphasis on faith over feeling. Ewart printed a terse quip, "Quit seeking blessings and experiences, and believe in the sacrifice of Calvary and receive the Holy Ghost."[99] Haywood lamented that the preoccupation with experiences and revelations was "playing havoc in the ranks," and that believers needed to trust "in the work of Christ on the cross of Calvary."[100] A New Issue evangelist later exhorted, "Let us preach not our EXPERIENCE, but the WORD."[101]

After the New Issue emerged, Ewart followed Palmer's directive that "acts of faith" are the appropriate means to lead believers into the new message. He noted that Durham had neglected to emphasize fully the believer's action in light of the truth of faith in Christ alone. The "three great acts of faith by which a sinner is identified with Jesus Christ" are repentance, water baptism in the name of Jesus Christ, and the reception of the Holy Ghost. Ewart made a qualitative distinction between the many Pentecostals whose "wonderful experiences" with God did not lead them to embrace the New Issue and those whose "repentance leads to godly sorrow," which was full identification with Christ through baptism in Jesus' name.[102] William Booth-Clibborn,

---

[96] Durham, "Sanctification – The Bible Does Not Teach," p. 1.

[97] Durham, "Personal Testimony," p. 47.

[98] *Ibid.*, p. 43. Elsewhere he blamed the spiritual poverty of many Christians on their disregard for the ordinance of baptism, "Identification with Christ," p. 30.

[99] Ewart, see brief entry in *Good Report* 1/10 (1 March 1914): 3.

[100] Haywood, "The Word of God," *Good Report* 1/6 (1 November 1913): 3.

[101] Westfield, "What Is Truth?"

[102] Ewart, "To Our Friends."

another Pentecostal pioneer, likewise exhorted readers, "Don't preach experiences – preach Christ!" by which he meant Acts 2:38.[103]

The New Issue expressed the same concern as Phoebe Palmer for Christians to ground their spiritual experience in Christ. This christo-centric thrust, initially an attempt to keep the experience of sanctify-cation from drifting into subjectivism, became in Pentecostalism a means for establishing a doctrinal rationale for the Pentecostal experience, and in Durham a more radical grounding of that experience in the atone-ment. The New Issue extended this christocentric shift even further, ultimately transforming "faith over feeling" into a doctrine that threat-ened to negate even the Pentecostal experience of Spirit-baptism itself.

b. From Gradual to Instantaneous

"THERE IS A SHORTER WAY!" So thundered Phoebe Palmer in exasperation: "This long waiting and struggling with the powers of darkness is not necessary."[104] With this cry, she challenged a major plank in Wesley's doctrine of sanctification. With it, she subverted the characteristically Wesleyan balance between crisis and process by privi-leging the former. She considered tarrying to be a lack of faith in the promises of God to grant holiness, especially when "He had com-manded her to possess it."[105] Furthermore, it was counterproductive to the Christian life: "One act of faith will do more for you than twenty years' hard toiling without it."[106] Because sanctification is in the atone-ment, one need only claim, appropriate, or possess what was provided by Christ: "As it has been purchased for you, it is *already* yours."[107] Instead of stages that may be spread over many years, she proposed three steps by which one can enter the sanctified life now – entire consecration, faith and testimony.[108]

The impact of Palmer's influence on Pentecostalism was to raise the expectation of immediate results. Though they would still encourage seekers to tarry for Spirit-baptism until they received, waiting was never considered to be meritorious in itself. Palmer's three steps were adapted in Pentecostalism to bring people quickly into Spirit-baptism.[109] In fact, there was concern if a preacher was not having im-

---

[103] William Booth-Clibborn, "Suddenly," *Meat in Due Season* 1/13 (June 1916): 4.

[104] Palmer, *The Way of Holiness – Is There Not a Shorter Way?* in *Devotional Writings*, p. 2.

[105] White, "Phoebe Palmer," p. 202. See also Faupel, *Everlasting Gospel*, pp. 63-64.

[106] Palmer, *Faith and Its Effects*, p. 351.

[107] *Ibid.*, pp. 53, 342.

[108] For a description of the three-step process, see White, "Phoebe Palmer," p. 205.

[109] White, "Phoebe Palmer," p. 207.

mediate results. Haywood speculated that the lack of victory among the faithful might have been due to "cowards" who did not have the courage to preach the "simple gospel."[110] For Parham, there was an added urgency to receive Spirit-baptism quickly, as tongues was a human language given by God to evangelize the world before the imminent return of Christ.[111]

Durham's Finished Work further telescoped the "full" gospel into the "simple" gospel by its singular focus on the atoning work of Christ. Though his three-step pattern was probably the same as other Pentecostals', Durham's theology shifted from a second work of grace to water baptism as an act of obedience toward God. Spirit-baptism did not demand long waiting but only a simple act of obedience – be baptized in water, "the only thing required ... between conversion and the baptism in the Spirit."[112] The threefold plan of salvation in Acts 2:38 was intended to chart the route into the full gospel as quickly as possible. If the hearers of Peter's sermon did not receive Spirit-baptism right away, "they stopped short of their privilege, and short of what the great preacher promised them if they would repent."[113] Though Spirit-baptism was a distinct experience from conversion, it was immediately available upon repentance and baptism.

New Issue theology built upon this simplification of the full gospel by treating the three aspects of Acts 2:38 as one inseparable event. For instance, Booth-Clibborn exhorted preachers to "preach the whole thing in a bundle," instead of preaching experiences, "days of tarryings and sundry waitings, and the different stages of salvation." God could wrap up all the promises from repentance to Spirit-baptism and healing "and deliver the whole business in ten minutes." To do so would yield spiritual results.[114] By treating Acts 2:38 as one unified event, Ewart could record that in the first wave of the New Issue Revival of 1914 "there was little need to tarry in order to receive the Holy Spirit baptism," and both Spirit-baptisms and healings followed immediately upon baptizing converts in the name of Jesus.[115]

---

[110] Haywood, "Be Strong in the Lord."

[111] Wessels, "Parham's Exegetical Journey," p. 8.

[112] Durham, "Two Great Experiences," p. 4.

[113] *Ibid*., p. 6.

[114] Booth-Clibborn, "Suddenly."

[115] Ewart, *Phenomenon*, pp. 33, 52. See a similar account by Haywood, *Birth of the Spirit*, p. 40, in *Seven "Jesus Only" Tracts*, ed. Donald Dayton (New York: Garland, 1985).

Phoebe Palmer's new doctrine, that sanctification is immediately available upon meeting God's conditions, eventually transmuted into a Pentecostal theology which expected Pentecostal results upon repentance and baptism in the name of Jesus Christ according to the "simple gospel" of Acts 2:38.

c. From End to Beginning

The instantaneous working of God that was taught from the time of Phoebe Palmer through the Pentecostal movement took another shift, from the end to the beginning of the Christian life. Whereas Wesley considered sanctification to be a goal of the Christian life (while never foreclosing on the possibility of attaining it now), Palmer could see no reason for God to withhold it from the honest seeker from the start: "If it is true that God gives sanctification in response to the believer's faith, then every Christian should be sanctified now."[116] Another Holiness writer likened the shift to that of "walking from the outer court of the Tabernacle into the Holy place and on into the Holy of Holies without stopping."[117]

Combined with her christocentric focus, Palmer's locating of sanctification at the beginning of the Christian life created the climate and conditions by which Durham's Finished Work theology would make sense. Essek Kenyon had also taken the same position on spiritual union with Christ: "While mystics and Higher Life advocates saw divine union as the *goal* of the Christian life, Kenyon held it as the *starting point.*"[118]

Parham brought water baptism near to Christian initiation with his doctrine of baptism as identification. Yet he taught that the new birth precedes Spirit-baptism, and with it one possesses the Holy Spirit. Durham, on the other hand, opened the door for a narrower version of the new birth by stating that the Spirit does not come to abide until Spirit-baptism. Combining his theology of the atonement (justification and sanctification) with the believer's identification with Christ by repentance and water baptism according to Acts 2:38, Durham initialized most aspects of the Christian life. Whereas Durham had reduced the three works of the Pentecostal holiness to conversion and Spirit-baptism, some of his New Issue disciples later further collapsed the two into one unified act of salvation. The result was a transformation of a revival service from the call to conversion (Revivalism), to sanctifica-

---

[116] White, "Phoebe Palmer," p. 204.
[117] Cited in Faupel, *Everlasting Gospel*, p. 247.
[118] Simmons, *Kenyon*, p. 99.

tion (Holiness), to Spirit-baptism (Pentecostalism), and finally to water baptism in the name of Jesus Christ (New Issue). A theology that so radically incorporated all three into one demanded an evangelistic practice that made room for all three.

6. Summary

On the eve of the Oneness "revelation," most of the doctrinal elements were in place. Patterns and themes had already been developed and debated in Holiness, Evangelical and Pentecostal circles. Most importantly, Durham had established Acts 2:38 as the pattern for identification with Christ and water baptism as the biblical prerequisite for receiving Spirit-baptism. The Finished Work doctrine was frozen in its infancy with Durham's sudden death, leaving many themes like loose threads waiting to be woven into a tapestry of doctrine and practice.

The New Issue leaders would develop Durham's legacy in their own inimitable way. A christocentric shift had been in progress since Phoebe Palmer, but Durham's Finished Work was the match that ignited a massive centripetal movement among the majority of Pentecostals toward Christ and his atoning work. The vacuum created by Durham's death only fanned the flame in the minds of certain disciples who were cast his mantle. Within a very brief period of time, Durham's teaching of the one act of grace was transformed into a distinctive doctrine of the one Name by which salvation comes, a Name that is appropriated only in water baptism, and a Name that reveals the nature of the true God who is one without eternal distinctions. Durham would have vigorously opposed these ideas, but it was he who forged the internal logic that demanded to be addressed.

6

Revelation of the Name

> The people were restless, inquisitive, and on the tiptoe of expectancy....
> The very suggestion of God's doing a New Thing struck fire in the
> minds and hearts of the saints, and from then on to the end of the camp
> one could hear expressions of the hope that God would soon do a New
> Thing for His people.[1]
>
> — Frank J. Ewart

The third stream of modern Pentecostalism, initially and unceremoni-
ously labeled the New Issue, was from the beginning claimed by its
followers to be a divine revelation. Though the doctrine was perceived
to be supernatural in origin, the visitation has an address and a history.

1. Encounter – April 1913

Fullblown movements are often initiated in embryonic moments. This
accurately describes the first stirrings of the New Issue. A reflective
statement is made by a speaker and received by a listener, quite unnoticed, long before it produces public action.

a. A New Thing Expected

The catalyst that spring-boarded the New Issue into existence appeared in a moment of deep fracture within the early Pentecostal
movement. The division was most keenly felt in the regions where
Durham's Finished Work teaching had taken root, especially the Los
Angeles area. Though there were efforts toward reconciliation with
the "Second Work" constituency, Faupel points out that the level of
anticipation of more apostolic truth being unfolded was running high:
"Many among them believed that even further revelation and a greater
outpouring of Latter Rain was coming as they sought to carry out

---

[1] Ewart, *Phenomenon of Pentecost*, p. 76.

their great commission to bring about the close of the age."[2]

The soil was further prepared by a major revival that exploded months earlier in Dallas, Texas, under the ministry of Maria Woodworth-Etter, a senior Holiness evangelist who had recently accepted the Pentecostal message. A two-week citywide crusade that began in July 1912 turned into a five-month revival that drew thousands nightly from across the nation. Many healings and unusual spiritual phenomena were reported, and anticipations of the imminent return of Christ mounted as the Revival progressed.

Woodworth-Etter was concerned to extend her distinguished healing ministry to reconcile the division created by Durham's ministry. She infused a spirit of "love and unity" into the atmosphere of the services by consistently drawing people's attention to Jesus.[3] Faupel argues that this persistent focus on Jesus in her appeals to sinners, the sick and saints alike, communicated the message, "seek for more of Jesus." Combined with the eschatological fervor that pervaded the Revival was an increased anticipation that, in the words of one leader, God was doing "a new thing."[4]

One who attended the meetings was R.J. Scott, a former Canadian then ministering in Los Angeles. Like Woodworth-Etter, he was burdened over the divisions in the new movement. After consulting with the evangelist, they agreed that God would have her conduct a "worldwide" Pentecostal camp meeting in the Los Angeles area, in hopes that this international event would unite the fractured movement. The camp meeting was scheduled to last four weeks, beginning on April 15, 1913.[5]

Scott prepared well for the camp meeting – a 5000-seat tent and adequate advertising. The location was in Arroyo Seco, a canyon basin outside Los Angeles where Scott had organized a camp meeting five years earlier. The event was moderately successful. Attendance was good though less than hoped for, and many healings were reported. The thematic focus on Jesus in preaching and healing was undoubtedly transferred to the new venue. A Canadian Oneness writer later commented that the familiar phrase used in prayer for healing, "in the

---

[2] Faupel, *Everlasting Gospel*, p. 272.

[3] C.J. Montgomery, "The Mighty Power of God in Dallas, Texas," and the observation by Stanley Frodsham that, "Jesus is the theme and they are not looking for another;" both cited in Faupel, *Everlasting Gospel*, pp. 274–75.

[4] Comment by M.M. Pinson, cited in Faupel, *Everlasting Gospel*, p. 275.

[5] R.J. Scott, "World-Wide Apostolic Faith Camp Meeting," *Word and Witness* (20 March 1913): 1.

Name of Jesus," might also have magnified the emphasis on the "Name" and its power.[6]

The spirit of expectancy begun in Dallas was carried to Los Angeles. According to Ewart who was present, "the people were restless, inquisitive, and on the tiptoe of expectancy." He recalled that the spiritually charged atmosphere was heightened by a sermon from Jer. 31:22, declaring that God was going to perform "a new thing" in their midst. Such a note resonated with the already expectant hearts, and "from then to the end of the camp one could hear expressions of the hope that God would soon do a New Thing for His people."[7] It is unlikely that Ewart's description can be generalized, since his own periodical, *The Good Report*, makes no mention of this mood of expectancy in its report of the camp meeting a month later.[8]

The goal of unifying the fractured Pentecostal movement that Scott and Mrs. Etter had envisioned was not met. Most of those who attended were from the Finished Work camp. Holiness Pentecostals were neither encouraged nor enthusiastic. Seymour was present but not invited to the platform.[9] Florence Crawford boycotted the event, calling it a "Compromise Camp."[10] The spirit of contention that had become so entrenched over the previous two years in the Los Angeles area militated against a repeat performance of the Dallas Revival. The legacy of the camp would not be unity within the ranks but a "new thing" that would precipitate yet another crisis.

b. The "Revelation" Declared

During the camp meeting a baptismal service was planned near the big tent, and R.E. McAlister, a Finished Work pioneer from Canada, was asked to preach. The moment came during the sermon, in which he observed that the Apostles baptized in the name of the Lord Jesus Christ, not in the triune formula. Some listeners were visibly startled, including Frank Denny, a missionary from China, who leapt onto the platform from the front row to warn McAlister that a Dr. Sykes so

---

[6] See Larden, *Apostolic Heritage*, p. 31.

[7] Ewart, *Phenomenon*, p. 76.

[8] "The L.A. Camp Meeting," *Good Report* 2/1 (1 June 1913): 4. The report was otherwise positive, mentioning nightly attendance of 1500 and 2500 on Sundays, accounts of healings and various missionary endeavors.

[9] Shumway, "A Study of the 'Gift of Tongues'" (B.A. thesis, University of Southern California, Los Angeles, 1914); cited in Faupel, *Everlasting Gospel*, p. 278.

[10] *Confidence* (July 1913), p. 146; cited in Faupel, *Everlasting Gospel*, p. 278.

baptized.[11] Notwithstanding McAlister's immediate effort to qualify his statement, it was too late. At least one little known listener by the name of John G. Schaepe (1870-1939) was immediately inspired to study and pray throughout the night. In the early hours of the morning he was heard running through the camp, shouting that the Lord had shown him the truth on baptism in the name of Jesus Christ.[12]

While Schaepe left no account of his revelation, and his name appears again only in an early clergy list of the Pentecostal Assemblies of the World,[13] Ewart was the one to bear the fruit of McAlister's observation. Since he and McAlister were colleagues and co-edited *The Good Report,* they reportedly spent many hours together after the camp meeting in discussion on the subject.[14] The impact on the whole camp appears to have been minimal at best. Woodworth-Etter, in her book *The Acts of the Holy Ghost,* made no mention of it in her account of the camp meeting.[15] Nor did Ewart himself comment on it in *The Good Report* a month later.[16] McAlister's interest at the time appears to have been an exegetical concern to harmonize the two passages, a point he later elaborated to Ewart:

> Lord, Jesus, Christ, being the counterpart of Father, Son, and Holy Ghost, ... made Jesus' words in Matt. 28:19, one of those parabolic statements of truth, which was interpreted in Acts 2:38 and other scriptures.[17]

c. The Kernel of an Idea

The content of Schaepe's "revelation" that night was probably little

---

[11] Ewart *Phenomenon*, p. 76. Denny and his wife were eventually baptized in Jesus' name and embraced the Oneness message through Ewart's ministry: "[Mrs. Denny] received a revelation of the present great light, and entered gladly and joyfully into the privilege of being baptized into the name of Jesus Christ," in "Sister Denny Called Home," *Meat in Due Season* (15 December 1915): 2. Dr. Sykes was apparently known in at least the Finished Work circles in the Los Angeles area, as Durham reported on "the miraculous healing of Dr. Sykes" during his meetings; see "The Outpouring of the Spirit in Los Angeles," *Pentecostal Testimony* 2/3 (1912): 15.

[12] Brumback, *Suddenly from Heaven*, p. 191; Arthur L. Clanton, *United We Stand – A History of Oneness Organizations* (St. Louis, MO: Pentecostal Publishing House, 1970), p. 15; Fred J. Foster, *"Think It Not Strange" – A History of the Oneness Movement* (St. Louis, MO: Pentecostal Publishing House, 1965), p. 52.

[13] *Minute Book 1919 (1907-1919)* – Pentecostal Assemblies of the World.

[14] Ewart, *Phenomenon*, p. 77.

[15] See Flower, "History," p. 24-A.

[16] "L.A. Camp Meeting."

[17] Cited in Ewart, *Phenomenon*, p. 77. It was not until December, 1915, that R.E. McAlister claims to have understood the theological significance of the new baptismal formula; see Larden, *Apostolic Heritage*, p. 87, and Ewart, *Phenomenon*, p. 99.

more than what he heard in McAlister's sermon, except for the spiritual force that personally attended the insight. It is not surprising that he described the moment as a revelation, given the prevailing milieu in which innovative interpretations of Scripture were often accompanied by claims of divine origin.

Though we do not know what he discovered from his night of study, one eyewitness, Harry Morse, was present and heard Schaepe expound his views. Morse, who later became a Oneness leader, recalled having listened attentively to "Brother Scheppe's new ideas on water Baptism and the oneness of the Godhead."[18] Since he likewise provided no details of Schaepe's views, it is probable that he was reading back his own Oneness beliefs into the event. Schaepe soon dropped out of sight, and Ewart never depended upon him or his ideas for his later formulation of the Oneness doctrine.[19]

With characteristic hyperbole Ewart heralded the camp meeting event "as startling and revolutionary as a thunder clap from a clear sky."[20] Yet it is clear from his comments that the "full" revelation of the name of Jesus and oneness of God did not crystallize until much later:

> It was long after this preacher [McAlister] had left the city of Los Angeles, where I had a pastorate, before the revelation of the absolute Deity of our Lord Jesus Christ, burst upon me. I saw that as all the fullness of the Godhead dwelt in Jesus, bodily; therefore, baptism, as the Apostles administered it, in the Name of the Lord Jesus Christ, was the one and only fulfillment of Matt. 28:19.[21]

He marked the time of the "revelation of the Name" one year later, 1914.[22] Characteristic of the Pentecostal movement as a whole, the

---

[18] Cited in Clanton, *United We Stand*, p. 16.

[19] Schaepe had a colorful but "worldly" history. German by birth, in his early years he worked on ships but later trained to be a "cowboy and bronco-buster," often finding himself on the wrong side of the law. Converted through the Salvation Army in Hawaii, he eventually came into the Pentecostal movement in 1907 while working in southern California. For the remainder of his life he lived within the vicinity of the Arroyo Seco campground; see Cecil M. Robeck, "Schaepe, John G.," *New International Dictionary of Pentecostal and Charismatic Movements*, p. 1042.

[20] Frank J. Ewart, *The Name and the Book*, p. 40. Ewart apparently regarded himself as the leading spokesperson for the movement, describing himself as "the ring-leader of the Oneness crowd," in *The Phenomenon of Pentecost*, p. 34. It is ironic that in 1913 he was chiding would-be leaders for their prideful self-aggrandizement, those who "want to invent something new, and become famous, by being the father of a new issue," in "False Teaching Regarding the Baptism in the Holy Ghost," p. 4.

[21] Ewart, *The Name and the Book*, p. 40.

[22] *Ibid.*, p. 80.

doctrinal formulation fashioned during the years between 1913 and 1916 has remained substantially the same to this day.[23]

The story of the birth of the Oneness movement as told by its followers begins with the 1913 World-Wide Camp Meeting. As we have seen, the event in fact had two moments – McAlister's sermon and Schaepe's "revelation." McAlister made no claim to revelation, but was venturing an exegetical resolution to a biblical enigma. Schaepe, on the other hand, left no account of his discovery, but claimed it as a revelation.

The Oneness narrative conforms to the ahistorical character of Restorationism. The movement's self-identity has continued to be one of supernatural origin in which the pure Apostolic doctrine and practice were divinely restored. This may explain why the story of 1913 as told by the bearers of the Oneness tradition depends more upon Schaepe's "revelation" in the night than McAlister's exegesis. The contours and content of the Oneness doctrine came a year later, this time from the tongue and pen of Ewart. But the catalyst occurred in the setting already prepared by Durham – a baptismal sermon.

2. Incubation and Birth – 1913-1914

a. Frank Ewart Prior to 1913

Frank Ewart was an Australian by birth, the son of a Scottish coal-miner. He had been a bush missionary with a Baptist denomination in the Victoria region.[24] Like his father, he was a "foot runner," but while still a young man, he developed a foot problem called pernicious anemia, which could only be alleviated by a change of climate.[25] This precipitated the move to Canada. While pastoring in the Winnipeg area he encountered the Pentecostal Revival, and later experienced the Pentecostal Spirit-baptism at a 1908 camp meeting in Portland, Oregon.

---

[23] See Grant Wacker, "Playing for Keeps," p. 213.

[24] Ewart, *Phenomenon*, pp. 4–5.

[25] Phone interview with Ewart's youngest daughter, Elvira Winters, 9 February 1996. Though Ewart's father was only nominally Baptist, he was disowned by his family when he married an Irish Catholic. Frank's mother died when he was only eight years old, while giving birth to her eleventh child. Throughout his life, Ewart would say, "I'll see my mother in heaven." In his ministry, Ewart was kind hearted toward young preachers. Many would visit Belvedere Tabernacle, hoping for the opportunity to preach in the Sunday morning service. Ewart would make every effort to find something for them to do in the service, which meant that often there would be as many as thirty people on the platform. Ewart's daughter recollects that her father's popularity and reluctance to turn anyone down made the Tabernacle a mecca for aspiring preachers, many of whom were misfits.

Finally forced to resign his pastorate because of his new Pentecostal views, Ewart accepted an invitation to assist William Durham at Seventh Street Mission in Los Angeles in 1911. Durham had stirred up both controversy and admiration on the West Coast, especially at the great Pentecostal centers of the Upper Room Mission and Azusa Street Mission. After planting the Seventh Street Mission, he recruited Ewart to be his associate. It was during this time that Ewart became convinced of Durham's Finished Work teaching. Though it is not certain that Ewart fully comprehended Durham's view on sanctification, he believed that his own more Reformed formation as a former Baptist made it "easy to apprehend the message for [I] had believed it while still in the Baptist Church."[26] From this early association, Ewart became an ardent follower of Durham's Finished Work teaching. Following Durham's death in July of 1912, Ewart became pastor, holding the post until the 1913 camp meeting.[27]

b. A Year of Study

In the spring of 1913 following the Arroyo Seco camp meeting, Ewart left Seventh Street Mission and attempted to establish his own work on Main Street in Los Angeles. R.E. McAlister remained to assist him along with Glenn Cook, a former Christian and Missionary Alliance minister from Indiana and Azusa Street veteran. Owing to a lack of adequate facilities, Ewart accepted an invitation to become an associate at Victoria Hall under Pastor Elmer Fisher. Following McAlister's return to Canada, G.T. Haywood, the prominent black pastor from Indianapolis, came as the featured speaker.[28] Haywood was by this time a disciple of Durham's Finished Work and was working closely in those circles in the upper Midwest. He was a friend of Ewart and frequent contributor to his periodical, *The Good Report*.

Throughout the winter of 1913-14, Ewart continued to study on the matter of water baptism, but baptized no one in the name of Jesus. Fisher and his assistant, A.G. Garr, encouraged him "to preach on the wonderful Name." Though he was accustomed to praying for the sick in the name of Jesus, ministerial restrictions were laid down regarding baptizing in the new name. Ewart later acknowledged that the topic had created a doctrinal struggle for him during that period: "For

---

[26] Ewart, *Phenomenon*, p. 75.

[27] *Ibid.*, pp. 6-7.

[28] Synan, *Holiness-Pentecostal Movement*, ch. 7; Ewart, *Phenomenon*, p. 50. For the story of Glenn Cook's conversion to Pentecostalism, see Brumback, *Suddenly*, p. 76, and Menzies, *Anointed to Serve*, p. 66.

months God was dealing with the writer about the name of God and its place in the gospel preached by the apostles."[29]

c. A Movement Is Born

Finally, Ewart revealed his growing convictions to Pastor Fisher, and was quietly released to begin his own work. He erected a tent in the town of Belvedere just outside Los Angeles and preached his "first public sermon on Acts 2:38, on April 15, 1914."[30] Just returning from an eastern trip, Glenn Cook was able to be present the opening night. He embraced Ewart's message and immediately became his assistant. The swiftness with which Cook followed Ewart's lead suggests that he and Ewart had been discussing the topic during the previous months, and he had already become convinced of Ewart's conclusions. Since neither one had been re-baptized, they procured a baptismal tank, set it up in the tent, and baptized each other during a service.

Like other Pentecostals, for Ewart vindication of the truth of a doctrine lay primarily in the spiritual effect it registered rather than in intellectual argumentation. Ewart reported that, as he preached and baptized in the name of Jesus,

> One of the greatest, most startling characteristics of that great revival was that the vast majority of the new converts were filled with the Holy Ghost after coming up out of the water. They would leave the tank speaking in other tongues. Many were healed when they were baptized.[31]

Franklin Small provided a similar account of his re-baptism on February 16, 1916: "I have been baptized in the name of the Lord Jesus and I have never felt more of His power and presence in my life, than since I obeyed His Word (Acts 2:38)."[32] It would be unconscionable in the minds of Ewart and other Oneness teachers to promote a doctrine without biblical justification. But in the world in which all competing interpretations appealed to the Bible, the deciding vote on a doctrine must be the manifestation of apostolic blessing and power.[33]

---

[29] Ewart, *Phenomenon*, pp. 50.

[30] Ewart, *Phenomenon*, pp. 51.

[31] Ewart, *Phenomenon*, pp. 52.

[32] Cited in Larden, *Apostolic Heritage*, p. 34.

[33] Six years later, Bell made a counter-claim using the same appeal to divine blessing. In a private letter to J.C. Brickey, a Oneness pastor in Jackson, TN, he recounted an occasion in which he had refused to baptize a woman in the name of Jesus solely on the grounds that she wanted it for the doctrinal reasons articulated by the New Issue advocates – reasons that Bell considered unscriptural. At the same service, he baptized a woman using a blended formula, "In the name of Jesus Christ, I baptize you into the name of the Father, and of the Son, and

Ewart's tent meeting in Belvedere was the first public occasion of baptizing in the name of Jesus that was guided by a self-conscious doctrine of the Name. Parham had baptized Howard Goss in the singular name in 1903.[34] Andrew Urshan reported that he began baptizing his converts in Jesus' name as early as 1910, though he did not associate with the new movement until 1919.[35] On his return to Canada in 1913, McAlister continued to preach the message he gave at Arroyo Seco, which resulted in the baptism of thirty candidates administered by Franklin Small. However, McAlister himself was not re-baptized until 1915.[36] The significance of these baptisms was primarily to conform to the apostolic practice, based upon his earlier exegetical harmonization of Matthew 28:19 and Acts 2:38. With Ewart, however, the practice received its rationale from a more comprehensive doctrine of the nature and name of God.

The bold and deliberate action by Ewart credits him with being the first to create an independent trajectory within the early Pentecostal movement. While others were exalting Christ in their ministry and a few were even baptizing in the name of Jesus, Ewart had been working on a theology that would provide the paradigm for the new baptismal practice.

3. The Revival Spreads – 1914-1915

The new message began to spread rapidly, especially on the West Coast and in the Midwest. Within a year Ewart began publishing a periodical, *Meat in Due Season*, which circulated from 1915 through the early1920's in North America and internationally to missionaries. This ensured the widest possible exposure to the Oneness message. He printed testimonies of prominent Pentecostal leaders who accepted the new doctrine and were re-baptized. Letters and reports from various churches and leaders were publicized. Testimonies of revivals and

---

of the Holy Ghost." As she came out of the water, she "fell under the power" and remained on the ground until she spoke in tongues. Bell then drew the happy conclusion: "This satisfies me that the Lord was well pleased with my refusal to baptize one simply in the name of the Lord Jesus Christ who had a wrong purpose and a wrong teaching for such an act, and pleased with the baptism which I have just described." See letter to J.C. Brickey, August 20, 1920, p. 2.

[34] Foster, "Think It Not Strange," p. 56.

[35] Andrew Urshan, *The Life Story of Andrew Bar David Urshan: An Autobiography*. Oneness Pentecostal Pioneer Series (Stockton, CA: WABC, 1967), p. 141.

[36] Larden, *Apostolic Heritage*, p. 32.

numbers of baptisms were reported. Ewart's popularity in the early days of the Pentecostal movement had won him many contacts and acquaintances, which increased his influence among ordinary people and leaders alike.[37]

To cast the net beyond the West Coast, Glenn Cook embarked on an evangelistic tour of the Midwest in January 1915. He preached the new doctrine for a week at Mother Mary Barnes' Faith Home in St. Louis, which led to Mother Barnes and her whole staff being re-baptized.[38] It was here that one of the leaders of the newly formed Assemblies of God, J. Roswell Flower (1888-1970), heard firsthand the new teaching. Though Flower had come into the Pentecostal movement under Cook's ministry, he was not convinced this time. On hearing that Cook was on his way to Indianapolis where Haywood was pastoring a prospering congregation, Flower sent a message warning Haywood that Cook was coming with a new doctrine. But he soon received this reply from Haywood: "Your warning came too late. I have already accepted the message and been re-baptized."[39]

Arriving in Indianapolis, Cook preached the message to another Pentecostal leader, L.V. Roberts, and his congregation. Reportedly, the first baptism in the name of Jesus Christ east of the Mississippi was held on March 6, 1915, with Cook first baptizing Roberts and then his entire congregation. Haywood, resistant at first, was soon convinced of the new message and was re-baptized along with 465 of his own members.[40]

The winning of Haywood was of immense significance for the future of the new movement. He was an influential leader and one of the most popular preachers in the Pentecostal movement at the time. He was the only nationally prominent black leader in the Finished Work ranks. Though he claimed never to have held credentials with the Assemblies of God, he had embraced Durham's Finished Work teaching and therefore formed most of his associations with those who eventually made up the Assemblies constituency.[41] Consequently, large numbers of the non-Holiness black Pentecostals eventually followed Haywood into the Oneness movement.[42]

---

[37] Ewart, *Phenomenon*, pp. 53-56, 79, 98-99; see Larden, *Apostolic Heritage*, pp. 86-87.

[38] Brumback, *Suddenly,* p. 192.

[39] Foster, *"Think It Not Strange,"* p. 54; Brumback, *Suddenly,* p. 193.

[40] Paul D. Dugas, ed. and comp., *The Life and Writings of Elder G.T. Haywood*, Oneness Pentecostal Pioneer Series (Stockton, CA: WABC, 1968), pp. 16-19; Ewart, *Phenomenon*, p. 53.

[41] Interview with Morris E. Golder, Grace Apostolic Church, Indianapolis, Indiana, 18 May 1974.

[42] A report in 1964 estimated that over half of Oneness Pentecostals were black. See Synan, *Holiness – Pentecostal Movement*, p. 163. This agrees approximately with the recent analysis

By the spring of 1915 the New Issue was spreading like wildfire "from mission to mission, assembly to assembly, until it became the issue of the day" within the new fellowship.[43] Rumors spread that the entire executive board of the newly formed Assemblies of God had accepted the new teaching.[44] By June, "this new advance message was sweeping Canada."[45] Small was re-baptized in 1915 at a convention in the Twin Cities, Minnesota. McAlister wrote a letter to Ewart that same year, declaring, "I have had a revelation to my soul of the one God in threefold manifestation." He too was soon re-baptized.[46] Through the efforts of McAlister, Small and numerous American evangelists, the Oneness movement made heavy inroads into the Assemblies of God fellowship in both the United States and Canada.[47] Louisiana lost all twelve of its Assemblies of God ministers to the new movement.[48]

4. Summary

The new teaching had caught the fragile Pentecostal movement by surprise and was spreading quickly. In an environment that was still feeling the lack of resolution within the Finished Work ranks, the New Issue was appealing to many. Also, the Assemblies of God had already gone on record at its first meeting in April 1914, stating the intention not to identify itself as "a sect, that is a human organization that legislates or forms laws and articles of faith."[49] But by the spring of 1915, many Trinitarian leaders were feeling the pressure to respond publicly.

by Talmadge French, who estimates that there are 1.01 million black Oneness adherents in the United States and 1.07 million whites; see Talmadge L. French, *Our God is One: The Story of the Oneness Pentecostals* (Indianapolis, IN: Voice and Vision, 1999), pp. 88, 108.

[43] Brumback, *Suddenly*, p. 193.

[44] E.N. Bell, "Editorial," *Word and Witness* 12 (June 1915): 1.

[45] Larden, *Apostolic Heritage*, p. 63.

[46] Both reports were printed in *Meat in Due Season* 1/9 (December 1915): 2

[47] Larden, *Apostolic Heritage*, pp. 88-89; Brumback, *Suddenly*, p. 197. When the Pentecostal Assemblies of Canada was first granted its charter in 1919, its ministers were Oneness in doctrine. But its decision to affiliate with the Assemblies of God in the U.S. in 1920 was a *de facto* break with that movement. This in turn led Franklin Small, a staunch Oneness leader, to form a continuing Oneness organization in 1921, The Apostolic Church of Pentecost. See R.A.N. Kydd, "Pentecostal Assemblies of Canada," *New International Dictionary of Pentecostal and Charismatic Movements*, pp. 961-64.

[48] Brumback, *Suddenly*, p. 197.

[49] *Minutes of the General Council of the Assemblies of God, 1914* (n.d.), p. 4.

7

Controversy and Rejection

> We still hold the necessity of having unity in the Spirit that we may
> come into the unity of the faith, but we see that diverse teachings and
> various explanations make for perplexity of mind and seemingly affect
> our keeping in the Spirit, often making it impossible to keep anything
> like unity.[1]
>
> – J.W. Welch

The new teaching was first known as the "New Issue."[2] In Canada,
Small frequently called it the "new advance message."[3] Though the
title appears to carry little doctrinal content – unlike Holiness and Finished Work labels – it is rich with millenarian innuendo. The "new
issue" was in fact discerned by its earliest advocates to be the "new
thing" prophesied in Jer. 31:22 and proclaimed at the Arroyo Seco
camp meeting. As a movement of the Latter Rain, it was in reality
perceived to be an old thing restored to perfection. Swept along by the
winds of eschatological anticipation, in less than a year it had blown
through the Finished Work ranks, gaining adherents, stirring controversy, and threatening unity.

1. Trinitarian Defense by E.N. Bell – Spring 1915

In March of 1915, E.N. Bell, an influential member of the Executive
Presbytery of the Assemblies of God and editor of their two maga-

---

[1] J.W. Welch, *Weekly Evangel* (24 June 1916).

[2] See E.N. Bell, "The Sad New Issue," *Word and Witness* 12 (June 1915): 2. After it
was no longer new, the movement was most popularly called by adherents and critics
alike simply "Jesus Only." This changed by 1930 to "Oneness" and "Jesus Name" in
response to charges that Jesus "only" implied a denial of the Father and Holy Spirit; G.T.
Haywood defended the teaching against these charges in an article, "Dangers of Denying
the Father," *Voice in the Wilderness* 2 (Nov. 13, 1922): 5, and *Pentecostal Outlook* 1 (April
1932): 3.

[3] Cited in Larden, *Apostolic Heritage*, pp. 64, 84, 92.

zines, *Weekly Evangel* and *Word and Witness*, felt the need to respond. He published a series of articles denouncing aspects of the New Issue teaching. His perception was that the new movement was largely contained on the West Coast, primarily in Los Angeles.[4] J. Roswell Flower, his assistant editor and later fierce opponent of the movement, published a report from California, which stated that the only prominent leaders were Ewart, Cook and George Studd.[5]

Numerous points of contention were raised throughout Bell's articles. First, he charged them with appealing to special "revelation." Quoting one advocate, Bell reported the claim that "this truth can only be discerned by the Spirit, and cannot be understood by the carnal mind."[6] Bell then made a plea for them to set aside such modern "revelations" and return to sound biblical doctrine.[7] He asked for a, "Thus saith the Lord," and a doctrine "standing alone on the written scriptures as illuminated by the Holy Ghost."[8]

Included in this new revelation was the introduction of new phrases that Bell rejected as unscriptural. When the Executive Presbytery met on May 11, 1915, in St. Louis to discuss doctrinal variations rising in the Pentecostal movement, it denounced as unfounded such statements as "the name of the Father, and of the Son, and of the Holy Ghost is Jesus Christ," and "Christ is the Holy Ghost."[9] The report closed with a caution to distinguish between extra-biblical revelations – or so it seemed to them – and openness to new insights from Scripture.

Second, Bell took issue with the New Issue insistence upon re-baptizing all believers. Ewart's interpretation, following McAlister's observation at Arroyo Seco, was that the early Church baptized exclusively in the christological formula, and did so in harmony with Jesus' words in Matthew 28:19. Therefore, re-baptism in the name of Jesus was mandated, because God was restoring in these Last Days the fullness of apostolic practice, including the revelation of the name of Jesus and how it was to be appropriated. To refuse re-baptism would be to stand against everything that God was doing in the Latter Rain outpouring of the Spirit.

---

[4] E.N. Bell, "The Great Outlook," *Weekly Evangel* 92 (29 May 1915): 3.

[5] J. Roswell Flower, "Mis-Statement Corrected," *Weekly Evangel* 99 (19 July 1915): 2.

[6] Cited in Bell, "Editorial," *Weekly Evangel* 86 (17 April 1915): 2.

[7] Bell, "Editorial Explanation on Preliminary Statement," *Word and Witness* 12 (June 1915): 1.

[8] Bell, "Great Outlook," p. 3.

[9] Bell, "Preliminary Statement."

Bell did not reject the validity of the Acts formula, and took great pains to show its legitimacy. But his resolution was that both formulas were valid, which thereby disqualified any requirement for re-baptism. Freedom to use the Acts formula should be permitted "when so *administered to a new convert.*"[10] He supported this position by referring to Parham's practice of baptizing in the name of Jesus Christ, which did not result in any doctrinal contention. He noted, "One of the Presbyters of the General Council of the Assemblies of God, H.A. Goss, was so baptized nine or ten years ago. Another Presbyter has for years so baptized whenever he felt like it."[11]

Bell's third criticism engaged his opponents on their interpretation of the "Name." Claiming that they had ritualized the name "Jesus Christ" into a scripturally unwarranted formula, he exegeted the "name" to mean "authority." To act in one's name was to act upon his authority, not use his name as a formula.[12] Bell thereby dismissed the Oneness claim of a *proper* and *revealed* name of God in both the Old and New covenants. For Bell, the Name had no revelatory quality to it, only a functional, authoritative one.[13] He provided no opportunity for Oneness refutation in his articles, but only referred to their non-trinitarian position, quoting one of them as saying, "The only God we know is Jesus Christ."[14]

Throughout this period, Bell maintained a conciliatory attitude, pleading for a spirit of acceptance on both sides. But by early June he was predicting the demise of the new movement: "We venture to predict it is now at high water mark, and that the old issue so needless will dwindle down, as it always has."[15] Not only was he wrong in his prediction, but also the summer was to bring changes – most notably in Bell himself – that would threaten the very foundation of the fragile new organization of the Assemblies of God.

---

[10] Bell, "The 'Acts' on Baptism in Christ's Name Only," *Weekly Evangel* 94 (12 June 1915): 1.

[11] Bell, "Sad New Issue," p. 3.

[12] Bell, "To Act in the Name of Another," *Word and Witness* 11 (May 1915): 2-3.

[13] Bell maintained his exegesis of the meaning of the name as authority throughout the controversy, repeating it as late as 1919. See Bell, "The Great Controversy and Confusion," *The Christian Evangel* 304/05 (6 September 1919): 6-7.

[14] Bell, "Sad New Issue," p. 2.

[15] Bell, "The 'Acts' on Baptism," p. 3.

2. Re-baptism of E.N. Bell – Summer 1915

External controversy can precipitate internal struggle, which appears to have been the case with Bell. As the summer of 1915 unfolded, he would make a decision that would reverberate throughout the fragile fellowship, both Trinitarian and Oneness. While they preached and prayed for unity, it was to elude them one more time. By summer they would encounter a major crisis similar to Durham's Chicago address in 1910.

a. Bell's Re-baptism

The Assemblies of God fellowship was conducting its Interstate Encampment in Jackson, Tennessee, from July 23 to August 1. H.G. Rogers was the host pastor, with Bell slated as the main speaker. Bell had apparently been in turmoil over the issue of baptism in Jesus' name prior to the camp. From the beginning of the meetings on Friday very little had happened. After disclosing his concern to Rogers, they cosigned a telegram to L.V. Roberts, the Oneness evangelist from Indianapolis, stating: "We want your message for the camp; take first train."[16] Upon his arrival, Roberts preached on the text of Acts 2:38, following which both Rogers and Bell announced publicly their intention to be baptized. Bell was the first, followed by Rogers and sixty-eight in all by the end of the week.[17]

Within a few weeks Bell was camp speaker at the Iowa State Camp Meeting in Davis City, Iowa, during which time he held private conferences with the other ministers over what he called the "exaltation of Jesus Christ as the Mighty God, in connection with Baptism in the name of the Lord Jesus." Although two or three disagreed, all gave him full liberty to preach the same. It was confirmatory for him that, without any appeal or call to baptism, "the people of their own accord soon began to come up after the meetings and requested to be baptized in the name of Jesus Christ."[18] Of the seventy-five or eighty who were baptized during the camp, about seventy requested that it be in the name of the Lord Jesus Christ.

Bell also observed the sense of joy and divine blessing that accompanied these baptisms: "The writer does not remember a single one

---

[16] Cited in a letter written to Ewart by L.V. Roberts immediately following the camp, in Ewart, *Phenomenon*, p. 99.

[17] Ewart, *Phenomenon*, p. 100.

[18] Bell, "Davis City Camp-Meeting Report," *Weekly Evangel* 105 (28 August 1915): 2.

coming up out of the water without a fresh anointing of the Spirit."[19] Applying a familiar Pentecostal test, Bell witnessed a divine confirmation of his decision by the unsolicited responses and the manifest presence of the power of God.

b. Bell's Editors

By the end of summer, the news of Bell's "defection" had spread throughout the organization. It was cause of rejoicing for some and dismay for others. Because of the confusion his re-baptism created at the headquarters, Bell absented himself from the office for the remainder of the year, leaving Flower to handle much of the editorial responsibility.[20]

In September, Bell submitted an article to the two periodicals entitled, "Who Is Jesus Christ?"[21] It was circulated among the presbyters prior to publication.[22] But owing to certain statements deemed objectionable to the editors, portions were deleted. Flower confessed only to having substituted the word "exalted" for "rediscovered" in the sub-title: "Jesus Christ, rediscovered as the Jehovah of the Old Testament."[23] But subsequent publication of the copy initially made available to the presbyters revealed strategic deletions, including Bell's reference to having been baptized.[24] In a comparison between the original and edited texts, Thomas Fudge concludes that Flower removed no less than twenty percent of the original text.[25]

3. The Truth According to Bell

Bell was a highly esteemed leader and coworker within the Finished Work fellowship. He had many friends in both camps with whom he

---

[19] Bell, "Davis Camp-Meeting," p. 2.

[20] Brumback, *Suddenly*, p. 198.

[21] Bell, "Who Is Jesus Christ?" *Weekly Evangel* 103 (14 August 1915): 1; *Word and Witness* 12 (September 1915): 5; see unedited manuscript in Oliver Fauss, *Buy the Truth and Sell It Not* (St. Louis, MO: Pentecostal Publishing House, 1965), ch. 2, and in tract form, *Who Is Jesus Christ?* (republished Houston, TX: Herald, n.d.).

[22] Clanton, *United We Stand*, p. 19.

[23] Flower, "History of Assemblies of God," p. 25.

[24] Clanton, *United We Stand*, p. 19.

[25] See Thomas A. Fudge's examination of the documents surrounding Bell's decision to be re-baptized and his doctrinal views. Fudge concludes that both Assemblies of God and Oneness representatives misrepresented Bell's intent and distorted his own words, and that Bell maintained a consistent position on the New Issue before, during and after his re-baptism in 1915; in "Did E.N. Bell Convert to the 'New Issue' in 1915?" *Journal of Pentecostal Theology* 18 (April 2001): 122-40.

had worked. His influential position as editor of two periodicals sent political ripples throughout the network. Consequently, any controversial move by Bell would not pass without notice – and sometimes not without exploitation.

a. An Experiential Hermeneutic

Bell maintained a unique mediating position within the highly polarized and politicized conflict. Though hailed by the Oneness camp as a convert, it is abundantly clear from his writings throughout this period that he had never renounced his Trinitarian belief.[26] However, a discernible shift occurred in his attitude, besides his re-baptism, that made his Trinitarian colleagues uncomfortable.

Deeply embedded in Bell's spirituality was the Pentecostal impulse to experience divine blessing and power. To be overwhelmed by adoration, joy, awe or godly sorrow, was a sign of God's manifest presence. Sometimes called an "anointing," it was not to be simply received passively, but earnestly sought. Seeking was not a selfish human endeavor but a divine mandate to accommodate God's desire to be experientially known in such states of spiritual liminality and transformation of life. Pentecostals also believed, as we have observed, that supernatural manifestations were a divinely authorized means for guiding the faithful. Manifestations were usually regarded as confirming beliefs or actions that conformed to God's will.

Though this spiritual hermeneutic took on a particular expression in Pentecostalism, its roots run far deeper in Revivalist and Pietist spirituality. Doctrine as head knowledge was of little use if it did not touch the whole person, including the affections.

How Bell described his experience is revealing. While he engaged in much study on the matter and defended his views with logic and clarity, the result was more "a brand new vision of Jesus" than a new intellectual insight. He graphically described the great emotional release that followed his re-baptism:

> I can say today, before God and all men, that His joy is rolling in my soul now as never before. As I write, His glory convulses my whole physical frame, and I have to stop now and then and say, "Glory," or "Oh, glory" to let some of it escape.[27]

---

[26] Clanton, *United We Stand*, p. 21. Clanton, a Oneness historian, believed that Bell denounced his belief in the Trinity. He registered surprise that one could receive so much truth and "then return to Trinitarian error," p. 21.

[27] Bell, "Who Is Jesus Christ," *Weekly Evangel*, p. l; *Word and Witness*, p. 5.

As with the Pietists and Revivalists before him, "gospel experience alone could convince of gospel truth."[28]

But biblical truth and personal experience were not antithetical to this tradition. It was not opposed to the primacy of biblical authority, but to ecclesiastical and doctrinal hair-splitting. Like his forebears, Bell had always insisted on scriptural support for new insights. The language in his article took on a more spiritual tone: "the lost Christ being re-discovered," "a new realization of Christ as the Mighty God," "a brand new vision of Jesus," and "the real vision of Christ as the Lord."[29] To some, this sounded perilously like the new revelations being heralded by the New Issue leaders. But Bell never abandoned his "Thus saith the Lord" policy. He was simply synchronizing his biblical doctrine with his spiritual experience.

b. A Christocentric Focus

If there was any change in Bell's thinking, it was likely a shift to a more christocentric focus. He reiterated his position that the baptismal formula was not the issue. It was secondary to the real issue, a vision of "the most glorious Christ you ever beheld."[30] His only dispute was the "unscriptural" arguments set forth by the New Issue teachers, such as their teaching that the name of Jesus means something other than divine authority and therefore must be used in a formulaic manner.

Bell never abandoned his belief in the doctrine of the Trinity, but his rhetoric suggests a more nuanced tone that resembles the christocentric Trinitarianism already observed in such writers as J. Munro Gibson.[31] Like the earlier evangelicals, he engaged in a comparative study of Old and New Testament passages to show that Jesus is "Jehovah," "eternal God and Creator," "the Mighty God," the "True God," "God with us," "Lord of Lords" and "one with the Father." The difference between classical Trinitarian thought and this tradition can be detected in the use of superlatives when referring to Christ. The reasons have varied, from defending the absolute deity of Christ against corrosive liberalism to the sufficiency of the atoning work of Christ against the diluting effect of seeking experiences. Bell's reason,

---

[28] Niebuhr, *Kingdom of God*, p. 108.

[29] Bell, "Who is Jesus Christ?"

[30] Bell, "Who is Jesus Christ?"

[31] *Ibid*. Bell included a parenthesis, "blessed be the Trinity," which was deleted in the supposedly "unedited" version by Fauss. This suggests that both sides in the debate were willing to exploit Bell's article for their own purposes.

as we shall see, is related more to the need for reassurance of Christ's presence and power in his own life and ministry.

Bell directed the reader's attention to the christological *classicus locus* for Oneness interpreters, Col. 2:9: "For in Him [Christ] dwelleth all the fulness of the Godhead bodily." He could even assure his Trinitarian readers that they need not be

> afraid the Father and the Holy Ghost will be left out.... You can't get Christ without getting God the Father also, even if you want to. God gives Himself only in the Son. Also, whoever gets Christ in His fulness gets the Holy Ghost.

How could one, then, exalt Jesus too much, seeing that "the whole Godhead, in all its fulness, is in Jesus?"[32]

c. An Alternative Name

Though Bell did not defect to the New Issue camp, he was drawn to a biblical study of the name of God. Not only did the study deepen his vision of the centrality of Christ, but he also sought to discover *the* Name in the New Testament that applied to Jesus. It is noteworthy that, unlike the New Issue leaders who were claiming that the new covenant name of God is "Jesus," Bell concluded that the name was "Lord." Since "Lord" was the proper designation for Jehovah in the Old Testament, to call Jesus "Lord" was to give him Jehovah's identity and revealed Name. In Phil. 2:9-11 and certain Acts passages, Bell concluded that "Lord" was God's proper name while "father" and "son" represented relationship only. It was this "discovery" that finally provided him with the scriptural justification for his re-baptism. He preferred "to use the real name common to both Father and Son, as the Lord commanded me to baptize in 'The Name,' not in a relationship phrase which is no proper name at all."[33] This section subtitled, "The Real Vision of Jesus Lost," which dealt with his argument for harmonizing Matt. 28:19 and Acts 2:38, was part of the deletions made by the editor in publication.

It is here that Bell was most articulate in his new view of baptism. He no longer believed that Christ intended Matt. 28:19 to be a formula. He burst forth in a prayer that the Lord would "help the dear brethren to see that Father and Son are, by no means, proper names." He believed further that "the Church has lost the secret of this name." The result of the loss for the church was "liberalism and formalism,

---

[32] Bell, "Who is Jesus Christ?"
[33] *Ibid.*, cited in Fauss, *Buy the Truth*, p. 15.

without understanding the true meaning and intent of the forms they were using." He then struck a note reminiscent of the Latter Rain motif, that "now God is restoring the spiritual vision of the mighty Jehovah-Christ."[34]

Bell discovered in the name "Lord" the key to the reason why the Apostles baptized in the name of the Lord Jesus; and more importantly, he discovered a Christ who is the full manifestation of the Godhead, the center of all things, and who was "becoming daily larger and more glorious to our vision."[35]

4. Bell's Defense of His Re-baptism

Bell's spiritual decision had caught him in a political vortex, one that he would be compelled to revisit for some time to come. The first challenge was to clarify his own intention in relation to his New Issue friends.

a. Bell's Relationship to the New Issue

Bell's article was largely a personal statement. He was still a Trinitarian, but consistently maintained an open, conciliatory and non–judgmental attitude toward all. On the issue of baptism, he reflected the liberal policy of the presbytery at that time:

> All may baptize with the phrase in Matt. 28:19 who feel so led, and I will love and fellowship them just the same; but personally, with my present light, I could not conscientiously do so any more.[36]

Bell never aligned himself with the New Issue movement, and there is no indication that he planned to leave his post with the organization. Though he could at last join in exalting Jesus Christ with similar fervor, he stoutly resisted any appeal to champion the new cause. When Ewart wrote to Bell requesting his written testimony, he received only "a mysterious and evasive reply asking that I please refrain from writing anything about his case until I heard from him again."[37] On one occasion, Bell publicly chastised Ewart for false advertising. Ewart had asked him to be guest speaker at a convention in Los Angeles on October 1, 1915, and had announced it in his periodical, *Meat in Due*

---

[34] Bell, "Who is Jesus Christ?" in Fauss, *Buy the Truth*, p. 15.

[35] *Ibid.*

[36] Bell, "Who Is Jesus Christ?" in Fauss, *Buy the Truth*, p. 15. Unfortunately, this statement was deleted in publication.

[37] Ewart, *Phenomenon*, p. 56.

Season, prior to receiving a response. Bell declined the invitation and proceeded to express his displeasure with Ewart's tactics in print.[38]

At the State Camp Meeting in Little Rock, Arkansas, held September 2-12, seven presbyters released a personal statement of their position on the issue of baptism. The signatures included those of Bell, Howard Goss, and H.G. Rogers, all of whom had been re-baptized, most in August. Bell's position remained basically unchanged. The statement denounced factionalism, recommended freedom in the use of the baptismal formula, discouraged re-baptism, and admonished visiting preachers to refrain from promoting their baptismal preference without express permission of the pastor.[39]

b. Bell's Reasons for Being Re-baptized

Why did Bell finally submit to being baptized in the name of the Lord Jesus Christ? In an open letter published in September he indicated there were three motives.

First, it was the personal matter of a long-standing doubt since his Spirit-baptism, "that it might please God for me now to be buried with Him in baptism."[40] In his letter to Brickey in 1920, he clarified the source of his anxiety:

> I had been half convinced that my baptism by the Baptists was unsatisfactory, and that possibly the Lord wanted me to be baptized in water by a man filled with the Holy Ghost, and that has bobbed up more or less during all the years that I have had the baptism experience.[41]

Bell's concern is a clear example of restorationist-millenarian thinking – Christian belief and practice are to replicate the apostolic pattern as perfectly as possible, constantly adjusting them as restored truth continues to unfold.

The second reason is an extension of the first; namely, that immediately prior to the camp meeting, he was intensely preoccupied with whether or not to be personally baptized. As the New Issue controversy was intensifying in churches and camp meetings, Bell's own internal doubt intensified correspondingly. He had already given much thought to the topic, as he had published a series of articles against the

[38] Bell, "'Meat in Due Season' Corrected," *Weekly Evangel* 108 (18 September 1915): 2; *Word and Witness* 12 (October 1915): 4.

[39] Bell, "Personal Statement," *Weekly Evangel* 108 (September 18, 1915): 2; *Word and Witness* 12 (October 1915): 1.

[40] Bell, "There Is Safety in Counsel," *Weekly* Evangel 108 (18 September 1915): 1; *Word and Witness* 12 (October 1915): 1.

[41] Bell, Letter to Brickey.

New issue in the spring. By the summer, he found it impossible to preach on any other topic, as "God took away every other message until I would obey."[42]

Finally, Bell became convinced that the Apostles had taught and practiced without variation baptism in the name of the Lord Jesus Christ. He was finally persuaded to this conclusion by his own earlier criterion – a "Thus saith the Lord."

In a letter written immediately following the camp meeting, L.V. Roberts revealed another reason, which Bell confided to him:

> A voice spoke to Brother Bell before going into this camp that if he did not preach water-baptism in the Name of Jesus Christ in this camp meeting, things would be a failure; he would dry up and it would be the worst meeting he had ever conducted.[43]

Apparently the long-standing struggle with his conscience blossomed into fear of failure if he refused to act. Flower later diagnosed this fear as an effect of spiritual and physical exhaustion.[44] Bell's account, both then and in 1920, indicates that the deeper motive lay more in his religious struggles and convictions than in physical exhaustion.

c. Dilemma and Illusion

The New Issue challenge to be re-baptized carried within it two subliminal messages that seemed to the unsuspecting ear difficult to refute. One was that to refuse to "obey" and be baptized in Jesus' name was perceived as tantamount to rejecting Jesus himself. If one loved Jesus as much as they declared, why would they refuse to take his name in baptism? Second, to reject the New Issue alternative by exalting the Trinity made it appear that one was diminishing, not exalting, Jesus. In a Jesus-centric religious culture, this created the illusion that Jesus was being affirmed only as "one of the Three," not the "fullness of God."

It is difficult to determine the role these dilemmas might have played in Bell's own journey. It is clear that he never departed from the Trinitarian faith, that he exegetically differed from the New Issue position on the "Name" of God, and that he rejected the insistence on re-baptism. All these were continuities throughout the crucial months. But it is difficult to sustain the argument that his journey lacked any discontinuity beyond a momentary lapse of judgment. The continui-

---

[42] Bell, "Safety in Counsel," p. 1.

[43] Cited in Ewart, *Phenomenon*, p. 100.

[44] Brumback, *Suddenly*, p. 199. Brumback himself accepts this analysis that it was not a "theological or ceremonial" reason but a psychological one.

ties did keep him in the Trinitarian camp, with the assistance of Flower and friends. But there is no evidence that the New Issue advocates were correct in their interpretation that the discontinuity was a Oneness revelation from which he later recanted.

The summer of 1915 was for Bell, if not a revelatory moment, at least an illuminating one. One cannot miss the intensity with which he was grasped by the fresh insight those months afforded him. By year's end he would not thank the New Issue leaders for the way they attempted to exploit his re-baptism and then malign his spiritual integrity. But the empathetic observer can at least admit that the Oneness movement set in motion an internal journey that deepened, enriched – and perhaps blessed – a Pentecostal pioneer who had experienced his Pentecostal faith in a new way without making it a "new issue."

5. Experiment in Liberality – Third General Council October 1-10, 1915

As summer and the camp meeting season drew to a close, it became apparent that the New Issue was not dying. Bell's re-baptism had only exacerbated the tension. The continuing fragile unity of the Assemblies fellowship was being threatened.

a. J.R. Flower – Champion of the Trinitarian Cause

Along with Bell, J.R. Flower shared responsibility for the organizational oversight of the fellowship and the editorial policy of the official periodicals. Observing the negative effect of Bell's re-baptism, he became concerned for the stability and direction of the new organization. He was not at all favorable to the New Issue, considering it patently heretical. He was trained as a lawyer, not a theologian. In the turmoil of the New Issue he had sought out a book on early church history, read about 4th-century Sabellianism, recognized the parallels, and straightway concluded that the New Issue was an ancient heresy, pure and simple. This gave him the single-mindedness to fight the new threat.[45] Also, because of his close association with Bell through the editorial office, Flower was a key figure in reclaiming him for a future in the Assemblies of God. As an unswerving champion of the Trinitar-

---

[45] Interview with William W. Menzies, Evangel College, Springfield, MO, 20 June 1973.

ian cause and an apparently persuasive leader, his contribution has since won him distinction as a "great bulwark of stability."[46]

Flower concluded by late summer of 1915 that a strong hand was needed to reverse the present confusion. Having acquired permission from some of the Executive Presbyters, he called the Third General Council of the Assemblies of God to be held in St. Louis on October 1-10, 1915.[47]

b. The Council in Session – Debate and Decision

The first three days of the conference were devoted strictly to spiritual matters, with preaching, prayer and testimonies, a "precedent established at Hot Springs and Chicago." The mood of conciliation and harmony that was established remained fairly constant throughout the next week of business and debate. A report following the conference hailed it a success: "Co-operative Fellowship Triumphs."[48]

The primary purpose of the meeting, however, was to address the New Issue. The focus was to be the formula used in water baptism. The format was one that had developed in early Pentecostalism as a way to address major disagreements: a public debate with presenters for each position followed by "free and full discussion."[49] The Council Committee selected J. Miller, A.P. Collins, G.T. Haywood and E.N. Bell to present their views. Following their addresses, many others were given the opportunity to expound.[50]

Those who may have wished for a clear and decisive conclusion to the matter were disappointed. In lieu of an exclusionary theological statement, the Council Committee presented a resolution advocating a spirit of liberality. In a strong statement of neutrality, the Council went on record that it refused "to attempt to bind the conscience of men on this matter." The statement disapproved of re-baptism on the grounds of formula alone, recommending that each minister be given "perfect liberty, without just censure from any one, to baptize such persons whose consciences are not satisfied that they have fully obeyed God in Christian baptism."[51]

---

[46] Menzies, *Anointed*, pp. 118, 115.

[47] Menzies, *Anointed*, p. 115. The call was published in *Weekly Evangel* 106 (4 September 1915): 1.

[48] J. Roswell Flower, "Great Victory in Fellowship," *WeeklyEvangel* 111 (16 October 1915): 1.

[49] *General Council Minutes of the Assemblies of God, 1915* (Springfield, MO: Gospel Publishing House, 1916), pp. 4-5; Menzies, *Anointed*, pp. 115-16.

[50] Flower, "Great Victory in Fellowship," *Weekly Evangel* 111 (16 October 1915): 1.

[51] *Council Minutes, 1915*, p. 5.

In an attempt to satisfy both parties, two days later the Council adopted a resolution, proposing that the two formulae be blended. It recommended that

> the substitution of the Name of "Jesus Christ" for the word "Son," (Matt. 28:19) would better harmonize Matt. 28:19 with the Book of Acts ... and, as a formula, would be preferable to the use of any one passage to the exclusion of the other.[52]

There is no record that this hybrid formula caught on, and it was eliminated in favor of another alternative in the conference of 1916.[53]

In a "Resolution on Doctrinal Matters," the Council approved a number of doctrinal statements that struck a blow to the New Issue. It rejected the teaching that "the Son is his own Father."[54] The Son and the Father were not to be confused. It also held as unscriptural the notion that Christ is identical with the Holy Spirit without distinction. As later Oneness writings confirmed, some were teaching that being born of the Spirit was synonymous with being baptized with the Spirit. This also the Council denounced as unfounded.[55]

The General Council of 1915 convened for the purpose of healing the widening rift within the ranks. Attention was directed primarily to the question of the formula to be used in Baptism. Since no consensus could be reached, it attempted to maintain a spirit of neutrality, liberality and respect for the rights of conscience among both ministers and local congregations. The Council did speak its mind on a number of doctrinal positions that had emerged. It identified and denounced aspects of the Oneness teaching on God and Christ that it believed to be at variance with biblical truth. The experiment in liberality was a mandate rooted in the very foundation of the Assemblies of God. But it was also a pragmatic decision to give more time to think and clarify

---

[52] *Council Minutes, 1915*, p. 6.

[53] *General Council Minutes, 1916*, p. 8.

[54] *Council Minutes, 1915*, p. 8.

[55] *Council Minutes, 1916*. The section, "The Spirit and the Blood," appears to have been directed at one element in early Oneness teaching, though it never persisted as part of the doctrine. Perhaps due to the untenable nature of the idea, it found no support and died. It is more likely, however, that it was a misunderstanding of some aspect of the new teaching; see Ewart's comments on the nature of the "quickened spiritual blood" of Jesus, in "What Is Truth?" *Meat in Due Season* 1/9 (December 1915): 2. Since the article appeared in the issue following the Third Council meeting, it was probably Ewart's effort to clarify what he had been teaching. The Council statement read: "The Scriptures nowhere declare that the blood of Christ is the Holy Ghost.... The blood is the blood, and the Holy Ghost is the Holy Ghost, not the blood. The Bible nowhere speaks of the spiritual blood of Jesus."

positions. At least some believed that they "should wait patiently for another year before arriving at a definite conclusion, allowing time for prayerful study of the word of God."[56]

6. Division on Doctrine – Fourth General Council, October 1-7, 1916

The Third Council's neutrality policy was an experiment that many had hoped would be respected. Some, however, believed that the problem would not disappear.

a. Mounting Unrest

Increasing unrest marked the year of 1916 prior to the Fourth General Council Meeting. It was to be a trial period. Though the reason was not clear, Flower observed that the New Issue leaders had chosen to remain within the fellowship following the Third Council meeting, even though the new teaching was not fully authorized:

> Tolerance had been shown on the part of those who had embraced the One Name doctrine and baptism in that name only, so that none of the advocates of the new doctrinal issue had withdrawn from the fellowship.[57]

But frequent references to controversy and division indicate that the Oneness advocates were aggressively spreading the new doctrine. It appears that they ignored the resolution approved by the 1915 Council, that "no such legal or fixed phrases are at all necessary in order to make it a Scriptural baptism."[58] The continued tension was also testing the patience of the Trinitarians who were tiring of this doctrinal irritant within their fellowship. Some began to use the time to clarify their doctrinal position.

The official publications of the Assemblies of God, *Weekly Evangel* and *Word and Witness*, were solidly under the editorial control of the Trinitarian majority.[59] They consistently called for a spirit of harmony, and refused to publish material of a controversial nature on the matter

---

[56] Flower, "History of Assemblies of God," p. 26.

[57] *Ibid.*, p. 27.

[58] *Council Minutes, 1916*, p. 5.

[59] Flower, "History of Assemblies of God," p. 27. Bell was now reduced to a contributing editor, while pastoring in Springfield, MO.

of baptism.[60] However, articles clearly supporting the Trinitarian position appeared in their columns, including one by E.N. Bell.[61]

One particular point of contention felt by the Trinitarians was the manner in which they had agreed to address controversial ideas that emerged within the fellowship. Early in the movement there had been general agreement that a minister would submit to the judgment of the ministerial fellowship before publicly preaching a "new revelation." Years later, Goss described the general procedure:

> There he was to submit it to his brethren in open session. If none of his hearers could tear it to pieces scripturally, or "shoot it full of holes," and if it came through still in one piece, all preachers would be at liberty to preach it, if they wished. For many years this was the common practice.[62]

It was this ministerial etiquette that the New Issue ministers appeared to flagrantly violate, as this strategy for maintaining doctrinal consensus had been established in the Assemblies of God as early as 1914.[63] Also, it was this policy that, in part, lay behind the Council's appeals to avoid contention and division outside the guidelines set down by the Council itself.

b. Fourth Council Agenda

As the hostility mounted, the new chairman, J.W. Welch, announced that the Fall Council would be a decisive meeting regarding the doctrinal issues facing the fellowship. He anticipated that "all that can be disturbed will be shaken into separation from that which is settled in God.... Lines will doubtless be drawn."[64] The Trinitarians went into the Fourth Council, held in St. Louis, with a favorable lead. The Credential Committee let it be known as early as June that it was carefully screening ministerial applicants according to the 1915 "Resolution on Doctrinal Matters."[65]

---

[60] "Controversy Discouraged," *Weekly Evangel* 108 (18 September 1915): 2; *Word and Witness* 12 (October 1915): 4; and "Editorial," *Weekly Evangel* 113 (30 October 1915): 2.
[61] Bell, "Bro. Bell on the Trinity," *Weekly Evangel* 114 (6 November 1915): 1; see M.M. Pinson, "What Think Ye of Christ? Whose Son Is He? Matt. 2:42," *Weekly Evangel* 116 (20 November 1915): 3; "The Holy Ghost a Person," *Weekly Evangel* 117 (27 November 1915): 2; "Editorial – The Mystery of God," *Weekly Evangel* 140 (20 May 1916): 1.
[62] Goss, *The Winds of* God, pp. 155-56.
[63] Brumback, *Suddenly*, p. 203.
[64] Cited in Brumback, *Suddenly*, p. 204.
[65] "Important Announcement by Request of the Credential Committee," *Weekly Evangel* 145 (24 June 1916): 8.

Once the Council was in session, the first step was the formation of a committee to draft a "Statement of Fundamental Truths."[66] The five-member committee consisted of D.W. Kerr, S.A. Jamieson, T.K. Leonard, S.H. Frodsham and E.N. Bell.[67] All were solidly Trinitarian; and even Bell had proved his orthodoxy sufficiently to regain the confidence of the Council.[68]

But D.W. Kerr was the hero for the orthodox Trinitarian faction. Although somewhat shy, he was one of the better educated ministers, having been trained for the ministry with the Christian and Missionary Alliance. He had studied and made "copious notes" for months, so was well prepared for the committee work.[69]

c. First Crisis: Formation of "Statement of Fundamental Truths"

The conference had opened with a mood of expectancy and tension. For many ministers present, the lines were already drawn. No one, in fact, could remain unaffected. "Every preacher and church was forced to take a stand on the New Issue."[70]

As the proposal for a doctrinal statement was presented, the Council was faced with its first open conflict. The issue dealt with the constitutional right of the Assemblies of God to formulate a "creed." The first Council in 1914 had made two statements that were now open to interpretation. On the one hand, it had disavowed any intention of being an organization "that legislates or forms laws and articles of faith." But it did recognize its responsibility to "disapprove of all unscriptural methods, doctrines and conduct."[71]

Now two years later, the Council was facing the supreme test: was a Statement of Fundamental Truths a binding creed or more generally the disapproval of unbiblical doctrines? The New Issue representatives protested that the leaders of the Council were actually imposing legislation. It was obviously to their advantage to rule out a Statement, as implementation of one would undoubtedly restrict their freedom to continue to propagate their teaching. Indeed, when the Statement was finally presented, the Oneness faction voted *en bloc* against each point. When asked why they were voting against sections with which they

---

[66] *Council Minutes, 1916*, p. 10.

[67] Flower, "History," p. 27; Menzies, *Anointed*, p. 118.

[68] Menzies, *Anointed*, p. 118.

[69] Brumback, *Suddenly*, p. 205.

[70] Menzies, *Anointed*, p. 118.

[71] *Council Minutes, 1914*, p. 4.

obviously concurred, Goss summed it up for them: "You are making a creed, and I am opposed to it."[72]

The Trinitarians, on the other hand, insisted that the Statement was "not intended as a creed for the Church, nor as a basis of fellowship among Christians, but only as a basis of unity for the ministry alone."[73] Following a lively debate, the motion was passed to allow a doctrinal statement to be drafted.

d. Second Crisis: Decision on the "Statement"

The second crisis arose when the Committee's proposed statement was submitted to the Council. Many prominent New Issue leaders were present and vocal – G.T. Haywood, Howard Goss, D.C.O. Opperman, L.V. Roberts, G.G. Rogers, Frank Ewart and others. Although Ewart did not hold credentials, he was allowed floor privileges.[74] Haywood hinted later that the planners had misrepresented the nature of the Council meeting by advertising it as an "open Bible council." Upon arrival, he had discovered that "we were not permitted to partake in any of the doctrinal discussions that took place" – presumably referring to the work of the five-member Committee.[75]

The Fourth Council was as hostile as the third one was conciliatory. Charges and counter-charges were hurled at each other. Frodsham, this being his first Council, described it as a "regular dog fight." One of the few moments of levity occurred when young Frodsham, a stranger to most, attempted to break the tension by introducing a hymn. Without thinking, he began singing the first song that came to mind: "This is like heaven to me!"[76] When the levity had died down and the final vote was tallied, the Trinitarian camp had won the battle. Realizing they were now barred from the fellowship, the Oneness contingent retired to the lobby, raising the question, "Where shall we go from here?" while the victors in the hall jubilantly sang, "Holy, Holy, Holy, ... God in three persons, Blessed Trinity."[77] When the dust had settled, 156 of the 585 ministerial membership were missing, and with them many assemblies. All black representatives present at the Fourth Council meeting followed Haywood from the hall.[78]

---

[72] Brumback, *Suddenly*, p. 208.
[73] *Council Minutes, 1916*, p. 10.
[74] Brumback, *Suddenly*, p. 208.
[75] Haywood, "St. Louis Council," *Voice in the Wilderness* 19 (1916): 1.
[76] Stanley Frodsham, personal letter to Robert Cunningham, 20 July 1963.
[77] Fauss, *Buy the Truth*, p. 34.
[78] Nelson, "For Such a Time as This," p. 254.

e. A Trinitarian Triumph

The "Statement of Fundamental Truths" was a 17-point document, the most detailed part of which was Section 13, "The Essentials of the Godhead." A well-crafted restatement of creedal doctrine, the strongly worded Trinitarian statement affirmed the propriety of the terms "Trinity" and "Persons" as being "in harmony with Scripture."[79]

The Statement declared that, while God was indeed one, the distinction of Persons was an eternal one, and not temporal as Sabellius had supposed. The Persons were distinct as to their relationships – the Father was the begetter, the Son was the begotten, and the Holy Spirit proceeded from the Father and Son. The Statement clearly defined the sonship of Jesus as an eternal relationship, regarding it a "transgression of the Doctrine of Christ, to say that the sonship is limited to the 'economy of redemption.'"[80]

On both points the Oneness position was excluded, since it had relegated both the Trinity and the sonship of Christ to the temporal realm. It regarded the Trinity as a threefold "manifestation" or revelation of the one God, while the sonship of Christ began with Mary. Elsewhere during the Council a resolution on the baptismal formula was passed, recommending that "all our preachers include in their formula used in connection with the act of Baptism the words used by Jesus in Matt. 28:19."[81]

To ensure that the Assemblies fellowship would remain purged of this "heresy," the Credential Committee was instructed personally to ascertain the doctrinal position of each applicant in relation to the Statement, refusing "those who seriously disagree."[82] To maintain continuance of doctrinal unity, the Council was empowered to discipline offenders, with the possible option to suspend credentials.[83]

7. Summary

As the New Issue spread throughout the early Pentecostal ranks, it created enough controversy by the spring of 1915 to bring about an open clash with its Trinitarian counterpart. Bell held center stage throughout the year. As the key spokesperson for the Trinitarian attack in the spring, his summer re-baptism only served to heighten his pro-

---

[79] *Council Minutes, 1916*, p. 10.

[80] *Ibid.*

[81] *Council Minutes, 1916*, p. 8.

[82] *Ibid.*, p. 14.

[83] *Ibid.*, p. 8.

file. While both sides claimed his allegiance in the fall, Bell theologi-cally represents a mediating position. Some did not acknowledge that he had remained Trinitarian. Fewer still understood his spiritual and theological reasons for being re-baptized. Though he was patient with differences, his tolerance for the increasingly sectarian spirit among the New Issue leaders was weakening.

The growing aggressiveness of the Oneness faction and efforts to sort out the theological implications of the new teaching coalesced to bring about a schism in 1916. Had the issues of re-baptism and the name of Jesus never been treated as an exclusive truth, there would probably have been insufficient energy to risk schism.

Bell represents a third and middle way in the conflict. Within a brief period of time, polarization had accelerated the tension beyond the capacity to negotiate. Schism had become inevitable by the summer of 1916.

8

From Issue to Doctrine:
Revelation of God and the Name

The Mighty God is Jesus, the Prince of Peace is He,
The everlasting Father, the King eternally,
The wonderful in wisdom, by whom all things were made,
The fullness of the Godhead in Jesus is display'd.

It's all in Him, it's all in Him,
The fullness of the Godhead is all in Him.
It's all in Him, it's all in Him,
The mighty God is Jesus, and it's all in Him.[1]

– George Farrow

The "New Issue" had taken the newly formed Assemblies of God by surprise. It did not come at first as a well-defined doctrine. Nor did its Trinitarian opponents always correctly understand it. But to all who embraced the new movement, it brought a freshness and immediacy that they could describe only as a "revelation."

1. Architects of the Doctrine

The route from revelation to doctrine in the New Issue is murky and complex, for a number of reasons. To begin, the new teaching did not make it to print immediately, as did Durham's Finished Work teaching. This means that much of what was being taught in the early months was primarily communicated orally at camp meetings, conventions and on evangelistic tours. By the Third General Council in 1915, there was a *mélange* of truth and myth, resulting in charges, counter-charges and disclaimers. Misunderstandings and extremes accompanied the first wave.

---

[1] George Farrow, "All in Him," *Sing Unto the Lord*, ed. Marvin Curry *et al.* (Hazelwood, MO: Word Aflame, 1978), no. 369.

One of the first doctrinal challenges was christological. In 1916, Ewart reported that some who had been re-baptized were teaching that "Jesus Christ the Son swallowed up the Father's identity in His own person ... [T]hey had withdrawn from our fellowship."[2] He acknowledged that this crisis called for a deeper study of the nature of Christ. He initiated that study in the same issue with an article, "The Record of the Son." Over the next decade, articles and comments on the proper identity of the Father appear in the literature, especially by Haywood, suggesting that this charge, though false, had struck a vulnerable spot in the infant Oneness doctrine.

Second, doctrinal development had come slowly. Ewart acknowledged in 1916 that it had taken him some time to formulate an exegetical and theological framework for the initial insight on re-baptizing in the name of Jesus. Beginning with Acts 2:38, "we saw that if the name of the Father, Son and Holy Spirit was Jesus Christ, then in some mysterious way the Father, Son and Holy Ghost were made one in the person of Jesus Christ. We saw from this premise that the old trinity theory was unscriptural."[3]

Finally, the doctrine that finally emerged was not the work of a single person. The evangelists for the New Issue were many, but the doctrinal formulators were few.[4]

Ewart was the instigator and initial apologist for the new doctrine. He had obviously been studying the subject between McAlister's baptismal sermon in 1913 and the day he and Cook re-baptized each other a year later. But it would be another year before two other major contributors to the doctrine would accept the message – Haywood and Small. The fourth theological pioneer, Andrew Urshan, did not affiliate with the Oneness movement until 1919. These four are selected because they wrote in the earliest period, their teachings became recognized in the movement as the foundational Oneness doctrine, and they had the means for wide circulation of their writings, primarily through their own periodicals and eventually their books. Their

---

[2] Ewart, "Editorial," *Meat in Due Season* 1/13 (June 1916): 2.

[3] Ewart, "The Unity of God," *Meat in Due* Season 1/13 (June 1916): 1.

[4] Glenn Cook was an associate with Ewart from the beginning. But his gifts were apparently in neither persuasive preaching nor doctrinal formulation, but primarily in management and organization. Consequently, it is the estimate of one leader that Cook's contribution has been neglected. He was one of the original signatories of the Azusa Street Mission, and Ewart's baptismal partner in the first official act of baptism in Jesus' name under the new doctrinal banner. He was influential in spreading the new message throughout the West and Midwest the following year (personal phone interview with David Gray, 9 February 1996).

writings set the direction and parameters for what would follow, an emerging Oneness orthodoxy.

As we shall see, there was much all four had in common. They all agreed on the necessity of re-baptism in the name of Jesus, the revelational character of the name of Jesus, and the radical oneness of God with its attendant rejection of the doctrine of the Trinity. But they did not agree on the meaning of Acts 2:38. Ewart and Small remained closest to Durham's initial vision of Acts 2:38 as full identification with Christ. Haywood and Urshan interpreted the same text as the new birth.[5] This difference led to a divergence that produced two distinct streams of thought within the Oneness movement, which in turn has had repercussions both internally and externally for nearly a century.

These next two chapters will survey the fundamental Oneness doctrine as it emerged from the works of these four theological pioneers. Other voices will be called upon, but these four are credited with laying the doctrinal foundation.

2. The "Revelation"

Unlike classical theology, Pentecostal theologies emerged from a milieu in which spiritual ideas and insights were perceived to be a direct work of the Spirit, what the writers themselves called "revelation." The Oneness doctrine was no exception, and in reality probably made the appeal more frequently than most others.

a. The Trinitarian Charge

What did the Oneness teachers mean by revelation? The Trinitarians found in this appeal an opportunity for frequent criticism. They set such revelations in contrast to the enduring truth of the Bible, suggesting that the Oneness view was the product of non-biblical speculation.

Carl Brumback, Assemblies of God historian, saw the movement as the result of extreme subjectivism in which one was likely to confuse "soulish mysticism" for "spiritual revelation."[6] J.R. Flower charged the new movement with "coining new phrases and seeking out new statements and revelations which have no foundation in the Word of God."[7] The Executive Presbytery in 1915 cautioned readers against the

---

[5] Within the "New Birth" stream, blacks and whites reflect a different history of applying the same doctrine, especially in their attitude to and relationship with other Christians.

[6] Brumback, *Suddenly*, p. 203.

[7] Flower, "Editorial," *Weekly Evangel* 95 (19 June 1915): 2.

New Issue: "We cannot accept a doctrine merely because some one claims to have a modern revelation to that effect."[8] One staunch Trinitarian blurted out, "Away with the revelations; let's hold to the full fundamental principles."[9] To the ears of the Trinitarians, the Oneness "revelation" was a doctrine of private interpretation and scripturally unfounded.

b. A Oneness Claim

At least to the charge of using the term "revelation," the Oneness movement had to plead guilty. Goss had retorted that the doctrine could not be grasped "by studying it out like some other doctrine. This comes by 'revelation.'"[10] R.E. McAlister wrote in 1915 of the "revelation to my soul of the one God in threefold manifestation."[11] And when asked why they rebaptized, they responded: "We got it by revelation."[12] Being more intent on disseminating the new teaching than explaining *how* they got it, there was never a defense of this claim to revelation or a clear explanation of what they meant. Most of the innuendoes were left to the Trinitarians.

The most conspicuous aspect of the claim to revelation was that it never appealed to a medium beyond Scripture, such as visions, trances, voices or angels. However foreign it may have sounded to listeners, Oneness teachers were convinced they were "rightly dividing the word of truth." As Small declared: "Every revelation or illumination effected by the Holy Spirit, must of necessity be substantiated, or be in harmony with the written Word of God."[13] Small's more Reformed beliefs interpret this position in a way that is not substantially different from the classical evangelical view of the "illumination" of Scripture by the Holy Spirit. Urshan articulated essentially the same view of revelation:

> By the word "revelation" ... we mean, "The Holy Ghost" illuminating our hearts and minds to actually understand certain scriptures on the Bible subjects.... For He, the blessed Spirit of Truth, is also the Spirit of wisdom and revelation. Yea, when He enters the true believer's heart and mind, He begins His blessed work of illuminating, revealing and un-

---

[8] "Preliminary Statement," *Word and Witness* 12 (June 1915): 1.
[9] Cited in Fauss, *Buy the Truth*, p. 33.
[10] Cited in Brumback, *Suddenly*, p. 202.
[11] Cited in Larden, *Apostolic Heritage*, p. 87.
[12] Cited in "'Have You Been Baptized In the Name of Jesus Christ?'" *The Victorious Gospel* (Early Spring 1915): 4.
[13] Cited in Larden, *Apostolic Heritage*, p. 64.

folding the infinite love and majestic personality of the One God of Israel in the Name and Person of His Son, Jesus Christ, to the believer who walks in the Spirit, and leads a holy life.

Revelation was not something new, independent of the objective truth of scripture. It was the progressive unfolding in history of God's act of restoring apostolic Christianity. Hence, Urshan could call it "further revelation."[14] This "revelational apologetic" grew out of neither an immediate revelation nor a particular metaphysical school. It was an expression, admittedly somewhat extreme, of an evangelical faith generated more than a generation earlier.

c. A Pentecostal Trait

Niebuhr's observation of American Revivalism that "gospel experience alone could convince of gospel truth" can be applied to the way in which many early Pentecostals approached the Bible.[15] The classic statement by Goss illustrates the prevailing attitude: "A preacher, who did not dig up some new slant on a Scripture, or get some new revelation to his own heart every so often ... was considered slow, stupid, unspiritual." Hence, the topic of conversation among preachers frequently was: "What new revelation have you received?"[16] Although this freedom spawned a considerable amount of "wild-fire fanaticism,"[17] they feared imposing heavy controls lest they miss some new light from God: "We must keep our sky-lights open so as not to reject any new light God may throw upon the old Word."[18]

This subjective confirmation of biblical truth was the principle applied by Charles Parham that established the Pentecostal doctrine of tongues as the "initial evidence" of the baptism of the Holy Spirit. In December of 1900, Parham had been teaching at Bethel Bible College in Topeka, Kansas, on the baptism of the Holy Spirit and had reached an impasse concerning the proper evidence of the experience. He departed for three days, leaving his students to study the Bible thoroughly on the subject and on his return report their findings. To his amazement, the unanimous decision was that speaking in tongues was the initial physical evidence of the baptism.[19] For Parham, the common

---

[14] Urshan, *Autobiography*, p. 137.

[15] Niebuhr, *Kingdom of God*, p. 108.

[16] Goss, *Winds of God*, p. 155.

[17] Edward Armstrong, "Sane and Insane Practices," *Weekly Evangel* 98 (10 July 1915): 1.

[18] "In Doctrines," *Christian Evangel* 52 (1 August 1914): 2.

[19] For Parham's account, see Brumback, *Suddenly*, pp. 22-23.

mind of the student body was sufficient sign for divine confirmation of the doctrine.

Parham applied this same principle two years later while struggling over the proper baptismal formula. As with the "initial evidence" doctrine, he received divine confirmation when he and his students were "waiting upon God that we might know the scriptural teaching on water baptism."[20] Even Brumback, who has disparaged the Oneness revelation as "soulish mysticism" and "fluctuating emotions," appealed to one man's vision as confirmation of the truth of the trinitarian position. During the heat of the controversy, A.F. Crouch had a vision of a gold chain with three links. Brumback recalled approvingly, "The Spirit impressed him with the truth that 'the three links are one chain but three *distinct* links.'"[21] Miss Carro Davis, an evangelist from Georgia, received a vision at the 1916 Council that confirmed for her the truth of the Oneness doctrine. While waiting for the committee to prepare a motion, "she waited on God in the auditorium and received a vision of the Lord Jesus Christ that greatly affected her life."[22]

For the early Pentecostals, a "revelation" was primarily a "new slant on a Scripture" or some new insight. Impatient with speculative ideas that had no appeal to the heart, the insights, which inspired them to pious worship and adoration, were considered to be the Spirit's work of "revelation to the soul." Occasionally, such subjective criteria were used to distinguish between true and false doctrine. There is no indication that the appeal was little more than the subjective confirmation of biblical truth to the soul.

The only difference between the Trinitarian and Oneness appeals was that the latter referred more frequently to their doctrine as a "revelation." Yet they made the same appeal to Scripture as did others, implying that nothing was added except the common Pentecostal presupposition of restored revelation. It is unfortunate that the Oneness apologists had not been less vociferous in their appeal to revelation, or had at least articulated more clearly its relation to Scripture.

d. A Latter Rain Hermeneutic

Another appeal common to other Pentecostals was the "revelation" of the Full Gospel being restored in the Last Days. As mentioned earlier, this frequently followed the language and pattern of the "Latter Rain" view of history. Following a familiar Protestant interpretation of his-

---

[20] Cited in Foster, *"Think It Not Strange,"* p. 71.

[21] Brumback, *Suddenly*, p. 200.

[22] Larden, *Apostolic Heritage*, p. 88.

tory, Assemblies of God teacher, David Womack, regarded the medieval period as one of captivity from which God had been slowly releasing His Church since the days of the Reformation. Each "revival" has championed its "new revelation of Christian truth." But the Pentecostal movement "has called for a complete return to the full gospel of the New Testament." According to his interpretation, the Pentecostalism and apostolic Christianity in this sense overlap.[23]

It was from this commonly accepted view of church history that Small interpreted the inbreaking of the revelation of Jesus Christ in relation to baptism:

> Up to this time the message in Canada relative to water Baptism was merely based on records only, without any illumination why it was so. But in the fulness of time when further illumination of the Scriptures came ... then it was clearly understood why the Apostles of Jesus used that exclusive rite.[24]

The early Pentecostals lived in the anticipation that as the *eschaton* drew near, God would continue to unveil more truth. Small saw doctrinal developments as just such truths, which in themselves put the participants "in a receptive attitude to receive further revealed truth, should it come."[25] Referring to the Arroyo Seco Camp meeting, Ewart called it "a move of God for the restoration of the Apostolic Faith on the earth."[26] S.C. McClain, a Oneness instructor of church history, simply added to the traditional "latter rain" concept of the restoration of apostolic power the "revelation of Jesus Christ," the restored full gospel that now incorporates the Oneness "truth." His chart of church history revealed that history had gone in a complete circle, with the Oneness revelation being the full latter-day restoration of apostolic Christianity.[27] No more major apostolic truth is to be expected – they now looked only for the second coming of Christ.

Small continued throughout his ministry and writings to interpret the Oneness message in terms of the Latter Rain paradigm.[28] From this

---

[23] David A. Womack, *The Wellsprings of the Pentecostal Movement* (Springfield, MO: Gospel Publishing House, 1968), pp. 74-75.

[24] Small, "Historical and Valedictory Account of the Origin of Water Baptism in Jesus' Name Only, and the Doctrine of the Fulness of God in Christ, in Pentecostal Circles in Canada," *Living Waters* 1/4 (April 1941): 1.

[25] Cited in Foster, *"Think It Not Strange,"* p. 60.

[26] Ewart, *Name and Book*, p. 39.

[27] S.C. McClain, *Student's Handbook of Facts in Church History* (St. Louis, MO: Pentecostal Publishing House, 1948), chapters 11-13. See church history chart on page 1.

[28] Small, "Historical and Valedictory Account," p. 1.

perspective, the Oneness movement was a unified piece with the early Pentecostal Revival – not a break – in which the new teaching was a progressive unfolding of latter day apostolic truth, even though 75% of the Pentecostal movement rejected it.[29]

3. The Plan

The New Issue revelation was not a speculative idea but was understood by its proponents to be part of God's plan of salvation. Its praxis centered in Acts 2:38 but included considerable reflection on the pivotal issue, the invocation of the Name in baptism.

a. The Plan – Acts 2:38

The New Issue began with and culminated in the act of baptism in the name of the Lord Jesus Christ. The initial catalyst had been a new way of harmonizing the Acts formula with Matt. 28:19. The final act of obedience to the new doctrine that emerged from it was re-baptism in that new Name.

The focal passage that illuminated the baptismal issue was Acts 2:38. By 1915 the new advocates were interpreting this passage as God's plan for the time of the Latter Rain. As most Pentecostals had already done with the baptism of the Holy Spirit, they simply added water baptism in the name of the Lord Jesus Christ, thereby interpreting Acts 2:38 as a prophetic fulfillment to restore the "full gospel" or New Testament Christianity before the end of this age: "God is bringing us back to Acts 2:38, His plan ... God's pattern is Acts 2:38, this is plain."[30]

This "divine plan" that had been sparked by the need to harmonize an apparent scriptural discrepancy was now developed into a logic of doctrine that challenged the traditional interpretations of God, Christ, salvation and the rite of baptism.

b. Key to the Plan – The Name

Beginning with McAlister's exegesis in 1913 that "Lord Jesus Christ" is the parabolic name of "the Father, Son and Holy Spirit," the early Oneness movement made the name of God the central feature of its

---

[29] Small, "Theological World Faces Reconstruction," *Living Waters* 1/1 (January 1930): 3.

[30] Fauss, *Buy the Truth*, p. 21. Chapter 4 is a summary of notes taken by Fauss at the 1915 Bible Conference in Elton, LA, where most of the Louisiana and Eastern Texas ministers and assemblies converted to the Oneness movement.

doctrine. The exegetical clue was found in Matthew's use of the singular form of the word "name" with reference to Father, Son and Holy Spirit. Excluding the charge that Matthew was a poor grammarian, Oneness teachers held that the only plausible explanation was that the Apostles knew something that had been lost to most of the Christian church since apostolic times; namely, that Jesus was speaking of his own Name. And this was confirmed, they contended, when in Acts the Apostles proceeded to baptize in the name of the "Lord Jesus" or "Jesus Christ."

Andrew D. Urshan, a Pentecostal missionary and evangelist who did not identify fully with the Oneness movement until 1919, wrote that he had understood the Trinitarian significance of the name, Lord Jesus Christ, as early as 1910:

> I understand, and learned then, that my Heavenly Father's adorable Name was 'Jesus' the Saviour; 'Christ' the Embodiment of the Holy Spirit; and 'The Lord' the external God, the Possessor of Heaven and Earth.[31]

He began then and continued throughout his ministry prior to 1919 to baptize according to Acts 2:38.[32] Urshan and other early teachers, however, interpreted the Name rather loosely, not always following McAlister's exegesis that the compound name, "Lord Jesus Christ," correlates with "Father, Son and Holy Spirit." But while they would variously identify the one name as "Lord Jesus," or "Jesus Christ," it became clear that the one consistent name was "Jesus."

In instructing on the "One Great Name" of Matt. 28:19, Ewart identified it simply as "Jesus."[33] Haywood, likewise, found it sufficient to state that "all who are baptized in the Name of Jesus are baptized in the name of the Father."[34] Fauss saw no inconsistency in advocating

---

[31] Andrew Urshan, *The Life Story of Andrew Bar David Urshan: An Autobiography.* Oneness Pentecostal Pioneer Series (Stockton, CA: WABC Press, 1967), p. 140; see also Urshan, *The Almighty God in the Lord Jesus Christ* (Los Angeles: By the Author, 1919; reprint ed. Portland, OR: Apostolic Book Corner, n.d.), p. 46.

[32] Andrew Urshan, *Life Story*, p. 141. Urshan himself had been rebaptized while on a missionary tour in Russia; see *Life Story*, p. 254. Since he baptized converts there in the name of Jesus, many Pentecostals were called "Jesus Only" or "Urshanites" (interview with Nathaniel A. Urshan, Calvary Tabernacle, Indianapolis, IN, 23 May 1973); see Steve Durasoff, *The Russian Protestants – Evangelicals in the Soviet Union, 1944-1964* (Rutherford, NJ: Fairleigh Dickinson University Press, 1969), p. 67; Hollenweger, *Pentecostals*, p. 269.

[33] Ewart, *Name and Book*, pp. 156-58.

[34] Haywood, "The Fatherhood of God in Christ," *Christian Outlook* 2 (June 1924): 385.

the full baptismal formula, "in the name of the Lord Jesus Christ," and simply asserting that the Apostles "did it in Jesus' Name."[35] While Urshan, like the others, taught extensively on the names and titles of God in the Bible, he was content to find his experience of God wrapped up "in that sweetest of all names, Jesus."[36]

As the Oneness doctrine developed, its proposals for the baptismal name were often fluid and imprecise, interchanging the terms "Lord Jesus Christ," "Lord Jesus," and "Jesus Christ." But the consistent singular name at the heart of the doctrine was "Jesus," because this name was the key that unlocked the door to the very nature and person of God.

4. The Oneness of God

The Oneness doctrine of God began with the baptismal formula that quickly shifted to a question of the theological character of the Name itself. Led by the work of evangelicals before them, Ewart and others set out on a biblical study of the names and titles of God in Scripture. But unlike their forebears, the study led the Oneness proponents to reject the traditional doctrine of the Trinity.

a. The Old Testament – Names of God

If the key to the trinitarian formula of Matt. 28:19 was found in the singular name of Jesus Christ, then, argued the Oneness Pentecostals, the very nature of God must be radically one. If God is one in name, He must also be one in person and nature.

This conclusion led them back to the monotheistic roots of the Old Testament. The *Shema* was regarded as foundational and certainly preferable to the later post-biblical innovations of Trinitarian doctrine. Following a debate in which he had taken the Trinitarian position at the Elton Conference in 1915, R.L. LeFleur later concluded that "the Scriptures did not teach a trinity of persons in the Godhead, or a second or a third person, but that the Lord our God was one Lord."[37]

The names and titles of God were studied with the singular intent of illuminating the supremacy of the one God in Jesus, and to disprove any basis for the Trinitarian doctrine. The primary task was to show that Jesus Christ filled the description ascribed to God in the Old Testament names. At the Elton Conference, Goss led a Bible study on the

---

[35] Fauss, *Buy the Truth*, p. 42.
[36] Urshan, *Almighty God*, p. 44; see pp. 47, 49.
[37] Fauss, *Buy the Truth*, p. 21.

"dispensational names of God," in which he attempted to show how such names as "Elohim," "Jehovah" and "Adonai" applied equally to God and Jesus. For instance, since "El-Shaddai" (which means "the Almighty") implies that there can be only one Almighty and Jesus declared himself to be "the Almighty" (Rev. 1:8), Goss concluded that Jesus could be no other than the Almighty God of the Old Testament.[38]

In the same manner, Haywood concluded an analysis of the names of God in the Old Testament with the rhetorical question, "which one of these do we find not incorporated in the Name of Jesus?"[39] For him, the purpose of the various names was to signify "a different relationship of the great Divine to mankind." But God had a "secret Name" as yet unrevealed, all other names being yet incomplete. That Name was finally revealed as "Jesus" in the angel's annunciation to Joseph: "The name of Jesus bears in it all that God's other name ever bore.... Thus in all things He is given pre-eminence and a name that is above every name."[40]

Urshan, on the other hand, turned his attention to the special significance accorded the name "Jehovah," because, unlike the others, it bore the special self-revelation of Israel's God:

> God has revealed Himself at different times in past ages by His excellent Names given to His people, but 'Yah-weh' (Jehovah), the Name of God, is the fullest explanation and manifestation of His great and infinite Being.[41]

Adapting a dispensational hermeneutic, Urshan resolved the three primary names of God into a unity by allocating each name to a different dispensation. "Elohim" was the name in the dispensations of Creation and Promise (Abraham), "Jehovah" was given in the period of Law (Moses), and "Jesus" was revealed in the Dispensation of Grace.[42] Since Jesus is the revealed name of God for "this gospel dis-

---

[38] Fauss, *Buy the Truth*, pp. 23-24.

[39] Haywood, *Divine Names and Titles of Jehovah* (Indianapolis, IN: Christ Temple, n.d.), p. 8.

[40] *Ibid.*, pp. 9-11.

[41] Urshan, *Almighty God*, p. 6. Urshan may have been influenced by a Jewish Christian "Sacred Name" publication, *Eusebia*, which was non-trinitarian, Christocentric, hebraicized the biblical names for God and Jesus, and believed in baptism in the Name of "YAH-SOUS." See reprints in *Almighty God*, pp. 24-36, 40.

[42] Urshan, "The Sevenfold Deity of Christ and the Divine Seven," *Witness of God* 1 (June 1920): 14; *Witness of God* 2 (July 1921): 1; *Life Story*, pp. 243-44; *Almighty God*, pp. 43-44, "Editorial," *Witness of God* 2 (July 1921): 1.

pensation," it is proper to "worship God, the Father, the Son, and the Holy Ghost in His new revealed Name."[43]

Small, as did Ewart, drew heavily upon the work of William Phillips Hall in his *Remarkable Biblical Discovery,* to argue that the "Name" is the key for declaring Christ as "the only GOD OF THE BIBLE for the identification of the human race with GOD. It explodes the TI-TANIC OF MODERNISM." This was the same approach taken by the earlier evangelicals to biblically prove the deity of Christ. But Small extended it to the Oneness revelation that he received in 1915; namely, that the "Name" was the foundation for the great affirmation "of GOD IN CHRIST and water baptism in the NAME OF THE LORD JESUS." He only despaired that the Pentecostal "latter rain" movement had largely turned its back on this great truth, and un-doubtedly referring to Hall's book, he concluded, "God is now raising up others to fill the gap and is moving on with his great work of reve-lation and restoration of truth on the outside of Pentecostal organization who are receiving the vision with open arms."[44]

"Jehovah" was the most important name in the Old Testament for the Oneness Pentecostals for three reasons. First, in that it was the Name given to Moses' for the deliverance of His people from Egypt. It was the "distinctive redemption name of the Deity."[45] It was also etymologically the name of "Jesus" in its Hebrew form, a derivative of Jehovah, meaning Jehovah – Savior. Finally, "Jehovah" is the name *par* excellence of divine self-disclosure, which designates God "in the es-sential eternality of His being."[46]

b. Doctrine of the Trinity Rejected

The themes of the radical unity and singular dispensational name of God became the primary theological weapons used to attack the doc-trine of the Trinity. As already mentioned, the idea of the Trinity with which most Pentecostals were likely to be familiar depicted the "three persons" as distinct intelligences and conscious wills, yet one God.[47] Accepting this view of the Trinity literally, the Oneness teachers ar-gued that to speak of three "persons" in the Godhead was nothing short of tritheism. They quickly charged the Trinitarians with believ-

---

[43] Urshan, *Almighty God*, p. 44.
[44] Small, "Theological World Faces Reconstruction."
[45] Ewart, *Name and Book*, p. 74.
[46] Ewart, *Name and Book*, p. 171.
[47] See above Chapter 4.

ing in "three Gods."[48] Urshan's preferred description of the Trinitarian view was "three separate and distinct persons."[49] But theological precision was not a chief characteristic of the debate in these volatile times. Urshan and others would occasionally contrast this description with what they called the "One God Doctrine."[50] Haywood taunted that the Apostles knew nothing of the word "Trinity" or "three separate Persons in the Godhead; they had not been informed that the Holy Ghost, the Spirit of God, and the Spirit of Christ were the Spirits of three Separate Persons." He concluded that to believe this would mean that, "we have on our hands three separate, distinct Gods."[51] He laid the cause of this great apostasy at the feet of the Roman Catholic Church at the beginning of what he called the "Dark Ages."[52]

Whether or not they had convinced themselves that Trinitarians really were tritheists, or only that the doctrine inevitably *implied* it, they consistently inserted the descriptive adjective "separate" whenever referring to the Persons in the Godhead. This persistent distortion served not only to attack the Trinitarians but also to "catechize" their followers that the doctrine of the Trinity was false teaching. While orthodox Trinitarian doctrine would insist on the Persons being eternally "distinct," it would eschew any hint that they were separate. In addition, Oneness teachers had defined the nature of God's oneness so narrowly and incorporated it into a new teaching on God's revelational Name, they could only conclude that the doctrine of the Trinity was nothing short of a dangerous distortion of biblical monotheism.

c. The Oneness Alternative

The Oneness alternative was in essence a form of Modalism. It was "unitarian" in a way that set it apart from the mainstream of historic Trinitarianism. But in terms of the divine threefold revelation of God in the world, it was basically "modalistic" and triadic.

The pioneers of the Oneness doctrine preferred the term "manifestation" to "person" as a designation for the threefold distinctions. Haywood preferred it because it was used in Scripture.[53] Ewart used it

---

[48] Fauss, *Buy the Truth*, p. 22.

[49] Urshan, *Almighty God*, p. 91.

[50] Urshan, "The New Light or the More Light," *Witness of God* 1 (September 1920): 2; see Fauss, *Buy the Truth*, p. 39.

[51] Haywood, *Victim of the Flaming Sword*, pp. 56, 58.

[52] *Ibid.*, pp. 57; Urshan, *Almighty God*, p. 91; Ewart, *The Revelation of Jesus Christ* (St. Louis, MO: Pentecostal Publishing House, n.d.) p. 25; Small, *Living Waters*, p. 76.

[53] Haywood, *Victim of the Flaming Sword*, p. 65; see Ewart, *Revelation of Jesus Christ*, p. 14.

as an alternative theological formulation of the divine relationships, "ONE in essence, with a threefold manifestation."[54] Urshan acknowledged "a divine threeness of one Divine Being,"[55] but described it as three "distinct, yet inseparable manifestations"[56] or "a threefold *relative-nature*."[57] Instead of rejecting the reality of the Trinity, he urged that the term be treated with respect.[58] His personal preference, however, was the terms "Tri-Unity"[59] or the "Three-One God."[60]

Small believed with the others that the term "manifestation" rather than "person" was the more biblical term, and defended its preference by Sabellius who he suggested "may have been as close to Christian orthodoxy as some of our good friends today who are contending for three Gods; for that teaching is 'Tritheism,' which the fathers condemned as heresy."[61]

The conclusion for all of them was that the Catholic and Protestant Trinitarians, not Oneness Christians, had departed from the biblical doctrine and language of the triune God.[62]

d. Analogies and Their Interpretation

The images used to convey the Oneness view of the divine tri-unity had been used throughout history to explain the nature of the Trinity. The sun and its rays, the elements of heat, light and power in fire, and the source, spray and power-thrust of the fountain – all were used by Urshan to explain the belief that in God the "three" were "distinct but not separate."[63] One of the favorite analogies was the tripartite view of the human person with body, soul and spirit. As a person is one being and one person with a body, soul and spirit, and since humans are

---

[54] Ewart, *Revelation of Jesus Christ*, p. 14.

[55] Urshan "The Trinity," *Witness of God* 4 (September 1923): 2.

[56] Urshan, "Sevenfold Deity of Christ," p. 12.

[57] Urshan, "The Trinity," p. 2.

[58] *Ibid.*, p. 1. Urshan's willingness in these early years to consider ways to reclaim the term "Trinity" illustrates the shift that frequently occurs in the process of institutionalizing an ideology. In this case, the politics of polemics demanded that the term eventually become a term of derision.

[59] Urshan, "The Trinity," p. 2; see Ewart, *Revelation of Jesus Christ*, p. 25.

[60] Urshan, *Almighty God*, pp. 6, 42, 78, 93.

[61] Small, "Historical and Valedictory Account," p. 6.

[62] Ewart, *Revelation of Jesus Christ*, p. 14.

[63] Urshan, "The Blessed Three-ness of the Godhead Slightly Revealed in Nature and Perfectly Demonstrated and Proved in the Person and Name of Our Lord Jesus Christ," *Witness of God* 4 (July 1923): 2.

made in the image of God (cf. Genesis 1:26), then the uni-personality of God is not destroyed by the threeness.[64]

Oneness teachers were unaware that the church had already traversed this territory and had understood the implications of denying eternal status to the threefold revelation of God. The theological distinction between ontology and revelation, between time and eternity, was never incorporated into the Oneness presentation. Urshan and Small could use the tripartite view of man – which illustrated a person's *ontological* being – but did so to support the Oneness preference for "manifestation," a *temporal* and *transitory* distinction only. Urshan's illustrations of three-in-one, which were effective in explaining the Trinity, did not make sense as an argument for the temporality implied in the term "manifestation."

This oversight may have occurred for two reasons. First, the question of time and eternity was not the issue for them. Their battleground was primarily the *nature* of the distinctions in the Godhead, i.e. the number of "persons." Behind that was their concern, extended from evangelicals before them, to argue for the "supreme" deity of Christ and his full identity as God. To use an analogy, though a person is tripartite, "his name is singular."[65] God, therefore, is *one* Person, not three. Their second concern was to demonstrate the centrality of Jesus as the "express image" of the *full* Godhead. Following J. Monro Gibson, who had warned of the danger in seeking "a *separate* knowledge of the Father, Son, and Holy Ghost," they argued that the whole Trinity was taken up and revealed in Jesus.[66] Just as the visible part of a person, the body, answers for the whole person, so the visible or human side of the Godhead, Jesus, represents the entire person of God.[67]

The basic Oneness position revolved around the paradoxical axes of immanence and transcendence, of visibility and invisibility. Their alternative to three divine persons was an omnipresent Deity who revealed Himself in a threefold way for the benefit of our salvation. Urshan explained that the baptism of Jesus was not a "trinitarian display, but a display of His infallible love and plan redemption." In Jesus' baptism we do not witness "three separate divine beings, but one God

---

[64] Urshan, "Blessed Three-ness," p. 2; Small, *Living Waters*, p. 94.

[65] Small, *Living Waters*, p. 94.

[66] Gibson, "Christianity according to Christ," p. 81; see Urshan, *Almighty God*, pp. 38, 79-83; Small, *Living Waters*, pp. 85-86.

[67] Urshan, "Blessed Three-ness," p. 2.

filling the Heaven, the air and the earth with His glory yet distinct in three manifestations." [68]

e. Charge of Sabellianism

While the charge of "Sabellianism" had already been laid, there was little understanding of the teaching, or of the implications of its conclusions. Also, there had been no theological links forged with it. It appears to have originated as an accusation from the Trinitarians. However, Haywood spoke approvingly of it, primarily because of its apparent preference for the term, "manifestation." On at least that point, he declared that, "the doctrine of Sabellius was more scripturally based than that of the Athanasian Creed."[69] Years later, Small wrote approvingly of Sabellius, declaring that, "Sabellianism appears to be more logical on the Godhead. It resolves the Godhead into Three Manifestations of God to man."[70] The observation seems to be a pragmatic one in which Sabellius fit their own Oneness purposes, and they had little or no fear of the charge of heresy that had been hurled at them since 1916. Urshan, conversely, rejected the label, because it taught that God was without personality, having "only divine attributes."[71] In contrast to Trinitarians, Arians and Sabellians, Urshan gave this summary statement of the Oneness position:

> We believe in *One Great and Eternal SPIRIT-GOD*, who is one Spiritual Being or person ... and that one God is none else but the Jehovah God of Israel.... We solemnly believe that Jesus Christ, our Lord, is that very Jehovah according to his Deity, and the Servant of Jehovah or the Son of God, and man according to his humanity.[72]

The Oneness writers were not patiently disposed to weigh the subtleties of the Trinitarian doctrine; nor did they strive to offer a comprehensive alternative. Their passion lay in another aspect of the doctrine of God; namely, a oneness that magnified the revelation of Jesus Christ as supreme Lord. It was this conviction that fueled their courage to repudiate the core doctrine of the Christian tradition.

---

[68] Urshan, "Sevenfold Deity of Christ," p. 10.

[69] Haywood, *Victim of the Flaming Sword*, p. 65.

[70] Small, "The Godhead – Questions and Answers," *Living Waters* 1/10 (September 1946): 7; also "Historical and Valedictory Account," p. 6.

[71] Urshan, "Editorial," *Witness of God* 2 (July 1921): 1.

[72] *Ibid.*, p. 2.

5. Summary

The term "revelation" was used primarily by Oneness advocates to describe the subjective confirmation of the objectively stated truth in the Bible. Confusion has been caused by their lack of precision or serious attempt to show how their revelation was related to Scripture. The notion was forged in the longstanding priority in evangelical faith that doctrine be readily appropriated to practical living and spiritual devotion. But it was more immediately a manifestation of the Pentecostal "Latter Rain" interpretation of history, which understood "further" revelation to be the activity of fully restoring apostolic Christianity. For most pioneer Oneness leaders, their "revelation" became the culmination of that great eschatological move of God.

The Oneness doctrine developed by beginning and ending with Acts 2:38. This chapter has dealt with the starting point of the "Plan" in Acts 2:38. Using the singular Name as the hermeneutical key, Oneness teachers studied the nature and name of God in the Old Testament to show that Christ fulfilled all the attributes of Deity. In rejecting the doctrine of the Trinity as they themselves defined it, Oneness proponents were attempting to re-establish the undifferentiated oneness of God. They then developed a modalistic interpretation of the Three-in-One that did not threaten the monarchy of God. The Old Testament understanding of the nature and name of God became the basis for interpreting Jesus and his name. To that task we now turn.

9

From Issue to Doctrine:
One Lord and One Baptism

> It shall be light in the evening time;
> The path to glory you will surely find
> Thru the water way; It is light today.
> Buried in His precious name,
> Young and old, repent of all your sin,
> Then the Holy Ghost will enter in.
> The evening time has come;
> 'Tis a fact that God and Christ are one.[1]
>
> – Hattie E. Pryor

Revelational moments had for some time included insights, ideas, or what many would classify as doctrine. Spiritual passion transmuted quickly into belief systems. Most of the time they were located in the writings of an individual or were not of the magnitude to create schism. This was not the case with Oneness Pentecostalism. What had begun as an exegetical quandary, within months took on doctrinal shape. Though the meanings were still fluid, the contours of the ideas were discernible. In this chapter, we will explore the emerging Oneness Christology and soteriology as they were being articulated for the first time.

1. One Lord Jesus Christ

Jesus was the burning passion of all Oneness Pentecostals. They believed themselves to be the blessed recipients of the "revelation of Jesus Christ." And whatever they believed about God and Christ was to find its key in this *one* person who was the full manifestation of the *one* God. But the doctrinal ramifications were considerably more com-

---

[1] Hattie E. Pryor, "The Water Way," *The Bridegroom Songs*, Christ Temple Edition (Indianapolis, IN: Christ Temple Bookstore, n.d.), no. 20.

plex, as their teachings were often worked out in the heat of argument and resentment.

a. Subordinate Sonship of Trinitarianism

The Oneness charge that Trinitarians were incipient tritheists was related to a more fundamental concern; namely, that Trinitarians minimized the full revelation of God in Christ. If only one person in the Godhead became incarnate, they believed the mathematical conclusion conflicted with Paul's clear teaching that "in [Christ] dwelleth all the fulness of the Godhead bodily" (Col. 2:9).[2] Trinitarians, they protested, taught a subordinate sonship. It was this conviction that was reflected in such Oneness designations for Jesus as "Absolute Deity,"[3] the "true God,"[4] the "only true God,"[5] and "the Mighty God."[6]

On the Trinitarian scheme, Jesus was neither the *full* revelation of the Deity nor the revelation of the *full* Deity. This was the point implied in Ewart's description of his revelation of "the absolute Deity of the Lord Jesus Christ."[7] Urshan accused Trinitarians who believed in the "absolute Deity" of Jesus with "trying to preach Him feebly as the Son, and by so doing they think they have gone to the limit of exalting 'the Lord of Glory.'"[8] Small accused Trinitarians of giving Christ an "inferiority complex" by limiting him to "second place in the Godhead in authority and power."[9] They considered it an inconsistency to credit Christ "with being the SECOND,"[10] when Jesus declared himself to be the *first* and the *last* (Rev. 1:11).

As with Trinitarians, Oneness Pentecostals applied the messianic prophecies to Jesus and transferred to him the prerogatives and characteristics of God Himself. Indeed, they frequently used the same arguments as Trinitarians to prove the deity of Jesus, but did so to discredit what they believed to be the Trinitarian doctrine of a divine but subordinate Son. Their dual insistence on the radical oneness of God and the one Name gave them a distinctive hermeneutic for the Son of Mary: he was not the incarnation of the Second Person of the Trinity, but the *full* revelation of the *one* God of Israel.

---

[2] Ewart, *Revelation of Jesus Christ*, pp. 6-7, 25.
[3] Urshan, *Almighty God*, p. 10; Ewart, *Name and Book*, p. 40.
[4] Fauss, *Buy the Truth*, p. 11.
[5] Haywood, *Victim of the Flaming Sword*, p. 10.
[6] *Ibid.*, pp. 56, 60, 65.
[7] Ewart, *Name and Book*, p. 40.
[8] Urshan, *Almighty God*, p. 10.
[9] Small, *Living Waters*, p. 90.
[10] Ewart, *Revelation of Jesus Christ*, p. 7.

b. The Father in the Son

It is not surprising that Trinitarians accused the Oneness exponents of denying the Father. E.N. Bell, who probably understood the Oneness position better than others, accused them of teaching that "Jesus is the Father and the Father is Jesus."[11] He implied further that they believed the Father and Spirit were "confined to the body of Jesus."[12]

In response, they insisted that they rejected only the belief that the Father was a "separate and distinct person" from the Son. Since God was an omnipresent Spirit, it was impossible to confine Him to a human body. Yet all that God was, was seen in Jesus Christ. As there were no hypostatic distinctions within the Godhead, the deity in Jesus was that of the Father, not the hypostatically distinct "eternal God the Son."[13] As Bell correctly understood, they held that "the 'Son' of God is only human, while the Deity is all of the Father. In this sense Jesus is God and man, all the God part being the Father and all the man part being the Son." Bell knew this was a departure from the doctrine of the Trinity in two ways: it "denies the eternal Son, and makes no distinction between the Father and the Deity of Christ."[14] In an effort to dissociate themselves from the charge of Patripassianism, both Urshan and Haywood outlined the Oneness alternative of the two-nature doctrine in terms of the Fatherhood and Sonship. Urshan described the position in terms of the dialectic of transcendence and immanence:

> [Jesus] was on earth yet at the same time He was in heaven. He was in heaven, yet He was on earth. So our Lord, as eternal God, the Spirit, is everywhere invisible; but, as God manifested in the flesh, He was on earth bodily. Not two Gods, but one Omnipotent God, who is the Son according to His blessed humanity, but God the Almighty, according to His absolute Deity.[15]

---

[11] Bell, "Questions and Answers," *Weekly Evangel* 200 (28 July 1917): 9.

[12] Bell, "Questions and Answers," *Weekly Evangel* 177 (17 February 1917): 9.

[13] Early Oneness apologists often bolstered their argument against the eternal Sonship of Jesus by referring to the popular commentary of early Methodist biblical scholar, Adam Clarke, who also rejected the concept of Jesus' eternal Sonship. It is not surprising that Clarke's teaching would be discovered by Oneness writers. The judgment of Old Testament scholar, Brevard Childs, is that "more credit for the Methodist revivals was due to the robust commentaries of Wesley's disciple, Adam Clarke ... Clarke's commentary was one of the few books which accompanied the settlers to the west," in "The Search for Biblical Authority Today," *Andover Newton Quarter,* 16/3 (January 1976): 202.

[14] Bell, "Questions and Answers," *Weekly Evangel* 200 (28 July 1917): 9.

[15] Urshan, "The Divinity of Jesus Christ, Or the Absolute Deity of the Son of God according to the Old and New Testament," *The Pentecostal Witness* 3 (1 April 1927): 2.

Urshan was influenced by J. Monro Gibson's christocentric Trinitarianism, in which "the Father, Son and Holy Ghost are all in Jesus Christ … so that our thoughts are not to leave Christ when they pass to the Father or to the Holy Spirit."[16] Gibson was less interested in speculating on the eternal distinctions between the divine persons than on encountering God by "sitting at the feet of Jesus and looking up into His face." As "your face is not yourself, it is only the outward expression or incarnation of your spirit,"[17] so the one Person *pro me* is the man Jesus who was "the face of God to us."[18] As Urshan summed up this view, God in Christ was "one *personality* and *one glorious* face."[19]

Small also carried forward this christocentric focus of the Godhead. He cited both J. Monro Gibson and a lecture series held in Winnipeg by Methodist scholar, Dr. Stanley L. Krebs, entitled, "Three Gods or One?" In both, Small found support for the theme that Christ is "the only image of the invisible three in one God seen in this world or the one to come." Since in his person Christ is the "only visible representation" of the Godhead, so Small argued that his Name is the only name by which the Godhead is known: "This is why there can be absolutely nothing added to the NAME of the Lord to make it more complete."[20]

In response to Trinitarians who were attacking the Oneness view on the grounds of 1 John 2:22, "He is antichrist, that denieth the Father and the Son," Haywood affirmed both the Father and the Son while denying the Trinitarian alternative, by insisting with Gibson and Urshan that "the Fatherhood of God is found only in the Son, who was God manifested in the flesh."[21]

For this reason, Small made a plea that Christ have restored to himself "His lost title 'Father' of which He was robbed during the dark ages." Trinitarians had segregated the Fatherhood of God and His Sonship into two eternally distinct "persons." But Christ could be absolutely God only if in his deity he was acknowledged as "Father." While his sonship was the "human phase of Christ," it was only in the Son that the Father was revealed. "The Sonship today holds first place

---

[16] Cited in Urshan, *Almighty God*, pp. 79-80; see Gibson, *Christianity according to Christ*, *passim*.

[17] Gibson, *Christianity according to Christ*, p. 59.

[18] Cited in Urshan, *Almighty God*, p. 80.

[19] Urshan, *Almighty God*, p. 81.

[20] Small, "The Godhead," *Living Waters* 1/2 (17 June 1918): 3.

[21] Haywood, "Dangers of Denying the Father," p. 3.

in all authority in heaven and earth because originally he is the Father of all things."[22]

It was the radically one God, the Father, not the Second Person or the eternal Son, who became incarnate in the human son of Mary. Oneness Pentecostals did not believe that their position in any way compromised God's transcendence in the incarnation. On this point there was no dispute with many fundamentalist Trinitarians who themselves opposed any kenosis in the incarnation. Bell acknowledged, "Christ's own deity was not and is not confined to such a body. While on earth in such a body Jesus spoke of himself as then in heaven, too," adding that, "Jesus is in the Father, just as much as the Father is in Jesus."[23] The point of difference was that the Oneness Pentecostals believed it was the *Father* who was incarnated in Jesus.

2. One Baptism

Baptism in the name of Jesus had been judged by the Trinitarian leaders of the Assemblies of God to be acceptable, since it was clearly a biblical practice. But the Oneness interpretation of the reason for and insistence upon re-baptism divided the Pentecostal movement. Among the New Issue pioneers themselves, however, there was difference as well as agreement on the meaning of Acts 2:38.

a. Acts 2:38 – The Gospel in Miniature

As there was only *one Lord*, there could be only *one baptism* that would express the *one faith* in the one Lord (see Eph. 4:5). Acts 2:38 became for Oneness Pentecostals the gospel in miniature, preaching it as the "full gospel" or "full salvation." It was God's plan for these times of the Latter Rain, "bringing us back to Acts 2:38; His plan."[24]

The three steps to full salvation were outlined in Acts 2:38: repentance, baptism in the name of Jesus Christ, and the baptism of the Holy Spirit.[25] Oneness Pentecostals saw this as the final restoration of New Testament or apostolic Christianity before the end of this age.[26]

---

[22] Small, *Living Waters*, pp. 103, 105, 104, 102.

[23] Bell, "Questions and Answers," *Weekly Evangel* 177, p. 9.

[24] Fauss, *Buy the Truth*, p. 21; see Haywood, *The Birth of the Spirit as in the Days of the Apostles*, reprinted in *The Life and Writings of Elder G.T. Haywood*, p. 25.

[25] See *What We Believe and Teach – Articles of Faith of the United Pentecostal Church* (St. Louis, MO: Pentecostal Publishing house, n.d.), p. 7. This threefold plan of salvation remains as the "basic and fundamental doctrine" of this Oneness organization.

[26] McClain, *Student's Handbook*, p. 62.

In its emphasis on re-baptism in the "Name" and its interpretation of the gospel, it presented not only a distinct alternative to the Baptistic heritage of the Assemblies of God but also not a little controversy.

b. Acts 2:38 – Proper Name and Formula

The first point of contention was the meaning of the word "name." Prior to his re-baptism, Bell had defended the Trinitarian formula on the grounds that "name" meant simply "authority." Therefore, to do anything, including baptizing, in the name of Jesus meant to do it in his authority, not merely to repeat a formula.[27] He was convinced that neither Jesus nor the Apostles insisted on a "fixed set of words," the consequence of which would be "formalism and legalism."[28] "The triune name was as much a proper name as Jesus."[29] This interpretation has been largely accepted by the Assemblies of God since that time.[30]

For the sake of unity and uniformity, the Council of 1916 stipulated that the words of Matt. 28:19 be incorporated in whatever formula a minister wished to use.[31] From the Assemblies of God side, A.H. Argue suggested a formula that understood "name" to mean "authority" and would blend the two formulae of Matt. 28:19 and Acts 2:38: "In the name of the Lord Jesus Christ, and on confession of your faith in Him, I baptize thee into the name of the Father, and of the Son, and of the Holy Ghost."[32]

Oneness Pentecostals did not accept this interpretation of the "Name." Based on their study of the name of God in the Old Testament, they insisted that whatever "name" meant, it was more than mere authority. It was God's *proper* name for this dispensation, his "revealed name."[33] The issue was a matter of distinguishing between a title or common name and a proper name. Thus Ewart concluded that the traditional interpretation of Matt. 28:19 was a "palpable case of confusing Names and Titles."[34]

[27] Bell, "To Act in the Name of Another," pp. 2-3.

[28] Bell, "Scriptural Varieties on Baptismal Formula," *Weekly Evangel* 97 (3 July 1915): 1.

[29] Bell, "The Great Battle for the Truth," *Christian Evangel* 300 and 301 (9 August 1919): 1-2; all "compromise formulas" based on this view were denounced by Ewart, *Phenomenon,* p. 78.

[30] Interview with Thomas F. Zimmerman, Assemblies of God Headquarters, Springfield, MO, 22 June 1973.

[31] *General Council Minutes, 1916,* p. 8.

[32] A.H. Argue, "Water Baptism and Its Formula," *Christian Evangel* 264 and 265 (30 November 1918): 8-9.

[33] Urshan, "Sevenfold Deity of Christ," p. 14.

[34] Ewart, *Name and Book,* p. 135

The confusion was resolved for Oneness theology by three mutually supportive ideas. First, the singular form of "name" prefacing the tri-une formula in Matthew 28:19 implied that the Name was indeed other than "Father, Son and Holy Spirit." Second, the use of the singular and proper name "Jesus" in Acts 2:38, together with the absence of the Trinitarian formula in the apostolic church, was evidence enough that the Apostles themselves made the distinction.[35] Finally, the conclusion was confirmed in the Pauline admonition that "whatever you do, in word or deed, do everything in the name of the Lord Jesus" (Col. 3:17).[36]

Although "Jesus" was a common Jewish name, its divine distinction was due to the invocation by the Angel in the annunciation, thereby binding the Name in an inseparable unity with the incarnate One. Furthermore, the identity was established by the designations "Lord" and "Christ."[37]

In the midst of the controversy, much of the rhetoric was reduced to the issue of the correct formula to be used in baptism. But the original core of the Oneness vision of the Name was a quintessentially Pentecostal one – the spiritual power it delivered. This power theme appears throughout the Oneness literature, which Ewart summed up well:

> Pentecost is power! What happened at Pentecost? .... What really happened at Pentecost was the declaration of a God-given charter to work miracles in the Name of the Lord Jesus Christ. A new power to create miracles! – a new power of signs and wonders – a new power of Christ-like works of supernatural healings
>
> ... a torrent of miraculous tongues that recommended the power of righteousness.... Power to deliver men from oppression, the delirium, the agony, the repulsive diseases of the devil.... That is Pentecost. It was a divine demonstration of the latent miracle working power in the Name of Jesus.[38]

---

[35] See Urshan, *Almighty God*, pp. 41-45, *The Doctrine of the New Birth or the Perfect Way to Eternal Life* (Cochrane, WI: Witness of God, 1921), p. 36; Ewart, *Revelation of Jesus Christ*, pp. 39-42, *Name and Book*, pp. 135-41; Small, *Living Waters*, pp. 92-95.

[36] Ewart, *Revelation of Jesus Christ*, p. 39; Urshan, *Almighty God*, p. 43.

[37] Small, *Living Waters*, pp. 97-98.

[38] Ewart, *Name and Book*, pp. 31-32. The theme of power as integral to Pentecostal faith, especially in black Pentecostalism, is explored in a provocative paper by Clarence Hardy, "'Take the Bible Way:' Charles Harrison Mason and the Development of Black Pentecostalism as Biblical Magic," Paper read at the 31st Annual Meeting of the Society for Pentecostal Studies, 14-16 March 2002, pp. 87-107.

Beneath the theological debates regarding the validity of baptism by correct formula lay the primordial Pentecostal mission of the Oneness evangelists for spiritual power. To be fully Pentecostal and employ the full force of the apostolic Pentecost, the whole Latter Rain Pentecostal movement and its adherents must be quite literally baptized into this supernatural reality through the invocation of the name of Jesus. To do less would be to thwart God's plan for the Last Days and consign the Revival to the anemic religion of the denominational world. Re-baptism was not about validity; it was about power.

c. Acts 2:38 – Identification with Christ: Ewart and Small

The second point of contention related to the three steps to "Bible salvation"[39] set forth in Acts 2:38. The doctrine that supported baptism in Jesus' name was the point upon which Bell argued for disfellow-shipping the Oneness constituency from the Assemblies of God. Excommunication could be warranted, not because an act of baptism was performed, but when that baptism was "connected with an un-clean life, or a factious, divisive, schismatic, unchristian spirit and with a denial of the Son of God, or of other truth essential to salvation."[40]

Acts 2:38 also became the major point of tension and disagreement *within* the Oneness movement. While all of the Oneness pioneers af-firmed the need for re-baptism, they did so for one of two theological reasons. Ewart and Small followed more closely Durham's Finished Work paradigm, interpreting Acts 2:38 as a full *identification* with Christ. In Ewart's writings, we find no effort to align this text with the new birth of John 3:5.[41] Rather, echoing Durham's cry, Acts 2:38 was

---

[39] Urshan, *Almighty God*, p. 21.

[40] Bell, "Questions and Answers," *Weekly Evangel* 213 (3 November 1917): 9; this statement was made in reply to the question, "Should one be disfellowshipped for baptiz-ing in Jesus' Name?"

[41] W.T. Witherspoon, an early fellow minister and leader in the United Pentecostal Church, reportedly confirmed that Ewart never taught Acts 2:38 as the new birth of John 3:5. Witherspoon's son, Arthur W. Witherspoon, conveyed this statement in a personal interview in Toronto, 23 July 1994. Ewart's daughter, Elvira Winters, confirmed Witherspoon's view (phone interview with Elvira Winters, 9 February 1996).

David Bernard, leading Oneness theologian with UPCI, however, believes that Ewart taught Acts 2:38 as the new birth, based on the opinion of a UPC minister, David Gray, who trained under Ewart, and an obscure reference in Ewart's *The Name and the Book*; see David K. Bernard, *Understanding the Articles of Faith: An Examination of United Pentecos-tal Beliefs* (Hazelwood, MO: Word Aflame, 1998), p. 46. A review of *The Name and the Book* reveals, on the contrary, that Ewart's interest was elsewhere: the revelation of the name of Jesus as the proper name of God for this dispensation, Acts 2:38 as the apostolic fulfillment of the Lord's Commission in Matt. 28:19, baptism as identification with

simply "normal" Christianity. When this "apostolic order" was followed, then apostolic life and power would follow:

> Back in 1914, when God revealed the apostolic order to the writer, and made known that He was going to raise up a new order of ministry who would do things according to the apostolic pattern, he never preached about nonessentials or abnormalities.... People were healed in the water and filled with the Spirit in the water by the thousands. It was the nearest thing to the apostolic pattern we have yet seen.[42]

Baptism in the name of Jesus was the "true baptism" in which the confessing sinner accepts the substitutionary work of Christ. But it was also, as with Durham, the "normal Scriptural way" to enter into the experience of Spirit-baptism. Elsewhere, Ewart called baptism the "True Christian Circumcision."[43]

The clearest articulation of Ewart's theology of Acts 2:38 appears in an article published in 1916. He began with Durham's teaching on identification with Christ, but added that Durham had been so preoccupied with the basis on faith alone that he had failed to elaborate on those acts of faith by which that identification was brought about.[44] Ewart then directed attention to Acts 2:38: "Repentance, water baptism in the name of Jesus Christ and the reception of the Holy Ghost are the three great acts of faith by which a sinner is identified with Jesus Christ, his great substitute according to the Scriptures." Like other Pentecostals, he clarified that the role of Spirit-baptism is "God's pledge of a part in the first resurrection."[45] In later years, he described the significance of baptism similarly: "Baptism into His Name is God's ordained way of expressing our belief. By believing in His Name, people identify themselves with Him in His death and burial and resurrection."[46] Ewart's theology of Acts 2:38 is, therefore, best understood in terms of Durham's central teaching on identification with Christ and the early Pentecostal paradigm of the full gospel or full salvation – what Ewart preferred to call "normal" Christianity.

Christ, and the spiritual power that attends the ministry carried out in the name of Jesus. These themes are consistent in Ewart's earlier and later writings.

[42] Ewart, "Like Precious Faith," *Apostolic Herald* 17/8 (August 1942): 7.

[43] Ewart, "The Significance of Water Baptism," *The Apostolic Herald* 16 (January 1941): 12.

[44] It is worth noting that the phrase, "acts of faith," is borrowed from Phoebe Palmer who made it a popular platform of her own teaching in *Faith and Its Effects* (see above).

[45] Ewart, "Identification with Christ," *Meat in Due Season* 1/13 (June 1916): 3.

[46] Ewart, *The Name and the Book*, p. 15.

Franklin Small is the other contributor to the "identification" inter-pretation of Acts 2:38. He was less influential in the United States for a number of reasons. Being located in Winnipeg, Canada, he devoted much of his evangelistic, teaching and organizational ministry to pro-moting the Oneness message throughout Canada. His periodical, *Living Waters*, was first published in 1918 and continued occasionally through mid-century. He is distinguished for being the only disciple of Durham's Finished Work teaching, Trinitarian or Oneness, committed to it beyond the first decade after Durham's death. Indeed, Small not only seems to have understood Durham's views on sanctification bet-ter than the others, he also developed the Finished Work doctrine in a direction that bore the mark of Small's own distinctive contribution.

Small's interest in the Finished Work and Oneness themes can be traced through his periodical. The dual focus of the Oneness message was simple: "GOD IN CHRIST and water baptism in the NAME OF THE LORD JESUS."[47] For Small this basically meant the oneness of God, the singular revelation of God in Jesus Christ, and the revealed name of Jesus as appropriated in baptism. He held the same doctrine of Spirit-baptism as most other Pentecostals – the promise that seals one for the first resurrection.

The focus and simplicity of presentation were evident in the early years. In the second issue of the paper, he wrote only two brief articles on "The Godhead" and "Water Baptism."[48] Five years later, he wrote an extensive article entitled, "Full Redemption," which reflected his Finished Work interest, but made no mention of the Oneness distinc-tives. He reflected Durham's distinctive teaching, that in conversion one receives a new nature as well as a new status: "The miraculous power of God operates upon his heart (nature) and creates it anew ...The first phase of redemption includes God's full standard of bless-ing."[49]

In a large issue in 1930 Small wrote four articles, two dealing with justification and the Finished Work, and two with the centrality of Christ and the Name.[50] In one, he introduced Hall's *Remarkable Biblical Discovery*, with its teaching on the name of God in Scripture. But Acts

[47] Small, "Theological World Faces Reconstruction," p. 4.
[48] Small, *Living Waters* 1/2 (17 June 1918): 3.
[49] Small, "Full Redemption," *Living Waters* 4/3 (November 1923): 3.
[50] Small, "Theological World Faces Reconstruction," "Fundamentalism or Modernism – Which? The Final Ultimatum," "Justification by Faith: Its Various Definitions during the Past Several Centuries," and "The Church the Body of Christ and Organization," *Living Waters* 1/1 (January 1930): 3-5, 7, 8-9, 19-20.

2:38 was not mentioned in any of the articles. Two highlights emerged: his comments on the Fundamentalist-Modernist battle raging at the time, and a painful attack on Pentecostal organizations. In the former, he revealed his bias on the side of the Fundamentalists as being more compatible with the Oneness teaching on Christ, stating that, "Fundamentalism rendered down and in its final analysis spells GOD IN CHRIST."[51] He also cited approvingly an excerpt of a personal letter from Dr. Roach Straton, a Baptist millenarian and staunch Fundamentalist, who affirmed with him the centrality of Christ.

In another article, he lashed out at Pentecostal organizations, which he believed were already stifling the Latter Rain Revival. Divine blessing had bypassed the restrictive denominations by raising up the Pentecostal movement, but the new Revival was now creating structures that were equally inhibiting: "They simply took for granted the Lord was through with REVELATION and so clapped on the organizational straps which today are clinched up good and tight."[52] Small's church polity was staunchly congregationalist, so he believed in granting freedom of conscience regarding the New Issue to ministers and local assemblies. He had witnessed the schism of 1916, and by 1921 he had had to form his own Canadian organization, The Apostolic Church of Pentecost, to preserve the Oneness voice, as the original Pentecostal Assemblies of Canada (of which he was a charter member) had turned Trinitarian and affiliated with the Assemblies of God. In 1941 he wrote a highly critical account of this eventual switch from an open conscience policy on the New Issue to a Trinitarian confession and affiliation.[53]

An article dealing with the new birth appeared in 1937, which was an open apologetic for the doctrine of eternal security. Nowhere did he refer to Acts 2:38 or distinctively Oneness soteriological themes.[54] Elsewhere in the issue he wrote an article on eschatology, in which he presented the classical Pentecostal teaching on those who qualified for the "first resurrection," namely, Spirit-filled believers.[55] Another article was on christology, in which he drew exegetical support from the

---

[51] Small, "Fundamentalism or Modernism," p. 19.

[52] Small, "The Church the Body of Christ and Organization," p. 9.

[53] Small, "A Historical and Valedictory Account."

[54] Small, "'Ye Must Be Born Again' *versus* The Probation Triangle," *Living Waters* (May 1937): 6-9.

[55] Small, "The First Resurrection, and the Rapture of the Church," *Living Waters* (May 1937): 9-10.

Methodist commentator, Adam Clarke, for the Oneness position that Christ was not the eternal Son, Second Person of the Trinity.[56]

Most of his major articles published in the 1940's dealt with the doctrines of the Finished Work and eternal security. In "The Sin Question," Small presented an accurate version of Durham's teaching, opposing those who taught that the "'old man' and the 'new man' exist concurrently in the believer." He declared, as did Durham before him, that, "Christ dealt a death-blow to the root of sin on the cross, which Adamic sin was a death penalty consisting of a fallen nature."[57] That is, inherent sin, the "old man," is removed, not just legally declared null. To distinguish his (and Durham's) view from the Keswick position – that the "old man" is still present but can be suppressed by the power of the victorious Christ – Small stated elsewhere his dislike for the phrase, "keeping the old man under."[58] Citing Kenyon, Small made mention in 1951 of earlier personal correspondence he received from Kenyon in response to his article, "The Sin Question":

> The late Dr. Kenyon of Seattle, Washington, once wrote to the Editor to say that a copy of Living Waters had been placed in his hand which contained a message on the subject of the "Sin Question"; he went on to say, "I have never had the pleasure of meeting you Pastor Small, but I wish to say, after reading your thesis on that subject, that you have a message far in advance of the average pastor of today; your message is timely and worthy of recognition among God's people.[59]

The degree of respect and support expressed in the letter strongly suggests that Kenyon recognized in Small, as he had in Durham, a strong resemblance to his own teaching.

Throughout his writings over the years, Small consistently drew upon the Latter Rain paradigm, that God was continuing to unfold lost apostolic truth – what he was fond of calling "the progressive aspect of doctrine."[60] He believed that the Assemblies of God leadership

---

[56] Small, "God Was in Christ," *Living Waters* (May 1937): 17-18. It is not unlikely that Adam Clarke's ideas assisted the early Oneness teachers in key aspects of their doctrinal formulation, in particular his denial of Christ's eternal Sonship and his equating the new birth in John 3:5 with Acts 2:38 (so Haywood and Urshan).

[57] Small, "The Sin Question," *Living Waters* 1/6 (February 1944): 2.

[58] Small, "The Fallen Nature – Total Moral Depravity of the Human Heart," *Living Waters* 1/8 (March 1951): 6. It is noteworthy that, on this one point in particular, Durham and Small represent more closely the teaching of Kenyon than conventional Keswick teaching.

[59] Small, "Editorial," *Living Waters* 1/8 (March 1951): 2.

[60] Small, "Christ's Death and Resurrection – The Finished Work of Calvary," *Living Waters* 1/8 (March 1951): 5.

had closed their minds to the revelation of the name of God in Scripture, a revelation that God was eventually giving outside the Pentecostal family in the work of Hall. Years later, he believed that his own teaching on eternal security was another moment of gradual unfolding. He explained why restored truth was also "deferred truth" that God could reveal only gradually:

> When the latter rain first fell about forty years ago, God had many things to say to His people at that time. Had it all come at once few there are that could have borne it, it was trying enough as it was for many. However, God did not withhold His initial blessing in starting the young movement away. There was deferred truth for the future and God gave grace to bear the tests for all who would pay the price.[61]

Though Small hints that his teaching on eternal security was a "deferred truth," he was probably referring to the slow acceptance within his own fellowship. He indicated elsewhere that, among other Pentecostal ministers, he was reputed to have held to what he then called, "eternal life" teaching, as early as 1919.[62]

In sum, Ewart and Small viewed Acts 2:38 as the Full Gospel pattern. Both gave considerable attention to developing a theology of the Name. Following Durham, Ewart and Small interpreted Acts 2:38 in light of the Pauline teaching on full identification with Christ. Acts 2:38 was the biblical pattern by which the believer fully identified with Christ, by taking on his name in baptism. But this particular interpretation of Acts 2:38 as identification with Christ has not enjoyed a strong influence in the Oneness movement, for at least three possible reasons. One is that neither Ewart nor Small was highly motivated to support centralized forms of church government. Ewart organizationally maintained a low profile. Small was involved on the Canadian scene, but preferred an association that permitted more local autonomy. Furthermore, concentrating on the movement in Canada militated against significant organizational leadership south of the border. A second reason is that neither one wrote a refutation or counter argument to the alternative interpretation that Acts 2:38 represented the new birth (see below). Concern to maintain unity in the movement may have been a contributing factor, especially with Ewart. Finally, Ewart and Small had other interests. Neither believed that the

---

[61] Small, "A Synopsis of Our Last Annual Conference, 1946," *Living Waters* 1/10 (September 1946): 1.

[62] Small, "Historical and Valedictory Account," p. 2.

unfolding of apostolic truth had stopped with the Oneness revelation.[63] This may have led to Ewart's flirting with controversial ideas that could have diverted his attention and possibly damaged his influence among his Oneness peers.[64] Small's interest was primarily in developing Durham's Finished Work teaching along the lines of the Reformed doctrine of eternal security, all of which in itself would have strained his relationship with the rest of the Arminian-oriented Oneness movement.

d. Acts 2:38 – The New Birth: Haywood and Urshan

By 1921 both Haywood and Urshan had developed another interpretation of Acts 2:38; namely, that it constitutes nothing less than the new birth. In comparison with the identification interpretation, the new birth teaching was potentially more radical, more isolationist, and more open to misunderstanding.

[63] We have already pointed out that Small believed in further unfolding of Apostolic truth, particularly his teaching on eternal security. Ewart, likewise, did not believe that the revelation of the Name was the last Apostolic truth to be restored to the church, and anticipated more truth to be revealed (phone interview with his daughter, Elvira Winters, 9 February 1996).

[64] In 1940, Ewart wrote an open letter during the process of applying for ministerial credentials with the Pentecostal Church, Inc., in response to criticisms that he was guilty of teaching doctrines unacceptable to the fellowship; see Ewart, "Statement of My Faith," *Apostolic Herald* 15/2 (February 1940): 5. In the Statement, Ewart recounted the teachings – Redemption of the Body, Spiritual Communion, and Final Restitution. He outright denied teaching Redemption of the Body – a belief taught earlier by Charles Parham that some Christians, called Overcomers (or the Man Child doctrine), will achieve a state of immortality without dying. He did publish at least two short articles on the subject but avoided any references to immortality in this life; see Ewart, "Who Is the Man Child?" and "Cyrus: A Type of the Man-Child," *End Time Witnesses* (n.d.). He acknowledged that while he had preached it was "unnecessary to partake of the literal elements at the Lord's Table ...I now regard the partaking of the literal elements of bread and wine as a great blessing to the saints, of which they should not be deprived." Finally, he openly acknowledged that he had believed but not taught for many years the Final Restitution doctrine, a version of universal salvation (called Pridgeonism after Charles H. Pridgeon, former Presbyterian Dean of Pittsburgh Bible Institite who became Pentecostal in the 1930's), which teaches that Hell is real but not eternal. Ewart qualified his own view: "I preach a Bible hell, as the retribution of rejecting Christ, and leave the heathen, who have never heard of Christ, to the mercies of God." Ewart had written approvingly of Pridgeon's doctrine in *The Name and the Book*, pp. 151-52. There was also an occasion in 1928 when he chose to join a small group of his church members who retired to a nearby mountain to await the return of Christ. In recounting the event, David Gray implies that Ewart believed the prediction; interview, 9 February 1996. Ewart's daughter, however, clarifies that her father did not believe it, but joined his church members out of pastoral concern. Interview, Elvira Winters.

The new birth as taught by these early Oneness leaders consisted of the application of the blood, the water and the Spirit to Christian initiation. The three steps of repentance, water baptism and Spirit-baptism in Acts 2:38 corresponded to these three elements of salvation – what Urshan called the "keys to the kingdom."[65] Adapting Adam Clarke's exegesis in his commentary on John 3:5, Urshan defined this three-step action to salvation as the "new birth," in which one is "born of the water and the Spirit."[66] Though he tried to reassure the Baptistic ears in the Assemblies of God that he was not "belittling the effect of the precious Blood of Jesus," Urshan insisted that water baptism still had a "fundamental place in the Christian faith."[67] While the blood was necessary, water was also part of our salvation, "which symbolizes the grave." And to neglect the baptism of the Holy Spirit would result in a merely humanistic gospel – a belief and a rite without the empowering presence of the Spirit.[68]

Likewise following Adam Clarke's exegesis, Haywood concluded that "born" of the Spirit (John 3:5) was synonymous with being "baptized" with the Spirit.[69] He acknowledged, indeed claimed, that other Christians agreed with Clarke's conclusion.[70] This is the theological point at which the Oneness new birth interpretation reverts to the classical Protestant interpretation that Acts 2:38 is a description of Christian initiation. But the Oneness variant was to interpret this "baptism" as the Pentecostal experience of Spirit-baptism with glossolalia. While most Pentecostals taught a two- or three-experience theology, many Reformed Fundamentalists recognized only conversion as the one foundational "crisis" experience for the believer. The Oneness version adopted this single-experience hermeneutic of Christian initiation and then redefined Pentecostal Spirit-baptism as the birth of the Spirit. That is, a person was born again only upon full reception of Spirit-baptism accompanied by glossolalia. Likewise, "born of water" was interpreted to mean water baptism, which of course for Haywood meant baptism in the name of Jesus. For Haywood, just as the blood and water are inseparable, so also are the

---

[65] Urshan, *Doctrine of the New Birth*, p. 25.

[66] *Ibid.*, pp. 37-38; see also *Witness of God* 2 (September 1921): 1.

[67] Urshan, *Autobiography*, p. 248.

[68] Urshan, *Doctrine of the New Birth*, p. 25.

[69] Haywood, *Birth of the Spirit*, pp. 15, 28-29.

[70] He claimed that, "no church, no creed, whatever their differences may be on other passages of the Scriptures, holds a contrary view on this matter," in Haywood, *Birth of the Spirit*, p. 14.

blood and the Name. Consequently, to appropriate fully the atonement, one needs to be baptized in the name of Jesus, because "the life of the Blood of Christ is connected with baptism when it is administered in His Name."[71]

The association of Acts 2:38 with the new birth was present in certain New Issue circles by 1916, though it is doubtful that by then it was well formulated in Haywood's thinking. Durham had already reported that some folk in the first decade of the Pentecostal Revival were teaching that one is not saved until Spirit-baptism," a view that he opposed as false doctrine.[72] Before Haywood published his teaching on it, a revealing article appeared in a 1916 edition of *Voice in the Wilderness*, by Pastor H.O. Scott, from St. Paul, Minnesota.[73] In it the author reflected on the atonement through the theme of blood, and integrated it with the familiar Acts 2:38 paradigm of salvation. He laid out three essential accomplishments of the Blood of Christ in the divine act of salvation – redemptive, cleansing and life-giving. The redemptive aspect directs one to the cross, "the place of payment of the purchase price that redeemed a fallen race." The cleansing work is accomplished in water baptism, which is not a "mere form" but a "vital part of the New Birth, in which figure no non-essentials." The life-giving benefit occurs with the coming of the Holy Spirit. He then concluded that the new birth was the result of this threefold atoning work of Christ's shed blood, and that "we can now understand Acts 2:38."[74]

An article that drew a similar conclusion, by correlating the birth-baptism parallels of John 3:5 with Acts 2:38, appeared in a subsequent issue. The author referred to John 3:5 and concluded that "according to these words there is but one way to be saved, and that is by being 'born of water and the Spirit,' or to repent, believe 'and be baptized in water and the Holy Ghost.'"[75] He then marked this experience as the key to entering the Kingdom of God.

---

[71] Haywood, *Birth of the Spirit*, p. 24.

[72] Durham, "False Doctrines," *Articles by Pastor Durham*, p. 40.

[73] H.O. Scott's name appears in this issue but also as the host pastor of the convention at which Franklin Small was re-baptized in the name of Jesus. See "Pastor Frank Small Baptized," *Meat in Due Season* 1/9 (December 1915): 2, and *Living Waters* 1/4 (April 1941):7.

[74] H.O. Scott, "The Blood of Jesus in Relation to the New Birth," *Voice in the Wilderness* 18 (1916): 3.

[75] "Entering by the Door," *Voice in the Wilderness* 19 (n.d., ca. early 1917): 2. The author is not identified, so we cannot be certain that it came from the pen of Haywood.

Haywood finally published an article about 1918 that appears to be his first public declaration on the subject of the new birth. He began by recalling how he and other followers of Christ from the time of the Apostles had suffered for the truth, including the early Pentecostals, and that now, "today we are facing another critical moment." Setting himself apart from other Pentecostal leaders who brought with them their "traditional 'way' of salvation," Haywood unapologetically appealed to the "Word of God" and launched into an exposition on the new birth and entrance into the Kingdom of God. Following the appearance of water and the Spirit in Jesus' baptism, he declared that to become a child of God, "we must need be baptized in WATER and the HOLY GHOST." He then drew the bold conclusion that the time was near when "the Gospel of Christ cannot be successfully preached without having WATER near at hand for the immediate immersing of penitent sinners."[76] Elsewhere he reiterated this requirement that salvation cannot be reduced to conversion, but that it is a dance between blood, water, and Name: "The blood and the Name of Jesus are inseparable. To be saved by water baptism, it must be administered in the name of Jesus.... It is not by water only, but by water and blood, and the blood is connected with His Name."[77] In other places, he included Spirit-baptism as the synonym for the Johannine "birth of the Spirit."

One significant development in the early formulation of the new birth doctrine is related to the relationship between repentance and baptism in the Acts 2:38 pattern. In order to hold both acts of faith together in this complex but integrated doctrine of salvation, Haywood distinguished between the biblical concepts of "forgiveness" and "remission" of sins. He likened forgiveness to the atonement sacrifice that was required each year under the Old Covenant. While God does not hold our sins against us, they still remain. An act of "remission" is required to remove them effectually. This, Haywood argued, is the symbiotic relationship between repentance and baptism: "The forgiveness of sins is to 'cease to hold the sins against' an offender after he has confessed and acknowledged his wrong; but the 'remission of sins' is to TAKE AWAY the sins out of one's life ...We may have our sins forgiven by confession and repentance, but the only way the Bible teaches for a man to obtain the 'remission' or 'washing away' of his sins, is by being baptized in water 'in the name of Jesus Christ.'"[78]

---

[76] Haywood, "The Word of God," *Voice in the Wilderness* (n.d., ca. 1918).

[77] Haywood, "A Uniform World Religion," *Voice in the Wilderness* 2/13 (1920): 11.

[78] Haywood, "Forgiveness and Remission of Sins," *Voice in the Wilderness* 2 (1920): 1.

This article is particularly illuminating in that the distinction between forgiveness and remission is reminiscent of Durham's view of sanctification. Durham claimed, as did Kenyon, that the "old man" or "Adamic nature" was removed, not just suppressed or juridically nullified. As Kenyon described it, the atonement secured for us both "legal" and "vital" righteousness. In Haywood, we can detect a reappropriation of these two soteriological functions of grace – forgiveness that legally reckons one guiltless in the act of repentance, and remission that removes the sin in the obedient act of baptism. In this new birth version of Acts 2:38, Durham's initializing of sanctification was retained as well as his emphasis on water baptism as an essential aspect of the believer's identification with Christ (Rom. 6:4 and Acts 2:38). Whereas Durham had incorporated both justification and sanctification in the first great experience of conversion, Haywood reassigned them to repentance and baptism respectively, under the salvific acts of forgiveness and remission of sins. In his earliest years, Urshan did not draw such distinction between forgiveness and remission. His 1921 monograph on the new birth makes no mention of it. According to his son, Nathaniel Urshan, it was not until some years later that he "understood the significance of 'remission' in Acts 2:38."[79]

In reviewing the two Oneness streams of interpretation of Acts 2:38 – Identification and New Birth – it is clear that Durham's influence lingered in important aspects of early Oneness soteriology. This gives some credence to the suggestion that this perceived wayward child of the early Pentecostal Revival embodies in important ways more faithfully than others the legacy of Durham and his Finished Work of Calvary teaching.

e. The Name and Baptismal Regeneration
Not only was the Oneness insistence on the efficacy of baptism uncongenial to the ears of the Assemblies of God but it also drew the charge of "baptismal regeneration."[80] Because their understanding of Acts 2:38 made it difficult to reduce the new birth to the spiritual born again experience of Revivalism, Oneness Pentecostals were forced to incorporate baptism into their salvation scheme in some integral way.

---

[79] Interview with Nathaniel Urshan, Calvary Tabernacle, Indianapolis, IN, 23 May 1973. Fudge traces the popularity of this innovative, but exegetically indefensible, interpretation from the 1940's through the 1980's among some Oneness thinkers. See Fudge, *Christianity without a Cross*, pp. 164-74.

[80] B.F. Lawrence, "Meat in Due Season Corrected," *Weekly Evangel* 202 (11 August 1917): 9; see Brumback, *Suddenly*, p. 192.

They first denied the charge of baptismal regeneration by affirming that the efficacy is in the *Name*, not the water. Urshan described the distinction between the two as that between essence and mode. While water is the "true mode of Baptism,"[81] the "essence of Baptism is in the Name of Jesus and not in the water, and the Name of Jesus is the saving Name of God our Saviour."[82] Water baptism did not save one, but it was the "symbolic way to salvation when one is dipped in the name of Christ," and it became "the test of a genuine faith and submission to the will of God."[83] The efficacy or "power" was not in the water but "in the faith of obedience in the name of the Lord Jesus."[84]

While they rejected a mechanical view of the effects of baptism, they understood it to be more than the believer's response of a good conscience toward God. Baptism in Jesus' name incorporated both the believer's act of *obedience* in faith toward God and God's act of *remission* of sin. Repentance and baptism, therefore, were inseparable as part of "New Testament born again salvation."[85] As Urshan taught, "Baptism and the real obedience go together and it takes both with Faith in the Name of Jesus Christ to save the repented sinner."[86] Indeed, both Urshan and Haywood taught that Acts 2:38 was the one way to enter the Church or Kingdom of God (cf. John 3:5).[87]

What status did such a doctrine accord Trinitarian believers? The difference was handled theologically in two ways. Haywood and Urshan based their theology of Acts 2:38 upon the belief that the threefold action constituted the new birth. Following the analogy, they drew a distinction between "begotten" or "conception" and "birth."[88] While begetting was from the father's side, the mother gave

---

[81] Urshan, *Doctrine of the New Birth*, p. 35.

[82] Urshan, "Twenty-seven Questions and Answers on the New Birth," *The Pentecostal Outlook* 12 (August 1943): 11. See also Haywood, "A Uniform World Religion."

[83] Urshan, *Apostolic Faith Doctrine of the New Birth* (By the Author, n.d.; reprint ed., Portland, OR: Apostolic Book Corner, n.d.): 14.

[84] Urshan, *Doctrine of the New Birth*, p. 13.

[85] Urshan, *Apostolic Faith Doctrine*, p. 14; see Ewart, "The Significance of Water Baptism," p. 12.

[86] Urshan, *Doctrine of the New Birth*, p. 34.

[87] Urshan, *Doctrine of the New Birth*; Haywood, *Birth of the Spirit*, p. 7. Both Urshan and Haywood taught that the "Church" is synonymous with the "Kingdom of God."

[88] This analogy has been used as early as Spener in 17th-century Pietism. Dale Brown summarizes: "In the mysterious process of regeneration there is a moment of complete passivity in a person which gives room to the omnipotent working of God. The decisive metaphor which serves as an approximation of Luther's *sola gratia* is not birth, but conception." Spener made the comparison to distinguish between "declared justification" and being "born again," the latter which represented a "completion and enhancement of

birth. Observing that many children who were conceived were never born, Haywood spiritualized the analogy to show that "many may have been begotten by the word but have never been born of the Spirit." While the Word may have begun life in many, the church (mother) "has had no 'strength' to bring them forth."[89]

Urshan adopted the same analogy, concluding that one who has not appropriated the blood, water and Spirit "cannot be the proper and full pledged child of God." Yet the Word of God has produced "spiritual conception."[90] He acknowledged that one who had not received the baptism of the Spirit was still a child of God, stating that "the difference is not in the relationship but in the fulness of life, or in the development of the spiritual condition."[91]

The second approach was based on the doctrine of the resurrection of the dead. Applying the Dispensational doctrine of the "Rapture" of the church or the "first resurrection," Haywood assured those who had never received the baptism of the Holy Spirit that "they take part in the last resurrection, and are given eternal life, while those filled with the Spirit have part in the first resurrection,"[92] thereby escaping the Great Tribulation period. The full requirement for the first resurrection was baptism "by both water and the Spirit."[93] Those who entered the Kingdom at the second resurrection included "all the righteous men of all ages who walked in all the light that they were given."[94] These included pagans, Jews and Christians of earlier genera-

---

the equally biblical juridical metaphor of justification," in *Understanding Pietism*, pp. 98-99. Like Wesley after him, the analogy was a useful heuristic tool to urge nominal Christians into a fuller life in Christ.

[89] Haywood, *Birth of the Spirit*, p. 11

[90] Urshan, *Apostolic Faith Doctrine*, pp. 13, 14.

[91] Urshan, "The New Birth and the Kingdom of God," *Witness of God* 2 (September 1921): 1. This statement strongly suggests that, in the early years, Acts 2:38 was generally understood as the charter for "full" salvation, not salvation proper. The rhetoric from the Trinitarian side accusing Oneness leaders of teaching that persons were not "saved" unless they were baptized in Jesus' name, suggests that there was much confusion on this point. It is probable that some enthusiastic Oneness preachers claimed exclusive rights to heaven for those who obeyed Acts 2:38, and likely many more Trinitarians heard the message that way. With the "evangelicalization" of the Pentecostal movement, the concept of full salvation has been pushed to the margins – a movement that is undoubtedly affecting the white segment of Oneness Pentecostals in particular. The result is the loss of categories within which to do theological reflection on a wide range of issues, including the status of those Christians who do not accept the Oneness message.

[92] Haywood, "Editorial," *Christian Outlook* 2 (April 1924): 325.

[93] Haywood, "First and Second Resurrection," *Christian Outlook* 1 (April 1923): 4.

[94] *Ibid.*; see *Birth of the Spirit*, p. 12.

tions. Haywood remained silent, however, on the status of the Trinitarian Pentecostals who had received Spirit-baptism.

Urshan believed so strongly that one must have the baptism of the Holy Spirit to enter eternal life, that the unbaptized who have walked faithfully in the light given them will receive their Spirit-baptism at the moment of resurrection, "shouting glory in the Heavenly language." That person's status, however, will be the same as the Old Testament saints, not "those who have been born of water and the Spirit." [95]

f. The Name and Persecution

Religious persecution and intolerance were not new to the first generation of Pentecostals. What they received at the hand of newspaper writers, cranky neighbors and irritable police was more than matched by scathing attacks from leaders within the Pentecostal fraternity. They continued to draw strength from the accounts of persecution and triumph in the Apostolic church.

Most of the New Issue leaders had already endured the onslaughts of rejection when they threw in their lot with Durham. In 1912, Ewart gave a dramatic report of the "bitter hostility" the Finished Work message was encountering along the West Coast from Oakland to Seattle:

> The finished work of Calvary was the issue, and many were the stories of the reproach and suffering that standing for this truth has entailed.... Brethren, this truth is of heavenly birth, and these are its birth-marks.... This truth has cost the church her richest blood.... This present message is God's ultimatum. The world will reject it, and God's ambassadors, and we will be called home. [96]

Now as part of the Oneness movement, leaders were able to credit the experience of rejection and reproach to their intimate association with the name of Jesus. Recalling accounts of apostolic persecutions for preaching in the name of Jesus (Acts 4:18, 5:28), they were convinced that persecution would naturally accompany their message. Urshan passionately warned the Oneness movement: "O beloved, the day is coming upon us soon, when we shall be singled out and bitterly hated by all men for that worthy Name, and probably suffer the loss of everything and even death for it." [97]

---

[95] Urshan, "New Birth and Kingdom," p. 1.
[96] Ewart, "The Work on the Coast," *Good Report* 1/3 (1912): 6.
[97] Urshan, *Almighty God*, pp. 56, 69; *Autobiography*, pp. 245-46.

Ewart, likewise, warned of those who hated the name of Jesus "with such an inveterate hatred that they would murder men for preaching it." He referred to Oneness missionaries being persecuted by other missionaries, to his own legal "persecution" by imprisonment for disturbing the peace with the large tent services in Los Angeles, and to the persecution of the Pentecostal movement by modernism.[98] Urshan did not hesitate to list the General Council of the Assemblies of God with the other persecutors of the Name. Calling Oneness believers the "faithful remnant," he charged the Assemblies of God with "accusing us through their magazines of wrong doing, seeking to stain our God-given character."[99]

Appeals to apostolic persecution for the name of Jesus, and reminders of the hostility generated by the rejection of 1916, provided early Oneness leaders with a way to account for the external criticism and any inferiority complex that may have resulted from that schism.

3. Summary

The new Oneness teachers attempted to turn classical Trinitarian Christology on its head by charging it with a kind of subordination-ism. A doctrine of three "equal" Persons in the Godhead could only subvert the "supreme" and "absolute" deity of Christ. They heralded the christological hymn of Col. 2:9 (in Christ all the "fullness of God" dwells) as the key to the revelation of God in Christ.

The name of Jesus was the heart of their Christology, but also the distinctive centerpiece of their soteriology. The apostolic "plan" of full salvation was the threefold pattern set forth in Acts 2:38. At this point, the Oneness movement divided into two schools of interpretation – identification and new birth. The insistence upon re-baptism by all and, at least in Haywood and Urshan, the belief in Acts 2:38 as the new birth, made this aspect of the new teaching the most offensive of all their doctrines. They championed a theology of salvation that, in its exclusivity, accorded all other Christians second-class status. But in each stream can be discerned the imprint of Durham's Finished Work teaching.

Rejection has its consequences. At the Fourth General Council, the New Issue ceased to be a family squabble. It was voted "outside the camp," only to reappear as a new and third alternative within a Re-

---

[98] Ewart, *Name and Book*, pp. 7, 45, 41, 64, 67.
[99] Urshan, *Almighty God*, p. 71; see *Autobiography*, p. 245.

vival that was barely a decade old. In the next chapter we will trace the organizational beginnings of this third stream of Pentecostalism.

10

From Issue to Organization

> One mind, one strength, and no division.
> One mind, one strength, and no division.
> One mind, one strength, and no division.
> That they all, that they all may be one.[1]
>
>   – David and Worthy Rowe

The expulsion of the New Issue from the Assemblies of God fellowship precipitated the birth of the third trajectory of modern Pentecostalism. The Assemblies of God would now be able to contend with their antagonists from a distance. That distance was long for two reasons. First, the New Issue teaching was sufficiently innovative that it created for adherent and opponent alike a boundary that restricted fellowship. Relentless accusations of heresy and apostasy produced the same distancing effect. The second reason is that organizational embodiment provided for the new movement an independence that allowed each stream to proceed unencumbered by countervailing forces. Those who had shared platforms and pulpits were now like distant relatives.

1. Organizational Beginnings

The adherents of the new doctrine were scattered only temporarily as they left the Fourth General Council of the Assemblies of God. Amidst rumors of their demise, they reappeared within a few months in organizational form. Under the leadership of such men as H.A. Goss, H.G. Rogers, and D.C.O. Opperman, who had been instrumental in the formation of the Assemblies of God less than three years earlier, a call for an organizational meeting was made for December

---

[1] David and Worthy Rowe, *"One Mind – One Strength – No Division"* (Apostolic Temple Church, Inc., 1973). This chorus was composed as a theme song for the Apostolic World Christian Fellowship.

28, 1916, in Eureka Springs, Arkansas. On January 3, 1917, business
was transacted for the organization of the General Assembly of the
Apostolic Assemblies.[2] The 154 names listed in the Ministerial record
represented ministers, missionaries, elders, deacons and evangelists.
Frank Ewart was counted among the ministers but held no official
position.

The immediate need for most of the ministers was an organization
with the legal status to issue ministerial credentials. But the timing was
complicated by the pending involvement of the country in the First
World War. The new group had been organized too late to receive
"proper recognition for the ministers of military age."[3] Fortunately, a
number of those present were also members of the Pentecostal Assemblies of the World. By now most of them had embraced the new
Oneness message, especially Ewart and Haywood. Haywood later
claimed that he had never held credentials with the Assemblies of God,
but only "P.A.ofW. credentials since 1911."[4] Probably in no small part
due to his influence with both the P.A.ofW. fellowship and the disen-
franchised ministers from the Assemblies of God, by 1918 the
P.A.ofW. was doctrinally ready to assimilate the membership of the
General Assembly of the Apostolic Assemblies.

The call went out to all Oneness Pentecostals to meet in St. Louis,
Missouri, in January of 1918. Although it disavowed any "intention of
forming a new organization," its real purpose was soon evident.[5] By
the end of the conference the two groups had merged, retaining the
title, "Pentecostal Assemblies of the World."[6] Three Oneness periodicals were being published during this time by members of the
organization – Ewart's *Meat in Due Season,* Haywood's *Voice in the
Wilderness,* and D.C.O. Opperman's *The Blessed Truth.* At its annual
meeting in 1919, the organization officially recognized all three.[7]

With Haywood as the prominent black leader in the movement, the
new organization was destined to be an experiment in racial integra-

---

[2] *Minute Book and Ministerial Record of the General Assembly of the Apostolic Assemblies* (By
the Organization, n.d.); Arthur L. Clanton, *United We Stand – A History of Oneness Organizations* (Hazelwood, MO: Pentecostal Publishing House, 1970), pp. 23-26; Fred J.
Foster, *"Think It Not Strange,"* pp. 73-74.

[3] Foster, *"Think It Not Strange,"* p. 73.

[4] Golder, *History,* p. 36.

[5] *Ibid.,* p. 46.

[6] Golder, *History,* pp; 46-49; Clanton, *United We Stand,* pp. 27-29.

[7] See "Second Annual Convention, Jan. 16-26, 1919," in *Minute Book 1919 (1907-
1919) – Pentecostal Assemblies of the World.*

tion.[8] The black membership was noticeably increasing on the rolls by 1919.[9] Synan claims that this circumstance turned the young Pentecostal Assemblies of the World into "one of the most fully interracial church bodies in the United States."[10]

While Ewart and Haywood had been present from the time of the merger in 1918, Andrew Urshan did not leave the ranks of the Assemblies of God until the early part of 1919. Due perhaps to his early association with evangelicals in Chicago as well as his alignment with Durham's Finished Work, Urshan's christocentric beliefs were evident early on. In a sermon preached at the convention in the Stone Church, Chicago, in 1911, he emphasized the work of the Spirit in revealing Jesus: "Beloved, let us walk in the Spirit, talk in the Spirit, think in the Spirit, sing in the Spirit, preach in the Spirit, testify in the Spirit, doing all things in the Spirit and in the understanding, and you will see Jesus."[11] The same attention to Jesus could be heard six years later. He took a familiar chorus as his theme:

> Jesus only, Jesus ever;
> Jesus all in all we sing;
> Saviour, Baptiser and Healer,
> Glorious Lord and coming King.

His single-minded focus on Jesus was evident throughout the sermon. In it, he declared that Spirit-baptism was the power that stirred the heart to exult in and exalt Jesus only:

> This holy thing [the Spirit within him] loves nothing but Jesus, and everything that has not Jesus in it has no charm for me. I can't read any book that is not about Him. If I read it I will hunt for Jesus Christ, but if I can't find Him, I will put the book aside.... The only thing that can stir this heart is Jesus.[12]

In a circular that Urshan distributed after he left the Assemblies of God, he acknowledged that, in Bell's words, he was "simply coming out with what was being put in his heart FOR YEARS."[13] In the same letter, he reported that he had been re-baptized in 1915 in Leningrad

---

[8] Clanton, *United We Stand*, p. 28; Foster, *"Think It Not Strange,"* pp. 74-75; Golder, *History*, p. 49.

[9] Golder, *History*, p. 53.

[10] Robert Mapes Anderson, *Vision of the Disinherited*, p. 191; Synan, *Holiness-Pentecostal Tradition*, p. 172.

[11] Urshan, "We Would See Jesus," *Latter Rain Evangel* 3 (June 1911): 9-11.

[12] Urshan, "United In and With Christ," *The Weekly Evangel* (15 December 1917): 4.

[13] E.N. Bell,"The Urshan Trouble," *Christian Evangel* 288 and 289 (17 May 1919): 6-7.

(then, Petrograd) while on his Russian mission trip.[14] Years later, he stated that he had also begun to baptize converts in Jesus' name. The numbers initially were not large – "180 souls in ice cold water" – but he was able to report that a revival had swelled their ranks to over a thousand by 1924.[15]

Following his return from Persia and Russia, he continued to preach and fellowship within Assemblies of God circles. He applied for and was issued ministerial credentials with the Assemblies of God in September of 1917.[16] When asked in his application whether he endorsed the Statement of Fundamental Truths approved at the 1916 General Council, he forthrightly stated, "Yes, except that I do not object [to] the formula which is written in Acts 2:38. Not as the New Issue folks explain it but simply because it is [the] written Word of God."[17]

As the months passed, he came under increasing suspicion of holding sympathies with the New Issue teaching. To answer the criticisms, he published a statement of belief in *The Weekly Evangel*, dissociating himself from any connection with "the advocates of the 'new issue' so-called." He affirmed his allegiance to the "one God, the Father, the Son and the Holy Ghost," who can be "only approached and seen *in* and *through* the person or face of Jesus Christ, the son."[18] He publicly

---

[14] E.N. Bell, "Andrew Urshan's New Stand," *Christian Evangel* 284 and 285 (19 April 1919): 9; J.L. Hall, "Urshan, Andrew David," *New International Dictionary of Pentecostal and Charismatic Movements*, p. 1167.

[15] Urshan, "Missionary Supplement," *Christian Outlook* 1/12 (January 1924): 3.

[16] "Certificate of Ordination," and "Application," Archives of the Assemblies of God, Springfield, MO. The Certificate certifies that Urshan was originally ordained as "Evangelist" in 1913, which he stated occurred at the 1913 World-Wide Camp Meeting in Los Angeles by an organization called, Rescue Mission Workers of America. There is a discrepancy in the Assemblies of God records, as one form indicates that William Durham ordained him in 1913. Since Durham died in 1912, Hall adjusts the date to 1910. Urshan's own account in the application, however, dates his ordination to 1913 at the Arroyo Seco Camp Meeting. It is possible, of course, that there were two ordinations by different ordaining bodies. The Assemblies of God Ministerial record indicates that Urshan's annual credentials were renewed in 1918 and 1919.

[17] Andrew Urshan, "Confession of Faith," *Weekly Evangel* 236 and 237 (20 April 1918): 13.

[18] Urshan, "Confession of Faith." His reference to the "face of Jesus Christ" suggests that he may have already been reading J. Monro Gibson, whose christocentric Trinitarian view emphasized the "face" of Christ as the only *visible* dimension of the triune revelation of God. Urshan published an essay by Gibson under the title, "The Trinity of Christ," *The Witness of God* 4/43 (July 1923): 4.

defended his christocentric baptismal practice on the basis of Paul's directive in Col. 3:17, to "do all in the Name of the Lord Jesus."

Urshan's reasons for desiring to remain in the Assemblies of God fellowship are not clear. Since he was an evangelist, it would certainly have provided a larger constituency of support for his ministry. His reluctance to leave may have been based upon a hope that the Executive would be lenient toward his baptismal practice.[19] This, however, was not the opinion of E.N. Bell and other Assemblies of God members, when he finally resigned in 1919. In two consecutive articles in *The Christian Evangel*, Bell denounced Urshan for being deceptive – though not purposely – for many years regarding his private beliefs, misleading the General Council, and creating a spirit of division by practicing re-baptism.[20] It is likely that Urshan was first persuaded of the necessity for using the christocentric name in baptism, but that he remained at least ambivalent about the New Issue doctrines until some time later. Following the relinquishing of his credentials, he immediately joined the ranks of the Pentecostal Assemblies of the World.[21]

Franklin Small, a Canadian from Winnipeg, continued to hold credentials with the Pentecostal Assemblies of the World for a number of years. The purpose was primarily for fellowship, as he had formed his own Oneness organization under a Canadian charter in 1921.[22] Though the reasons are unclear, Ewart's name did not appear on the roster from 1920 onwards.[23]

2. The Issue of Race

The years from 1920 to 1924 gradually revealed serious racial tensions within the restructured organization. More blacks were joining the ranks as a result of Haywood's influence and his moving the headquarters from Portland, Oregon, to Indianapolis.[24] This meant a national demographic shift in which "the blacks ... constituted a majority in the North, while the whites bulked larger in the South."[25]

---

[19] This is the reason given by his son, Nathaniel Urshan. Interview at Calvary Tabernacle, Indianapolis, IN, 23 May 1973.

[20] Bell, "Andrew Urshan's New Stand," and "The Urshan Trouble."

[21] His name appears on the ministerial list of the Pentecostal Assemblies of the World in 1920; Golder, *History*, p. 67.

[22] Larden, *Our Apostolic Heritage*, p. 92.

[23] Golder, *History*, p. 71.

[24] *Ibid.*, p. 67.

[25] Anderson, *Vision of the Disinherited*, p. 191; see Synan, *Holiness-Pentecostal Tradition*, p. 172.

Because of segregation policies in the South, it was practically impossible to hold an integrated convention in that part of the country.
Consequently, the annual conventions were held in the North, which
strained the financial resources of the southern white ministers to attend each year. Tensions were aggravated in 1921 when the southern
white constituency scheduled a Bible Conference in Little Rock, Arkansas, for November 3-12, 1922. The stated purpose was "to work
for greater unity.... The south had long looked and hoped for true
fellowship and unity and we believe this meeting will do a great deal
to bring it about."[26] But while it did unify the southern fellowship, it
deepened the growing rift with the blacks.[27] The undercurrents of
racial unrest began to appear in a number of ways throughout the organization – misunderstandings, false reports, and complaints over
black officials signing ministerial credentials for southern white ministers.[28] The issue of credential signing was particularly sensitive, as
Haywood was General Secretary at this time.

The tension mounted as the ministers gathered for the annual meeting in St. Louis, October 4-6, 1923. Undoubtedly inspired by the
southern Bible Conference, a compromise resolution was passed that
recommended a "division by color" in the matter of signing credentials. The policy would be that "two white Presbyters sign the
credentials for the white brethren (especially in the southland) and two
colored Presbyters sign the papers for the colored brethren."[29] The
final decision was that two ministers, T.C. Davis (black) and H.A.
Goss (white), be authorized to sign the certificates for those who demanded it. Others were processed normally.[30] But this small
compromise solution was not sufficient to stem the tide of dissension
as they prepared for the annual meeting of 1924. Rumors of a split
were noised throughout the ranks.[31] Within a month of the meeting,

---

[26] Taken from a pamphlet comprising the minutes and events of the conference by
William E. Booth-Clibborn, *A Call to the Dust and Ashes* (St. Paul, MN: Privately published, 1922), p. 2; cited in James L. Tyson, *The Early Pentecostal Revival: History of
Twentieth-Century Pentecostals and The Pentecostal Assemblies of the World, 1901-30* (Hazelwood, MO: Word Aflame, 1992), p. 257.

[27] Foster, "*Think It Not Strange,*" pp. 75-76; Clanton, *United We Stand*, pp. 29-30.

[28] Golder, *History*, pp. 67-68, 71, 78.

[29] *Minute Book of the Pentecostal Assemblies of the World, 1922-1923*, p. 10. There were a
few white ministers who disapproved of the resolution, Tyson, *Early Pentecostal Revival*, p.
244.

[30] Haywood, "An Open Letter," *Christian Outlook* 1 (October 1923): 208.

[31] Haywood, "Division Coming?" *Christian Outlook* 2 (June 1924): 374; Haywood,
"One Convention," *Christian Outlook* 2 (August, 1924): 418.

Haywood was sounding a note of pessimism – "It may be the last united Convention."[32]

Immediately prior to the Conference, the white constituency from Texas met in Houston to draw up an alternate proposal. It recommended changing the name of the organization, but, more offensively for the black constituency, it proposed restructuring into two racially separated administrations under one organization.[33] The General Conference convened in Chicago on October 14-19, 1924. The proposal made it to the floor of the General Conference, but served only to ignite a major confrontation that resulted in the final schism. The majority of the whites withdrew to Andrew Urshan's church in Chicago, cutting the rolls of the Pentecostal Assemblies of the World by over 50%.[34] The new, white organization that emerged from the dissident group was called The Apostolic Churches of Jesus Christ.[35] The name was changed again a year later to The Pentecostal Ministerial Alliance, when they discovered that another church by that name had been registered.[36]

The schism of 1924 left a legacy of hostility on both sides. It was a particular affront to the black members who had struggled so tirelessly to maintain the unity of the fragile movement.[37] As the white members rationalized it, they were relieved to be free of racial handicap in the South, in order that they might evangelize more effectively and "spread the glorious gospel."[38]

[32] Haywood, "Editorial," *Christian Outlook* 2 (September 1924): 441.

[33] Clanton, *United We Stand*, pp. 31-32; Tyson, *Early Pentecostal Revival*, p. 247. This is the same proposal that was implemented by the Church of God (Cleveland, TN) for many years, Synan, *Holiness-Pentecostal Tradition*, p. 172.

[34] *Minute Book of the Pentecostal Assemblies of the World*, 1924 (By the Organization, n.d.); Golder, *History*, pp. 82-83.

[35] "Minutes of Meeting, October 16 and 17, 1924," *Witness of God* 6/59 (November 1924): 2.

[36] Reported in *Witness of God* 7/62 (March 1925): 13; Clanton, *United We Stand*, p. 36.

[37] Haywood, "New Organizations," *Christian Outlook* 2 (October 1924): 466; Haywood, "United Methodism – North and South," *Christian Outlook* 2 (November 1924): 481; Haywood, "Unity," *Christian Outlook* 3 (July 1925): 124; Haywood, "To Our Brethren of Color," *Christian Outlook* 4 (January 1926): 3.

[38] Clanton, *United We Stand*, p. 33. This was the rationale used as well by W.E. Kidson. He illustrated by relating an event in which he was harassed by the police and mayor of a southern city for holding an integrated service; interview at the headquarters of the International Ministerial Alliance, 1312 North Sixty-seventh Street, Houston, TX, 6 July 1973.

3. Segregation and Re-Organization

The years from 1924 to 1931 were slow, struggling years for both segments of the movement. Growth was slow for the Pentecostal Assemblies of the World in particular.[39] While the white segment grew faster, there was a fractious spirit among its members. One pastor in Malvern, Arkansas, confessed in 1930 to have gotten "so discouraged over the division among the brethren that I decided to go into the Trinity movement."[40] However, by 1930 he was sufficiently heartened by the progress in the Oneness movement to remain within its ranks.

While the predominantly black constituency continued in the Pentecostal Assemblies of the World, the white segment divided quickly into two main groups. By 1925 there was dissatisfaction with the Pentecostal Ministerial Association for being primarily a ministerial fellowship with no provision for congregational affiliation. The result was the formation of Emmanuel's Church in Jesus Christ, a group of ministers representing the tri-state region of Oklahoma, Texas and Louisiana.[41] It in turn merged in 1927 with a small group that had been formed in St. Louis, under the new name of Apostolic Church of Jesus Christ.[42] This group tended to emphasize the "new birth teaching," which equated the water and Spirit-baptisms in Acts 2:38 with being born again, though there were exceptions to this teaching within the membership.[43]

The Pentecostal Ministerial Alliance was a looser association, with little centralized authority. Its attitude toward the "new birth teaching" of Acts 2:38 was mixed, many believing that it was important only that believers walk in the light they had. The new birth would have been constituted by a conversion experience apart from water baptism and the baptism of the Holy Spirit.[44] In 1932, the organization

---

[39] The number of names on the official lists from 1925 to 1930 remain substantially the same, *Minute Book of the Pentecostal Assemblies of the World, 1925-1930* (By the Organization, n.d.).

[40] Claude P. Kilgore, "Letter," *Apostolic Herald* 5 (March 1930): 9.

[41] G.C. Stroud, "By Way of Explanation Concerning the Movement Formulated at Houston, Texas," *Pentecostal Witness* 2 (1 February 1926): 1-2; Clanton, *United We Stand*, pp. 52-61.

[42] Editor, "General Joint Convention Report," *Pentecostal Witness* 4 (1 December 1927): 8; Clanton, *United We Stand*, pp. 59-61.

[43] Foster, *"Think It Not Strange,"* p. 85.

[44] W.E. Kidson, "The Pentecostal Ministerial Alliance, Inc.," *Apostolic Herald* 2 (January 1927): 3; Clanton, *United We Stand*, p. 47; Foster, *"Think It Not Strange,"* p. 78.

was restructured to provide greater organizational strength, at which time it changed its name to Pentecostal Church, Inc.[45]

4. Attempts to Re-Unite and Further Fragmentation

There was continued dissatisfaction and unrest throughout this period as the small movement saw itself in its dividedness and not in its unity. As early as 1926, an abortive merger attempt was made between the Pentecostal Ministerial Alliance and Emmanuel's Church of Jesus Christ.[46] Another attempt was made between the two groups in 1930, but it too failed.[47] To their credit, the desire for unity among the various factions of the new movement had not died. Undoubtedly the fragmentation into small, struggling groups was depleting their resources.

Correspondence was exchanged between The Pentecostal Ministerial Alliance and the Apostolic Church of Jesus Christ in the fall of 1930, which eventually led to a large Unity Conference of all Oneness Pentecostals in September 1931, in Columbus, Ohio. The hope was that the badly fractured movement might be inspired toward unity.[48] From that meeting came a surge of negotiations. Both white groups then turned to the Pentecostal Assemblies of the World. The Pentecostal Ministerial Alliance proposed a separate administrative system similar to the proposal in 1924.[49] However, the enthusiasm was apparently less than whole-hearted, and the proposal failed in the negotiation stage.[50]

Almost simultaneously the Apostolic Church of Jesus Christ (formerly Emmanuel's Church) organized a special meeting with the ministers of the Pentecostal Assemblies of the World. On November 18, 1931, a merger was quickly accomplished, and its name changed to the Pentecostal Assemblies of Jesus Christ.[51] The principles adopted provided for an integration of racial balance into one administrative system, not two separate ones. But the new merger had been so hastily

---

[45] Kidson, "The Eighth Annual Conference," *Apostolic Herald* 8 (February 1933): 4.

[46] "Consolidation of Emmanuel's Church in Jesus Christ and Pentecostal Ministerial Alliance at Present Impossible," *Pentecostal Witness* 3 (1 December 1926): 3; Oliver F. Fauss, "Letter from P.M.A.," *Pentecostal Witness* 3 (1 January 1927): 1-2.

[47] Kidson, "Minutes of the Conference," *Apostolic Herald* 6 (November 1931): 5-7; Clanton, *United We Stand*, pp. 107-11.

[48] "Unity Conference," *Pentecostal Witness* 7 (September 1931): 13.

[49] Kidson, "Minutes of the Conference," pp. 5-7.

[50] Kidson, Interview.

[51] "The St. Louis Conference," *Pentecostal Outlook* 10 (January 1932): 2-3, 14.

devised that major decisions were made without due process. Consequently, the new creature was soon being attacked by certain members
of the Pentecostal Assemblies of the World as "illegal and unofficial."[52]
Black leaders claimed that the notice of the meeting had been given
without sufficient notice or proper sanction from the General Convention. The swiftness with which the meeting was called raised
suspicion and fear by blacks that insincerity and opportunism were the
motives of the white organization.[53] The leaders of the newly organized group denounced the rumors in a counter-charge, claiming that
"the legality of this conference cannot be questioned, and it will stand
the test of any court."[54]

But the charges, the compromise to change the name of the organization, and the abandonment of the episcopal form of government
practiced since 1925 were too much for many black leaders to bear. A
few ministers, including Samuel Grimes, E.F. Akers and A.W. Lewis,
took swift action to consider re-organization. In the midst of the turmoil, the original Pentecostal Assemblies of the World charter had
disappeared. It was eventually found in the home of a person who was
apparently unaware of its value, and was quickly salvaged just prior to
its expiration date. There was immediate suspicion of foul play, as
Pentecostal Assemblies of the World supporters hurled accusations that
the charter had been "stolen and hidden away."[55] The re-organization
meeting was held in Dayton, Ohio, and the Pentecostal Assemblies of
the World was re-established under its original charter and given the
motivation to begin again under its zealous leaders.

The newly formed organization, the Pentecostal Assemblies of Jesus
Christ, was able to continue. But owing to the selection of the southern city of Tulsa, Oklahoma, as the site of the 1937 General
Convention, black ministers from the North were politely informed
that there were no integrated accommodations. With this affront,
nearly all of the Pentecostal Assemblies of the World leaders who had
joined the new experiment returned home.[56] Except for a counter-
proposal made by the Pentecostal Assemblies of the World in 1932
(which was rejected), no further efforts between the two groups were

---

[52] W.T. Witherspoon, "Official Board Meeting," *Pentecostal Outlook* 1 (April 1932): 12.
[53] Golder, Interview, Grace Apostolic Church, Indianapolis, IN, 22 May 1973.
[54] "Our Organization," *Pentecostal Outlook* 1 (April 1932): 4.
[55] Golder, *History*, p. 97.
[56] Clanton, *United We Stand*, p. 86.

made. All that lingered was the accumulated bitterness from failed attempts to bridge the racial divide organizationally.[57]

Two other occasions weakened the early leadership of the Pentecostal Assemblies of the World. The first was the loss of R.C. Lawson, a prominent black pastor in Columbus, Ohio, who left the organization in 1919 over a dispute with Haywood regarding marriage and divorce, with Lawson stating that re-marriage is not allowable under any circumstance.[58] He moved to New York City, where he founded the Refuge Temple Church of Our Lord Jesus Christ, which later became the mother Church for the organization, Church of Our Lord Jesus Christ of the Apostolic Faith, Inc.[59] Lawson remained Presiding Bishop until his death in 1961.

The second loss was a schism in 1957, in which Bishop S.N. Hancock left the P.A.ofW. during a power struggle over the selection of Presiding Bishop. Controversy also centered on his own peculiar version of adoptionist christology, which had been denounced by the leadership. A number of churches and ministers followed Hancock in the forming of the Pentecostal Churches of the Apostolic Faith Association, Inc.[60]

With the unsuccessful attempts at a merger during this period, the white segment continued in two organizations, the Pentecostal Assemblies of Jesus Christ (mostly white membership by 1937) and the Pentecostal Church, Inc. (formerly the Pentecostal Ministerial Alliance). The only other effort to unite prior to 1944 was in 1936, which again was unsuccessful.[61]

The only significant schism within the white constituency during this period was led by L.R. Ooton of Indiana, in 1941. He took nearly one thousand ministers from the tri-state region of Indiana, Ohio and West Virginia, making his organization the third largest Oneness group at the time. Ooton began his ministry in the Pentecostal Assemblies of the World, and following the schism joined the white Pentecostal Minsterial Alliance, becoming its first Secretary. He grew increasingly discontent with moderates such as Howard Goss and W.E.

---

[57] The lingering pain was evident in an interview with a former Presiding Bishop of the Pentecostal Assemblies of the World, Ross P. Paddock, at Apostolic Temple, South Bend, IN, 16 May 1974.

[58] Golder, *History*, p. 94.

[59] See *The Discipline Book of the Church of Our Lord Jesus Christ of the Apostolic Faith, Inc.* (rev. ed.; New York: By the Organization, 1969.)

[60] Golder, *History*, pp. 140-42.

[61] Clanton, *United We Stand*, pp. 113-15.

Kidson who did not preach Acts 2:38 as the new birth, which led him in 1927 to switch to the Apostolic Church of Jesus Christ. Though he was an official in the newly merged organization, the Pentecostal Assemblies of Jesus Christ (1931), he became displeased with its strong centralized government, especially what he called the "dictatorial methods" of some of the leaders.[62] At about that time he organized a loose ministerial fellowship called the Tri-State Council, which became the basis for his organization, the Apostolic Ministerial Alliance.[63]

5. Formation of United Pentecostal Church

This persistent drive for unity within the three largest Oneness organizations finally bore fruit for the white segment. In 1944 the invitation was extended again by one of the groups, and in September 1945, both organizations, the Pentecostal Assemblies of Jesus Christ and the Pentecostal Church, Inc., strategically held their annual conventions in St. Louis. The result was the birth of the United Pentecostal Church.

The major issue to be overcome was not sociological but theological. The major point of tension was the interpretation of Acts 2:38 as identification or new birth. All agreed on the truth of the practice, but not all could agree that Acts 2:38 constituted the new birth.[64] The two views were largely aligned organizationally, with most of the ministers in the PAJC holding to the new birth teaching and the majority of the PCI constituency embracing the identificationist position. Though this tension has been minimized by the later official interpretation of the merger, Fudge claims that the contest was vigorous, each side fearing that the other would gain supremacy under the new arrangement. Much of Fudge's study comprises oral interviews that complement and

[62] Interview with L.R. Ooton at his home in Tipton, IN, 17 May 1974. Ooton reported that he confronted W.T. Witherspoon and S.G. Norris about their "dictatorial methods."

[63] Interview, Ooton; Interview with Kidson. There is a discrepancy regarding the date when Ooton left the PMA; Ooton states that he left in 1927 following the conference in Indianapolis in which there was sharp disagreement over the new birth teaching. Kidson states that he left the PMA in 1929. Ooton indicates that he had a "division of fellowship" with Franklin Small in Canada over Small's belief in eternal security and holiness standards, shortly before he died.

On a personal note, Ooton and Andrew Urshan were acquaintances of Paul Rader, the evangelical preacher and radio speaker, and often attended Rader's church in Chicago. According to Ooton, Rader acknowledged that he had received the baptism in the Spirit, and had once invited Ooton to visit his church to pray for a "Pentecostal revival." Ironically, this relationship brought the charge of "compromiser" from Witherspoon.

[64] Clanton, *United We Stand*, p. 120.

sometimes challenge the official account of the tensions that led up to the merger. While organizational unity was achieved, it was not accomplished without negotiation and a willingness to make provision for each camp. The merger was indeed to be a test of fraternal compromise.[65]

An indication of the doctrinal challenge facing the new organization is evident in the Statement of Fundamental Doctrine that was finally ratified. A portion of the Statement reads: "We shall endeavor to keep the unity of the Spirit until we all come into the unity of the faith, at the same time admonishing all brethren that they shall not contend for their different views to the disunity of the body."[66] Though the two views have technically continued to co-exist within the organization, the new birth view eventually became the dominant position. It is the official position maintained by most of the leadership appointments, schools and publications. The UPCI owns and operates the only Oneness publishing house, a successful enterprise that reflects in its books and educational material primarily the new birth alternative.[67]

Why did the Identification position, a strong alternative within the Oneness constellation of doctrines in 1945, virtually disappear? We have already suggested reasons for the failure of Ewart and Small to exert a stronger influence in the 1920's and 30's. It is important to note that, while black Oneness groups have faithfully followed Haywood's new birth teaching, they have also continued his generous interpretation of the doctrine with regard to other Christians. The new birth position as represented in the UPCI is a radicalized version of the teaching, accomplished only by suppressing the earlier voices that addressed the spiritual condition of others and resisting any serious

---

[65] Thomas A. Fudge, *Christianity without the Cross: A History of Salvation in Oneness Pentecostalism* (Parkland, FL: Universal Publishers, 2003), pp. 95-100. Fudge's work is a case study of the history of this doctrinal tension within the UPCI. A strength of the study is the valuable information gleaned through extensive oral interviews. This data provides the basis for an alternative interpretation, which at times challenges the official UPCI interpretation of its origins and development. In particular, Fudge records the voice of the "identification" advocates – many of them with close connections to the key players in the merger – and traces the ways in which he argues their presence has been organizationally minimized and marginalized from 1945 to the present. While Fudge's thesis is undoubtedly controversial, its strength lies in the meticulous gathering of the oral history and the alternative story that emerges from it.

[66] Clanton, *United We Stand*, p. 121.

[67] French reports the annual volume of publications: "1.5 million pieces of Sunday School literature, over 123,000 books, 855,000 periodicals, 3,803,000 tracts," in *Our God is One*, p. 109.

theological reflection upon a doctrinal matter of central importance. Fudge points out one reason for the virtual disappearance of the Identification position within the UPCI is that their leading representatives published very little on the core doctrine.[68] Their interest was broader than that of those in the new birth camp who tended to be preoccupied with Acts 2:38. More importantly, they were more tolerant of the diversity and resisted contending for their view, in the spirit of maintaining unity. As Fudge states, "The conclusion is unavoidable: the PAJC, in general, contended for their views while the PCI, concomitantly, continued to live by the merger agreement."[69] Others have suggested that personalities were a factor, that the PCI leaders were "gentler, kindler souls ... who were not contentious by nature ... so they lost."[70] Finally, Fudge concludes that, while the PCI was better organized, its doctrine of Acts 2:38 was less defined.[71] As a result, the lack of clarity eventually became the weakness that a more assertive camp was able to exploit to its advantage.

The United Pentecostal Church suffered two splits in the early years. W.E. Kidson from Houston led the first schism in 1954.[72] Dissatisfied with the growing power and "authoritarianism" of the organization, he formed a small fellowship with twenty ministers who were likewise so disturbed, called the International Ministerial Association.[73] It has continued to provide ministerial fellowship for, but exercise no authority over, its membership. Prominent Texas minister, Murray Burr, initiated a split in 1969 over discontent with the centralized government of the United Pentecostal Church and a desire for

---

[68] Fudge, *Christianity without the Cross*, p. 104. It is Fudge's conclusion that their interest was more pastoral than narrowly doctrinal. He suggests this is particularly true of Goss and Yadon, the latter being the dominant UPC leader in the Northwest.

[69] Fudge, *Christianity without the Cross*, p. 335.

[70] Cited in Fudge, *Christianity without the Cross*, p. 338.

[71] Fudge, *Christianity without the Cross*, p. 162.

[72] W.E. Kidson, *In the Service of the King – Autobiography of W.E. Kidson* (Houston, TX: By the Author, n.d.), p. 30.

[73] Kidson, Interview. The occasion that prompted the schism was Kidson's infringement of the organizational policy to refrain from official and public fellowship (such as granting "platform courtesy" in a worship service) to any minister who previously had been disfellowshipped from the organization. Kidson invited The Rev. David Cootes to preach at his church, a minister who had been disfellowshipped from the United Pentecostal Church a few years earlier over the "Latter Rain" doctrine. Upon receiving a strongly worded letter of admonition by the District Board, Kidson made the decision to leave.

stricter "holiness" standards. The new group, the Apostolic Ministers Fellowship, is now Apostolic Churches International.[74]

There have been a number of defections from the UPCI over the years, both nationally and internationally. Domestically, most have become independent or joined other small organizations or ministerial associations. The effect has been a further dilution of those who adhere to the Identification teaching. The numerical and organizational strength of the UPCI remains strong. It is presently the fourth largest Pentecostal organization in the U.S., claiming 600,000 adherents and an international membership of 1.9 million.[75]

6. Assessment

The UPCI represents approximately one-half of the total numerical strength of the Oneness movement in North America. The remainder of the white Oneness adherents can be found within a variety of small groups or ministerial associations, many of them regionally based. Many tend to be classified as Independent, having little use for central-ized authority. In some cases they follow a charismatic leader, a pattern not uncommon in Pentecostalism.

The Pentecostal Assemblies of the World has been less successful in unifying black Oneness Pentecostals, but still retains approximately 45% of all black adherents, with 450,000 in the U.S. and a total global constituency of one million.[76] Haywood's influence on the black One-ness movement has resulted in over one million black

Pentecostals in the U.S. adhering to the Oneness faith, nearly half the total Oneness population.[77] Most of the black groups retain some

[74] The "Preamble" of their Manual reflects a highly negative attitude toward any form of centralized church government, *Apostolic Ministers Fellowship* (By the Organization, n.d.), pp. 1-2.

[75] The story of the tensions and defections within the UPCI since 1945 is chronicled by Fudge, *Christianity without a Cross*.

[76] The Pentecostal Assemblies of the World has tripled in size in the last 25 years. Ac-cording to the head of the organization in 1977, Presiding Bishop Francis Smith, of Akron, OH, a census that was nearing completion pointed to an adult membership strength of from 125,000 to 150,000 (telephone interview with Bishop Francis Smith, in Akron, OH, 1 October 1977).

[77] French's study includes a list of 428 Oneness groups in the world, with relatively ac-curate approximations of numerical strength in terms of the number of churches and adherents (see French, *Our God is One*, p. 86). It should be noted that there are a few interracial congregations in the UPCI, as it engages in ministry among blacks. The largest UPCI church in Canada, Faith Sanctuary in Toronto, is predominantly black. The PAofW, though mostly black, maintains a rigorous interracial policy on theological

form of "episcopal" governance that is able to combine charismatic leadership with centralized authority.

Like the Pentecostal movement in general, a small segment of the Oneness movement can be found on the fringes of the mainline organizations. There are numerous Independent churches that have affiliation with no organization and are frequently founded and pastored by a single leader. There are between fifteen and twenty small Sabbatarian groups. A few of them are Yahwists or devotees to the Sacred Name of Yahweh, that practice baptism in the name of Jesus (or Yahshua in Hebrew) and believe in the Oneness doctrine.[78] A third group is the "Branhamites," an isolated cluster that follows the teachings of the late William Branham. Branham was a leading Pentecostal healing evangelist from the 1940's and 1950's who embraced the Oneness doctrine in his later years.[79] His followers now regard him as an inspired prophet whose teachings are to be preserved on printed page and tape.[80] Because the followers are represented in both Independent churches and small house clusters that meet together to listen to the tapes, it is difficult to determine their numerical strength. Finally, at least some of the snake-handling sects in the Appalachian mountains of West Virginia, Tennessee and Kentucky adhere to rudimentary Oneness beliefs.[81]

Because of their beliefs, the Oneness groups are isolated from the wider Pentecostal movement, including such pan-Pentecostal organizations as the Pentecostal World Fellowship and the Pentecostal and Charismatic Churches of North America. Lacking the critical mass of the UPCI, many smaller groups experienced the need for a common Oneness identity and fellowship. The result was the formation of the Apostolic World Christian Fellowship in 1971. The UPCI has never joined, ostensibly because the father of the initiator of the fellowship had been dismissed from the UPCI in the early 1950's for teaching a

---

grounds. White ministers have held episcopal office, including Presiding Bishop.

[78] For details of these groups and their distinctive doctrinal beliefs, see *Directory of Sabbath-Keeping Groups* (4th ed.; Fairview, OK: The Bible Sabbath Association, 1974).

[79] Richard Crayne, *Pentecostal Handbook* (Morristown, TN: By the Author, 1963), pp. 21-22.

[80] See the magazine, *Wings of Life* (Texarkana, TX: Privately published, n.d.), pp. 1-7. For an illustration of the *verbatim* teachings of Branham, see William M. Branham, *The Spoken Word* (Jeffersonville, IN: Spoken Word, 1972).

[81] See Robert K. Holliday, *Tests of Faith* (Oak Hill, WV: The Fayette Tribune, 1966), pp. 19-20, 47-52. For a brief description of snake-handling Pentecostals, see H.D. Hunter, "Serpent Handling," *New International Dictionary of Pentecostal and Charismatic Movements*, pp. 1052-53.

version of adoptionist christology. The AWCF currently represents 153 organizations worldwide, for which it is a means of "demonstrating unity, assessing numerical strength, and coordinating evangelistic efforts."[82]

The continuing story of Oneness Pentecostalism is one of evangelism and growth, as it shares in the bounty of the global Pentecostal movement. Its history is one of deep fracture from its parent Trinitarian body. But in many parts of the world, the story of its traumatic birth is unknown. People hear only the story of *one* God who is revealed in Jesus, and they enter gladly into those acts of faith set forth in Acts 2:38. For them, the message is simple and the tools are adequate for the journey.

But the plot thickens as the movement matures. Its global strength of fifteen to twenty million will command attention if not approval. But success is not partial to its host. Numerical strength will effect deep changes within Oneness Pentecostals, and they will be obliged to give an accounting for their existence. This will occur at many levels of their life, including their singular claim to the Apostolic gospel. Like other Pentecostals, their beliefs were born in popular religion, with little knowledge of and only antipathy toward the classical formulations of the Christian faith. As they prepare to enter their second century, they will need more provisions for the journey. And they will not be able to ignore the wider fellowship of Christians any more than that larger body can pass them by.

[82] D.A. Reed, "Oneness Pentecostalism," *New International Dictionary of Pentecostal and Charismatic Movements*, p. 940.

Part III

Theology of Oneness Pentecostalism

11

Theology of the Name

> God's *name* is his enacted identity, God's sheer irreducible particularity as *this One* who is and acts *thus*. God's name is his incomparability, his uniqueness. Bearing this name, God is not simply holy mystery, the nameless and voiceless whence of some sense of the numinous, an ineffable and indefinite deity. In his unalterable and unassailable mystery he is the one who he is: the self-determining one, wholly beyond the reach of any comparison or class.[1]
>
>   – John Webster

Heterodox movements are notoriously difficult to grasp. They often appear on the stage of history by the force of a charismatic leader and a popular thirst for something beyond conventional offerings. They usually appear as a surprise, unexpected and unpredicted, and are frequently greeted with defensive resistance. Reasoned attempts to understand their beliefs and practices vary from ideal typologies to contextual analysis. The former attempts to understand the movement and its ideas in terms of a set of normative beliefs or theoretical models, which may or may not take into account the historical and social context.[2] Contextual studies, conversely, focus on the social, economic or political dimensions and may thereby miss the force of beliefs. At its best, the church bears responsibility to test the theological ideas that present themselves within its life, which should include listening carefully to the times and circumstances within which those ideas are cradled.[3]

---

[1] John Webster, *Holiness* (Grand Rapids, MI: Eerdmans, 2003), p. 36.

[2] An excellent example of applying a theological "Chalcedonian Pattern" to the practice of pastoral counseling, see Deborah van Deusen Hunsinger, *Theology and Pastoral Counseling: A New Interdisciplinary Approach* (Grand Rapids, MI: Eerdmans, 1995).

[3] An excellent illustration of a theological and contextual assessment of Oneness Pentecostalism in Mexico, see Kenneth D. Gill, *Toward a Contextualized Theology for*

1. Lenses and Labels

Oneness Pentecostalism is a popular religious movement that emerged within the matrix of late 19th-century evangelical Protestantism and the early Pentecostal movement. The task of Part III is to explore in a more systematic fashion the foundational doctrines that constitute a distinctive Oneness theology. The task of settling on a theological lens or paradigm through which to interpret this movement is more complex than the Oneness ideas themselves.

The earliest efforts were more like labels than lenses. The first term to be used was the "New Issue," a generic tag that was accepted by both sides and functioned largely as a rhetorical device within the early controversy. As the Issue became less new, it gradually waned in usage. A more theologically specific label, "Jesus Only," emerged at about the same time. As indicated in Part I, this phrase was not uncommon among early evangelicals, especially of the Keswick variety. But in this controversy it gradually became theologically freighted as a title of derision by the Trinitarians to accuse the new movement of "denying the Father." As early as 1922, Haywood's celebrated article, "Dangers of Denying the Father," signaled concern by the proponents of the new movement that the Trinitarians were deliberately distorting – or at least misunderstanding – its teaching.[4] But as a term of self-designation, the term "Jesus Only" was slow in dying, and continued to be used through the 1930's.[5] The pejorative connotation of the term, and likely the consolidation of the movement's theological identity, finally resulted in the shift to a more satisfactory designation. Consequently, it is now rare for a Oneness representative to accept the label from others without protest.

---

the *Third World: The Emergence and Development of Jesus' Name Pentecostalism in Mexico* (New York: Peter Lang, 1994).

[4] Haywood, "Dangers of Denying the Father," *Voice in the Wilderness* 2 (13 November 1922): 5; *Pentecostal Outlook* 1 (April 1932): 3.

[5] See the following sampling of references: "They were satisfied with what we are pleased to term the 'Jesus Only' faith," Andrew D. Urshan, "The Blessed Three-ness of the Godhead," *Witness of God* IV/43 (July 1923): 3; "We ... firmly stand for the blessed message of Jesus Only," L.R. Ooton, "Mighty Holy Ghost Revival in Saint Paul, MN," *Apostolic Herald* I/6 (December 1926): 1-2; calling for a merger, reference in an open letter to the "amalgamation of all 'Jesus Only' people," *Pentecostal Witness* VI/11-12 (September-October 1930): 1; reference to the Pentecostal Assemblies of Jesus Christ as "a heaven-recognized 'Jesus Only' movement," *Pentecostal Outlook* III/10 (October 1934): 5; "Jesus Only" tracts advertised as late as the *Pentecostal Herald* XXI/3 (March 1946): 6.

Three labels that have endured to become acceptable to Oneness as titles of self-designation and recognized by others are: "Apostolic," "Jesus' Name," and "Oneness."

While "apostolic" clearly has a currency outside Oneness and even Pentecostal circles, the new movement embraced it to define its commitment to full apostolic practice according to Acts 2:38.[6] A number of organizations, especially African-American groups, have incorporated the term in their name.[7] It is more favored within the movement than by Trinitarians, except in settings where it has become commonly recognized nomenclature. "Jesus' Name" has been an enduring preference within the movement, especially as the designated alternative to "Jesus Only."[8]

"Oneness" as a self-designation begins to appear in the literature about 1930. The title suggests a shift in focus to the doctrine of God. G.T. Haywood uses the term as early as 1910, but as a reference to the unity of God's people: "This is the Lord's paper, published for that 'Oneness' amidst God's saints throughout the land, as our Lord prayed in John 17:17, 21 and 22."[9] Ewart uses the term in 1916 with reference to the unity or "oneness" of the two natures in Christ.[10] It may be noteworthy that the term "Oneness" emerges as a desired title during a period of great fragmentation in the early movement and failed efforts at unity. In a 1930 editorial, W.E. Kidson uses it to describe the new movement: "Formerly the largest organization of ministers, evangelists and missionaries standing for the present day truth – generally known as the 'Oneness Movement' – was the Pentecostal Assemblies of the World."[11] That the term emerges within a white group which eventually becomes part of the largest Oneness organization, the United Pentecostal Church, may explain in large part why "Oneness" has become the most familiar term, both inside and outside the

---

[6] The appeal here and among predecessors of the Oneness movement was the Restorationist goal of recapitulating in their day the pure Apostolic faith and practice.

[7] Conversations with leading representatives suggest there is no discernible racial dynamic involved with the term "Apostolic."

[8] Note the subtitle of Gill's book on the Mexican Oneness movement, *The Emergence and Development of Jesus' Name Pentecostalism in Mexico.*

[9] G.T. Haywood, *Voice in the Wilderness* 2 (July 1910): 2.

[10] Ewart, "The Unity of God," *Meat In Due Season* I/13 (June 1916): 1.

[11] W.E. Kidson, "The Purpose of the PMA," *Apostolic Herald* V/7 (July 1930): 5. In a 1934 editorial, Kidson writes as if the term is becoming commonplace: "We cannot see how anyone believing in the ONENESS can afford to use anything different than our own ONENESS SUNDAY SCHOOL LITERATURE," in *Apostolic Herald* 11/7 (July 1934): 2.

movement. The term "Oneness" is used throughout this study for the
following reasons: (1) it is an acceptable term among Oneness Pentecostals, (2) there are no discernible traces of racism in the choice of the
term, and (3) it is recognized as a neutral term within the wider North
American Christian community (which is the focus of this study).[12]

A more theological label which has dogged the Oneness movement
since its inception is "heresy." It emerged as a serious charge by Trinitarians during the two years prior to the General Council decision in
1916 to remove the New Issue advocates from its fellowship. It continues to be the official position of the Assemblies of God, but has
been taken up with zeal by other evangelicals.[13] Anti-cult internet sites
regularly include in their list of cults or heretical groups references to
the Oneness movement and the UPCI.

Like the Assemblies of God before them, the evangelical litmus test
is a combination of Scripture and identified heresies of the early Christian centuries.

Some form of Sabellianism or modalism emerges as the defining
culprit regarding the doctrine of God, and a suspicion that the Oneness insistence on re-baptism transgresses the boundary of salvation.
The assessments are often accurate in their analysis of specific theological ideas. But while there may indeed be a place for such analysis, this
approach is often simplistic or reductionistic, especially among evan-

---

[12] One group in which there is tension over the choice of "Oneness" as a descriptor
is Franklin Small's Canadian organization, The Apostolic Church of Pentecost. For
some in the organization, the term "Oneness" implies a strict sectarian doctrine that
totally rejects the doctrine of the Trinity, insists upon re-baptism, and highly restricts
fellowship with other Christians. ACOP holds more loosely to a "tri-unity" view of
God, which makes provision for those in its fellowship who consider themselves to be
Trinitarian. While some regard themselves as Oneness, the tolerance for diversity is a
result of a merger in 1953 with a small regional Trinitarian group, Evangelical
Churches of Pentecost (phone interview with the moderator, Gil Killam, 19 April
2001). The ACOP is an illustration of a more open approach to the New Issue that
continues to exist on the margins of the mainstream Oneness movement, mostly in
ministerial fellowships and independent ministries.

Other examples are the Full Gospel Ministerial Fellowship that thrived in the
northeast U.S. and Canadian Maritimes until the 1940's, and continues as a small
independent fellowship; the ministry of Bethel Temple in Seattle, founded by W.H.
Offiler (Trinitarian but baptized in the name of the Lord Jesus Christ), and Bethesda
Missionary Temple in Detroit, a center for the Latter Rain Revival in the 1940's. See
Chapter 14.

[13] Two prominent examples are Gregory A. Boyd, *Oneness Pentecostalism and the
Trinity*, and E. Calvin Beisner, *"Jesus Only" Churches* (Grand Rapids, MI: Zondervan,
1998). The latter is part of the Zondervan Guide to Cults and Religious Movements.

gelical anti-cult groups. It is often based upon a plain reading of written materials, which has the disadvantage of narrowing the analysis to only what one reads and to the segment of the movement that publishes the material – in this case, the UPCI. It further ignores the fact that Oneness Pentecostalism is a popular religious movement that was reacting – indeed, overreacting – to a set of religious and social circumstances, failing to grasp the complexity of a doctrine that had been hammered out in controversy over more than four centuries.

Given that Oneness Pentecostalism is a distinctive movement that shares much with its evangelical and Pentecostal heritage (unlike groups such as the Jehovah's Witnesses and the Mormon Church) and is still in the early stages of its own doctrinal development, it is both charitable and ecclesially desirable to engage in open but irenic debate. Further, many Christians feel ecumenically bound to recognize an affinity with Oneness Pentecostals, especially those whose ministry is received in the wider church. In this case, it is relatively inconsequential that there are those within the Oneness tradition who are reluctant to fellowship outside their organizational boundaries.

The Roman Catholic ecumenical scholar, Ralph Del Colle, offers a more responsible and theologically nuanced alternative; namely, that Oneness Pentecostalism is a "heterodox" presence within the larger Christian family. Following the definition of the 19th-century European theologian, Friedrich Schleiermacher, he argues that while heresy is "tantamount to a denial of the faith," heterodoxy is often naïve or excessive in its claims. In the end, it performs an important ecumenical function in helping the wider church to clarify and deepen its claims and to re-examine instances of exaggeration or neglect.[14] Such an approach radically alters the way we engage with Oneness Pentecostals, demanding much more in terms of critical assessment and a spirit of humility. As a former Oneness Pentecostal and lifelong observer of this movement, I do not find the charge of heresy compelling. It is strained at best and takes no account of the spiritual character of those it condemns, or, as Del Colle points out, the "right" shape of its worship. Heterodoxy, on the other hand, generously locates the movement within the broad stream of Christian history, a place that for the moment may not offend even Oneness Pentecostals.

---

[14] Ralph Del Colle, "Oneness and Trinity: A Preliminary Proposal for Dialogue with Oneness Pentecostalism," *Journal of Pentecostal Theology* 10 (1997): 85-110. One detects a similar approach in Gill's study of Oneness Pentecostalism in Mexico, *Toward a Contextualized Theology for the Third World.*

Within this broader general context, I have sought a more theological interpretive lens or paradigm, for two reasons. One is to help locate Oneness doctrine within the broader field of Christian theological ideas; the other, to explore its distinctive beliefs as a coherent whole. The theologian knows that one can enter the doctrinal room through many windows. Further, one can select a single doctrine for study or examine the system as a whole. In this section, I propose to explore the three foundational doctrines that constitute the Oneness belief system, and to offer a paradigm or interpretive lens through which these doctrines cohere.

In my first attempt over thirty years ago I described Oneness Pentecostalism as an expression of "Evangelical Unitarian Pentecostalism,"[15] an effort to locate the movement within its evangelical, non-Trinitarian, Pentecostal milieu. While there is some justification for it, the label can be as confusing as enlightening. I eventually became convinced that the 'Name" is a central and cohering feature in Oneness thinking, though underdeveloped by Oneness writers. I discovered that its theological interests (in the doctrine of God and Christology) lay historically with the early Antiochene school of thought, the tradition that leaned most heavily on its Jewish roots. On that basis I constructed the paradigm, "Jewish Christian Theology of the Name."[16] But it eventually became apparent that the term "Jewish Christian" was confusing for some, even though I attempted to define the term. While the following pages will continue on the same trajectory relatively unchanged, the title is simplified to "A Theology of the Name."

Though a theology of the Name may appear ecumenically anachronistic and limited to the study of early Jewish Christian faith, a potential contribution today is its significance as an element in the doctrine of revelation, the locus of the Church's knowledge of the God who acted in Israel and definitively in Jesus of Nazareth. And that is where we begin, with the Jewish Christian roots of the Name.

---

[15] See David Reed, "Aspects of the Origins of Oneness Pentecostalism," in Vinson Synan, ed., *Aspects of Pentecostal-Charismatic Origins* (Plainfield, NJ: Logos International, 1975). This essay was initially read while I was a graduate student at Boston University, at the third meeting of the Society for Pentecostal Studies at Lee College, Cleveland, TN, in 1973.

[16] This is the paradigm I used in my Ph.D. thesis, "Origins and Development of the Theology of Oneness Pentecostalism in the United States" (Ph.D. diss., Boston University, 1978). I carried this into my essay, "Oneness Pentecostalism," in the first edition of Stanley M. Burgess and Gary B. McGee, *Dictionary of Pentecostal and Charismatic Movements* (Grand Rapids, MI: Zondervan, 1988).

2. Constructing the Paradigm

A theology of the Name appropriately begins with the witness of the People of God in the Old Covenant and in particular the ways in which their understanding of Yahweh is transferred to Jesus and reinterpreted in light of his coming. This means that the first use of the term, "Jewish Christian," must be reserved for those earliest Christians whose roots and identity were Jewish. But as we shall see, a theology of the Name with its particular reference to Israel's God can also be used in a non-ethnic, theological way. This study draws upon the works of Jean Daniélou and Richard Longenecker in their respective studies of early Jewish Christian Christology, and from that to the possibility of a non-ethnic theological understanding. This will be the starting point for applying a theology of the Name to Oneness Pentecostalism.

Daniélou identifies at least three recognizable groups of early Jewish followers of Jesus. One was the heterodox Ebionites, those "who acknowledged Christ as a prophet or Messiah, but not as the Son of God."[17] The traditional orthodox group identified with the Christian church in Jerusalem of which James, the brother of Jesus, was the leader. These were strict monotheists and followed the Jewish customs but were distinct from the Ebionites in that, in their acknowledgement of the messianic role of Jesus, they "implied the divinity of Christ."[18] The third category was "a type of Christian thought expressing itself in forms borrowed from Judaism,"[19] but which bore no *direct* relationship to Judaism. Paul and those involved in the Gentile mission represent this pattern of breaking with the mandatory Jewish laws and customs but continued theologically and morally to regard the Scriptures of Israel to be their own.

It is this third type that is of interest for this study. Though Daniélou limits the period of influence for the third type to the middle of the second century, he opens the way for the development of an exclusively *theological* approach, one in which distinctively Jewish themes are revived and called to serve the interests of another time and place.

Richard Longenecker agrees. He first highlights a number of distinctly Jewish Christian themes, including the Sacred Name, in his

---

[17] Jean Daniélou, *The Development of Christian Doctrine before the Council of Nicaea*, vol. I: *The Theology of Jewish Christianity* (ed. and trans. John A. Baker; London: Darton, Longman & Todd, 1964) p. 7.

[18] *Ibid.*, p. 8.

[19] *Ibid.*, p. 9

study of early Jewish Christian Christology.[20] But he observes that, as
these themes suffer neglect over time due to their Jewish identity, the
conditions are created for that perennial possibility of reform-minded
sectarian groups to revive certain motifs they believe were forgotten or
neglected by the Church:

> In the general christological consensus, being formed in the apostolic pe-
> riod, there was also a basis for the rise of sectarian attitudes.... In reaction
> to the direction that the crystallization of thought in mainstream Christi-
> anity was taking, some undoubtedly latched onto earlier titles which they
> felt were being ignored and certain perspectives which they considered
> illegitimately relegated to an inferior position in the structure of Christian
> thought.[21]

The history of the Church is witness to the number of sects whose
existence can be explained in large part by the desire to restore certain
early Jewish Christian motifs and perspectives. These themes are *theological* in nature, separate from Judaism or any historical movements
within Christianity. These movements are often sectarian in nature
and appear during periods of social or religious change.

A sect or movement in this third category will have an affinity with
one or more biblical themes identified as distinctly Jewish, for instance,
the Sacred Name, Sabbatarianism, Millenarianism and the restoration
of an Israelite state. Further, the distinctly Jewish theme becomes the
point of identity for the sect. Such a movement is generally distinguished from mainstream Christianity in its attempt to relegate to
secondary rank all other doctrines in the service of this theme. The
phenomenon itself is not necessarily schismatic, since it may function
as a reform movement within the larger institutional body.

Alternately, in the denominational and sectarian culture of North
America a myriad of religious groups or denominations simply co-exist
as a competitive fraternity. An extreme sectarian spirit separates from
the wider church and claims absolute truth for itself alone. Since any
movement exists in its own historical and religious setting, a certain
degree of contextualizing will occur, thereby intermingling, consciously or not, the borrowed doctrine with the various forces and
interests of its own culture. The following is an attempt to illustrate
how Oneness Pentecostal doctrine functions as one expression of this
third category of Jewish Christian theology.

---

[20] Richard N. Longenecker, *The Christology of Early Jewish Christianity* (Studies in
Biblical Theology, 17; Naperville, IL: Alec R. Allenson, 1970), pp. 41-46.

[21] *Ibid.*, p. 153.

3. Contextualizing the Paradigm

Since the distinctive Oneness doctrines to be examined in this section are God, Christ and salvation, the application of a Jewish Christian paradigm should demonstrate the ways in which Oneness theology reflects the third category described above. That is, in these doctrines the *Name* and *nature* of the divine reality and presence will in some way bear the marks of Jewish Christian motifs. Old Testament categories and metaphors that are transferred into the earliest strands of the New Testament church are picked up, often isolated, and applied to the concerns of the particular movement or sect.

a. Doctrine of God

i. Name of God. There are three aspects of the doctrine of God in Oneness theology that reflect distinctly Jewish Christian themes. One of the most important is the "the Name."[22] Behind the Name as christological designation in the New Testament lies the Jewish belief in the name of God. For Israel and early Jewish Christian alike, "the Name of God stands as a symbol for His sole deity, His glory, and His character as righteous and holy."[23] Signifying more than mere nominalistic naming, "the Name is used to designate Yahweh in his ineffable reality."[24] It is not insignificant that such a theological regard for the name of God gradually disappeared over the course of the early Christian centuries. Daniélou suggests that the Name was "a Semitic equivalent of what the divine οὐσία was to be for the Greeks."[25] When Christianity became largely Gentile, the Name became less intelligible and important in the Greek environment.

There continues to be little serious theological effort to understand and mine the resources of the Name. Since the concept is so deeply embedded in the Old Testament and given less than central importance in the New, it is an unlikely candidate for theological

---

[22] For a detailed discussion of the name of God in Scripture, see D. Preman Niles, "The Name of God in Israel s Worship – The Importance of the Name Yahweh" (PhD diss., Princeton Theological Seminary, 1974); William C. Strickland, "The Meaning of the Name of God in Biblical Theology" (ThD diss., Southern Baptist Theological Seminary, 1953); and more recently David S. Norris, "No Other Name: A Socio-Historical Approach to the Argument of Luke-Acts (Pierre Bourdieu)" (Ph.D. diss., Temple University, 2000).

[23] C.H. Dodd, *The Interpretation of the Fourth Gospel* (Cambridge: Cambridge University Press, 1953), p. 93.

[24] Daniélou, *Jewish Christianity*, p. 148.

[25] *Ibid.*

exploitation outside the field of biblical theology, a discipline that itself struggles to regain acceptance in the field of contemporary biblical studies.[26] Emil Brunner is the only major theologian of the 20th century to give serious consideration to the Name as a theological idea.[27] Unless and until it is discovered to have relevance for the church in the future, it is likely to lie fallow in the field of theology. But its importance in the Scripture as a way by which the People of God understand themselves and the God they follow means that it is likely to reappear from time to time, and it is most likely to reappear among sectarian movements whose primary concern is to call the church back to its roots.

ii. Nature of God. The monotheistic identity of Israelite religion is indisputable, a conviction that was protected and enshrined in the *Shema* (Deut. 6:4). This creed functioned throughout Israelite history to distinguish Yahweh from the gods of Israel's pagan neighbors. But the nature of that unity has been a matter of debate. Though the quasi-hypostatic dignity given to Wisdom, the Word and the Name in late Judaism may have assisted the later Christian doctrine of the Trinity,[28] it was an early Jewish Christian conviction to maintain a "strict monotheism,"[29] or an "undiminished monotheism."[30]

Hans-Joachim Schoeps, referring to the Ebionites in particular, points out that these Jewish Christians were so "oriented exclusively toward the divine monarchy, it was inconceivable that there could be any other kind of revelation."[31] There is increasing indication that, during Second Temple Judaism, the unique identity of Yahweh was being understood less as a monadic oneness than a dynamic unity that involved the "personifications" of divine Word and Wisdom.[32]

---

[26] For a review of this eclipse, see Brevard S. Childs, *Biblical Theology in Crisis* (Philadelphia: Westminster, 1970); and a constructive proposal more recently, *Biblical Theology: A Proposal* (Philadelphia: Fortress, 2002).

[27] Emil Brunner, *Dogmatics*, vol. I, *The Christian Doctrines of God* (trans. Olive Wyon; Philadelphia: Westminster, 1950), ch. 12.

[28] Daniélou, *Jewish Christianity*, pp. 148, 151.

[29] *Ibid.*, p. 8.

[30] Dom Gregory Dix, *Jew and Greek – A Study in the Primitive Church* (London: Dacre, 1953), p. 28.

[31] Hans-Joachim Schoeps, *Jewish Christianity-Factional Disputes in the Early Church* (trans. Douglas R.A. Hare; Philadelphia: Fortress, 1969), p. 72.

[32] See especially the recent work by Richard Bauckham, *God Crucified: Monotheism and Christology in the New Testament* (Grand Rapids, MI: Eerdmans, 1998). In ch. 1, Bauckham argues that already in Second Temple Judaism the Word and Wisdom functioned in an almost quasi-hypostatic fashion, sufficient to provide early Jewish Christians a conceptual framework for incorporating the identity of Jesus fully within

As the Christian movement became more influenced by the Hellenistic world, the particular Jewish Christian interest in preserving its monotheistic identity became more evident. As J.N.D. Kelly observes, the second Christian century revealed an "intense concern for the fundamental tenet of monotheism" over against the paganism and Gnosticism of the Hellenistic world. When the emerging Logos doctrine began to show signs of threat to the divine unity, the reaction in the West in particular to preserve the divine unity was manifested in a movement called Monarchianism.[33]

Throughout the history of the Church there have been Christians suspicious that the creedal doctrine of the Trinity was an unwarranted and sub-Christian departure from its identity in Judeo-Christian monotheism and was, in effect, a crypto-tritheism. The Oneness movement shares this bias that there can be no true oneness without preserving the "numerical unity" of God.

iii. Presence of God as "Dwelling." A third aspect of the doctrine of God that reflects its distinctively Jewish character is the mode of Yahweh's presence in the world. One of the characteristic Old Testament metaphors is the "dwelling place" of God. While the transcendence of God was a marked feature of Jewish religion, Yahweh's immanence was described as "dwelling" in the midst of His people. Yahweh's presence was both localized in a place or epiphany and transitory. Arthur Michael Ramsey points out that "this 'localized' conception is held in tension with a deepened conviction that Yahveh is transcendent and never to be confined to any earthly dwelling."[34] God even occasionally "withdraws his presence."[35]

Several places that marked the divine dwelling were the Ark of the Covenant (Num. 10:35-36), the Tabernacle (Exod. 40:34) and the Temple (1 Kgs 8:27-29). The presence of God in a place was frequently described as "glory" (*kabod*), a term that came to refer to "the revealed being or character of Yahweh."[36] The appearance was frequently attached to "a local theophany, on Mount Sinai or in the tabernacle and the temple."[37]

the unique identity of Yahweh.

[33] J.N.D. Kelly, *Early Christian Doctrines* (2nd ed.; New York: Harper & Row, 1960), pp. 108-109.

[34] Arthur Michael Ramsey, *The Glory of God and the Transfiguration of Christ* (New York: Longmans, Green & Co., 1949), p. 15.

[35] Dale Moody, "Shekinah," *The Interpreter's Dictionary of the Bible*, vol. IV, George A. Buttrick, ed. (New York: Abingdon, 1962), p. 317.

[36] A.M. Ramsey, *The Glory of God*, p. 10.

[37] *Ibid.*, p. 15.

In later Rabbinic Judaism, one characteristic expression for dwelling was "*shekinah.*" It became a "circumlocution to express the reverent nearness of God to his people."[38] In a period that was placing emphasis on Yahweh's transcendence, the *Shekinah* became a way of speaking about God so that it conveys the truth of his omnipresence, accessibility and special activity within the created world without infringing the doctrine of His transcendence.[39]

During this time the concepts of glory, tabernacle and dwelling coalesced into a unified pattern in such a way that one image could be implied in another. Ramsay observes that "this unified imagery is the background of much of the thought of the writers of the New Testament,"[40] especially in their Christology. One of the most prominent dwelling places of Yahweh was in the "Name." "Yahweh chooses to dwell with Israel by putting his 'name' in a special place" (Deut. 12:5, 11, 21).[41] For instance, Yahweh's name might accompany His glory as when Moses asked to see His glory and was told that when the "glory" passed by His Name would accompany it (Exod. 33:17-18).

The Jewish concept of "dwelling" constitutes part of the intellectual and theological framework for early Jewish Christians to express the nature of God's presence in Jesus. Instead of using the Greek language of metaphysics, Jewish Christians found such concepts as tabernacle, temple, glory, and Name to be ready vehicles for interpreting their experience of Jesus.

b. Christology

To reiterate Ramsay's observation, the New Testament writers employed these metaphors inherited from the Old Testament to set forth their understanding of Christ.

i. Name of God in Jesus. As the name of God (especially the revelational and "proper" name, Yahweh) is so closely identified with divine self-revelation in the Old Testament, it is not surprising to find special theological significance attached to the Name in the New Testament. Longenecker observes that, "as a christological designation, 'the name' appears almost exclusively in materials that reflect the Jewish Christian mission and Jewish Christian interests." New Testament writers drew

---

[38] See Moody, "Shekinah."
[39] A.M. Ramsey, *The Glory of God*, p. 19.
[40] *Ibid.*, pp. 20, 26.
[41] Moody, "Shekinah."

the same Jewish conclusion; namely, that the Name points to divine presence and power.[42]

Daniélou even sees in the use of the Name a Jewish Christian equivalent for the pre-existent Logos and a firm attestation of Christ's divinity.[43] He observes how New Testament writers, by directly quoting Old Testament texts, attach the name of Yahweh to Jesus (e.g. Acts 2:21; Rom. 10:12).[44]

Among the names bearing theological significance, the name "Jesus" itself is part of the early Jewish Christian strand of Name christology. Longenecker cites the importance given the name of Jesus in the Gospel of Matthew, beginning with the Angel's announcement of the name to Joseph (Matt. 1:21-25).[45] Referring to the same text, Hans Bietenhard says of Jesus that, "at God's command He receives the name of Jesus, which expresses His humanity and also His divine mission."[46] Wilhelm Bousset, in his study of early Christology, observes that in the Fourth Gospel, "the name of Jesus plays the same role as the name of the Old Testament Yahweh."[47] Kittel notes the significance of the common practice in the New Testament to offer all prayer in the name of Jesus (e.g., John 14:13-14; 15:16; 16:23, 26).[48] In reference to the name "Lord" in the christological hymn of Phil. 2:9-11, Longenecker goes so far as to suggest that for early Jewish Christians it would be more accurate to say that, "since Jesus is the name of God, it is appropriate that the Old Testament title for God be his as well."[49]

Whatever emphasis should be placed upon the name of Jesus, there is strong indication that such a christological strand emerged for a short time in the early Jewish Christian community. Daniélou suggests that the final disappearance of the whole phenomenon of a Name Christology may have been due to its "richness in Jewish tradition."[50] Similarly, Longenecker thinks that when Christianity had finally

---

[42] Longenecker, *Christology*, pp. 44, 45.

[43] Daniélou, *Jewish Christianity*, p. 407.

[44] *Ibid.*, p. 149; cf. Longenecker, *Christology,* p. 44.

[45] Longenecker, *Christology*, p. 44.

[46] Hans Bietenhard, ὄνομα κτλ, *Theological Dictionary of the New Testament*, vol. V (Grand Rapids, MI: Eerdmans, 1985), p. 272.

[47] Wilhelm Bousset, *Kyrios Christos – A History of the Belief in Christ from the Beginnings of Christianity to Irenaeus* (5th ed.; trans. John E. Steely; New York: Abingdon, 1970), p. 215.

[48] ὄνομα, p. 276.

[49] Longenecker, *Christology*, p. 128.

[50] Daniélou, *Jewish Christianity*, p. 147.

shifted to a predominantly Gentile environment, the concept may have "either suffered subordinationistic interpretations or been considered equivalent to the Greek οὐσία."[51] It appears that an embryonic Name Christology emerged within the earliest Jewish Christianity to express not only Christ's humanity but also the nature of the divine presence in him, using categories of thought from their own Jewish tradition.

ii. Presence of God in Jesus. Besides the use of the Name, how did the early Jewish Christians describe the presence of God in Jesus? Their focus seems to have been primarily on Jesus' redemptive activity. While they were less interested in the Hellenistic language of ontology (though Hellenistic concepts are clearly present throughout the New Testament), the categories they used to describe Christ connoted the unique presence of God in Jesus. Longenecker states that, "while the Christology of the earliest Jewish believers was primarily functional, it presupposed and carried in substratum ontological commitments."[52] To illustrate, the use of the Name as applied to Jesus was a potent image of the presence and power of Yahweh and may in fact have functioned for certain early Jewish Christians to express the deity of Christ.[53]

More recently, New Testament scholar Richard Bauckham has argued that for these earliest Jewish Christians the key christological concept was the *unique identity* of Yahweh and of Jesus, rather than more familiar categories of function and ontology. He summarizes his view this way:

> The unique divine sovereignty is a matter of *who* God *is*. Jesus' participation in the unique divine sovereignty is therefore also not just a matter of what Jesus does, but of *who Jesus is* in relation to God. Though not primarily a matter of divine nature or being, it emphatically *is* a matter of divine identity. It includes Jesus in the identity of the one God.[54]

In other words, early Jewish Christians were persuaded that in Jesus they were not only witnessing divine activity but also divine presence.

A category well suited to express the presence of God in Jesus is the familiar concept of "dwelling." It was a ready metaphor for transferring the dwelling "places" of the Old Testament to Jesus. Daniélou is convinced that "dwelling is the Semitic category best suited to express

---

[51] Longenecker, *Christology*, p. 46.
[52] *Ibid.*, p. 155.
[53] Daniélou, *Jewish Christianity*, p. 151.
[54] Bauckham, *God Crucified*, p. 41.

the Incarnation."[55] Dale Moody likewise believes that "it is only a step from this belief that God could dwell in a particular place to the Christian belief that God dwelt in his fullness in Jesus Christ." But a "dwelling" Christology never matured in the early church, perhaps due to the emergence of Hellenistic terminology and the association it might create with the polytheistic heresy of Gnostic dualism.[56] Christians were concerned to affirm that this divine presence is a permanent union, not a temporary visitation like the prophetic Spirit in the Old Testament.

The *locus classicus* for a "dwelling" Christology is John 1:14 (see also Col. 1:19; 2:9). "The event of the Incarnation is nothing less than the glory of God pitching a tent ... in human flesh."[57] Even among the Ebionites, who did not associate the "Spirit of revelation" or "True Prophet" with God's nature, the concept of dwelling formed the imagery of the presence of the True Prophet in Jesus: "Having appeared first in an incomplete way in the prophets of the Old Testament, the 'True Prophet' has reached completion in the Messiah Jesus and has come to rest 'for ever.'"[58] The distinctiveness of Jesus was not in the nature of the dwelling but simply in its finality.

In the Old Testament, Yahweh chooses to dwell in particular earthly habitations. It has already been pointed out that Yahweh dwells in the Name. Another dwelling place is the Temple. Jesus' own comparison of the Temple in Jerusalem with himself constituted blasphemy for the Jewish leaders during his trial (Matt. 26:61-65). In making such a parallel, "he was declaring himself to be the presence of God."[59] Indeed, even though the Temple was regarded as the divine dwelling place, "the true temple ...is the body of Jesus."[60] Prior to the building of the Temple, Yahweh dwelt in the "Tabernacle." In the New Covenant, the body of Jesus becomes the new and true Tabernacle. In his excellent study, Yves Congar highlights the christological significance of the Tabernacle motif in the Transfiguration story.[61]

---

[55] Daniélou, *Jewish Christianity*, p. 156.

[56] Moody, "Shekinah," p. 319.

[57] *Ibid*. p. 319.

[58] Schoeps, *Jewish Christianity*, p. 72.

[59] Jean Daniélou and André Chouraqui, *The Jews – Views and Counterviews – A Dialogue between Jean Daniélou and André Chouraqui* (New York: Newman, 1967), p. 24.

[60] Moody, "Shekinah," p. 319. See also the study of the Temple by Yves Congar, *The Mystery of the Temple; Or, The Manner of God's Presence to His Creatures from Genesis to the Apocalypse* (trans. Reginald F. Trevett; New York: Newman, 1962).

[61] Congar, *Mystery of the Temple*, p. 133.

The "glory of God" also becomes a form of dwelling in Jesus. Rooted in the Old Testament expectation of the Messianic Age, a "theology of glory" was soon applied to the life and mission of Jesus. Ramsey points out how the images of glory, tabernacle, and dwelling of Yahweh had already begun to coalesce in the Septuagint. This unified pattern "was familiar to the Greek-speaking Jews of the time of the apostles, and it lay to hand for the Christian church to use and to build upon."[62]

The imagery of dwelling did not develop apart from the Jewish view of Yahweh. Rather, it was a way to acknowledge Yahweh's presence while at the same time maintaining the divine mystery and transcendence, admitting no confinement or confusion between the two. For this reason, Jewish Christian Christology is marked by this tendency to assert a theological distance if not an actual separation between the humanity of Jesus and the divine presence within him. It shares the characteristics of the ancient Antiochene Christology. In his study of early Christologies, R.V. Sellers turns to this very point; namely, that in the Antiochene school the Logos is described as "taking man's nature as an 'indwelling.'"[63] Schoeps extends the characterization to a determination "to 'separate' the two natures of Godhead and manhood in Christ."[64] Antiochene Christologies consistently demonstrate their preference for Jewish Christian patterns and interests.

In sum, in applying particular Jewish characteristics of the doctrine of God to Christ, we find a christological model that is marked by a theology of the Name – in some cases specifically the name of Jesus – and the distinctly Jewish concept of "dwelling," to communicate the mode of the presence of Yahweh in Jesus.

c. Salvation

A Jewish Christian theology of the Name follows consistently into the life of the believer and the Christian community as a whole.

i. Identity with the Name. The purpose of Yahweh's self-revelation is to create a covenantal relationship. One means by which God actualizes this covenant is in the giving of his Name. As Brunner states, "the disclosure of a name creates communion."[65] As the name of Jesus is

---

[62] A.M. Ramsey, *The Glory of God*, pp. 26, 37.

[63] R.V. Sellers, *Two Ancient Christologies – A Study in the Christological Thought of the Schools of Alexandria and Antioch in the Early History of Christian Doctrine* (London: SPCK, 1940), p. 162.

[64] Schoeps, *Jewish Christianity*, p. 73.

[65] Brunner, *Doctrine of God*, p. 124.

given in the Annunciation to Mary, it connotes the divine mission of Jesus to the extent that the name of Jesus itself "embraces the whole content of the saving acts revealed in Jesus."[66] Those who call on the divine Name for salvation bear that Name and are identified as God's People. When the Name is invoked in the Christian community, "the name determines the fellowship of the Christians. In the community, people are to accept everyone who comes there in the name of the Lord." As Jewish people were identified by the covenant with Yahweh, followers of Jesus are unified "by the name of Jesus."[67] Christians become literally a people of his Name.

ii. Baptism in the Name. In the New Testament, the distinctive mark of this identity with Jesus is baptism, especially as it involves the invocation of the Name. The invocation is regarded as an essential element, whether one uses the christocentric formula following the pattern in Acts, or the Trinitarian formula of Matt. 28:19. In so doing the believer is identified with the risen Lord. As Bousset states, "the name of Jesus is plainly the means of grace effective (along with water) in baptism."[68]

There is good reason, however, to conclude that the more archaic formula was some form of Lord Jesus Christ.[69] As Bousset notes, it is likely that baptism in the Pauline community was practiced in the name of Lord Jesus. He also joins other scholars in speculating that in the case of Matt. 28:19, "the trinitarian formula was only later inserted."[70] Schoeps adds that Ebionite baptism was in the name of Jesus.[71] Finally, it is the opinion of Daniélou that the "triune formula and triple effusion" do not derive from Jewish Christianity."[72]

We can now see the application of an early Jewish Christian understanding of the Name to Christian initiation in the rite of water baptism. Daniélou at least detects other possible marks of Jewish Christianity in baptism, such as the belief that baptism imparts the Holy Spirit, and that the purpose of baptism is to incorporate the believer

---

[66] ὄνομα, p. 273.

[67] Bousset, *Kyrios Christos*, pp. 292-93.

[68] *Ibid.*, p. 295.

[69] For further discussion on the formula used in baptism, see Philip D. Stairs, "The Problem of the Formula Used with Water Baptism" (Master's thesis, Winona Lake School of Theology, 1968); see also Adolf Harnack, *History of Dogma* (7 vols.; trans. Neil Buchanan; New York: Dover, 1961), I, p. 72 n. 2.

[70] Bousset, *Kyrios Christos*, pp. 130, 299.

[71] Schoeps, *Jewish Christianity*, p. 106.

[72] Daniélou, *Jewish Christianity*, p. 323.

into the community of the People of God, a sign rooted in Jewish circumcision.[73]

iii. Power of the Name. A believer's incorporation into Christ and receiving of the Spirit places them within the realm of the power of the risen Lord and his strong Name. G.W.H. Lampe points out that the name of Yahweh functioned much the same for the Jews, as "both a sign given to the people of the Covenant to distinguish them from the outside world, and a powerful weapon against their adversaries." In the New Testament, the "potent name of Jesus ... is a powerful defence against the forces of the devil."[74]

The power of the name of Jesus is clearly illustrated in Acts through the signs and wonders performed by the Apostles – exorcisms, healings, prayer and the power to draw persecution when proclaiming the Gospel (e.g. Acts 5:28). This relationship between power and the Name – as used for instance in Acts 4:7 – is already present in Ps. 54:1, "Save me, O God, by thy name, and vindicate me by thy might" (RSV). And unlike the magical connotations commonly practiced in the Gentile world, Jesus is proclaimed as Lord and accorded the same divine sovereignty as Yahweh. To illustrate, "healing does not take place by pronouncing a set formula, but through the Lord in answer to the prayer which calls upon Him in faith."[75]

In the act of Christian initiation into the community of Jesus, a Jewish Christian theology of the Name serves to express the identity of the believer and the whole Christian community with its Lord. This identity is established initially in the giving of the Name in baptism. There is some evidence that in earliest Christianity the mark one received at baptism was that of the Name, not the sign of the cross that appeared much later.[76] Following initiation, the name of Jesus becomes a powerful presence and tool for Christian believers, helping them to achieve the signs of the kingdom, those "greater things" which Jesus himself had promised.

4. Summary

I have attempted to sketch out a paradigm to assist in the task of interpreting Oneness Pentecostalism within a larger theological framework.

---

[73] *Ibid.*, pp. 326, 329.

[74] G.W.H. Lampe, *The Seal of the Spirit* (New York: Longmans, Green & Co., 1951), pp. 284, 285.

[75] ὄνομα, pp. 277, 278.

[76] Daniélou, *Jewish Christianity*, p. 154.

The movement is viewed as a modern sectarian expression whose dominant metaphors are extracted from particular strands of early Jewish Christian theology, especially the concepts of the Name and the presence of God as dwelling.

I have sought to construct the model for a theology of the Name from these distinctively Jewish Christian themes with reference to the doctrine of God, early Jewish Christian Christology, and the relationship of the Christian to Christ. Though no coherent system of thought representative of Jewish Christianity existed, these themes and metaphors point to a distinctive outlook that left its mark on the early Jewish converts to Christianity. The more immediate interest here, however, is to discover the forms in which those concepts, which largely fell into disuse in mainstream Christian thought, have reappeared in often innovative and idiosyncratic ways in later sectarian movements. This study is devoted to an examination of these ideas and their function in the theology of one of those movements, Oneness Pentecostalism. That remains the task of the following pages.

12

One God and One Name

> He's the great I Am,
> the everlasting Father,
> He's the Prince of Peace,
> The great eternal Wonder,
> Holy Counselor and Zion's righteous Gov'nor,
> He's the great, He's the great I Am.[1]
>
> – Mrs. S.K. Grimes

The Oneness theology of the Name establishes its belief in a particular interpretation of the biblical understanding of the Name, beginning with the Old Testament. For both Oneness and Jewish understanding, the Name is more than a nominal designation. It bears the presence and power of the divine nature. This is particularly true for the revelational name, Yahweh.[2]

1. The Name of God

The name of God in Scripture, especially the Old Testament, bears a number of characteristics that are taken up in Oneness theology to support its strict monotheistic confession, and more particularly the futuristic implications for a full and final revelation of that Name in the new covenant.

a. The Name as Revelational Presence

In ancient cultures, names were believed to bear the personality and character of the person, including deity. This was particularly true for the Jews, who understood and followed a God who revealed himself in many forms, but significantly in the giving of his Name. The

---

[1] Mrs. S.K. Grimes, "The Great I Am," *The Bridegroom Songs*, no. 84.

[2] For the remainder of this study, the name "Yahweh" will be used to designate God in the Old Testament. "Jehovah" will be used only when it appears within quotations.

unique name given by God, "Yahweh," was believed to bear in it the very nature of Yahweh.[3] But as Emil Brunner explains, this name applies in particular to the divine presence as revealed in the world:

Thus the name of God means the indissoluble unity of the nature of God with the revelation not only in the sense that it is the nature of revelation, but that it is the nature of the God of revelation.[4]

In other words, one meets God and no other in the encounter with his Name. For instance, when Moses asked Yahweh to see his glory, God gave him his Name (Exod. 33:18-19).

Similarly, Oneness theology locates its particular view of the name of Jesus in this understanding of the unity between Yahweh and the Name. Ewart's comments are indicative: "the name and nature of God are synonymous."[5] More specifically, "God's presence and power and glory were all in His Name." The Name is the "self-expression, or self-declaration, of God's Own Being."[6] More recently, Oneness theologian, David Bernard, draws the same conclusion. God's presence, character and purpose are revealed through the use of various titles and names for God. But for Bernard there is both an incomplete and progressive character to the revelational names in the Old Testament. Even the redemptive name of Yahweh, so prominent in the New Testament when referring to God, is partial. None of the names and titles constitutes "a complete revelation of God's nature."[7] One awaits the full revelation in the New Testament.

[3] See Edmond Jacob, *Theology of the Old Testament* (trans. A.W. Heathcote & P.J. Allcock; New York: Harper & Row, 1958), pp. 84-85.

[4] Brunner, *Christian Doctrine of God*, p. 127. This observation is important in the following discussion regarding the traditional Trinitarian charge against Sabellianism, which separates the true being of God from the manifestations in the divine economy, or as Rahner puts it, the economic Trinity *is* the immanent Trinity. I will argue that a mature theology of the Name is the unique feature in Oneness theology that mitigates the weakness in a modalistic view of God and bridges the Sabellian discontinuity between the immanent and economic Trinity.

[5] Ewart, *Revelation*, p. 15.

[6] *Idem, The Name and the Book* (Chicago: Daniel Ryerson, 1936), pp. 5, 26.

[7] David K. Bernard, *The Oneness of God, Series in Pentecostal Theology*, vol. I (Hazelwood, MO: Word Aflame, 1983), p. 49. Bernard is currently the most recognized theologian in Oneness Pentecostalism. A prolific writer with at least a dozen books in print, he is pastor with and leading spokesperson for the official Oneness position of the United Pentecostal Church International. Hence, his views reflect the currently dominant view of UPCI; namely, that the soteriology of Acts 2:38 constitutes the new birth. For a detailed study of the origins and development of the doctrine of salvation in the UPCI, see Thomas A. Fudge, *Christianity without the Cross*.

Oneness theology attributes its understanding of the relation between God and the Name given in revelation to this unique Semitic
way of affirming both the transcendence and the integrity of the revelation. Specifically, in the Name one encounters more than a temporal
manifestation or transitory theophany; the Name embodies and bears
the divine reality in person, character and purpose, without violating
the divine transcendence.

b. The Name as One

Scholars and Oneness thinkers alike have studied the various names
and titles for God in the Old Testament. The purpose is usually to
identify the characteristics of God they regard as being fulfilled in Jesus.[8] Generally, the name of Yahweh holds a place of distinction
among all the others. It is the one name that identifies Yahweh as God
acting in salvation history. It is the Name revered and held sacred by
the Jewish people. It is the Name distinctive of God's covenant relationship with his people. Whatever its origin in ancient religion, Exod.
3:13-15 states that Yahweh is the Name by which God would be remembered by future generations.[9] Nathaniel Urshan (1920–), son of
Andrew Urshan and prominent Oneness leader, proposes that the
name of Jesus – transliterated meaning "Yahweh who saves" – is the
fulfillment of the promise made by God to continue his Name: "Here
is a memorial and a name established unto all generations, and adopted
by the Lord God Almighty."[10] While Oneness writers attach importance to the various titles and names for understanding the person and
ministry of Jesus, Yahweh holds a special place, in part because it is
embedded within the very name of Jesus.

In Oneness thinking, the Name also serves as a window into the
singular nature of God's being. For Ewart in particular, the confession

---

[8] Andrew Urshan was strongly influenced – and undoubtedly others through him – by
the lectures on the "Names of Deity" by F.L. Chappell, millenarian and disciple of A.J.
Gordon, at about the turn of the last century. The six lectures were published by Urshan
in *The Witness of God* and reprinted in six consecutive, bi-monthly issues of *The Witness of
God*, from March, 1968, to February, 1969, under the editorship of his son, Nathaniel A.
Urshan, following his death; see also G.T. Haywood, *Divine Names and Titles of Jehovah*.

[9] Exod. 3:13-15, "God said to Moses, 'I AM WHO I AM ... this is my name for ever,
and thus I am to be remembered throughout all generations" (RSV).

[10] Nathaniel A. Urshan, *Consider Him – David's Son and David's Lord* (St. Louis, MO:
Pentecostal Publishing House, n.d.), p. 29. Urshan was for many years pastor of Calvary
Tabernacle, Indianapolis, Indiana, and radio preacher for the official UPCI radio broad-
cast, "Harvestime." He became General Superintendent of the United Pentecostal
Church International in 1978, a position he held until his retirement in 2001.

of monotheism is reflected in the one Sacred Name itself, a point he highlights from the prophet Zechariah: "And the LORD will become king over all the earth; on that day the LORD will be one and his name one" (RSV).[11] Ewart was initially led to the relationship between the singular name and the oneness of God through a study of the baptismal name. He concluded that if water baptism is to be administered in the singular name of Jesus, there must be a biblical and theological reason. In 1916 he wrote:

> As God began to confirm the truth and open the scriptures to us, we saw that if the name of the Father, Son and Holy Spirit was Jesus Christ, then in some mysterious way the Father, Son and Holy Ghost were made one in the person of Jesus Christ.[12]

In other words: "The unity of God is sustained by the absolute unity or oneness of His name."[13] Elsewhere he reverses the argument to draw the same conclusion:

> Since it has been established beyond dispute that ... God is essentially One, then that one God only has and needs one Name; and that one Name ... designates Him in the essential eternality of His being.[14]

For Oneness theology, the oneness of God that is revealed through this mutual witness of divine name and nature in the Old Testament must logically be extended to the New Testament as the foundation for understanding Jesus as both the fullness of God's self-revelation and the singular name which reveals the one God. One of the more strained efforts to establish the monarchy of God through the singular name of Jesus is the traditional Oneness claim that the triune baptismal name in Matt. 28:19 (Father, Son and Holy Spirit) is not a proper name but descriptive titles of divine activity. Ewart exclaims: "This is a little short of impiety to maintain that there are three distinct names ... when God's Word so explicitly and emphatically declares that there is only ONE NAME."[15] In other words, the "one God and one Name" theme becomes a hermeneutic used almost universally by Oneness exegetes to interpret the christological and Name texts of the New Testament. As Ewart explained in 1916, the journey that led him to reject the doctrine of the Trinity and confess the oneness of God originated with the christocentric baptismal formula and the theologi-

[11] Ewart, *Revelation*, p. 33.
[12] Ewart, "The Unity of God."
[13] Ewart, *Revelation*, p. 21.
[14] Ewart, *Name and Book*, p. 171, see also *Revelation*, p. 19.
[15] Ewart, *Revelation*, p. 16.

cal significance of the singular name of Jesus. This theological conviction continues to find its basis in the Old Testament texts on the oneness and name of God.

To summarize, the Oneness preference for the name Yahweh undoubtedly is related to the following: (1) it connotes the full presence of the divine being, (2) it is the one Name that points to a future self-revelation of God which is to last for all time, (3) it is embedded in the name of Jesus itself, and (4) it is associated with God in redemptive activity, culminating in Jesus as "Yahweh our savior."

c. The Name as Proper Name

Oneness theology further distinguishes the name of Yahweh from other names for God by interpreting it as God's "proper Name." It was originally a means by which Israel set apart its God from the gods of its neighbors. Brunner suggests that "so long as a plurality of 'gods' formed part of the thought-world of the time the 'Proper Name' of the True God was a necessity."[16]

Several Oneness writers emphasize the importance of the name of God being more than a functional title or product of human religious construction. One early Canadian Oneness writer, John Paterson (1898-1998), makes the declaration that "there is one name known in the Old Testament as THE NAME ... it is JEHOVAH."[17] Similarly, Andrew Urshan claims that, because it is the Name that is to be carried into the future, it is the "memorial name of the Three-One God."[18] A corollary is that the deity of Christ is implied in this Name. Ewart suggests that, since the Name was promised for the future, it is "carried on in the Hebrew name, 'Yahoshua,' and 'Jesus' is the equivalent in the Greek."[19] Indeed, this ineffable and unutterable Name finally "was retained in the Name of the ... Lord Jesus Christ, and constituted the ONE NAME OF GOD, throughout time and Eternity."[20]

Not all Oneness writers agree that Yahweh is the final name of God for the new covenant. Haywood believes that the "proper Name" had not yet been given in the Old Testament, that God had a "secret

---

[16] Brunner, *Christian Doctrine of God*, p. 119.

[17] John Paterson, *The Real Truth about Baptism in Jesus' Name* (Hazelwood, MO: Pentecostal Publishing House, 1941), p. 13. The late John Paterson was a Canadian Oneness minister who had been associated with the Oneness movement since its early years. In his writings he shows some awareness of the christological and Trinitarian controversies in history and offers an apologetic for the Oneness position.

[18] Andrew Urshan, *Almighty God in the Lord Jesus*, p. 6.

[19] Ewart, *Revelation*, p. 20

[20] Ewart, *Name and Book,* p. 126.

name" which was hidden until the fullness of time, the advent of Christ. As Haywood explains, "Jehovah had a name which was to be 'above all His names.'" When the Name was finally revealed, "all the titles that Jehovah ever bore are comprehended in this one name Jesus." The point is clear: there may not have been only *one* name in the Old Testament that could be carried into the New, but Haywood's *terminus* is the same as the other Oneness teachers – Jesus is the only final, definitive and proper name of God.[21] It is unclear, however, whether or not Haywood makes any clear distinction between titles and proper names in the Old Testament.

Andrew Urshan does make such a distinction. Certain names such as "*Adonai*" and "Lord" are non-revelational names used by believers to indicate some aspect of the nature of God. Applying a dispensational hermeneutic, he concludes that there are three revelational and proper names which are given for particular dispensational ages – Elohim, El-Shaddai and Yahweh, which designate God's activity in the dispensations of creation, promise and law, respectively. Jesus, however, is the greatest name of God for this the greatest dispensation of all, the dispensation of grace, because it is the name of God for the salvation of all humankind.[22]

David Bernard believes that the various names used for God in the Old Testament are part of God's plan of progressive revelation: "None of them is a complete revelation of God's nature." They are all eventually taken up in the full and final revelation of God's redemptive name in Jesus: "Jesus is the culmination of all the Old Testament names of God. It is the highest, most exalted name ever revealed to mankind." Following Ewart, he appeals to the "one name" prophesied in Zech. 14:9, that in the future there will be one God and one Name by which God will be known.[23]

In summary, there is no agreement among Oneness exegetes regarding the distinction between names and titles for God in the Old Testament, or the relationship between the name of Yahweh and other names for God. But there is preference given to the name Yahweh, and all are finally agreed that Jesus is the one proper name of God for the new age of universal salvation.

---

[21] Haywood, *Divine Names*, pp. 8, 10, 11.
[22] Andrew Urshan, "The Name of God," *Pentecostal Outlook* 9 (February 1940): 5
[23] David Bernard, *Oneness of God*, pp. 49, 51.

d. The Name as Promise

The sacred Name given to Moses in Exod. 3:14 bears a futuristic element in that it can literally mean, "I WILL BE WHAT I WILL BE." Lutheran theologian, Wolfhart Pannenberg, suggests that this name incorporates the Old Testament revelation that Yahweh will ultimately act in the future.[24] Zimmerli likewise believes that the formula, "I am Yahweh," presents Yahweh as Promiser. Yahweh carries out his promises in history in order to reveal himself: "The history that God brings forth is the carrying out of the revelation of God's person that took place in revealing His name."[25]

This futuristic aspect of the name of Yahweh is picked up by Ewart and applied to Jesus. Like David Bernard, he observes in the Old Testament revelation of the Name the promise of a progressive revelation: "I AM THAT I AM" means "to become," thereby "promising a continuous and increasing self-revelation." The *telos* of course is the final revelation of Jesus, and the prophecy was fulfilled when "Jesus called this lost name out of obscurity."[26]

For Oneness theology this hidden and futuristic aspect of the name Yahweh in the Old Testament is a messianic prophecy. The one who will bear this new name in its redemptive mode will be the full and final revelation of Yahweh.

2. The Monarchy of God

Oneness Pentecostalism is a departure from traditional Trinitarian faith. For historical and theological reasons, it rejects the complex, philosophically laden creedal formulations of the Christian era that are perceived to compromise the monotheistic foundations of the Christian faith. This concern leads Oneness theologians to revisit and reaffirm with Israel the first principle of their own belief, the confession of the one and transcendent God.

a. The Shema

The *Shema* (Deut. 6:4) is unquestionably the creed *par excellence* of the Hebrews. It confesses the sole and sovereign lordship of Yahweh over the world, and establishes God's absolute monarchy or oneness. Al-

---

[24] Wolfhart Pannenberg, "The Revelation of God in Jesus of Nazareth," in *Theology as History*, vol. III, *New Frontiers in Theology*, ed. James M. Robinson & John B. Cobb, Jr. (New York: Harper & Row, 1967), pp. 119-20.

[25] Cited in Robinson and Cobb, *Theology as History*, p. 44.

[26] Ewart, *Name and Book*, pp. 76, 120.

though the Word, Wisdom and Name are mentioned in personal terms, these "personifications"[27] do not violate or compromise the claim of unity in Yahweh's being.

Early Jewish Christianity zealously defended the monarchy of God. According to Patristics scholar, J.N.D. Kelly, this concern to preserve the integrity of monotheism was deeply ingrained in these early Christians. The second-century Apologists, who were using the materials of Hellenistic philosophy to construct their theology, struggled to explain their triadic Christian experience of God within the monotheistic framework of their Jewish heritage. Even into the latter part of the third century, the various expressions of the Monarchian reaction to the new Logos theology came from a "tradition which antedated the whole movement of thought inaugurated by the Apologists."[28]

The Oneness movement can be counted among a long historical line of protestors against the creedal outcome of the debates. Each movement has had its reasons. Some simply did not understand the complex christological and Trinitarian debates of those early centuries. Others rejected the set of philosophical ideas and language within which those doctrines were framed. Still others protested against the ways in which they perceived the church hierarchy to have manipulated the final creedal formulations as a means to control or persecute those who dared to disagree. And finally, some decided that the doctrinal decisions took the church dangerously far from its true biblical heritage. Certainly for many, including Oneness adherents, the reaction to the historic doctrine of the Trinity is rooted in the Jewish and Jewish Christian resolve to preserve the inheritance of an unadulterated monotheism. To distinguish themselves from a Trinitarian doctrine that is regarded as a fundamental departure from its biblical roots, some Oneness exponents refer to themselves as "Christian monotheists."[29]

---

[27] G.B. Caird, "The Development of the Doctrine of Christ in the New Testament," *Christ for Us Today*, ed. Norman Pittinger (London: SCM Press, 1968), p. 79. See also Bauckham, *God Crucified*. Bauckham claims that the role of Word and Wisdom as "personifications" begins in Second Temple Judaism, a development that already understands the oneness of God to be more complex than a solitary undifferentiated divine monad. It will be important for Oneness theologians to reconsider the fundamental reason for their resistance to a more complex understanding of divine oneness. A helpful direction will be to revisit the reasons for the birth of the movement: beginning with Durham, it was a "Christo-centrizing" protest against the multiplicity of crisis experiences being taught and sought in the early Holiness Pentecostal movement.

[28] Kelly, *Early Christian Doctrines,* p. 125.

[29] See Kenneth V. Reeves, *The Godhead* (Granite City, IL: By the Author, 1971), p. 9;

Oneness theology, therefore, self-consciously identifies with this monotheistic Jewish tradition. One Oneness writer, Kenneth Reeves, asserts that Oneness Pentecostalism stands for the same belief as Jewish monotheism, "with the exception that the Son of God is the Messiah, and that this One God has sent His Spirit in and upon the people as the Holy Ghost."[30] As Thomas Streitferdt, another Oneness writer, explains, Jewish monotheism is "the bed in which God planted the seed of salvation," which was corrupted in part by Greek philosophy. "Not only Judaism, but all true believers in God, rest on this concept – the strict monotheism of God."[31] David Bernard begins his book on *The Oneness of God* with the chapter, "Christian Monotheism," in which he also concludes that the Bible teaches a "strict monotheism."[32]

Oneness literature is replete with references to the *Shema* and the oneness of God as the fundamental tenet of its doctrine.[33] One prominent Oneness teacher, the late S.G. Norris, makes the large claim that the Bible either stands or falls on this significant truth.[34] Citing John 4:24, a favorite Oneness description for God is "God is Spirit."[35] Similarly, God is the "one, Holy, Eternal Spirit,"[36] "ONE ETERNAL SPIRIT,"[37] the "Holy One of Israel,"[38] "the absolute ONE."[39] And God has "only one personality."[40]

Ralph V. Reynolds, *Truth Shall Triumph – A Study of Pentecostal Doctrines* (St. Louis, MO: Pentecostal Publishing House, 1965), p. 86; "Christian Monotheism," in Bernard, *Oneness of God*, ch. 1.

[30] Reeves, *Godhead*, p. 9. Reeves is a retired Oneness pastor in Granite City, IL. He is affiliated with the United Pentecostal Church International.

[31] Streitferdt, *The Word Became Flesh* (Orange, NJ: Lutho, 1961), pp. 11, 52. Thomas Streitferdt was a Oneness pastor in New York City, affiliated with the predominantly black Pentecostal Assemblies of the World.

[32] Bernard, *Oneness of God*, p. 21.

[33] See the *Articles of Faith* of the United Pentecostal Church in *What We Believe and Teach* (St. Louis, MO: Pentecostal Publishing House, n.d.), p. 1. Oscar Vouga, *Our Gospel Message* (St. Louis, MO: Pentecostal Publishing House, n.d.), p. 27. Morris E. Golder, *The Principles of Our Doctrine* (Cincinnati, OH: Apostolic Light, n.d.), p. 4.

[34] S.G. Norris, *The Mighty God in Christ* (St. Paul, MN: Apostolic Bible Institute, n.d.), p. 1.

[35] See Reynolds, *Truth Shall Triumph*, p. 87.

[36] Haywood, *Divine Names*, p. 12.

[37] Ewart, *Revelation*, p. 14.

[38] Clifford E. Hobbs, *Whom Say ye that I am?* (Lansing, IL: Lansing Apostolic Church, 1971), p. 56.

[39] Ewart, "The Oneness of God," *Apostolic Herald* 19 (January 1944): 3.

[40] Melvin R. Springfield, *Jesus the Almighty* (2nd ed.; Portland, OR: Parry Mail Advertising Service, 1972), p. 7. Springfield is a Oneness pastor affiliated with the United Pentecostal Church. His book, *Jesus the Almighty*, is in the form of a basic catechism on

Ewart was one of the more speculative Oneness thinkers. A typical example is his attempt to use a modern illustration from Einstein's theory of relativity to deduce a theological truth about God. He first points out that, since the theory holds to "only ONE, ABSOLUTE," with all else being relative, there must inevitably be a distinction between time and eternity – the latter being absolute, not just endless time. Since God alone is eternal, all else is subordinate to God. Ewart then uses this argument to discredit the Trinitarian projection of the hypostatic distinctions back into the eternal Godhead.[41] Elsewhere, he more specifically states that a belief in the oneness of God must presume a mathematical unity: "If God is not a numerical one, why does He declare in Isaiah, '... The HOLY ONE of Israel'?"[42]

b. God as Transcendent Spirit

At first glance, Oneness language for God appears to be notoriously general and impersonal. To express God's transcendence, Oneness writers are fond of using the term "invisible."[43] Andrew Urshan describes God as "an unapproachable, mysterious, incomprehensible, hidden spiritual BEING."[44] This is of course the language of classical Christian theism to affirm God's otherness. More specifically, Oneness thinkers are struggling to identify with the Jewish belief in the transcendence of God, but a God, nevertheless, who reveals himself. The language of invisibility is borrowed from a Oneness favorite Pauline text that describes Jesus as the "image of the invisible God" (Col. 1:15). The particular Oneness interest in this terminology is to clarify that the one true God is without parts or distinctions, and that Jesus is the full and final revelation of this *one* invisible God. But it is important to remember that, while Oneness theology expresses its affinity with Jewish monotheism and a monarchical view of God as Spirit, its primary religious identity is defined and shaped by the modern Pentecostal movement, of which it is a part.

the Oneness doctrine.

[41] Ewart, "The Einstein Theory," *Apostolic Herald* 17 (September 1942): 2.

[42] Ewart, *Revelation*, p. 6.

[43] *Ibid*. See also Ewart, *Name and Book*, p. 98: Reeves, *Godhead*, p. 10; John Paterson, *God in Christ Jesus* (Montreal: By the Author, 1964), pp. 7, 9, 15.

[44] Andrew Urshan, *Almighty God*, p. 75.

3. God as Three-In-One

While Oneness Pentecostals rhetorically draw attention to their belief in the radical oneness of God, they cannot avoid the biblical tripartite language of Trinitarian discourse. But Oneness theology builds its modalistic view of God and understanding of the meaning of "person" in ways that are radically different from the classical Trinitarian approach. A necessary first principle for any dialogue must be an effort to understand the language and how it functions in the ideas of each partner.

a. The Dialectic

The Oneness doctrine of God is distinguished from the classical Trinitarian doctrine primarily in its insistence upon permitting no distinctions, especially Trinitarian ones, in the nature of God as God exists apart from revelation. Since Oneness theologians hold to the monarchy and transcendence of God, the basic theological principle is that the Three-In-One is a simple dialectic of transcendence and immanence.

The Oneness view is that if God is a single transcendent, eternal Being, God's threeness is limited to the act of divine self-disclosure in history. Any distinction in the Godhead is the dialectic of otherness and expressibility. This dialectic is incarnationally expressed in the New Testament as Father and Son.

"Visible and invisible" seem to clearly indicate that the matchless, invisible loveliness and beauty of the Father's character was made visible and mentally apprehensible in the Son.[45]

Reeves describes these polar realities of God's transcendence and Word as "the two sides of God." In New Testament language, "Father and Son are fitting terms to describe God in His Omnipresent and eternal aspect from the particular aspect into which he projected Himself." Similarly, he identifies these two "aspects" or "elements" in God's being as Spirit (transcendence) and Word (expression). But Reeves appears to restrict this dialectic to God's activity in "time and creation," and does not indicate whether or not such a distinction exists within God's being in any form other than that of abstract principle.[46] Another Oneness writer, Melvin Springfield, does propose that the Word represents an eternal dimension of God's eternal being,

---

[45] Ewart, *Name and Book*, p. 98.
[46] Reeves, *Godhead*, pp. 10, 14, 20, 21, 24.

though he fails to elaborate the point: "The Word, or God's Expression, has always been in existence."[47]

This dialectical principle of transcendence and immanence becomes a hermeneutic for defending the monarchy of God and at the same time allowing for some form of threefoldness. Whereas Trinitarians attribute eternal reality to both the one and the three, Oneness theologians attribute the oneness of God solely to his transcendent being and the threefoldness to his activity in history. Christologically, the Father-Son relationship and the two natures in Christ are understood in terms of the dialectic of transcendent eternal Spirit and God in revelation. That is, in good modalistic fashion, Oneness theologians refuse to accept any Trinitarian element beyond that of the economy of salvation. The one exception is the notion that the Word exists eternally as the "expression" of the mind of God.

b. God as Uni-Personality

One of the constant points of debate with Oneness theologians is the understanding of the term "person." The discussion is clouded by the confusion between the "person" of Christ and the "persons" in the Godhead, two different but related issues.

Though there is no consensus among Oneness writers, they are generally agreed that God is Spirit and personhood is a term attributable only to Christ. Since Oneness theology does not take its reference point from the classical discourse, it is important first to identify the Oneness definition of the terms and how they are used.

Undoubtedly to counteract what they consider to be a crypto-tritheism in the term "three persons," Oneness teachers generally select their definition of "person" from a modern dictionary. For example, Oneness pastor and teacher, Clifford E. Hobbs, defines person as "an individual in bodily form."[48] With or without the bodily form, John Paterson regards person as "a distinct being."[49] So long as such definitions persist within Oneness thinking, the suspicion of tritheism in Trinitarian doctrine will not disappear.

---

[47] Springfield, *Jesus the Almighty*, p. 19.

[48] Clifford E. Hobbs, *Whom Say Ye That I Am?* p. 69. Hobbs was for many years an Independent Oneness pastor of Lansing Apostolic Church, Lansing, IL, whose influence was extended through a radio broadcast, bi-monthly publication called *The Last Angel Message* and other writings. His teachings include the "sleep of the dead" during the intermediate state and a repudiation of the observance of Christmas.

See also Oneness minister, G.K. Jensen, *When God Became Flesh* (New Westminster, Canada: Plowright Printing Co., n.d.), p. 4.

[49] Paterson, *God in Christ Jesus*, p. 38.

Ewart equally resists the language of persons but draws his conclusion from Scripture: "The word 'Person' is never used in the original languages as describing God."[50] Rather, God in transcendence is better described as "substance" or "Eternal Spirit." The terms "Spirit" and "person" aptly illustrates the Oneness dialectic of transcendence and immanence. In Ewart's words, "God the eternal Spirit was incarnated in the person of His Son." To contrast his view with Trinitarianism, he goes on to say: "Instead of the second person of the Deity being incarnated, it was God Himself, the whole Deity." [51]

Haywood likewise uses the same Spirit-person terminology. Since the Apostles taught that God was a Spirit who came "in the Person of Jesus Christ," it is impossible for God to exist in three separate persons, Spirits or personalities. Rather, there is "but One God, and that God is manifested in the Person of the Lord Jesus Christ."[52]

Andrew Urshan does attribute personhood to God. In describing the Father in the Father-Son relationship, he asserts that there is only "one single divine Being or Person" but fails to relate the concept to the Trinitarian distinctions.[53] Reeves defines person according to the Latin *persona*, which means mask, but then restricts the term to Jesus in his humanity: "The only mask that God wore in the New Testament record is the flesh of Jesus Christ."[54]

Theodore Fitch, a heterodox Oneness teacher, applies the same Spirit-person principle in an almost Arian fashion. Though he rejects any suggestion that the Christ was merely a "created" being, he diverges from mainline Oneness theology in his teaching that Christ the Word was not eternal but had a beginning prior to creation: "Jesus was the first Person to exist BEFORE creation started." Since God as Spirit and the One who is called Father "has no form," then personhood is the omnipresent Spirit that takes on the form of humanity, albeit a spiritual form or being prior to creation. Sonship is a descriptive title reserved for the incarnation.[55] It is important here only to

---

[50] Ewart, *Name and Book*, p. 98.

[51] Ewart, *Revelation*, pp. 43, 22.

[52] Haywood, *Victim of the Flaming Sword*, pp. 56, 58. See also p. 15; *The Finest of the Wheat* (Indianapolis, IN: Christ Temple, n.d.), p. 35; Vouga, Oscar, *Our Gospel Message* (St. Louis, MO: Pentecostal Publishing House, n.d.), p. 29.

[53] Andrew Urshan, *Life*, p. 248.

[54] Reeves, *Godhead*, p. 5.

[55] Fitch, Theodore, *God the Father's Omnipresent Spirit* (Council Bluffs, IA: Privately printed, n.d.), pp. 6, 9, 13, 17. Fitch was an Independent Oneness preacher and teacher in Iowa. Although he was in close association with the organizational Oneness movement as early as the 1930's, his divergent teaching of the pre-existent body of Christ has proba-

observe that, while Fitch does not fit well within the broad stream of Oneness theology, he shares the same understanding of "person" and Spirit-person principle we see generally in Oneness theology.

Oneness resistance to defining God as "person" must not be construed to imply that God is without personality or is a mere impersonal spiritual force. Rather, Oneness theology uses the language of "Spirit" to describe God's singular otherness in transcendence. Personhood, on the other hand, is reserved for that divine projecting forth of God's mind, the dynamic of unveiling. It is God in the act of revealing, lifting his hiddenness, facing himself toward that which is other than Himself – the creation. "Personhood" in God refers to that revelational aspect of God that takes on form and is finally consummated in the human form of Jesus Christ.

c. God in Three Manifestations

The Oneness language for God intentionally frees it from association with the doctrine of the Trinity in two ways: the language of "Spirit" safeguards the monarchy of God, and "person" is reserved for the human Jesus. This provides Oneness theology with a linguistic shape for its alternative to the trinitarian terminology of "three persons."

Oneness writers are fond of describing the threefold doctrine of God as "three separate and distinct persons."[56] The implication for them is that there are three centers of consciousness or more radically three divine Beings,[57] all of which sounds to them like "modified tritheism."[58] Any suggestion of three personalities threatens the fundamental Christian commitment to the sovereignty of the *one* God. Besides the threat to Christian monotheism, it also diminishes the centrality of Christ. Three "equal" persons in the Godhead means, mathematically at least, a shift away from God's purpose to set forth Christ in his divine fullness. This is the point being made by Norris,

---

bly been a contributing factor in his independent status.

[56] See Nathaniel Urshan, *Consider Him*, p. 18; Andrew Urshan, *Almighty God*, p. 81; Reeves, *Godhead*, Hobbs, *Whom Say Ye*, p. 68; Golder, *Principles*, p. 8. The classical Trinitarian view that most closely approximates this view is the "social analogy" theory. For an example of the social analogy theory of the Trinity, see Leonard Hodgson, *The Doctrine of the Trinity* (New York: Charles Scribner's Sons, 1944). The doctrine of the Trinity developed by the Eastern Fathers accentuates the threefoldness of the divine nature in ways that appear to threaten the unity of God.

[57] See Paterson, *God in Christ Jesus*, p. 38.

[58] Reeves, *Godhead*, p. 30.

that according to Col. 2:9, the *fullness* of the Godhead is revealed in Christ, "not just part of it."[59]

The Oneness alternative to the "three persons" is three "manifestations." Taking the language from another christological hymn, 1 Tim. 3:16 ("he was manifested in the flesh"), Oneness theology extends the language of "manifestation" to the whole threefold divine reality. In so doing, it expresses what Oneness people hope to maintain – the monarchy of God and the reality of the triune revelation. Nathaniel Urshan summarizes the view: "We realize there are three in one. The Father, the Word and the Holy Spirit are in, and manifested through Jesus Christ."[60] Haywood likewise calls the Trinity a "three-fold manifestation."[61] Reeves writes that it is God revealing Himself "in three basic ways."[62] Howard Goss even attempts to retrieve the term "Trinity" for the Oneness movement, observing, "We believe that we are the true trinitarians because the word trinity means tri-unity – three in one."[63] He proceeds to explain that the threefold manifestation of God in the New Testament is "not three eternally separate, distinct persons or Gods."[64] In the early years following his conversion to the Oneness movement, Andrew Urshan experimented with language in an attempt to redeem some form of Trinitarian terminology. One rather crude example is the difference he made between "TriUnity" and "Tri-units."[65] The former is the true meaning of the word "Trinity" and therefore acceptable to Oneness theology, while the latter implies the incipient tritheism of the traditional doctrine of the Trinity.

Occasionally Oneness writers prefer to describe the tripartite reality as "offices," all of which are taken up and manifested in Jesus Christ. Nathaniel Urshan, for instance, teaches that "we believe in three offices which are filled by one person," Jesus Christ.[66] Gordon Magee likewise refers to these "offices in one person."[67] The highly imper-

---

[59] Norris, *Mighty God in Christ*, p. 13. Col. 2:9 is one of the classical Oneness texts, "For in him [Christ] the fullness of deity dwells bodily" [RSV].

[60] Nathaniel Urshan, *Consider Him*, p. 18

[61] Haywood, *Victim*, p. 12

[62] Reeves, *Godhead*, p. 8.

[63] Reeves, "Godhead," *Pentecostal Herald* 23 (December 1948): 7.

[64] *Ibid.*

[65] Andrew Urshan, "The Doctrine of the Trinity and the Divinity of Jesus Christ," *Pentecostal Witness* 3 (1 December 1926): 1-2.

[66] Nathaniel Urshan, *Consider Him*, p. 12.

[67] Gordon Magee, *Is Jesus in the Godhead or is the Godhead in Jesus?* (Pasadena, TX: By the Author, n.d.), p. 30. Magee was an Independent Oneness pastor in Houston, Texas. Formerly from Ireland, he was a popular debater and conference speaker in Oneness

sonal connotation of this terminology is unfortunate, and is only compensated in part by the emphatic christocentrism of the Oneness doctrine.

Oneness theologians by and large consign the Trinity exclusively to the realm of divine self-disclosure in the world. There is seldom a hint of the threefold nature of God – only an affirmation of a threefold revelation. Andrew Urshan, however, speculated early on regarding such a possibility, but failed to elaborate or discern the significance of his position. He writes about a "divine threeness of the Divine Being"[68] and "our blessed and adorable THREE-ONE GOD."[69] He refers to God as having "a three-fold relative nature, which is reflected in the triune nature of man."[70] In one passage he states more boldly than any other Oneness teacher a position comparable to that of Trinitarians:

> I personally cannot refrain from believing that there is a plurality in God's mysterious Being, and that this plurality is shown as a three-ness, not three separate, distinct Beings or Persons of God, but a mysterious, inexplicable, incomprehensible three-ness.[71]

Urshan wrote these lines shortly after he left the Assemblies of God fellowship. It is clear that he was struggling to formulate a moderate position that was not Trinitarian but one that gave serious consideration to the Trinitarian witness. It is unfortunate that his limited understanding of the doctrine of the Trinity and apparent lack of awareness of the Trinitarian implications of his own proposal in part prevented him from developing his ideas. It is likely that these early speculations were so similar to the orthodox Trinitarian doctrine that they threatened the identity of the new movement.

d. The "Us" Passages in Genesis

The "Us" passages in Genesis (Gen. 1:26, "Let us make man in our image;" 3:22, "Behold, the man has become like one of us, knowing good and evil") are frequently argued by popular Trinitarian writes as evidence of the Trinity in the Old Testament.[72] Oneness teachers gen-

circles. This popular booklet was widely circulated during the 1950's and 60's as a readable and persuasive apologetic for the Oneness doctrine.

[68] Andrew Urshan, "Doctrine of the Trinity," p. 1.

[69] Urshan, *Almighty God*, p. 45.

[70] Urshan, "Doctrine of the Trinity," p. 2.

[71] Urshan, *Almighty God*, p. 77.

[72] See Carl Brumback, *God in Three Persons* (Cleveland, TN: Pathway, 1959), pp. 39-42; F.J. Lindquist, *The Truth About the Trinity and Baptism in Jesus' Name Only* (Minnea-

erally respond by proposing that God is speaking to angels. Magee argues that "angels were present when God made the world, and they applauded His creative acts.... God is addressing the Cherubim or elect angels."[73] Reeves notes that this as a common Jewish interpretation, and concurs with it.[74] Paterson, echoing that strand of Oneness teaching, which holds that the Word had a distinct status before the incarnation, believes that God was conversing with the Word, "the embodiment of the invisible God."[75] This "embodiment" is apparently of a spiritual nature, similar to a hypostatic distinction. But he emphasizes that this in no way threatens the oneness of God: even "Elohim," a plural name for God, is not a plurality of persons but a "plurality of attributes."[76] Bernard reviews a variety of interpretations, concluding only that to view such plurality as denoting "persons" in the Godhead would be to "contradict the rest of Scripture."[77]

e. Analogies

Like Trinitarians, Oneness exponents turn to the world around them to find analogies that illustrate their particular view of the Three-in-One. One of the most popular analogies is the triune nature of man, "the most absolute unit we know: Body, soul and spirit, but one man."[78] Andrew Urshan elaborates on this analogy: while each element is different, they "cannot be separated without causing death."[79] Likewise, God consists of "three sublime elements, yet there is only one God."[80] Nathaniel Urshan offers a similar analogy of a person in relationship. A man can be a son, a father, and a husband, and thereby "fill different positions" without compromising his existence as a single person.[81] Other analogies come from the world of nature such as the

polis, MN: Northern Gospel, 1961), p. 13; Luke Miller, *A Review of the "Jesus Only" Doctrine* (Austin, TX: Firm Foundation, 1959), p. 8; Charles W. Walkem, *The Jesus Only Theory: A Brief Analysis of the Trinity* (Los Angeles: The Church Press, n.d.), p. 4.

[73] Magee, *Is Jesus in the Godhead*, p. 26. See Also Nathaniel Urshan, *Consider Him*, p. 20; Springfield, *Jesus*, p. 42.

[74] Reeves, *Godhead*, p. 40.

[75] Paterson, *God in Christ Jesus*, p. 39.

[76] Paterson, *God in Christ Jesus*, p. 39. See also Magee, *Is Jesus in the Godhead*, p. 27.

[77] Bernard, *Oneness of God*, p. 151.

[78] Ewart, "Oneness of God," p. 3.

[79] Andrew Urshan, "The Blessed Trinity of God Revealed in Nature and Demonstrated or Personified in Jesus Christ Our Lord," *Pentecostal Witness* 3 (1 July 1927): 2-3.

[80] *Ibid.*, p. 3; see also Reynolds, *Truth Shall Triumph*, p. 94; Small, *Living Waters*, p. 94.

[81] Nathaniel Urshan, *Consider Him*, p. 25.

one tree with its roots, branches, and sap;[82] a light ray which gives illumination, warmth and power; and fire which also gives light, heat and power.[83]

The difficulty with the Oneness selection of analogies is that, owing to a limited or erroneous understanding of the Trinitarian doctrine and lack of awareness of the Trinitarian implications of the analogies, Oneness apologists fail to prove their point.

The analogy of a human being as body, soul and spirit may illustrate the threefold nature of a single person, and by extension the unipersonality of God. But the analogy breaks down since a person's body, soul and spirit are integral to their being, but, Oneness thinkers argue, this does not apply to God. They are attempting to show precisely that the three manifestations are *not* part of God's being but belong only to the realm of self-disclosure. The analogy functions much better as an illustration of an Augustinian understanding of the Trinity. It is ironic that if Oneness theologians would take their analogies more seriously, they would discover this aspect of their doctrine at least to be within the broad scope of Trinitarian faith.

f. Functions of the Three Manifestations

There is little attention in Oneness writings devoted to exploring the "functions" of the Father, Son and Holy Spirit that would distinguish their views from Trinitarian doctrine. Their focus has been almost exclusively devoted to reiterating their distinctive Oneness doctrine that the Three are really only one, divine, uni-personal Spirit making himself present in the world in a threefold way. Oneness teachers do not hesitate to attribute personality to the three, even though terms like "manifestation" and "office" are impersonal. The Oneness distinction is that God is one divine Being whose essence is revealed as Father *in* the Son and Spirit *through* the Son. The Oneness christocentrism becomes apparent because as humanity Jesus *is* the Son, and as Spirit (i.e. in his deity) he reveals, indeed *is* the Father, and sends, indeed *is* the Holy Spirit as the Spirit of Christ.

The task of Oneness theologians is to demonstrate that the Father, Son and Holy Spirit are all present in each manifestation. It is interesting to note that the following explanation by Andrew Urshan is a classic Trinitarian statement of *perichoresis*, the idea that when one Person in the Godhead acts, the other Persons are equally present:

---

[82] See Andrew Urshan, "Blessed Trinity," p. 2; Theodore Fitch, *God the Father*, p. 2.

[83] Andrew Urshan, "Blessed Trinity," p. 2.

Whenever you find the Holy Spirit in function, there you find the Father and the Word also in function. And wherever the Son is in activity, there you find the Father and the Holy Spirit in activity. And, wherever you observe the Father in operation, there and then you find the Holy Spirit and the Word also in operation.[84]

From a christological point of view, Magee lists a series of biblical texts intended to show that Jesus is the Father, the Son and the Holy Spirit.[85] For all the impersonal language of function and manifestation, he argues that Christ in his divinity *is* the Personal God, making clear his response to those who accuse Oneness theology of denying personality to the Spirit, "How could we if we believe the Spirit is Jesus?"[86] A similar argument is made by Andrew Urshan: since the Holy Spirit is called the Spirit of Truth, and Jesus himself says, "I am the Truth," "the Holy Spirit, therefore, must be the life, the Spirit of the Son, just as He is the Spirit of the Father."[87]

The three "offices" follow predictably the traditional roles of the Father, Son and Holy Spirit in Trinitarian thought. For instance, Reeves regards the Father as God in His Omnipresence (unrelatedness), the Son as the human mediator, and the Spirit as "God's particular presence in and for believers."[88] Golder describes the functions in terms of creation, redemption and indwelling, respectively.[89] Nathaniel Urshan likewise sees their functions as those of creation, redemption, and presence in the world, to bring humanity to repentance.[90] Bernard prefers the term "manifestation," and indicates that the Father, Son and Spirit are not separate persons or personalities but can "only denote different aspects or roles of one Spirit-being."[91]

---

[84] Andrew Urshan, "The Holy Spirit's Relationship," *Pentecostal Herald* 38 (December 1963): 3.

[85] Magee, "Is Jesus in the Godhead," pp. 14–16; see also Streitferdt, *Word Became Flesh*, pp. 45–50.

[86] *Ibid.*, p. 17.

[87] Andrew Urshan, "Holy Spirit's Relationship," p. 3.

[88] Reeves, *Godhead*, p. 19.

[89] Morris E. Golder, *The Principles of Our Doctrine* (Cincinnati, OH: Apostolic Light, n.d.), p. 8. Golder was a prominent Oneness leader and teacher. He ministered for most of his life in Indianapolis, IN. He was affiliated with the Pentecostal Assemblies of the World.

[90] Nathaniel Urshan, *Consider Him*, p. 12.

[91] Bernard, *Oneness of God*, p. 134.

4. Classification of the Oneness View of God

Oneness Pentecostalism is a modern, sectarian reaction to the traditional doctrine of the Trinity, much the same as the Monarchian reaction to the new Logos theology in the third century.[92] Some form of Modalism or Sabellianism is the most common label.[93] Since Oneness leaders historically have not been concerned to conform to either traditional orthodox doctrine or its various heretical counterparts, such accusations caused little offense in the early years of the movement.[94] There are obvious parallels with certain aspects of second-century pre-Nicene views. Kelly states that even the second-century Apologists viewed the divine Triad not as three coequal persons but a "single personage, the Father who is the Godhead Itself, with His mind, or rationality, and His wisdom." The "intense concern for the fundamental tenet of monotheism" was still the primary driving force in their theology.[95] Though the theology was not thoroughly developed, these Church Fathers affirmed some form of Trinitarian distinctions within the Godhead prior to the incarnation.

Early 3rd-century theologians Hippolytus and Tertullian attempted to develop the Logos doctrine in a way that affirmed real distinctions within the Godhead. Their view is generally recognized by the title "economic Trinitarianism." While the Trinitarian distinctions were generally located in the "economy" of salvation, Tertullian coined the term "economy" to designate a "dispensation" prior to creation in which "the one only God has also a Son, His Word, who has issued out of Himself."[96] Both he and Hippolytus taught that the three persons were "severally manifestations of a single indivisible power." But here the distinction was understood more as "distribution" than "separation," on the analogy of a light from the root of a tree. The point was to elaborate on the extension of the Son from the Father, not his separation from him. Even the terms πρόσωπον (*prosopon*) and *persona* in their earlier usage had the dynamic imagery of face, expression or role, not "otherness or independent subsistence," which they later came to mean. As Kelly points out, never "was the idea of self-consciousness nowadays associated with 'person' and 'personal' at all

---

[92] Kelly, *Early Christian Doctrines*, p. 109.

[93] See James Bjornstad and Walter Bjorch, *Jesus Only – A Modalistic Interpretation* (Wayne, NJ: Christian Research Institute, 1970); Brumback, *God in Three Persons*, p. 23; Menzies, *Anointed to Serve*, p. 112.

[94] See Haywood, *Victim*, p. 6; Streitferdt, *Lord Became Flesh*, p. 15.

[95] Kelly, *Early Christian Doctrines*, p. 108.

[96] Cited in Kelly, *Early Christian Doctrines*, p. 113

prominent."[97] Patristic scholar G.L. Prestige's succinct description of the distinction between the one and three in this period is that God is "one object in himself and three objects to himself."[98] Elaborating on this distinction, J.S. Whale adds:

> In the One God ... there are three divine organs of God-consciousness, but one center of divine consciousness. That is, as seen and thought, God is three; as seeing and thinking, he is one.[99]

If Kelly and Whale are correct, one distinctive mark of the "economic Trinity" during this period is that, while holding to the one center of consciousness, it maintained the three distinctions not merely as temporal manifestations but as "real distinctions in the immanent being of the unique, indivisible Father."[100]

One form of the "Monarchian" reaction to the prevailing theology championed by Tertullian and others was the Modalistic Monarchianism identified with Sabellius and his followers. It distinguished itself from the prevailing Logos doctrine in its view that God is a monad "which expressed itself in three operations." These operations are transitory manifestations or "modes of self expression" of the one essence.[101] There is some evidence that Sabellius regarded the manifestations as being successive appearances, with one form disappearing as another came on the scene. An overall criticism has persisted that in any variation of this view the *real* God remains hidden and appears only indirectly as a manifestation or theophany. As historian J.F. Bethune-Baker points out, in the Modalism of this sort there can obviously be "no real incarnation."[102] But theologian Harold O.J. Brown, in his extensive study of heresy in the church, sums up well the spirit of Modalism in the early church and in particular the shift that occurred between the Councils at Nicaea (AD 325) and Constantinople (AD 381):

> Nicene orthodoxy was rather close in spirit to modalism. By Constantinople, 'consubstantiality' had come to mean the equality of the Persons. In 325 the church was monotheistic, but in a Trinitarian way; by 381 the church had become Trinitarian first, monotheistic second ... At Nicaea

---

[97] Kelly, *Early Christian Doctrines*, pp. 113, 115.

[98] Cited in J.S. Whale, *Christian Doctrine* (Cambridge: Cambridge University Press, 1963), p. 119.

[99] *Ibid.*, p. 119.

[100] Kelly, *Early Christian Doctrines*, p. 108.

[101] *Ibid.*, pp. 119-22.

[102] J.F. Bethune-Baker, *An Introduction to the Early History of Christian Doctrine* (London: Methuen, 1954), p. 106.

the emphasis was on the oneness of nature, after Constantinople on the equality of nature.[103]

In its general teaching on the One-in-Three and concern to preserve the "unrevised" monarchy of God, Oneness doctrine conforms to some form of modalism – the manifestations appear either *successively* through sequential historical periods or *simultaneously*. Occasionally Oneness language such as "dispensational manifestations" suggests the former. The early Andrew Urshan, for instance, refers to the "three distinct manifestations, operations, *in three dispensations*" [emphasis mine].[104] Ewart describes the Three as "the ONE ELOHIM in dispensational manifestations."[105] Urshan and others, however, reject the label of Sabellianism as representative of Oneness theology.[106]

It should be remembered that much of Oneness rhetoric tends to be imprecise and under-developed. Since Oneness views did not develop through direct and informed influence from these early heresies, it does not follow immediately that the attending criticisms of the latter necessarily apply to Oneness Pentecostals. For this reason, it is a prudent first step to examine the way in which an idea functions in a given context, since the practice of a theological belief may vary from one cultural setting to another.

In the form of modalism most typical of Oneness theology, all three manifestations are simultaneously present in the divine activity. Commenting on the work of the Holy Spirit, Paterson probably has Sabellianism in mind when he assures his readers that, "I do not say that the Holy Spirit did not exist previous to the glorification of the Son of Man…. But I do say that the manifestation of God as the abiding Comforter was utterly impossible until Jesus was glorified."[107] Here he still wants to speak of the Holy Spirit as in some way being contiguous with the earthly life of Jesus, even though the Spirit's work as Comforter does not begin until Christ's ascension. Similarly, Reeves's summary of the Oneness position focuses on the work of each "manifestation": "God in His Omnipotence, His particularity in Christ and

[103] Harold O.J. Brown, *Heresies: Heresy and Orthodoxy in the History of the Church* (Peabody, MA: Hendrickson, 1988), p. 138.

[104] Andrew Urshan, "The New Light or the More Light," *Witness of God* 1 (September 1920): 1.

[105] Ewart, *Revelation*, p. 18.

[106] Paterson, *God in Christ Jesus*, p. 21; Andrew Urshan, "Editorial," *Witness of God* 2 (July 1921): 1-2.

[107] Paterson, *God in Christ Jesus*, p. 33.

His Impartation to Believers as the Holy Ghost."[108] But we note that all three are still present, the Father and Son carrying on their functions simultaneously with the Spirit. This functional distinction, however, contrasts sharply with the relational distinctions articulated in the classical trinitarian formulation of the Nicene Creed: the Father as *ungenerated*, the Son as *begotten*, and the Holy Spirit as *proceeding*.

Two concerns in particular present themselves in the Oneness doctrine of God: a lack of permanence and personality in the manifestations. These appear in two aspects of the doctrine: (1) the triune "manifestations" or functions are temporal only and therefore appear to preempt access to the real God,[109] and (2) the Holy Spirit is the Spirit of God by "emanation."[110] But Oneness doctrine attempts to work out some basis for the *permanent* and *personal* aspects of the divine revelation through its distinctly christocentric orientation. In contrast to the Sabellian notion that the three manifestations somehow separate us from the "real" but inaccessible essence of God behind the mask of revelation, Oneness theology self-consciously teaches that in Christ we do encounter the real God. Following Col. 2:9 ("in him the whole fullness of deity dwells bodily"), the Oneness position is that the "fullness" of God is encountered in the one person of Jesus Christ.

This is developed theologically through the usual Oneness definition of "person" (the traditional modalist view that the term "person" is reserved for the one personal God, not three subsisting realities within the Godhead) in combination with the theology of the name of Jesus as the revealed and proper name of God for this dispensation of grace (that in the invocation and appropriation of the name of Jesus one encounters the one true and personal God). This reflects more accurately the standard Oneness view of the Trinitarian reality. An example is the summary statement of the doctrine by John Paterson: "We have found that Jesus is Father in His Godhead, Son in His humanity, and Comforter in the body of His elect."[111] Streitferdt's statement is almost identical: "Jesus Christ is the Father as to divinity, Son as to His humanity, and the Holy Spirit in His emanation."[112] The language is plainly modalistic, in which the *one* and only person in the Godhead appears or acts in three modes or manifestations. But it is

---

[108] Reeves, *Godhead*, p. 30.

[109] For example, Oneness theology has historically taught that the "Sonship" of Christ will cease at the close of this age. This view will be addressed in Chapter 15.

[110] See *What We Believe and Teach*, p. 3; Streitferdt, *Word Became Flesh*, p. 50.

[111] Paterson, *God in Christ Jesus*, p. 37.

[112] Streitferdt, *Word Became Flesh*, p. 50.

noteworthy that both Paterson and Streitferdt identify this one divine Person as "Jesus," a reference to the Oneness distinctives of radical christocentrism and Name theology. These unique elements in Oneness theology need to be taken into account in any assessment of or comparison with classical modalism.

The second concern is the language of "emanation," which can be traced back to the early modalistic controversies. It also has a long history in Oneness doctrine, including the Articles of Faith of the Pentecostal Church, Inc., one of the early Oneness organizations that entered the 1945 merger to form the United Pentecostal Church International. It remains unchanged in the UPCI Articles of Faith as part of the section on "The One True God": "This one true God has revealed Himself as Father, through the Son, in redemption; and as the Holy Spirit, by emanation." Commenting on this confusing term, David Bernard is aware of the charge of impersonalism and is quick to clarify the denomination's official position: "To some, the description of the Holy Spirit as God revealing Himself 'by emanation' may imply that the Spirit is only an impersonal force. The UPCI does not intend any such implications."[113]

It is apparent that, while the term "emanation" is unhelpful and misleading as a theological description for the Holy Spirit, it does not function in a Oneness Pentecostal ethos as it might have done in a fourth-century religious culture. The Oneness Pentecostal emphasis on the experience of the Holy Spirit, its radical christocentrism, and its distinctive theology of the Name, all are theological ideas that were not actively present in the early Monarchian controversies. All three elements are mitigating factors in the customary criticism of impersonalism. Bernard states this difference clearly: "The Spirit is revealed and received through the name of Jesus ... the Holy Ghost comes in the name of Jesus."[114] So while a particular term or aspect of Oneness theology may fit the profile of an ancient heresy, the equation changes when the doctrine is studied as a whole. In this sense at least, it is important to qualify any description of Oneness theology as modalistic.[115]

---

[113] David Bernard, *Understanding the Articles of Faith: An Examination of United Pentecostal Beliefs* (Hazelwood, MO: Word Aflame, 1998), pp. 8, 27.

[114] Bernard, *Oneness of God*, p. 129.

[115] For an example of the danger of directly extending theoretical conclusions without first engaging in contextual analysis, see Harold O.J. Brown's assessment of the christological implications of modalism in his otherwise excellent volume, *Heresies: Heresy and Orthodoxy in the History of the Church*, p. 99: "Logically, modalism makes the events of redemptive history a kind of charade. Not being a distinct person, the Son cannot really represent us to the Father. Modalism must necessarily be docetic and teach that Christ

The following areas in particular deserve future theological reflection by Oneness theologians. One involves the Oneness commitment to preserve the uni-personality of God. The typical Oneness perception of the official doctrine of the Trinity is something akin to the traditional "social analogy" theory of the Trinity. While this approach is enjoying current popularity in contemporary studies, it is still only one possibility.[116] The model of three distinct centers of consciousness in the Godhead is not a necessary derivative of either the Scripture or the creeds, according to one of its chief advocates, Leonard Hodgson. A broad range of views recognized as legitimately within the parameters of the historic doctrine of the Trinity have been put forward. The "psychological" model, most coherently developed by Augustine, points to one single center of consciousness that exists in three ways or modes. And a combination of the two has even been suggested, involving "three hypostatical consciousnesses but only one self-consciousness." [117] The limited understanding of the doctrine of the Trinity by Oneness theologians has in part inhibited them from exploring their own doctrine in greater depth. Instead, they conclude that the only theologically legitimate form of oneness is an absolute, undifferentiated monarchy.

It is important to remember that, while the theological *conclusions* of the doctrine of the Trinity took centuries to formulate, the theological *implications* were present in the Scriptural witness. The earliest Christians acknowledged the mystery of a threefold encounter with the God they confessed to be one. For this reason, the Trinity is first and foremost a mystery of God to be received in faith, not a metaphysical riddle to solve.

The very character of the divine self-disclosure as triune requires us to consider the implications for the nature of God. Catholic theologian, Karl Rahner, sums up the consistent conclusion in his famous statement, "The economic Trinity is the immanent Trinity."[118] Likewise Mennonite theologian, Gordon Kaufman, points out the

---

was human in appearance only…while Christ was fully God, he only appeared to be man." This assessment does not accurately describe the Oneness view of Christ.

[116] For example, see Colin Gunton, *The Promise of Trinitarian Theology* (London: T. & T. Clark, 1991), and James Torrance, *Worship, Community and the Triune God of Grace* (Downers Grove, IL: InterVarsity Press, 1997). For a helpful critique of this communitarian view of the Trinity, see Mark D. Chapman, "The Social Doctrine of the Trinity: Some Problems," *Anglican Theological Review* 83/2 (Spring 2001): 239-254.

[117] See Claude Welch, *In This Name – The Doctrine of the Trinity in Contemporary Theology* (New York: Charles Scribner's Sons, 1952), pp. 40, 133-34, 152-53.

[118] Karl Rahner, *The Trinity* (New York: Herder & Herder, 1970), pp. 99-100.

inconsistency of maintaining the separation between the nature of God and God in revelation. All we can ever possibly know about God comes through "the relationships in which we stand." To acknowledge the truthfulness of what is given us in those relationships means that "the true understanding of God given in his revelation ... is his *true essence for us*." [119] This means that as God's self-revelation is indeed a triune one – which Oneness theologians acknowledge – then God's essence itself must somehow bear a triune character. Not to acknowledge this relationship is to leave open the possibility that God is not just more than but is explicitly *other* than what he is in his self-revelation.

Bernard, as do other Oneness theologians, leaves the door open for precisely this criticism, since for him there is nothing exclusive in the three manifestations. His conclusion is based on the Oneness view that, since the "three" are confined to the temporal realm, they hold no permanence. Consequently, there is nothing "special" or unique in them that would hinder God from revealing himself in another way. The three manifestations serve to reveal the nature and purpose of the *one* God and the *Name*. It is implied that any further manifestations would at least consistently serve the same purpose. As Bernard states:

> The recognition of these three manifestations does not imply that God is limited to three manifestations or that a threeness exists in the nature of God. Moreover, there is not a total distinction of one manifestation from another.... We cannot confine God to three or any other number of specific roles and titles. Neither can we sharply divide Him because He is one. [120]

Oneness theology has yet to provide a coherent explanation of why God's revelation in Scripture is consistently and exclusively threefold. At the least, a re-examination of the implications for the nature of God based on the recognition of the triune character of God's revelation is warranted.

A second important area is an examination of the term "person" in its various meanings and connotations, and the ways in which it has been used throughout history by Trinitarians. The historical context and popular understanding with which the term was developed is inadequate for the future. Oneness theologians are now aware that the theological meaning of the term is both different from and more com-

---

[119] Gordon D. Kaufman, *Systematic Theology: A Historicist Perspective* (New York: Charles Scribner's Sons, 1968), pp. 100-101.

[120] Bernard, *Oneness of God*, p. 143.

plex than a modern dictionary meaning. For example, of possible interest to them might be the observation made by theologian Cyril Richardson, that the word "person" in Latin originally carried with it the idea of *confrontation*, not a center of self-consciousness – a perspective that fits well with the Oneness view of God's internal dynamic toward expressibility.[121] Further, the language of "person" is preferred to the impersonal language of "manifestation" or "office," in even focusing on the one God. For example, encounter with any one "person" in the triune revelation is a personal encounter with the *one* God. To speak of the "Person" of the Holy Spirit is at least to affirm that the Spirit is not just an impersonal force but is the "personal presence" of God Himself; i.e. the Spirit *is* God.[122]

Finally, while Oneness Pentecostalism may be rich in the experience of the Holy Spirit, it is theologically weak. Owing in part to its christocentric focus and description of the Spirit as an "emanation" of God, there is little theological framework for or incentive to explore the rich and distinctive identity and mission of the Spirit.

5. Summary

The fundamental building blocks for the Oneness doctrine of God are the undifferentiated oneness of God's being and the revelation of God's name. While the movement's views conform most closely to historic modalism, there are voices in the tradition that are suggestive of a kind of economic Trinitarian thought. Further, Oneness theology does not fit neatly into the mold of classical modalism on two counts: its radical christocentric orientation, and its theology of the Name which particularizes and personalizes the revelation of God in the name of Jesus as God's "proper" name for this dispensation.

After nearly a century since its inception, there are signs of theological development in its doctrine of God, though progress has been slow. Since 1916 Oneness Pentecostalism has consciously molded its

---

[121] See Cyril C. Richardson, *The Doctrine of the Trinity* (New York: Abingdon, 1958), p. 63.

[122] In a stimulating theological essay on Oneness and Trinitarian views of God, Amos Yong models the kind of theological dialogue that will help in advancing ecumenical discussion; see "Oneness and the Trinity: The Theological and Ecumenical Implications of Creation *Ex Nihilo* for an Intra-Pentecostal Dispute," *Pneuma* 19/1 (Spring 1997): 81-107. See also Ralph Del Colle's essay, in which he argues for the recognition and theological significance of the Oneness Trinitarian and Pentecostal experience of God, "Oneness and Trinity: A Preliminary Proposal for Dialogue with Oneness Pentecostalism," *Journal of Pentecostal Theology* 10 (April 1997): 85-110.

identity as an *anti*-Trinitarian movement. The public rhetoric in speech and print is sufficient to demonstrate this claim. For much of the century it has devoted its energy to honing a Oneness "orthodoxy" in contrast to the Trinitarian faith, and in ways that have exacerbated an already polarized relationship with the wider Pentecostal and Christian fellowship. Consequently, until recently there has been little serious effort within the movement to pursue a theological inquiry in a spirit of *rapprochement*.[123] One critical loss for the movement is that, by hermetically sealing its doctrine from review and critique in the protective shield of special "latter day" revelation, it deprived itself of the opportunity to develop and otherwise amend its inherited formulations. The effect has been an unfortunate perpetuation of misunderstandings and misrepresentations that enfeebles all parties.

Present signs signal an increasingly congenial environment for pursuing theological questions concerning the doctrine of God. One ecumenical move forward for Oneness theologians would be to recognize the theological value of Trinitarian language and thought, and incorporate those elements from that tradition which accord with sound theological principles, but without the expectation that formulations currently repugnant to Oneness leaders be embraced.

---

[123] The one exception – now largely marginalized and theologically underdeveloped – is the alternative descriptor, the "Tri-Unity" of God. This was first proffered by Andrew Urshan and continues to be a point of self-identity for individuals and groups on the margins of the Oneness movement, such as the Canadian organization founded by Franklin Small, the Apostolic Church of Pentecost.

13

The Name and Christology

> Do you know Jesus, our Lord, our Savior,
> Jesus the Son of God?
> Have you ever seen him, or shared of His favor?
> Jesus the Son of God.
>
> O sweet Wonder! O sweet Wonder!
> Jesus the Son of God; How I adore Thee![1]
> — G.T. Haywood

The earliest followers of Jesus believed that the Scripture which was theirs as faithful Jews, also pointed to him as its fulfillment. They believed that in Jesus they encountered Yahweh, and they worshipped him. For some, a sacred name was his as well, so they worshipped, preached and cast out demons in the name of Jesus. Oneness Pentecostals believe that in Jesus is revealed a God who is radically one, and in his name is unveiled God's bestowed name for the era of the New Covenant.

1. The Name of God in Jesus

Oneness Pentecostals teach that there is a direct relationship between God's giving of his name in the Old Testament and the giving of the name of Jesus in the New Testament. Messianic prophecies also bear within them the promise of the new Name.

a. Proper Name as "Jesus"

For Oneness exegetes, the name of Yahweh is one among many names and titles of God recorded in the Old Testament. But it holds the special distinction of designating God's very essence, not just an

---

[1] G.T. Haywood, "Jesus the Son of God," *The Bridegroom Songs*, no. 5.

attribute. Because the Name can be interpreted as futuristic ("I will become who I will become"), some Oneness writers believe that "Yahweh" itself points to another "ineffable" and "secret" Name, holding within itself the dynamic potential of a future, full revelation.[2] Within that name is fixed both his divine identity and his function:

> When he [God] wished to proclaim through the medium of ONE SU-
> PREME NAME both the exalted personal position of the Mediator of
> the "new and better covenant" ... He did it by the use of this same glori-
> ous name, "JESUS," "JEHOVAH the Saviour."[3]

For Oneness theologians the name of Jesus is theologically and etymologically identified with the name of Yahweh, because Yahweh's name signifies God's personal self-disclosure and that name is embedded in the name of Jesus. This is the basis for the Oneness description of the name of Jesus as "the supreme Name of God."[4]

Certain passages are hermeneutically pivotal, one of the most prominent being the annunciation to Joseph in Matt. 1:21, "You will call his name Jesus, for he will save his people from their sins." Oneness interpreters find in this command by the angel to name the child "Jesus" the fulfillment of a promise made centuries earlier and written into the name of Yahweh itself.[5] The allusion in Heb. 1:4 that Jesus received his name by inheritance ("the name he has obtained is more excellent than theirs" [the angels]), implies that Jesus is God's proper name. Linking it with Matt. 1:21, Oneness teachers agree with Reeves that while "Lord Jesus Christ" is indeed a compound name, "the name 'Jesus' in particular is God's name.'"[6] Further, Jesus' own statement, "I have come in my Father's name" (John 5:43), is regarded as a claim by Jesus that quite literally his name is divine.[7] Oneness writers occasionally describe this name as God's "family" name; as Oneness pioneer, L.R. Ooton, concludes, the son must bear both the father's name and his nature.[8] Again, this name is both a revealed and proper name. Bernard

[2] See Ewart, *Name and Book*, p. 75; Fitch, *Pray to the Man Jesus – He Is Our Heavenly Father* (Council Bluffs, IA: By the Author, n.d.), p. 31.

[3] Paterson, *Real Truth*, p. 14.

[4] Paterson, *God in Christ Jesus*, p. 64.

[5] See Paterson, *Real Truth*, p. 14; Ewart, *Name and Book*, p. 6; Springfield, *Jesus*, p. 12; Reeves, *Godhead*, p. 57.

[6] Reeves, *Godhead*, p. 65; see also Fitch, *The Man Jesus*, p. 31; Ewart, *Revelation*, p. 32; idem, *Name and Book*, p. 77.

[7] See Ewart, *Revelation*, p. 32; Paterson, *Real Truth*, p. 16; Hobbs, *Whom Say Ye*, p. 50.

[8] L.R. Ooton, *Sermons from the Sermon on the Mount* (Tipton, IN: By the Author, 1970), p. 19.

understands the Name in terms of the Old and New Covenants: as Yahweh was the redemptive name of God in the Old Testament, so "Jesus is the redemptive name of God in the New Testament."[9]

The reference to the salvific implications of the Name in Acts 4:12 ("there is no other name ...by which we must be saved") is harmonized with Matt. 1:21 to substantiate the claim that "Jesus" is indeed the redemptive name of God for this new age.[10] Ewart links the Name with the work of Christ, specifically with the atonement:

> The Name of God deified the blood of Jesus. The name has in it the virtue and power of the cross.... Every accredited compendium of theology admits that Jesus had to be God in order to make Atonement for sin.... He came in and with his Father's Name. Jesus is God's redemptive Name.[11]

Finally, the highly exalted name in Phil. 2:9-11 is generally interpreted by Oneness exegetes to be the name "Jesus," not "Lord" as commonly understood.[12]

We have already observed that the Trinitarian name in Matt. 28:19 is given a christological interpretation by Oneness writers.[13] They argue that the name of the Father is Jesus (John 5:43), the name of the Son is Jesus (Matt. 1:21) and the name of the Holy Spirit is Jesus (John 14:26).[14] The exegesis follows that, since the singular "name" is used in Matt. 28:19, the appellation "Father, Son and Holy Spirit" being three, cannot possibly be the Name.[15] Rather, they are mere descriptive titles pointing to the one personal and proper name of Jesus.[16]

It is customary for Oneness theology to classify "Christ" and "Lord" as important descriptive titles to specify the identity of "Jesus" as the revealed name. This is Paterson's view: "JESUS is His Name, and the titles merely distinguish Him from all others."[17] While Reeves calls "Lord Jesus Christ" a "compound name" for the whole Godhead, he quickly clarifies that "the name 'Jesus,' in particular, is God's name."[18]

---

[9] Bernard, *The Oneness View of Jesus Christ* (Hazelwood, MO: Word Aflame, 1994), p. 24.

[10] See *What We Believe*, p. 4.

[11] Ewart, "Like Precious Faith," *Apostolic Herald* 8 (August 1942): 7.

[12] Paterson, *God in Christ Jesus*, p. 64; Haywood, *Divine Names*, p. 9.

[13] This aspect of the Oneness doctrine will be discussed in the next chapter.

[14] Andrew Urshan, "Why I Was Baptized in the Name, Lord Jesus Christ," *The Voice of Calvary Tabernacle* 13 (April 1957): 9.

[15] Reynolds, *Truth*, p. 44.

[16] Paterson, *Real Truth*, p. 30.

[17] Paterson, *God in Christ Jesus*, p. 59.

[18] Reeves, *Godhead*, p. 65.

Because some combination of the Name is always used in the baptismal formulas in Acts, and the fact that the titles distinguish the particular identity of this Jesus, the full name is used by Oneness Pentecostals in their baptismal formula.

b. Some Exceptions

There are exceptions to this traditional Oneness view of the singular name "Jesus" as the name of God. One comes from Franklin Small, who interprets the compound name, "Lord Jesus Christ," to be itself the full name of the Father, Son and Holy Spirit.[19] He correlates the two triune names in the Great Commission as follows:

> "Go ye, therefore, baptizing them in the Name (singular) of the Father (which is the LORD), and the Son (Jesus), and of the Holy Ghost (Christ the Anointed)," which said is LORD JESUS CHRIST.[20]

Small believes that the name of Yahweh is "Lord," not "Jesus." It is probable that he developed this interpretation from his study of William Phillips Hall's work, *A Remarkable Biblical Discovery.*[21] This echoes R.E. McAlister's attempt to harmonize the two formulas of Matt. 28:19 and Acts 2:38 in his baptismal sermon at the 1913 Arroyo Seco camp meeting.[22]

Another exception is that of E.J. Kolenda, a former Independent Oneness pastor and conference speaker from South Bend, Indiana. Kolenda teaches that, while Jesus is the redemptive name of God, it is the "Name of His HUMILIATION." That is, by itself it refers to his humanity. The full name is "Lord Jesus Christ," which Kolenda correlates with the name of the Trinity. In contrast to Paterson and others, he believes that the compound name is a valid name, on the basis that "Lord" and "Christ" are considered to be names, not titles.[23]

Two identifiable groups represent a third class of exceptions. There are those who consider themselves to be Trinitarian, but teach that the name of God is "Lord Jesus Christ." This teaching provides the exegetical basis for the use of the apostolic formula in water baptism while

---

[19] Small, *A Synopsis of the Name and Deity of Christ* (Winnipeg, Canada: Zion Apostolic Church, n.d.).

[20] *Ibid.*

[21] See Small, "Theological World Faces Reconstruction," *Living Waters* 1 (January 1930): 3-5.

[22] See Ewart, *Phenomenon of Pentecost*, p. 77.

[23] E.J. Kolenda, *For Remission – The Purpose of Calvary* (Sound Bend, IN: Apostolic Publishing Association, 1960), pp. 98, 99, 100, 101.

holding to the traditional doctrine of the Trinity.[24] A second grouping consists of a number of "Yahwist" sects who adhere to a modalistic view of God and baptism in the name of Yahshua.[25]

c. Name and Deity of Jesus Christ

For Oneness theology the name of Jesus is itself one of the most significant doctrines for establishing the deity of Christ. This hermeneutic departs from traditional interpretation that views the name of Jesus as a reference to his human identity.

Following more closely the Jewish notion that the name of God bears the divine presence, Ewart could confidently acclaim that, "in the Apostles' doctrine, Jesus was the visible manifestation of the invisible God, both in name and nature." The "inherited Name" of Christ in Hebrews 1:4 is sufficient proof that "His oneness with the Father is overwhelming."[26] One detects in Oneness representatives like Ewart the same zeal and conviction expressed by William Phillips Hall when he made his "remarkable discovery" of the name of God in Scripture:

> It appears that there never would have been any doubt whatever among Christians of the Deity of the Lord Jesus Christ during the Christian era had the original apostolic interpretation of the words, "the name of the Father and of the Son and of the Holy Spirit" ...been clearly understood and taught by men from the apostolic age until the present time.[27]

For Hall, the discovery of the Name is directly associated with the battle a century ago to defend the deity of Christ against theological skeptics. Oneness Pentecostals linked it to the radical reaction of William Durham to a perceived over-emphasis on spiritual crisis experiences. For both, the Name is foundational to Christology, but for Oneness adherents, the name of Jesus above all titles bears the stamp of divinity.

---

[24] Three notable representatives are W.H. Offiler, *God and His Name* (2nd ed.; Seattle, WA: Privately published, 1932); Patricia Beall Gruits, *Understanding God* (Detroit, MI: Evangel Press, 1972); and Ernest B. Gentile, *God and His Word – A Catechism of Bible Doctrine* (rev. ed.; Hong Kong: Asian Outreach, 1971).

[25] Yahwists are a sectarian Jewish Christian sect whose primary aim is to restore to the Church the original Hebrew name of God, YAHWEH, and of His Son, YAHSHUA. The various groups are listed and identified by their distinctive doctrines in the *Directory of Sabbath-Observing Groups* (4th ed.; Fairview, OK: The Bible Sabbath Association, 1974).

[26] Ewart, *Name and Book*, pp. 77, 118.

[27] Hall, *Remarkable Biblical Discovery*, p. 16.

2. The Person of Christ

Besides the inseparable link between the person and name of Jesus, Oneness christology bears a distinctive character that we would argue is directly associated with its starting point in the Old Testament understanding of God and the Name.

a. Jewish Christian Characteristics

We have already discussed in Chapter 11 certain marks of Jewish Christian theology that are potentially formative elements in a particularly Jewish Christian Christology – in particular, the Oneness application of a theology of the Name to its own doctrinal identity. Four other characteristics of Jewish Christian theology make their way into Oneness theology, which are reflected in its distinctive christological formulation.

First is the emphasis on the *transcendence* of God. As with Jewish Christian theology, Oneness theologians teach that God as Spirit is totally boundless in his existence, without form and appearance. God's "otherness" is at times interpreted in terms of holiness, a characteristic that becomes interpreted by some Oneness theologians to mean that God cannot countenance Christ's bearing of our sins on the cross.

A second mark is the care taken to preserve the *monarchy* of God against intimations of tritheism. Oneness theology shares with Jewish Christian theology a concern to avoid any explanation of the pre-existence of Christ that would compromise the monarchy. Rather, both interpret such distinctions in terms of the more dynamic Jewish concepts of Word and Wisdom instead of Greek hypostatic distinctions.

Third, one finds in Jewish Christian theology a tendency to emphasize the *distinction* between the two natures in Christ. If God is so markedly "other" than humans, then God's "presence" in Christ must be conveyed in ways that preserve his "otherness." The imagery used to describe the relationship is borrowed from the motif of divine "dwelling" in the Old Testament. In later christological formulations, Jewish Christian theology risks denying a real union of the two natures in Christ, a risk that appears in Oneness theology as well.

Finally, Jewish Christian theology tends to accentuate the *humanity* of Jesus. In heterodox Ebionitism, Jesus is viewed as a man who acquires his "sonship" by "adoption" when the Father bestows the Holy Spirit upon him at his baptism. In Oneness theology, when one sets aside the emphasis on the Name and the priority of Christ's divinity being the "full" deity of God, the identity and role of the humanity of Jesus is underdeveloped.

b. Oneness Model of Christology

Oneness Christology is distinctive in many ways. In particular, it builds its doctrine intentionally with images and metaphors drawn from the Old Testament accounts of Israel's encounter with God. Owing in part to its Monarchian interest and intense biblicism, Oneness theology reflects the motifs of its Jewish Christian predecessors.

   i. New Testament Shema. The *Shema* of the Hebrews (Deut. 6:4) is a pivotal text for Oneness theologians in their defense of the monarchy of God. But the New Testament text, Col. 2:9, in practice achieves the confessional status of a "Christianized" *Shema*: "For in him [Christ] the whole fullness of deity dwells bodily." The appeal to this text constitutes an important part of the rhetoric against what they perceive in Trinitarianism to be a diminishing of the *full* revelation of God in Christ. They believe that by positing hypostatic distinctions within the Godhead Jesus is neither the full revelation of the deity nor the revelation of the full deity.

   Ewart is in effect attacking this perceived christological reductionism when he writes about the revelation he received of "the *absolute* Deity of the Lord Jesus Christ" [emphasis mine].[28] Such division of the persons implies a kind of subordinationism of the Son in his deity. Andrew Urshan estimates the negative effect on the preaching of Christ in the Trinitarian subordination of Christ:

> In these days of ours, not only are thousands of so called Christians denying the absolute Deity of our Lord, but those who believe it are trying to preach Him feebly as God the Son, and by so doing they think they have gone to the limit of exalting "The Lord of Glory."[29]

Small is likewise convinced that Trinitarianism "gives Christ an inferiority complex in the eyes of the world." Being only the second person of the Godhead relegates Christ "to second place."[30] On the other hand, they believe that their own doctrine "takes Him out of a secondary position and gives Him Lordship."[31] This for them is the core message of Col. 2:9.

---

[28] Ewart, *Name and Book*, p. 40.
[29] Andrew Urshan, *Almighty God*, p. 10.
[30] Small, *Living Waters*, p. 90.
[31] Nathaniel Urshan, *Consider Him*, p. 17.

In this sense at least, Emil Brunner shares a similar concern for what he calls "the naïve way in which the three Names were placed alongside of one another" in the baptismal formula of Matt. 28:19. The image was certain to create an impression of a "little Christian Pantheon." Applying the image literally, Oneness writers see in it a division and an alongside-ness of the three persons in the doctrine of the Trinity, which for them endangers the centrality of Christ in the Christian revelation. Oneness theologians would likely applaud Brunner's proposal for a more dynamic and biblical expression to describe the relationship between the Father and the Son; namely, that we have "the Father *through* the Son, *in* the Son; but we do not have the Father *alongside* the Son, and the Son *alongside* of the Father."[32]

This difficulty of perception raised by Oneness theologians might be ameliorated in their dialogue with Trinitarians if there could be agreement on a more adequate expression of the biblical dynamic of revelation and greater clarity of the centrality of Christ in Trinitarian theology. It would render pointless much of the logic used by Magee in his argument that Trinitarians require two Fathers for Christ, "the First Person of the Trinity, to whom He prayed (they say), and the Holy Spirit, Who performed the miracle act of paternity in the virgin womb."[33] Such naïve reasoning can make sense only on the basis of a literal and simplistic application of the image created in the Trinitarian formula itself when separated from its historical dynamic.

ii. A "Dwelling" Christology. Probably the most prominent image used by Oneness theologians to describe the divine-human reality in Christ is that of "dwelling." As we have already observed, the concept is borrowed from the Jewish experience of the divine presence residing in localized dwelling places, and the early Jewish Christian transference of the concept to its Christology.

The favorite christological text for Oneness theologians and also one of the most prominent passages used to describe the relationship between the two natures of Christ is Col. 2:9: "For in him the whole fullness of deity *dwells* bodily" [emphasis mine] (cf. Col. 1:19). It defines the basic Oneness paradigm of one Spirit "in" the one human person. Ewart describes it succinctly:

> The human body was TAKEN ON by Him [God] in the fullness of time. When He BECAME flesh the Godhead dwelt in His person from His birth to His Ascension. He carried His human body with Him to

[32] Brunner, *Doctrine of God*, pp. 220, 227.
[33] Magee, *Godhead in Jesus*, p. 17.

Heaven, and in His glorified body now and ever, dwells the fullness of God.[34]

Throughout Oneness literature one detects this dichotomy between the two natures in Christ. Simply put, "the Godhead which is Spirit is in the person of Lord Jesus Christ."[35] Or more crudely stated, "Jesus is God in a body."[36] Occasionally the principle is expressed in terms of the Father and the Son, the Father being the Spirit and the Son the flesh: "*The Son is the flesh or humanity*. The Father is the great eternal Spirit Who indwelt the Son" [author's emphasis].[37] Magee finds in Jesus' claim that "the father who dwells in me does his work" (John 14:10) sufficient proof that it is the Father who indwells the human body of the Son.[38] Any emphasis on the Word is generally irrelevant here, since Oneness theologians do not recognize hypostatic distinctions within the Godhead. Hence, Hobbs can state that Jesus became the Son at birth "yet not losing His identity as being the Father," and still claim, "God became eternally visible when He, the Word, became flesh."[39]

Predictably, the Old Testament dwelling places of Yahweh become the primary metaphors for a Oneness "dwelling" christology. We have already observed that for Israel the presence of God dwells in his Name. Yahweh also dwells in such places as the Tabernacle, Ark of the Covenant, and Temple. Commenting on Col. 2:9, Paterson makes the christological application, "all the ark contained and all it represented is today found in Jesus."[40] Andrew Urshan similarly calls Jesus "the temple of God, in whom the Father of lights dwelleth and manifesteth His full grace and glory."[41]

Probably the most popular metaphor is the Tabernacle in the Wilderness. The term itself often becomes a synonym for dwelling. In a paraphrase of John 1:14, Reeves states that he Word "tabernacled among us."[42'] Norris writes, "the presence or Spirit of God ...finally dwelt (tabernacled) in Jesus Christ."[43] Golder likewise states that "the

---

[34] Ewart, *Name and Book*, p. 173.

[35] Hobbs, *Whom Say Ye*, p. 74.

[36] Streitferdt, *Word Became Flesh*, p. 62; see also Reeves, *Godhead*, p. 43.

[37] Magee, *Godhead in Jesus*, p. 13.

[38] *Ibid.*, p. 28.

[39] Hobbs, *Whom Say Ye*, pp. 78, 100.

[40] Paterson, *Real Truth*, p. 20.

[41] Andrew Urshan, *Almighty God*, p. 94.

[42] Reeves, *Godhead*, p. 15.

[43] Norris, *Mighty God*, p. 11.

Word (God-Spirit) was made flesh ...and tabernacled with men."[44] This comparison is not made unconsciously. Like many evangelicals, Oneness teachers are fond of interpreting the Tabernacle typologically to show that Jesus is the true and perfect Tabernacle. F.E. Curts, an early Oneness writer, carries out a detailed study of the Tabernacle and its furniture in an effort to establish the Oneness doctrines of Christ and salvation and that Jesus is "the true tabernacle."[45] Haywood likewise finds compelling the Tabernacle dwelling motif for christology: "The birth of Christ was the beginning of the manifestation of God's Tabernacle or dwelling place among men."[46] Reeves refers to the human Son as "the Particular Tabernacle Wherein the Shekinah Glory that used to dwell in the Tabernacle of Moses indwelt."[47] Norris echoes the same theme, that Jesus is the "permanent tabernacle of God. In the Old Testament God had only temporary dwelling places. He needed a permanent place to complete His work of salvation." Therefore, the Son "was to become His PERMANENT BODY or Tabernacle."[48]

For Oneness theology a "dwelling" christology is more than a formal borrowing from the Old Testament. It is definitive for understanding the divine-human reality in Christ. As we shall see, the Oneness interpretation of the union of the two natures is shaped significantly by this metaphor of "dwelling."

iii. A "Glory" Christology. A sub-theme interwoven in this Oneness "dwelling" Christology can best be described as a "glory" Christology. Like the image of "dwelling," the origin of this metaphor is in the Jewish "glory" tradition, especially the period of late Hellenistic Judaism. As A.M. Ramsey suggests, the rich images of glory, Tabernacle and dwelling coalesced into a "composite pattern," as illustrated in the Septuagint.[49]

Oneness Christology integrates the metaphor of dwelling with the "glory" tradition through the images of "manifestation," "image," "form" and "face." Key christological passages are 2 Cor. 4:10 ("face"), Phil. 2:7 ("form"), 1 Tim. 3:16 ("manifestation") and Heb. 1:3 ("image").

---

[44] Golder, *Principles*, p. 6.

[45] F.E. Curts, *The Tabernacle in the Wilderness* (St. Louis, MO: Pentecostal Publishing House, n.d.), pp. vi, 44.

[46] Haywood, *Before the Foundation of the World* (Indianapolis, IN: Christ Temple, 1923), p. 63.

[47] Reeves, *Godhead*, p. 35; see also Hobbs, *Whom Say Ye*, p. 93. Fitch, *Lovely Titles of Jesus* (Council Bluffs, IA: By the Author, n.d.), p. 30.

[48] Norris, *Mighty God*, pp. 12, 17.

[49] See A.M. Ramsey, *Glory of God*, p. 26.

They all express the divine-human reality in terms of the Spirit-person dialectic in which the humanity is a showing forth or epiphany of the divine reality. In Christ the hidden God becomes "manifest." He who is without form takes on the "form" of the servant. The Invisible One reveals Himself as in a mirror, Christ being His "express image." Though Oneness theologians seem only occasionally to study the relationship between the "glory of God" and Christ, they borrow heavily for their christology from the variety of images in the rich "glory" tradition of Jewish Christianity.

Accounts of the divine appearances or theophanies in the Old Testament enrich the Oneness "glory" Christology. Here the idea of "dwelling" and "manifestation" coalesce. Magee, for instance, points out that theophanies in the Old Testament were "temporary materializations of God in Angelic form. Now in this dispensation JESUS is the IMAGE of the invisible God.... That human form called 'the Son' is God's perfect, complete and permanent theophany."[50] Norris likewise teaches that "God used this angelic body as a *temporary* dwelling place."[51] Ewart defines an epiphany as "God in a body," and then applies the same christological hermeneutic: as every theophany was an imperfect expression of God's full revelation, it pointed to the one who would be "God's final theophany." Here Ewart is referring to Heb. 1:3 ("[Christ] reflects the glory of God and bears the very stamp of his nature") to show that Christ is manifested as "God's permanent visible Person."[52] Reynolds interprets the various dwelling places in the Old Testament as earthly occasions for divine manifestations – creation, Mount Sinai, the theophanies, the Tabernacle – but that, "in the incarnation Christ is the express image of the invisible God."[53] Andrew Urshan applies the same principle to the image of Christ as "the face of God." Quoting 2 Cor. 4:6, in which Paul describes "the glory of God in the face of Christ," "face" refers to the revelation and manifestation of God: "The Lord Jesus Christ has been and will be forever the manifestation and revelation – the face of God." In an attack on the doctrine of the Trinity, Urshan objects that God cannot have "three distinct, separate faces" but only "one personality ... and one glorious face." He then adds that the revelation or face of God is the epiphany of God's glory.[54]

---

[50] Magee, *Godhead in Jesus*, p. 31.

[51] Norris, *Mighty God*, p. 3.

[52] Ewart, "The Last Theophany," *Pentecostal Herald* 21 (January 1946): 4, 15.

[53] Reynolds, *Truth*, p. 89.

[54] Andrew Urshan, *Almighty God*, pp. 81, 83, 82. For other references to the manifes-

To summarize, the foundation stones for Oneness Christology are the Jewish Christian concepts of "dwelling" and "glory." One of the most prominent christological applications is the recurring theme of Christ as the "express image" of God or the "manifestation" of God.[55] As with the early Jewish Christian usage, it is impossible to separate the images of "dwelling" and "manifesting" in Oneness theology. They form a composite that sums up the heart of the Oneness Christology: "The great mystery of godliness is the incarnation – God manifest in the flesh."[56]

c. Fatherhood: Deity of Jesus

i. Pre-Existence Defined. In an essay on New Testament Christology, G.B. Caird provides a helpful description of the Jewish, and in particular rabbinic, understanding of pre-existence in God: it is that which occurs eternally "first in the mind of God." As such it is not a hypostatically distinct person, but the plan, purpose and even predestination on the part of God in eternity prior to its becoming actualized in creation and history. For instance, the Torah was said to pre-exist within God's eternal purpose. Caird shows how early Christians transferred this concept to Jesus:

> They ascribed pre-existence to Jesus because they wanted to claim for him all that the Jews had claimed for the Torah, because they believed that in him God's purpose for man, and therefore for the whole cosmos, had become an earthly reality.[57]

This form of pre-existence implies no division within God, thereby preserving his monarchy.

ii. Pre-Existence in Eternity. Caird's observation reflects what appears to be a consensus among Oneness theologians regarding the pre-existence of Christ. They describe three stages in the divine self-disclosure. The first stage is God's utter transcendent being which has existed from all eternity. God is described as Spirit or omnipresent Spirit. He is the undifferentiated Godhead, "invisible, incorporeal,

---

tation of the glory of God in Jesus, see Paterson, *God in Christ Jesus*, pp. 29, 44; Fitch, *God the Father*, p. 23.

[55] For a few examples, see Nathaniel Urshan, *Consider Him*, pp. 19, 21; Magee, *Godhead in Jesus*, pp. 3, 6, 31; Norris, *Mighty God*, pp. 2, 4, 6, 11, 17; Paterson, *God in Christ Jesus*, pp. 8, 36, 52; Reeves, *Godhead*, pp. 16, 23, 39; Hobbs, *Whom Say Ye*, pp. 15, 19, 20, 43.

[56] Magee, *Godhead in Jesus*, p. 3.

[57] Caird, "Doctrine of Christ in the New Testament," pp. 77, 79.

without parts, without body, and therefore free from all limitations."[58]
Paterson implies that even at this stage God is called "Father," render-
ing the Hebrew title of "everlasting Father" in Isa. 9:6 as "Father of
Eternity."[59]

Before God emerges out of eternity, God ordains the creation and
redemption of the world. Following the declaration in Rev. 13:8 that
Jesus is the Lamb slain "before the foundation of the world,"
Haywood comments that before creation, "His plan was complete
from beginning to end."[60] He believes this to be the meaning of Jesus'
statement in John 17:5, when he prays to be glorified with the glory
he had before the world was made: "This glory for which Jesus prayed
was ordained before the foundation of the world through the foreknowledge of God in the beginning even as was also the slaying of the
Lamb."[61] Springfield takes Christ's pre-existence initially to mean that
"the Son pre-existed in the mind of God only."[62] Hobbs likewise describes pre-existence as exclusively divine foreknowledge or the
"thought of God."[63] Commenting on John 17:5, Magee calls it "the
Idealic existence of the Son before the foundation of the world or His
existence in God's mind or thought."[64] In other words, this first stage
of Christ's "pre-existence" was exclusively in the form of God's eternal purpose for the world. In commenting on John 1:1, Ewart
concludes that even the Logos at this stage exists only in a pre-
expression form simply called "absolute Deity."[65]

iii. Pre-Existence in "The Beginning." The second stage is initiated by
the act of divine *self-expression* with regard to that which is other than
God. It precedes the creation of the world but is divine activity with
reference to creation. It is this pre-creation "beginning" to which
Gen. 1:1 refers. Reeves teaches that the nature of God now has two
distinguishable but inseparable elements, "Spirit and Word." While
"Spirit" refers to God's eternal being outside creation, "Word" is
God-in-relation or "God in time."[66] As the "form" of God, Magee

---

[58] *What We Believe*, p. 3.

[59] Paterson, *God in Christ Jesus*, p. 28.

[60] Haywood, *Before Foundation of the World*, p. 12.

[61] Haywood, *Victim*, p. 34.

[62] Springfield, *Jesus*, p. 19.

[63] Hobbs, *Whom Say Ye*, pp. 17, 66.

[64] Magee, *Godhead in Jesus*, p. 29.

[65] Ewart, "Last Theophany," p. 4.

[66] Reeves, *Godhead*, p. 14.

describes Christ's pre-existence as "the full equation in a majestic form of the invisible God."[67]

It is this stage of divine self-disclosure in which Oneness teachers introduce their understanding of the Logos. Predictably, they reiterate that the Word is not to be distinguished from God in any hypostatic fashion. Rather, the Word is that which comes forth from God, and is nothing other than God in divine self-disclosure. "The Word was the visible expression of the invisible God.... But the Word was, essentially, nothing less than the eternal God Himself."[68]

By their insistence upon the full deity of the Word, Oneness theologians mean to emphasize that he is neither a created being as in Arianism[69] nor an eternally distinct person "separate as to individuality" as in Trinitarianism.[70] Rather, as the expression of God, "the fullness of the Godhead dwelt in Him."[71] The Word is in reality everything that can be implied by personification without positing a second personality.

Because the Word is the expression and form of God, many Oneness theologians identify him with Old Testament appearances.[72] It was "the Word that spoke from the burning bush."[73] Haywood writes that, "Melchizedek was Christ before His incarnation."[74] Paterson believes that Yahweh Himself is the Word: "This visible expression of the Eternal Spirit – this Word or *Memra* – appeared to men under the exalted name of Jehovah."[75] In various ways Oneness theologians attempt to articulate a Logos theology that holds in balance the radical oneness of God and the distinctive reality of the Word.

iv. Fatherhood in Jesus. The third stage of the divine self-disclosure is the incarnation. Following the modalistic emphasis on the equality of Christ with God, Oneness theologians variously describe Christ's deity as "Word," "Father," and "the whole Trinity." God is Spirit without division and without form. When God takes on form, the undifferentiated deity is present. In Ewart's words, "Instead of the second person of the Deity being incarnated it was God, Himself, the whole Deity."[76] As the "form" of God, Jesus is the pre-existent Word in flesh. But in

---

[67] Magee, *Godhead in Jesus*, p. 7.

[68] Paterson, *God in Christ Jesus*, p. 7.

[69] See *ibid.*, p. 47; Reynolds, *Truth*, p. 91.

[70] Ewart, "Last Theophany," p. 4; see also Nathaniel Urshan, *Consider Him*, p. 18.

[71] Ewart, *Name and Book*, p. 173.

[72] See Magee, *Godhead in Jesus*, p. 31; Norris, *Mighty God*, p. 3; Springfield, *Jesus*, p. 19.

[73] Hobbs, *What Say Ye*, p. 99.

[74] Haywood, *Victim*, p. 28.

[75] Paterson, *God in Christ Jesus*, p. 15.

[76] Ewart, *Revelation*, p. 22.

his deity, he is indwelt by the undifferentiated Godhead. Or as Nathaniel Urshan states, in Jesus "dwells the Father, the Son, and the Holy Spirit."[77]

Because "Fatherhood" signifies God in undifferentiated being, Oneness theologians think it is only consistent to say that it is the Father, albeit through the Word, who takes on flesh. If only the second person of the Trinity becomes incarnate, the truth of the "fullness" of the divine revelation is lost. It is in this sense that "Jesus is the Father as well as the Son."[78] In contrast to the tendency in modalism to veil the real God from revelation, Oneness Pentecostalism believes it is fighting a battle to preserve the truth that the real God in His fullness as the Father is present in Jesus.

This Father-Son relationship is best understood in terms of the Oneness Spirit-person dialectic. The Spirit (Godhead, Father) is revealed in the human person (Son), and that person (Son) reveals the Spirit (Father). The following statement by Magee is a response to the frequent charge Jesus is his own Father: "WE DO NOT BELIEVE THAT THE FATHER IS THE SON. But we do believe that the Father is *in* the Son."[79] Using Oneness definitions, "if we deny the FATHERHOOD of Jesus, then we deny that He is God."[80] The dialectic is expressed as simply "the Father in the Son, and the Son in the Father."[81] In order to maintain the radical oneness of God, the deity of Jesus must be described in terms of the Father, Spirit or Godhead. Since there is no eternal Son, sonship is restricted to Jesus' humanity. Andrew Urshan attempts to clarify the conundrum for Trinitarian critics that God seems to collapse into the humanity of Jesus or that Jesus is an unresolved split identity. He emphasizes that the omnipresent Father-God is always transcendent, even during the period of the incarnation:

> He [Jesus] was on earth yet at the same time He was in heaven. He was in heaven, yet He was on earth. So our Lord, as Eternal God, the Spirit,

---

[77] Nathaniel Urshan, *Consider Him*, p. 14. One of the problems with this way of stating the doctrine is that in Oneness theology the "Son" refers exclusively to Jesus' human nature. So to suggest that the Son dwells in Jesus contradicts the Oneness belief that the Son *is* Jesus in his humanity. It would be more consistent to state that in Jesus dwells the Father, "Word" and Spirit.

[78] Haywood, *Victim*, p. 17.

[79] Magee, *Godhead in Jesus*, p. 9.

[80] *Ibid.*, p. 15.

[81] Hobbs, *Whom Say Ye*, p. 64.

is everywhere invisible; but, as God manifested in the flesh, He was on earth bodily.[82]

Bernard expresses the dialectic in terms of the two natures in Christ:

> We can easily understand all of this if we realize that Jesus has a dual nature. He is both Spirit and flesh, God and man, Father and Son. On his human side He is the Son of Man; on His divine side He is the Son of God and is the Father dwelling in flesh.[83]

In his celebrated article defending the Fatherhood of God, Haywood states that Oneness adherents "acknowledge the Father and the Son in Christ Jesus.... The Fatherhood of God is found only in the Son."[84] In other words, Oneness theology holds the view that the deity of Christ is the one Spirit who proceeds from eternity, through the Word, into the human person of Jesus.

v. Divergent Oneness Views of Christ's Pre-Existence. There is relatively little variation among mainstream representatives of Oneness theology regarding the core doctrines of God and Christ. But a greater variety exists on the margins of the movement in persons and groups that maintain an identity with the Oneness movement but hold to views of Christ that differ in important ways from orthodox Oneness teaching. Theodore Fitch is included here because of the way he literalizes Christ's pre-existence as a "spiritual body." For him Jesus in his pre-existence had a prepared body in human form. In the beginning God "suddenly formed a body for Himself." Jesus in his pre-existence was God's "First-begotten" and later the "Jehovah-Angel" who finally became the Son in Mary.[85] Fitch attempts to avoid the trap of Arianism by stating (using the Spirit-person dialectic) that the Word "is the FIRST and ONLY person of God."[86]

C. Haskell Yadon, former district superintendent with the United Pentecostal Church, represents a similar position in an edited work, *Jehovah-Jesus – The Supreme God: Son of God, Son of Man.*[87] Not unlike

---

[82] Andrew Urshan, "The Divinity of Jesus Christ, or the Absolute Deity of the Son of God according to the Old and New Testaments," *Pentecostal Witness* 3 (1 April 1927): 2.

[83] Bernard, *Oneness of God*, pp. 69-70.

[84] Haywood, "Dangers of Denying the Father," *Voice in the Wilderness* 2 (13 November 1922): 5.

[85] Fitch, *LORD*, pp. 3, 4.

[86] *Idem, God the Father*, p. 6.

[87] Robert D. Weeks, *Jehovah-Jesus: The Oneness of God; The True Trinity* (New York: Dodd, Mead and Co., 1876), republished as *Jehovah-Jesus – The Supreme God: Son of God, Son of Man*, ed. C. Haskell Yadon (Twin Falls, ID: By the Editor, 1952). Yadon was a leader in the United Pentecostal Church and president of Conquerors Bible School in

the Oneness orthodox view, the author teaches that God is absolutely one and Jesus Christ is fully God. Likewise, Christ is not God the Son, but in his divine nature he is the Father. Yadon departs from traditional Oneness theology, however, by proposing that the "Son of God" is "begotten" before the creation of the world. Following the conventional understanding of the word "begotten," the Son "cannot be eternal." Yadon, therefore, argues for a hypostatically distinct being called the Word who is God's agent in creation. He is "not the divine alone, nor the created alone, but the twofold Person. God and the Son, the uncreated and the first created, united." Yadon denies the charge of Arianism on the grounds that the Son is not merely a creature but is "in union with the divine nature of God the Father."[88] This position is reminiscent of a pre-Nicene view of the divine Logos. But to modalistically inclined Oneness ears, it sounded more like a binitarian-like move to reinstate two "persons" in the Godhead.[89]

A similar doctrine exists in one strand of the African-American Oneness movement. Bishop S.N. Hancock (now deceased), formerly with the Pentecostal Assemblies of the World, had published a small book, *The Great Godhead*, in which he proposed that Jesus in his pre-existence was not "God" but the "Son of God."[90] The Son was subordinate to the Father, even in the second stage of his pre-existence. Though Hancock's views were divergent from the traditional Oneness position, they were apparently never regarded as heretical by his denomination. When he left the Pentecostal Assemblies of the World to form his own organization in 1957, the issue was apparently not one of doctrine but the result of a political struggle for the position of Presiding Bishop of the PAofW following Haywood's death.[91]

Portland, Oregon. He discovered the book by Robert Weeks in a used bookshop, and republished it under his own editorship. The position of the original author, and later Yadon himself, is a digression from orthodox Oneness christology. At the request of the church authorities, Yadon withdrew the book from circulation. Yadon remained in good standing as a District Superintendent with the organization until his retirement and subsequent death in 1997.

[88] *Ibid.*, pp. 33, 44, 45.

[89] This was the concern expressed by Nathaniel Urshan, then Assistant General Superintendent of the United Pentecostal Church and pastor of Calvary Tabernacle in Indianapolis – undoubtedly the representative opinion of the official leadership of the UPC at the time (interview with Nathaniel Urshan, Calvary Tabernacle, Indianapolis, IN, 23 May 1973).

[90] The basic teaching of the book was gleaned through a personal interview with Robert Little, at Apostolic Temple, South Bend, IN, 14 May 1974.

[91] This is Golder's conclusion. See Golder, *History*, p. 140. My perusal of the first Minute Book of Hancock's organization reveals no distinctive doctrine. See *Pentecostal*

The doctrine did remain alive, however, in Hancock's new organization, The Pentecostal Churches of the Apostolic Faith Association. Many of the ministers who followed Hancock accepted his teaching, though adherence was not mandatory.[92] Nevertheless, a schism did occur in May 1974, when one of Hancock's leaders, Bishop David Collins, formed a new organization, The True Churches of the Apostolic Faith Inc., for the explicit purpose of preserving Hancock's teaching.[93] According to Elzie Young, the Presiding Bishop of the continuing PCAF, Collins and his supporters had added substantially to Hancock's original teaching.[94]

The variant view of Christ taught by Collins appears to be a curious but crude form of Adoptionism.[95] Jesus in his pre-existence was neither God nor Son of God, but was present only potentially in the literal "seed" of Adam and "came out of Adam" as did all humanity. The redemptive line through Abraham and David carried the seed from which would come the Savior. It is not clear whether the "seed" is spiritualized in a theological interpretation of Jesus' genealogy or is literalized as the "seed" of David, as Young suggests.[96] By either means Jesus had his beginning in Mary as the "Son of God," being the fulfillment of the sonship God began when He "fathered" Adam. He was Son of man, as the "seed" or "Son" of Abraham, David and Mary. He received the Spirit of God at Jordan, but only "in a greater measure than us." Here we have a highly unusual form of Adoptionism, with Jesus' pre-existence being defined exclusively in terms of the human seed in Jesus' family tree.

Another highly unusual and innovative form of Adoptionism appeared in a book in the early 1950's by G.B. Rowe, *Reincarnation of Adam as Jesus Christ, Or Adam, Then and Now.*[97] Rowe had been an

---

Churches of the Apostolic Faith Assn., Inc. – Ministerial Record, Codified Rules and Minutes, 1975-1958 (Indianapolis, IN: Christ Temple, 1958).

[92] Robert Little, Interview. It appears that the doctrine was not a requirement for ministerial membership, since some of the ministers did not hold wholeheartedly to Hancock's doctrine.

[93] Telephone interview with David Collins, Detroit, MI, 1 September 1974.

[94] Interview with Elzie Young, Apostolic Temple, South Bend, IN, 15 May 1974.

[95] The contents of the doctrine were gleaned from the interviews with Bishop David Collins and Bishop Elzie Young.

[96] Young's impression is that Collins believes that the literal "seed of David" was hidden for centuries, finally making its way sovereignly into the womb of the Virgin Mary (interview, Elzie Young.)

[97] G.B. Rowe, *Reincarnation of Adam as Jesus Christ, Or Adam, Then and Now* (South Bend, IN: Apostolic Publishing Association, n.d.).

early Oneness pioneer and leader in the United Pentecostal Church, and for many years was pastor of Apostolic Temple, Mishawaka, Indiana. When the book appeared he was dismissed from the United Pentecostal Church for holding heretical beliefs.[98] His doctrine of Christ can be summed up as "Adam reincarnated." According to this view, God created only one son, Adam. Reminiscent of the "Adam-myth" – the view taught by certain early Ebionite sects that the Messiah was the reincarnation of Adam – Jesus was literally the first Adam re-incarnated.[99] In Mary, God "created a second body for the first Adam in spirit to dwell in," thereby designating Jesus at his birth only as the new Adam. Regarding his deity, "Jesus was not God, nor the Son of God, until he was baptized in the river Jordan."[100] Further, the pre-existence of Jesus is neither in eternity nor before creation, but in the person of the first man, Adam. While Rowe's doctrine of the name of Jesus is traditionally Oneness, his Christology bears marks similar to the early Ebionite sects of Jewish Christianity.

A significant deviation from orthodox Oneness Christology presently circulating within UPCI circles is called the "divine flesh" teaching.[101] It originated with Teklemariam Gezahagne, General Superintendent of the Apostolic Church in Ethiopia, a member organization of the UPCI with over one million members.[102] Gezahagne was reared in the Ethiopian Coptic Church, and therefore the Monophysite tradition, which historically holds to the belief that Christ's true nature is divine, not human. Gezahagne's highly spiritualized, nearly docetic, Christology echoes this tradition. Similarly to other dualistic traditions, the reason for Christ's singular divine nature is that if he were fully human he would be tainted with sin and therefore could not atone for the sins of humanity. Gezahagne states, "Christ did not come to partake of our earthly clay, but came instead that we may partake of His divine nature." Christ did not share Adam's inherited nature but, like Adam, was "directly begotten by

---

[98] Interview with Cleveland M. Becton, United Pentecostal Church International, Hazelwood, MO, 15 June 1973.

[99] See Daniélou, *Jewish Christianity*, pp. 68-69.

[100] Rowe, *Adam*, pp. 10, 22.

[101] Other terms include "celestial flesh," divine flesh," and "heavenly flesh." I am indebted for information on this teaching to Vonelle Kelly's unpublished paper, "The UPCI and 'Divine Flesh.'"

[102] Gezahagne's book is now published in English; see Teklemariam Gezahagne, *Bible Writers' Theology* (Arkansas: Ozark Mountain, 1999). His teaching is gaining a hearing not only in Ethiopia but among some ministers within the American UPCI.

God."[103] Unlike the other Oneness heterodoxies that lean toward the Judaistic sects, the "divine flesh" teaching reflects the dualistic tendencies of Hellenism.[104]

With the exception of the "divine flesh" teaching, the foregoing examples of heterodox views illustrate that Oneness theology as a whole conforms sufficiently to Jewish Christian thought forms to produce the strengths and weaknesses which that tradition bears.

d. Sonship: Humanity of Jesus

i. Sonship in History. The sonship of Christ in Oneness theology begins with the birth of Jesus. Undoubtedly the highly personal terms of Father and Son would signify a hypostatic distinction were the term applied to Christ's pre-existence. The term "begotten" is taken in its human meaning "to give birth." It is generally argued that the words "eternal" and "begotten" are contradictory.[105] Therefore, the Godhead, which is called "Father," prepares a human tabernacle in which to dwell, and that body is called the "Son." Bernard rejects the Trinitarian teaching of the "eternal Son," stating that the Son "was formed during the time of the law and in the womb of a woman."[106]

ii. Sonship and Subordination. Oneness theologians readily acknowledge the subordinate role given to the Son. Unlike the Trinitarian claim that the Son is eternal but incarnate in Jesus, Oneness theology restricts the sonship to the humanity. In Jesus' statement that the Father is greater than he (John 14:28), Oneness exegetes see a recognition of the subordination of the Son. But the qualification is that, in Reeves's words, "there is no inferiority in Jesus Christ in His undivided Deity as God."[107] Rather, "He who was the eternal God became the Son, and accepted voluntarily as to His flesh and as to His humanity ... an inferior and subordinate position relative to His essential Deity." Highlighting the contrast in beliefs, Magee prefers this solution to the Trinitarian subordination of the "ETERNAL Son."[108] Not understanding the historic considerations that led to the Trinitarian doctrine of the incarnation, they can make the charge that Trinitarians "have a

[103] Gezahagne, *Bible Writers' Theology*, pp. 169, 174; cited in Kelly.

[104] Gezahagne's "divine flesh" teaching is a particularly interesting case of contextual theology, in which a traditional and culturally deep-seated Coptic belief is carried over into a Oneness Pentecostal setting.

[105] Magee, *Godhead in Jesus*, 20; see also Paterson, *God in Christ Jesus*, p. 20; Reeves, *Godhead*, p. 34.

[106] Bernard, *Oneness View of Jesus Christ*, p. 68.

[107] Reeves, *Godhead*, p. 24.

[108] Magee, *Godhead in Jesus*, pp. 22, 25.

real dilemma – One Co-Equal Person GREATER than another CO-EQUAL Person!"[109]

iii. Sonship and Atonement. The human Sonship in Oneness Christology has a distinct purpose. Following much of the Fundamentalist theology of the atonement at the turn of the century, Oneness exegetes establish their doctrine on the Old Testament Levitical sacrificial system of the shedding of blood. Only God's requirements are sufficient to redeem the world. The purpose of God's work in the virgin birth of Christ is for this very purpose: "The Virgin birth made it possible for our God to assume human flesh and a bloodstream not contaminated by 'Adamic depravity' thereby making it capable and suitable for redemption."[110] This unique birth was God's act of preparing "a body of flesh and blood" which could accomplish the work of redemption.[111] Occasionally, a highly literalistic interpretation of the blood leads to the belief that having no earthly father, from whom comes the blood, Jesus was free from original sin, which is passed on biologically.[112]

iv. Sonship and Christ's Humanity. The work of the Son, or the humanity, spans the period from his birth to the *eschaton*, fulfilling the purposes of redemption, mediation, the millennial reign and final judgment.[113] To emphasize the role of humanity in redemption, Reeves comments on 1 Tim. 2:5, that "it is the *man* Christ Jesus, not the God Christ Jesus who is the mediator."[114] Redemption requires not only a name and deity but also a humanity that, patterned after the Jewish Christian affinity for separation of the two natures, has its well-defined role distinct from the indwelling Spirit.

Parallel to the emphasis on the deity of Christ is the importance of his full humanity. Oneness writers have given little attention to the nature of Christ's humanity other than to acknowledge it and point to the purpose of the body as God's prepared atoning sacrifice. Reeves, however, makes the point that Christ was born with "body, soul, and spirit (as have we) plus the Word."[115] Paterson likewise stresses Jesus' full humanity, applauding the contribution made by Nestorius. Jesus

---

[109] Springfield, *Jesus*, p. 38.

[110] Golder, *Principles*, p. 6; see also Springfield, *Jesus*, p. 36; Reynolds, *Truth*, p. 24.

[111] S.R. Hanby, *The Apostles' Doctrine* (Hazelwood, MO: Pentecostal Publishing House, n.d.), p. 2.

[112] See L.R. Ooton, *Sermons from the Sermon on the Mount* (Tipton, IN: By the Author, 1970), p. 35; see also Fitch, *LORD*, p. 18.

[113] See Magee, *Godhead in Jesus*, p. 16; Reynolds, *Truth*, p. 91.

[114] Reeves, *Godhead*, p. 18.

[115] *Ibid.*, p. 68.

was complete with spirit, soul, and body, as well as a human will that was real.[116] He makes this particular response to attempts to gloss over the limitations Jesus experienced: "Why are they afraid that if Christ had a complete human personality He might have succumbed to temptation?"[117]

To summarize, Oneness theology teaches a sonship that is exclusively human. By virtue of his virgin birth he is the unblemished humanity that is finally given as a blood sacrifice for sin on the cross.

e. Unity of the Two Natures

It is evident by now that Oneness theology bears the mark of Jewish Christian Christology in its concern to maintain the separation of the two natures. A "dwelling" Christology supports this tendency.

i. Birth of Jesus. Oneness teachers are concerned to affirm a genuine union of the two natures in Christ, an event different from the abiding presence of the Spirit in believers. Streitferdt's intention is clear: "In Him Divinity and humanity were FUSED but not CONFUSED."[118] Reeves contrasts the Spirit in Christ and in us as that between "fusion" and "engrafting."[119] Norris likewise believes Christ's birth signifies a presence of greater significance than the Spirit that descended on the prophets: "The fullness of that wonderful presence of the Lord's SPIRIT BEING, not just a part of it, was incarnated in the body of Jesus Christ." The body became God's "permanent abiding place."[120] Andrew Urshan likens the union to the unity we find in a human person.[121]

Springfield expounds an odd and highly Nestorian view of the unity of the two natures. Because God cannot "associate with sin in any way," it is impossible for a full indwelling of the Godhead in a body that "was capable of sinning."[122] Hence, God could dwell fully in Jesus only after the resurrection. At face value, it is questionable whether this is anything more than a moral union.

For Oneness Christology, the Jewish Christian tendency to preserve the transcendence and otherness of God in the incarnation, combined with the use of such images as "dwelling," reveals a tentativeness in

---

[116] Paterson, *God in Christ Jesus*, pp. 49, 51.

[117] *Ibid.*

[118] Streitferdt, *Word Became Flesh*, p. 36; see also Reeves, *Godhead*, p. 17.

[119] Reeves, *Godhead*, p. 17.

[120] Norris, *Mighty God*, pp. 13, 14.

[121] Andrew Urshan, "Divinity of Jesus Christ."

[122] Springfield, *Jesus*, p. 25.

ascribing permanency to the union of the natures. This seeming depreciation of the incarnation appears ironic given the otherwise high and central role of Christ in Oneness theology. It is possible, however, that the key lies implicitly in the theology of the Name. Here is a potential theological resource for deepening an understanding of the permanency of the union, particularly in attending to the giving of the name of Jesus at the annunciation and the Spirit's agency in the conception. The name of Jesus is permanently and hypostatically "united" with the person, and carries within it the promised presence of God. It is possible that the Oneness emphasis on the strong name of Jesus bears such intimations of a high Christology that the doctrine intuitively depends upon the Name for much that others would accomplish with the aid of other theological concepts such as the two natures. There appears, however, to be no conscious effort in Oneness writings to develop the theology of the Name in support of this important doctrine. Currently, the Name functions primarily to show Christ's deity as the full embodiment of Yahweh.

ii. Ministry of Jesus. It is in the life and ministry of Jesus that the Oneness view of the dual nature of Christ begins to show its inherent weakness. The principle most popular among Oneness people to express the Father-Son relationship is put forth by Magee as a key principle: "Ask yourself – Is Jesus acting as a man now or is He acting as God?" While Magee attempts to affirm a full union in the statement, "divinity and humanity were fused, but not confused," the relationship appears more like a loose affiliation than a union. Magee states that, because the two realities are not to be confused, Jesus "could speak from two different standpoints." As God, he walked on the water and performed miracles. As a human, he wearied, was hungry and could suffer. When he declared that he and the Father were one, he "spoke out of the depth of His Divine Consciousness." But when he prayed in the Garden, it was "humanity praying to Divinity."[123] Magee, however, never deals with the problem of whether or not each reality knows what the other is doing. In Magee's explanation, Jesus appears to have a dual personality, switching from one center of consciousness to another as the occasion demands.

This is the way in which Oneness theologians have attempted to resolve the nature of the union of the two natures. For example, Ewart states that the humanity of Jesus did not turn the water into wine but

---

[123] Magee, *Godhead in Jesus*, pp. 7, 8, 11.

rather "it was the Deity dwelling inside the flesh that did it."[124] Streit-ferdt teaches that "what Jesus did not know as man, He knew as God; ...what He did not know as Son, he knew as Father."[125] Hobbs implies that the relationship is one of will wherein the human ego employs the divine reality when needed: "In that He was God in the form of man, He could at any time use the power from which He was begotten.... When Christ used the divine nature of God at His own will, He was God – His equal."[126]

Oneness theologians, however, do make an effort to avoid the crude impression that Jesus was praying to himself or simply being a ventriloquist, though there is evidence of this sort of explanation being employed in the early years.[127] But traditional Oneness interpretation sees the issue as one of Spirit and person in the same way as they counter the charge of denying the Father. Jesus as the human Son is praying to the Father in his transcendence, not in His "expressive de-ity" which indwells the Son. In Springfield's words: "He is not praying to Himself, but rather to the Spirit of God, or Godhead, Who hears all, sees all, and understands."[128]

Oneness theology is not totally unaware of the importance of the unity of the two natures, even if it consistently bears the marks of a Nestorian Christology. Reeves, for instance, describes the union as God's ability to "particularize" himself in flesh without separation.[129] Here he expresses his desire to offer a more "fully-orbed view of God" in an effort to balance the more narrow Jesus-centrism of Magee and others, by giving more attention to God in his transcendence and the incarnation.[130]

Ewart describes the relationship of the two natures during the life of Jesus as a real one in which Jesus acted as one person:

> That life was so dominated and controlled by an invisible and divine ego, and the manifestation of this ego, which He insisted was His Father, was so complete that it was impossible to discover a separate identity.[131]

---

[124] Ewart, *Revelation*, p. 35.
[125] Streitferdt, *Word Became Flesh*, p. 40.
[126] Hobbs, *Whom Say Ye*, p. 62.
[127] Interview with W.E. Kidson; Paterson, *God in Christ Jesus*, p. 49.
[128] Springfield, *Jesus*, p. 14.
[129] Reeves, *Godhead*, p. 24.
[130] Interview with Kenneth Reeves at United Pentecostal Church International, Hazelwood, MO, 12 June 1973.
[131] Ewart, *Name and Book*, p. 84.

Here Ewart perceptively describes the effects of the union. However, as we shall see, the union does not hold at the cross. Paterson
sounds classically Nestorian in his statement that "there existed side by
side two distinct and complete natures." Yet he teaches that the union
was real and the humanity of Jesus was real: "He received no help
from the fact that He is God as well as man." The union is complete
but without divine coercion, as Jesus "had a will distinct from His
Father's will." Paterson avoids the excesses of Magee and others by
refusing to play one ego off against the other. Instead, the unity is a
real one in which the Godhead "resides *permanently* in His glorified
body."[132] Jesus is living and acting as one unified person through the
complete obedience of his human will to that of the Father.

Paterson believes that the problem of explaining the two natures in
Christ is not simply a Oneness issue. While Oneness theologians view
the problem in terms of the unity of the Father and the Son, Trinitarians have added "a second and unrelated mystery – the 'Second Person'
theory."[133] Since Paterson and other Oneness writers articulate a theology of the Word, more dialogue needs to occur with Trinitarians. It
appears that Oneness theologians have not yet grasped the reason for
the traditional Trinitarian insistence upon the eternal Sonship in the
incarnate state. Simply put, the belief in the inseparability of the two
natures secures the theological conviction that in the incarnation it is
God, not merely a prepared human vessel, who has entered human
history and assumed flesh for the salvation of the world. The one who
is called Son is truly God in this humble state, and therefore the only
one qualified to represent humanity before the Father. This view of
Christ is markedly different from the Oneness belief in which redemption is achieved by a human body prepared by God.

iii. Cross of Jesus. The cross becomes the first real test of the union of
the two natures for Oneness theologians, and here there is no consensus. The critical text is Jesus' cry of dereliction: "My God, my God,
why hast thou forsaken me?" (Matt. 27:46). But the interpretation of
what occurs in this moment is influenced by a particular reading of the
divine necessity in procuring salvation for the world. This is the belief
that the body of Jesus, at this point quite separate from the divine
Spirit and prepared for this moment by his virgin birth, endures death
by shedding of blood. This can be the only way for God to accomplish

---

[132] Paterson, *God in Christ*, pp. 25, 50, 51, 52.
[133] *Ibid.*, p. 52.

salvation, since a holy God cannot associate with human sin except in and through a specially prepared and perfect human sacrifice.

Here Oneness interpreters differ. One view is that at this moment of utter dereliction on the cross, the Spirit of God withdraws from Christ. Springfield states emphatically: "God will never, never has, and did not then tolerate sin.... God, in order to remain Holy, had to withdraw."[134] Ewart draws the same conclusion, in contradiction to his own otherwise strong statement on the unity of the two natures: on the cross God "had to vacate the body for the flesh to die." This was the redemptive plan, as it was in this body itself that God "provided a Lamb that taketh away the sin of the world."[135] Andrew Urshan likewise follows this interpretation, commenting that this was the only time God was separated from His Son. He knows, however, that even if the sacrifice occurs only in a human body, this act of separation pierces the very heart of God, and calls it a "terrible tragedy to the Godhead." To the extent that God can suffer, God suffered the pain of this separation "that we might be united to Him through that death."[136] The Spirit and body were re-united on the third day bringing forth Christ's resurrection. Norris describes Christ on the cross as the Lamb "dying without God." However, with the culmination of God's great act of atonement, He re-entered the body permanently, "NEVER to leave that BODY again."[137]

Magee and Streitferdt, however, reject the above interpretation. For Magee, the cry of Jesus on the cross came from the momentary spiritual weight of the sins of the world. As the sin-bearer, he "had to feel as any man feels under sin, that is, God-forsaken." Though in his humanity he felt separated from God, the Spirit of God remained with him "until he had offered full and satisfactory sacrifice for your sins and mine."[138] Streitferdt makes precisely the same point, that the Spirit was "integrally abiding in the body of Jesus" until his death. The feeling of dereliction on the cross was Christ's human response, not a real abandonment.[139] Bernard shares this view, pointing out that Jesus' cry on the cross cannot be abandonment, because "Jesus is the Father."

[134] Springfield, *Jesus*, p. 15.
[135] Ewart, "Oneness of God," p. 13.
[136] Andrew Urshan, "Holy Spirit's Relationship," p. 3.
[137] Norris, *Mighty God*, pp. 18, 19.
[138] Magee, *Godhead in Jesus*, p. 8.
[139] Streitferdt, *Word Became Flesh*, pp. 38, 39.

The cry indicates only that the human nature was "feeling the wrath and judgment of God upon the sins of mankind."[140]

We note, however, that the language used suggests only a moral union, one in which God remains *with* the Son rather than the Son *being* the divine reality present in and effecting the salvation of the world, the God incarnate who alone is able to present the human family before the unbegotten Father. This Nestorian tendency is not an exclusively Oneness problem, but an inherited weakness from its evangelical forbears. An over-emphasis on the atonement in some Protestant circles has had the unintended consequence of separating that work from Christ's identity (incarnation) and ministry, especially the way in which it narrows the understanding of Christ as "sinbearer" to the moment of his death.

This exclusive attention to the human body of Jesus is further reinforced by the manner in which some teachers focus on the literal shedding of blood. Though most realize that the blood symbolizes the giving of the life, the significance is that it is the total *living* and *giving* of the life that matters. The blood symbolizes the sacrificial nature of divine self-giving love that culminated in death on the cross. The christological application in the New Testament of the offering of an unblemished sacrificial lamb to atone for the sins of the people undoubtedly has contributed to a popular understanding that focuses almost exclusively on the sinless body of sacrifice. Its limitation, not error, is that it does not sufficiently account for the doctrine of the incarnation. For Oneness theology, the weakness of its "dwelling" Christology is perhaps no more evident than here.

iv. The Eschaton. The work of redemption stretches into the future where the Son gives the kingdom to the Father, following which he himself "will also be subjected to him who put all things under him, that God may be everything to everyone" (1 Cor. 15:28). Oneness Pentecostals generally regard this as the completion of the mediatorial and redemptive work of the human Son, at which point the sonship ceases. Because the humanity of Christ has always performed an exclusive function for God, it is dispensable when its work is complete. However, as in other areas, there is no clear consensus of teaching nor is there much significant explanation of the teaching.

Paterson approaches the topic by distinguishing between Christ's Godhead and Lordship, the former spanning from eternity to eternity with the latter representing a temporary office for the purpose of

---

[140] Bernard, *Oneness of God*, p. 178.

bringing about the kingdom. He states in one place that God "resides permanently in His glorified body." But elsewhere he teaches that the mediatorial work will come to an end, "His humanity being subjected to His glorious divine nature as God, the Father."[141] But he nowhere explains what he means by this final subjection of the humanity.

Others simply reiterate this position that the sonship will cease, God having "completed His work through His Beloved Son – His Flesh – His humanity."[142] He will "dismiss His body and will then again enter into the fullness of HIS GLORY and POWER."[143] As Streitferdt states: "Jesus will be eternally known as Jesus the Mighty God."[144] Haywood affirms the purpose of the human and subordinate Son, but urges his readers to view him within the eternal and final vision of him as the "all in all" and "the Almighty God."[145] Magee echoes this concern: "I do not want Him to be eternally known as the subject Son. I want Him to be eternally known as The Mighty God."[146] Bernard agrees with the Oneness consensus, reflecting the transitoriness of the Son's role:

> The "Son of God" refers to a specific role that God temporarily assumed for the purpose of redemption. When the reasons for the Sonship cease to exist, God (Jesus) will cease acting In His role as Son, and the Sonship will be submerged back into the greatness of God, who will return to His original role as Father, Creator, and Ruler of all.[147]

There are few variations on this Oneness teaching. One curious proposal, taught by Theodore Fitch, is the view that humanity is a temporal phase following which Jesus "will become exactly as He was BEFORE He was born of Mary."[148] The only Oneness figure with whom I am familiar, who teaches that the sonship ceases *before the end*, is S.C. Johnson, founder of the predominantly African-American Oneness organization, *The Church of the Lord Jesus Christ of the Apostolic Faith*. Sonship is reserved for the days of Christ's flesh between his

---

[141] Paterson, *God in Christ Jesus*, pp. 25, 42.

[142] Hobbs, *Whom Say Ye*, p. 65.

[143] G.K. Jensen, *When God Became Flesh* (New Westminster, Canada: Plowright Printing Co., n.d.), p. 8

[144] Streitferdt, *Word Became Flesh*, p. 43.

[145] Haywood, *Victim*, p. 42.

[146] Magee, *Godhead in Jesus*, p. 25; see also Nathaniel Urshan, *Consider Him*, p. 21.

[147] Bernard, *Oneness of God*, p. 106; see also *Oneness View of Jesus Christ*, pp. 79-80.

[148] Fitch, *God the Father*, p. 41. This hints of a kind of Gnosticism in which the world is a spiritualized space, the consequence of which is that nothing that occurs within time and space is of any material significance. Fitch is likely unaware of this tradition or would follow its conclusions.

birth and death. But because the resurrected existence is "spiritual," Jesus can no longer be called "son": "The man died, then the divine life entered into that body and he went back to what he was ... Spirit." So having now given up the sonship of flesh, "He is Father."[149]

Not all Oneness writers teach the termination of the body of Jesus. Reeves at least vaguely proposes that, though the sonship will not cease, "the particularity will flow over into God's eternality and Generality."[150] Norris believes that, following the Spirit's re-entry into the body of Jesus after the crucifixion, Jesus becomes the permanent and inseparable dwelling place even into eternity: "In heaven, the only God you will ever see is the Lord Jesus." Norris regards this quality of permanence to be the distinguishing mark of the full and definitive self-disclosure of God over against the "divers manifestations of God."[151] Ewart likewise sees no closure to the existence of the body. Following the Ascension, He lives "in His glorified body now and ever."[152]

There is little divergence then from the Oneness teaching that the sonship at least passes through a change when the kingdom is given over to the Father. By identifying Christ's sonship with his humanity, which itself is soteriologically understood in a rather utilitarian way, the sonship is set apart for a particular and temporal role. One can at least understand why Oneness theologians conclude that the sonship of Jesus will cease at the end of history, on the basis of 1 Cor. 15:28. Whereas sonship for Trinitarians theologically demands an eternal identity in a Father-Son relationship, Oneness theologians regard the sonship more functionally. Even the birth of Jesus is viewed as the preparation of a body for a specialized task. And for at least some, the body will have accomplished its divinely appointed mission with the consummation of redemption. This conclusion is another indication of the consistent way in which Oneness theologians work out their "dwelling" Christology.

Oneness writers have reflected little on the theological implications of their position of temporal sonship in the future state. It is likely that

[149] S.C. Johnson, *Is Jesus Christ the Son of God Now?* (Philadelphia: By the Author, n.d.), pp. 3, 6. Johnson, now deceased, was an autocratic leader whose teachings and standards of "holiness" were restrictive and harsh. He had little association with other Oneness groups. His teaching continued under the leadership of his immediate successor, S. McDowell Shelton. The organizational headquarters remains in Philadelphia, Pennsylvania, under more moderate oversight.

[150] Reeves, *Godhead*, p. 66.

[151] Norris, *Mighty God*, p. 19.

[152] Ewart, *Name and Book*, p. 173.

their vision is not unlike that of other Pentecostals and Fundamental-ists, except that their distinctive doctrine of sonship logically leads many of them to interpret 1 Cor. 15:28 as a final dissolution of that which was always temporal and functional – the human body. The change is not likely to be some mystical re-absorption into deity, but the consummation in salvation history of the One whom they knew as Redeemer and Mediator but in the End as the "Lord of Glory." Yet serious questions remain, especially as Oneness theologians extend the logic of their position to questions of sonship, the identity of Jesus, and eschatology. The lack of consensus among Oneness thinkers is itself a hopeful sign that this teaching is not a necessary conclusion but only a logical and formal consequence of their Christology.

3. Classification of Oneness Christology

Oneness Christology is both simple and difficult to classify. It is simple in that many of its ideas are recognizable in strands of historical movements, especially pre-Nicene modalism and less so in the doc-trine of the economic Trinity. It is difficult in that there are *sui generis* elements in its theology, such as its theology of the Name. So much of its theology is as yet underdeveloped that a number of directions are theologically possible. Three models come to mind: a Logos Christol-ogy, a Spirit-christology, and a Name Christology. The first two have substantial history in the pre-Nicene period, while the third is only hinted at in early strands of Jewish Christianity.

One possible direction is the development of a Logos Christology that might begin with but must move beyond the lines of pre-Nicene theology. Because of their divergent teaching on the sonship of Christ, Oneness theologians have devoted considerable attention to exploring the temporal and eternal distinctions of the Word. As observed earlier, some aspects of Oneness teaching of the Logos are similar to that of the second century Apologists, and following them, the economic Trinitarians. For instance, the early Apologists were still "ardent monotheists," and believed the solution to the pre-existence of Christ was to place him as "the Father's thought or mind, and that, as mani-fested in creation and revelation, He was its extrapolation or expression."[153]

This is similar to the consensual Oneness view of pre-existence, and for the same reason. It holds that the Logos, whether only *in potentia*

---

[153] Kelly, *Early Christian Doctrines*, p. 95.

or as the expression of the mind of God, it is in essence God. That is, the Logos is neither an eternally distinct reality nor merely a created being.[154] Also, early views that only spoke of the Son with reference to Christ's humanity, taught that Christ's "divine Sonship dates from the incarnation." Even in the third century, Hippolytus "was reluctant to designate the Word as Son in any other than a proleptic sense till the incarnation."[155] Though for different reasons, Oneness theologians are equally reluctant. Reynolds summarizes their view of sonship as being neither "eternal" nor "created" but "begotten."[156]

A second alternative leads in the direction of a Spirit-christology, an expression also developed in the pre-Nicene period generally spanning the period from Clement and Ignatius in the second century to Hippolytus and Tertullian a century later. According to Kelly, Spirit-christology identifies one of the earliest attempts by Christians to grasp the mystery of the divine-human reality in Christ. It teaches that "in the historical Jesus Christ the pre-existent Son of God, who is divine spirit, united Himself with human nature." In some proposals the Spirit simply indwells the person; in others he becomes human.[157] In either case, we have an early Christology still dominated by the Jewish Christian ideals of the monarchy of God and the divine dwelling in the world.

Oneness theology exhibits traits that resemble some form of Spirit-christology. Its characteristic Spirit-person hermeneutic is similar to the approach taken by the earliest writers. In simplest terms, Hobbs states, "the Godhead which is Spirit is in the person of the Lord Jesus Christ."[158] The "Spirit" may be named variously as "Godhead," "Father," even "Father, Son and Holy Spirit." But it signifies the eternal Spirit of God in the human person of Jesus. Even when there is an effort to articulate a Logos Christology, the primary purpose is not to adapt a philosophical concept for a christological purpose, as did some

---

[154] This assessment differs from that of the Assemblies of God minister and writer, Carl Brumback, who regards Yadon and Fitch as Arians, and erroneously identifies them as representative spokespersons for the Oneness position. See Brumback, *God in Three Persons*, p. 104; see also Paterson's rejoinder to Brumback's charge: "Let me assure you that any person ... who would assert that Jesus is ONLY a created being would be promptly disfellowshipped by the United Pentecostal Church, and would be disowned by every other Oneness organization. This charge is absolutely without foundation," *God in Christ Jesus*, p. 66.

[155] Kelly, *Early Christian Doctrines*, pp. 42, 112.

[156] Reynolds, *Truth*, p. 91.

[157] Kelly, *Early Christian Doctrines*, pp. 142-44.

[158] Hobbs, *Whom Say Ye*, p. 74.

of the early Christian philosophers. Rather, it intends to express the dynamic of God's self-disclosure according to its own theological Spirit-person dialectic. An excellent contemporary effort to recast Oneness christology as a Spirit-christology has been made by Ralph Del Colle, a Roman Catholic theologian with interests in the Pentecostal and charismatic movements. In it he ably demonstrates a viable trajectory for future Oneness theology.[159]

The third alternative is some form of Name Christology. There are only hints of such an approach in the earliest Jewish Christian tradition, more on the order of raw materials for such a task. Subsequent interest in the Name has appeared throughout history in sectarian movements whose interests are not the development of a comprehensive theology of the Name. Its broader theological contribution, however, lies in an articulation of the particularity of the biblical revelation of the God of Israel and Jesus Christ.[160] Old Testament scholar, Christopher Seitz, argues that a recovery of the theological significance of the Name is crucial for a biblical understanding of salvation history. Neither Israel's God nor the God of Jesus can be reduced to a monotheistic abstraction that claims, "we all worship the same God." Seitz's bold claim is otherwise:

> Here it is significant to note that for Christian theology, what receded in terms of particularity in the divine name YHWH, which is everywhere present in the Old but completely absent in the New, is matched by the emergence of the very specific name Jesus. The same reverence for the name enjoined in the Old attaches to the name Jesus in the New. In modern debates about "God language" the Christian starting point remains the name of Jesus. It is only through Jesus that we share in the divine life at all, being at one time strangers to the commonwealth of Israel. The specificity of the personal name YHWH, for Israel, naming her God and the only God, is now matched for Christians by the specific name Jesus.[161]

---

[159] Ralph Del Colle, "Oneness and Trinity: A Preliminary Proposal for Dialogue with Oneness Pentecostalism," *Journal of Pentecostal Theology* 10 (1997): 85-110. See also his larger study, *Christ and the Spirit: Spirit-christology in Trinitarian Perspective* (New York: Oxford University Press, 1994). A Pentecostal scholar, Harold D. Hunter, is also proposing a Spirit-christology as a way forward for future Pentecostal-charismatic theology. See H.D. Hunter, *Spirit Baptism: A Pentecostal Alternative* (Lanham, MD: University Press of America, 1983); and "The Resurgence of Spirit Christology," *EPTA Bulletin: The Journal of the European Pentecostal Theological Association,* 11/1 & 2 (1992): 50-57.

[160] Brunner's contribution has already been noted. See Brunner, *Christian Doctrine of God.*

[161] Christopher Seitz, *Word without End: The Old Testament as Abiding Theological Wit-*

The Oneness understanding of the Name is unique in that, unlike the conclusions derived from a study of the titles of Jesus, the name of "Jesus" itself is the revealed and proper name of God. "A mark of the divine sonship of Jesus is His ability to make known this name of God to men."[162] Oneness theology develops its theology of the Name primarily to establish two fundamental doctrines: the radical oneness of God disclosed in the singular name of Jesus, and the deity of Christ in which only the bearer of God's name is qualified to be the full revelation of God and Savior of the world.

But there are exegetical difficulties with the traditional Oneness approach to establishing a New Testament theology of the name of Jesus, especially in its failure to account for the variety of "titles" that are given the status of "name" for God. For instance, the name in the Lord's Prayer is probably "Father";[163] the name in Phil. 2:9-11 may be "Lord," not "Jesus";[164] the name in Heb. 1:4-5 is likely "Son."[165] Furthermore, the triune name in Matt. 28:19 must be taken at face value, as a theological elevation of that which is otherwise a common title to the status of proper name. Thus it is doubtful that any meaningful distinction between "title" and "name" in the New Testament can be defended, except in the theological sense that in Jesus and his name we have the only basis for the Christian claim of salvation.

4. Summary

The Christology of Oneness Pentecostalism is a non-historical sectarian expression of Jewish Christian theology. Its distinctive characteristics are a theology of the name of Jesus, a christological model based on "dwelling" and the "Glory of God," a zealous defense of the monarchy and transcendence of God, and the affirmation of the full humanity of Jesus reminiscent of the Antiochene and particularly Nestorian traditions.

As a sectarian movement, the distinctive Oneness beliefs have demarcated but also marginalized it from the rest of the Christian

---

ness (Grand Rapids, MI: Eerdmans, 1998), p. 260. For an incisive rendering of the theological significance of the "personal" name in the Old and New Testaments, see ch. 3, "The Divine Name in Christian Scripture."

[162] ὄνομα, p. 272.

[163] See Brunner, *Christian Doctrine of God*, p. 206.

[164] See Oscar Cullmann, *The Christology of the New Testament* (rev. ed.; trans. Shirley C. Guthrie & Charles A.M. Hall; Philadelphia: Westminster, 1963), p. 234.

[165] *Ibid.*, p. 310.

community. One of the effects has been an impeding of its theological development. The movement is presently at an important juncture in its life, with numerical growth and improved educational standards undoubtedly bringing this generation into increasing contact with the wider Christian community. Though it could react to a perceived threat to its identity, an alternative strategy is to develop and refine its theological ideas through respectful engagement with others.

It is naïve to assume that such involvement will not alter some cherished Oneness beliefs. But part of the process of reassessment is often the discovery that a cherished belief does not a confession make! In this chapter we have sketched out possible directions for the future of Oneness Christology. We now turn to an examination of the ways in which the distinctive Oneness doctrines of God and Christ become employed in the doctrine of salvation and the Christian life.

14

The Name and the Christian Life

> Preach in Jesus' name, Teach in Jesus' name,
> Heal the sick in His name
> And always proclaim it was Jesus' name,
> In which the power came;
> Baptize in His name, enduring the shame,
> For there is vict'ry in Jesus' name.[1]
>
>   – G.T. Haywood

The theme of the Name runs through Oneness literature far deeper than the rhetoric of the oneness of God and its Jesus-centric piety. It carries out the logic of its convictions most conspicuously in its doctrine of salvation and vision for the Christian life. It is also here where we are confronted with its most sectarian and divisive elements, creating the point of greatest controversy with other Christians and within its own fellowship. While Oneness theologians do not always agree on how to apply their distinctive belief, the Name remains a cohering force for their identity.

1. The Name in Salvation

Historically for most Oneness Pentecostals, the name of Jesus carries within itself the very promise and fulfillment of salvation. They would affirm Hans Bietenhard's conclusion in Kittel's *Theological Dictionary* that the name "embraces the whole content of the saving acts revealed in Jesus." Therefore, "the whole life of the Christian stands under the name of Jesus."[2] The foundation for their theology of salvation lies in this biblical appeal. One of their favorite passages is Acts 4:12: "There

---

[1] G.T. Haywood, "Do All in Jesus' Name," *The Bridegroom Songs,* no. 43.
[2] ὄνομα, pp. 273, 274.

is salvation in no one else, for there is no other name under heaven given among men by which we must be saved."[3]

It is no surprise then that the Name is inseparably bound up with Christ's atoning work on the cross. All would in some way agree with Ewart that "the name has in it the virtue and power of the cross."[4] But the question remains how the benefits of the cross are related to the Name. Oliver Fauss, a pioneer in the "new birth" tradition, provides a clue to the more exclusive side of the Oneness movement when he states that it is impossible to "claim the cleansing of His blood, without accepting and believing on HIS NAME. The blood is in His NAME."[5]

All Oneness theologians agree that the atoning work of Christ on the cross is efficacious for salvation. And because the name of Jesus is the saving name of God and therefore inseparably linked with the salvation event, appropriating that Name cannot be a mere human act of self-identification but God's own act of marking or "sealing" the believer as His own. They would find support in G.W.H. Lampe's description of the Name as the divine seal, "the invisible imprint of the potent and tremendous name of God which marks the believer as God's property."[6] Through this identification of the name of Jesus with the act of salvation, Oneness theology lays the foundation for a soteriology that makes the Name indispensable. The act that most definitively appropriates the Name for the believer is water baptism.

2. The Name in Baptism

Before the New Issue emerged in 1914, William Durham had already, and in some ways unwittingly, set the stage for the controversy over water baptism, in his Finished Work of Calvary teaching that the believer is most fully identified with Christ in the act of baptism. Durham began with his key text of Rom. 6:4 ("we were buried therefore with him in his death") and then shifted attention to Acts 2:38, describing it as a parallel text that carries the same meaning.[7] All this was picked up in R.E. McAlister's baptismal sermon on Acts 2:38 in

---

[3] See Reynolds, *Truth*, p. 45; *What We Believe*, p. 5.

[4] Ewart, "Like Precious Faith," p. 7.

[5] Oliver F. Fauss, *Baptism in God's Plan* (Hazelwood, MO: Pentecostal Publishing House, 1955), p. 26.

[6] G.W.H. Lampe, *The Seal of the Spirit* (New York: Longmans, Green & Co., 1951), p. 284.

[7] See Chapter 4 above.

1913, and culminated a year later in Ewart's launching of the new movement.

a. One Practice, Two Theologies

Baptism for Oneness theology is the living point of coalescence between the *Name* and *salvation*. It is peculiarly located between the evangelical-conversionist emphasis on salvation by simple faith and confession in Christ as Savior and the traditional Pentecostal teaching of Spirit-baptism. Elements of both traditions are taken into Oneness soteriology, but reinterpreted and integrated with its own theology of baptism.

Following its Restorationist heritage, the Oneness movement has been agreed from the beginning that Acts 2:38 represents the apostolic pattern for Christian experience. Where it has not gained consensus is in the soteriological meaning of this text. Two traditions of teaching have coexisted from the early years. John H. Dearing (1880-1940) acknowledges this as he launches into a study of the new birth: "We enter into this study fully realizing that it is a subject that has caused a great deal of controversy."[8] W.T. Witherspoon, a leading member of General Presbytery of the newly formed United Pentecostal Church, in 1947 frankly acknowledges the existence of these two groups within the fellowship, with an allusion to the tension created by the different views: "As is well known, the 'Jesus Name' group has been divided into two camps. The dividing line between these camps is the question of the New Birth."[9]

One trajectory follows the evangelical-conversionist tradition in which the "new birth" is the appropriation of the saving work of Christ by an act of faith and personal conversion experience. Witherspoon states:

> [It] contends that a thorough conviction attended by confession, repentance, restitution, etc., brings about a condition in the soul of a seeker that could be none other than the New Birth. Later experiences such as baptism in Jesus' name and reception of the Holy Ghost with the Bible

---

[8] John Dearing, "Born of the Spirit, John 3:5," Lesson 43, Part 1, *Bible Study Notes.*

[9] W.T. Witherspoon, "Our Present Faith," published in the *Pentecostal Herald* following a meeting and with the permission of the Board of General Presbyters and Executive Board of the United Pentecostal Church on 11 June 1947; cited in Reynolds, *Cry of the Unborn: Understanding the Spiritual Birth Process* (Hood River, OR: Alpha Bible, 1991), p. 105.

evidence of speaking in other tongues are *privileges* of the Christian.[10] [emphasis mine]

This view is similar to the theology of the Assemblies of God: salvation is made effective through conversion and commitment, and all else – water and Spirit-baptism – is *subsequent* to that salvation experience. This group would contend, however, that Acts 2:38 is the "Bible standard of full salvation," and to be appropriated in all aspects.[11]

David Bernard and UPCI historian, J.L. Hall, acknowledge but give little historical importance to this view. Hall states that both traditions agreed on the "essentiality of water baptism" and that the qualified language of "Bible standard" and "full" was included only "to show patience toward ministers who practiced Acts 2:38 but who held to the view that salvation – at least in part – occurred at faith and repentance."[12] This minimalist interpretation, however, does not correspond with Witherspoon's account. Though Fauss recollected that both groups believed essentially the same, another minister reported that there were "many" doctrinal differences.[13] Whatever the proportions, the visibility and conviction of each group were sufficient to warrant serious counsel by Witherspoon. And if this tradition believes that baptism in Jesus' name as essential (as Hall asserts), the question is: *essential for what?* As Witherspoon indicates, this group already regards those who repented to be saved. For them – as the salvation qualifiers above suggest – it is probably essential to restore full apostolic practice, to do all in the name of Jesus, to conform to biblical teaching and practice, and undoubtedly to reap the blessings of God for such obedience. Also, most Oneness believers draw on an early Pentecostal distinction between the "saved" and the Spirit-baptized who are in the Church, the Bride, the Kingdom, partakers in the First Resurrection

---

[10] Witherspoon, "Our Present Faith."

[11] This phrase is still the language of the Articles of Faith of the UPCI; see *Manual* (Hazelwood, MO: United Pentecostal Church International, 1999), p. 22.

[12] David Bernard, *A History of Christian Doctrine: The Twentieth Century*, vol. III, *A.D. 1900-2000* (Hazelwood, MO: Word Aflame, 1999), p. 120.

[13] Fudge, *Christianity without the Cross*, p. 75, fn. 5 and 6. Fudge's book is a meticulous account of these two soteriological traditions that inhabited the membership of the UPCI. His concern in particular was to retrieve the voice of those who identify with the evangelical-conversionist stream but whose presence within the ranks has dwindled over the years and whose writings have been less prolific than the stream that has become the "orthodox" position of the UPCI. For a review of the early years of this tradition as reconstructed through oral interviews, see especially pp. 83-95.

(Rapture). While the records indicate that they agreed on the *practice* in Acts 2:38, their theology differed.

The second group teaches that Acts 2:38 as a whole, including water and Spirit-baptism, constitutes the new birth. In Witherspoon's words, this group contends that the experience of confession and repentance "is but a turning toward God and that they are not in the Kingdom until they have entered it by birth of water and Spirit."[14] By interpreting Acts 2:38 in light of the Johannine new birth in John 3:5 ("unless one is born of water and the Spirit, he cannot enter the kingdom of God"), this group rejects the classical Pentecostal view that Acts 2:38 refers to a Spirit-baptism of empowerment in favor of a soteriological interpretation in which the constellation of events constitutes in itself what it means to be born again. This view signals a surprising departure from the evangelical-conversionist tradition within which the Oneness movement was born.

The irony is that this more exclusive view of Acts 2:38 is in some ways similar to the soteriological interpretation by such New Testament scholars as James D.G. Dunn and Max Turner. For Dunn, the three elements in this text constitute the early church's experience of "conversion-initiation." As the paradigmatic text for Christian identity, it is "the only verse in Acts which directly relates to one another the three most important elements in conversion-initiation: repentance, water-baptism, and the gift of the Spirit."[15] Turner echoes Dunn's conclusion that Acts 2:38 is a primary soteriological text: "As Dunn has rightly argued, we should conclude Luke regards believing, repenting, being baptized, and receiving the Spirit, as belonging together as a theologically unified conversion-initiation complex."[16] The

---

[14] Witherspoon, in Reynolds, *Cry of the Unborn*, p. 105. This is Witherspoon's position.

[15] J.D.G. Dunn, *Baptism in the Holy Spirit: A Re-Examination of the New Testament Teaching on the Gift of the Holy Spirit in relation to Pentecostalism Today* (Philadelphia: Westminster, 1970), p. 91.

[16] Max Turner, "The Spirit in Luke-Acts: A Support or a Challenge to Classical Pentecostal Paradigms?" *Vox Evangelica* 27 (October 1997): 75-101. For an extended treatment of the Holy Spirit in Luke-Acts, see Turner, *Power from on High: The Spirit in Israel's Restoration and Witness in Luke-Acts* (Sheffield: Sheffield Academic Press, 1996). Turner and Dunn have challenged the classical Pentecostal theology of subsequence. See Dunn's *Baptism in the Holy Spirit*, and response by Ervin, *Conversion-Initiation and the Baptism in the Holy Spirit: A Critique of James D.G. Dunn's Baptism in the Holy Spirit* (Peabody, MA: Hendrickson, 1984). Turner in particular has been in dialogue with Assemblies of God scholar, Robert Menzies. See Menzies, *The Development of Early Christian Pneumatology with special reference to Luke-Acts* (JSNTS 54; Sheffield: Sheffield Academic Press, 1991), and *Empowered for Witness: The Spirit in Luke-Acts* (JPTS 6; Shef-

parallel with Oneness Pentecostals does not go unnoticed by Turner: "*With the clear exception of Oneness Pentecostals,* most classical Pentecostal *praxis* separates conversion-initiation from Spirit-endowment by a considerable passage of time" [emphasis mine].[17] The "evangelical" critique of classical Pentecostal theology by Dunn and Turner, and their agreement with this group of Oneness Pentecostals that Acts 2:38 is a soteriological text, is a vivid enough illustration of how divergent this particular Oneness tradition is from the rest of the Pentecostal family.

Of course, at another level the praxis within the Oneness conversion-initiation stream is far from the views of Dunn and Turner. Beyond the agreement that the text is soteriological, and that repentance is a constituent element, this Oneness tradition insists upon administering baptism in the name of Jesus and theologically shifting the coming of the Spirit from the moment of conversion to Pentecostal Spirit-baptism. The strength of this interpretation is that it holds more theological promise for a comprehensive understanding of salvation, since the text explicitly incorporates elements of ecclesiology (water baptism) and pneumatology (gift of the Holy Spirit). A comparison of the paradigmatic soteriological texts of John 3:16 and Acts 2:38 vividly illustrates the point. The weakness of this view is that it confines these theological verities exclusively to its own distinctive praxis.

The evangelical-conversionist interpretation, conversely, underlines the Protestant emphasis on the priority of God's grace in salvation and one's appropriating that grace through faith alone. It will, however, have to confront the same critique of the doctrine of subsequence already directed to its fellow Pentecostals. We now turn to an examination of how Oneness theologians interpret the triple themes of Acts 2:38.

b. Acts 2:38 in Three Acts

i. Repentance – Belief unto Obedience. When on the Day of Pentecost the onlookers asked what they must do to be saved, Peter proclaimed that they must first *repent.* Repentance for Oneness Pentecostals is the definitive expression of the act of believing in Christ. It distinguishes them from the wider Pentecostal and evangelical world, for which salvation is a simple act of confession in Jesus Christ as Savior. Faith is

---

field: Sheffield Academic Press, 1994).
    [17] Turner, "The Spirit in Luke-Acts," p. 96.

more than a mere act of the will, or worse, mental assent. Rather, "saving faith," as Reynolds describes it, is "a faith unto obedience. If one is believing to the saving of his soul, he is also repenting and obeying the gospel."[18] Repentance and obedience are the active elements without which faith is not active or salvation achieved. This understanding of faith draws the ire of evangelical critics who charge the Oneness movement with preaching a gospel of "grace plus works."[19] Such acts of human cooperation with divine grace would likely be treated more sympathetically from the Wesleyan tradition.

Repentance is also more than conversion, the latter being treated by some Oneness Pentecostals as merely an "experience" of God.[20] Conversions are the staple of Revivalism, with all the subjective elements associated with it. They fit within the evangelical-conversionist paradigm in which conversion is perceived, at least by Oneness theologians, as "all you need" to be saved, with nothing more to do. It is likely that the Oneness evangelical-conversionist stream is more sympathetic to the language of conversion, since in this soteriological scheme conversion is seen as sufficient for salvation. It is interesting to note that the Pentecostal Church Inc., the organization most identified with this tradition to enter the UPC merger, included in this section of its Articles of Faith the heading, "Repentance and Conversion." It was retained in the UPC Articles of Faith until 1995 when it was deleted in favor of the single heading, "Repentance."[21] This may indicate the strengthening of the conversion-initiation leadership to distinguish further the UPC from the broader Pentecostal and evangelical world.

Neither a mental affirmation of faith nor conversion experience suffices for Oneness doctrine. Repentance has both spiritual and moral content perceived to be lacking in the other appeals. Yet the following fine summation of the relation between faith and baptism in the New Testament by Baptist scholar, G.R. Beasley-Murray, challenges distortions inflicted by both Oneness and Revivalist Christians, and would be difficult to argue against by either side:

---

[18] Reynolds, *Truth*, p. 33.

[19] This criticism comes primarily from Reformed evangelical circles in which repentance is in itself a work of enabling grace in response to divine initiative. Cf. e.g. E. Calvin Beisner, *"Jesus Only" Churches*, pp. 51-72.

[20] Without defining its theological significance, J.L. Hall acknowledges that "United Pentecostals accept that a person can have a genuine experience with God before water baptism or before receiving the Holy Spirit" (emphasis mine), in *The United Pentecostal Church and the Evangelical Movement* (Hazelwood, MO: Word Aflame, 1990), p. 36.

[21] Bernard, *Understanding the Articles of Faith*, p. 29.

In the New Testament faith is no mere intellectual acceptance of a set of religious propositions. It has the Lord Christ as its object and calls forth a response of the whole man to Him. To confess Christ is to acknowledge the truth of the Gospel about Him, to turn from the world and self to the God revealed in Him for mercy and deliverance, and in grateful acknowledgement of the divine love, to make of obedience the total surrender of the self. Mind, heart and will are involved in the faith that turns to the Lord, even as the Lord redeems the whole man in his "spirit and soul and body" (1 Thess. 5:24).[22]

Apart from the misrepresentation of evangelical praxis, what is distinctive and crucial for Oneness Pentecostals is that repentance is not an autonomous act of being saved but the first act designed more specifically to direct the convert toward the next act. Repentance defines faith and belief in such terms of action as to prepare the believer for the ultimate act of obedience – baptism in the name of Jesus. To follow the example of the evangelicals would threaten to undermine its underlying belief that water and Spirit-baptism are in some way essential for full Christian discipleship.

ii. Baptism – Appropriating the Name of Jesus. True repentance is *belief that obeys*, and obedience is primarily the act of being baptized in the name of Jesus. This is the second act in God's "Bible standard" of salvation. Oneness theologians in both traditions turn to the Pauline injunction: "Whatever you do, in word or deed, do everything in the name of the Lord Jesus" (Col. 3:17). Such passages are frequently used to taunt the Trinitarians who appear to be inconsistent at best and disobedient at worst. As Paterson's rhetorically asks: "Why do some preachers use Jesus' name to cast out devils, to heal the sick, in prayer of all kinds and in giving, yet they persistently refuse to use it in baptism?"[23]

If true belief leads to baptism, it is specifically in baptism that *faith is united with the Name*. As Ewart states: "Baptism into His Name is God's ordained way of expressing our belief."[24] For J.T. Pugh, prominent UPCI leader, believing is not a matter of words alone but "sinking ourselves into the very death, burial, and resurrection of Jesus Christ through repentance, baptism in Jesus' name, and the infilling of

---

[22] G.R. Beasley-Murray, *Baptism in the New Testament* (Grand Rapids, MI: Eerdmans, 1962), pp. 267-68.

[23] Paterson, *Real Truth*, p. 21; see also Andrew Urshan, "Why I was Baptized in the Name, Lord Jesus Christ," p. 10.

[24] Ewart, *Name and Book*, p. 15.

the Holy Ghost."[25] Repentance and baptism in Jesus' name are so inextricably linked in Reynolds's mind that he believes Oneness Pentecostals "have the right to challenge an individual on whether or not he is believing if he refuses to be baptized in Jesus' Name."[26] Bernard concurs, stating that "obedience is the only course open to us if we truly accept the Bible as our sole authority for faith and practice and if we truly desire to make Jesus the Lord of all of our life, including our thoughts, values, beliefs, and practices."[27]

One of the most offensive practices for other Christians is the Oneness insistence upon re-baptism, as it appears schismatic and is a declared denial of the validity of Trinitarian baptism. Oneness Pentecostals, on the contrary, regard it as essential, since "a person is not baptized who has never been baptized in the name of Jesus."[28] For the evangelical-conversionist Oneness position, this may simply mean that a baptismal formula that has no precedent in the apostolic tradition nullifies the act itself; conformity to biblical praxis is of the highest priority. For those with a stricter doctrine of the Name, a baptismal rite without the invocation of the proper name of God is invalid. While one is saved through faith, the kind of faith required for salvation is faith that acts in obedience to God's will. True faith leads believers to be baptized in the name of Jesus Christ if they intend to be faithful and obedient to the apostolic practice.

One of the more contentious issues in Oneness baptismal theology is the meaning of baptism. Whatever disagreements Oneness Pentecostals have among themselves, they generally reject the common accusation (especially by fellow Pentecostals and evangelicals) that they teach baptismal regeneration. Their opposition has less to do with the rite than the theological conviction that the efficacious agent is the Name, not the water. In baptism the name of Jesus links salvation and removal of sins.[29] Ewart disavows any efficacy in the water itself: "*Water baptism* cannot save anyone." Its efficacy is "in the Name of Jesus."[30] Andrew Urshan distinguishes between *mode* and *essence* to make the same point. While the proper mode of baptism is immersion, he recalls

---

[25] J.T. Pugh, *How to Receive the Holy Ghost* (St. Louis, MO: Pentecostal Publishing House, 1969), p. 32.

[26] Reynolds, *Truth*, p. 34.

[27] Bernard, *In the Name of Jesus* (Hazelwood, MO: Word Aflame, 1992), p. 48. See also his more detailed treatment of the relationship between grace, faith and acts of obedience in ch. 2, *The New Birth* (Hazelwood, MO: Word Aflame, 1984), pp. 31-64.

[28] Reynolds, *Truth*, p. 44; see also Paterson, *Real Truth*, pp. 24-25.

[29] See Reynolds, *Truth*, p. 42.

[30] Ewart, "Significance of Water Baptism," p. 12.

that he "had not seen yet the essence of the baptism and the stress upon that part which Our Lord put." This "essence" to which he refers is the "Name."[31] Likewise for Haywood, "to be saved by water baptism, it must be administered in the name of Jesus.... The life of the blood of Christ is connected with baptism when it is administered in His Name."[32] The UPCI continues to distance itself from other traditions that teach baptismal regeneration, though some individual ministers have no difficulty in accepting the label.[33]

For observers who are not familiar with the centrality of the Name in Oneness doctrine and praxis, the distinction is either not grasped or considered inconsequential. For many, it is the requirement of water baptism itself as part of the salvation scheme that is problematic. Gregory Boyd, a pastor-theologian and former Oneness Pentecostal, recognizes the importance of baptism as a normal part of the salvation experience in the New Testament, but adds: "This is not, however, the same as saying that salvation was ever seen as being directly contingent upon baptism."[34]

While baptism does hold a central place across the spectrum of Oneness theology and praxis, Oneness Pentecostals themselves differ on what occurs in the act of baptism – most predictably along the lines of the two soteriological traditions within the movement. This difference and tension between those who do and those who do not understand Acts 2: 38 as the pattern for the new birth has existed in Oneness circles from the earliest years.[35] The evangelical-conversionists among them believe that sins are removed by grace through the act of faith, prior to water baptism. Baptism itself is an act of identification with Christ through taking on his Name and acting in obedience as the outward expression of faith. As Oneness theologian, Robert Sabin, states following his departure from the UPCI,

> It was after I left the UPCI that ... the message of the cross became more clear to me, that is, the message that Jesus accomplished on the cross my salvation, my justification, and that I did not save myself by my observing the three steps of Acts 2:38.[36]

---

[31] Andrew Urshan, *The Doctrine of the New Birth* (Cochrane, WI: Witness of God, 1921), pp. 35, 36.

[32] Haywood, *Birth of the Spirit*, p. 24.

[33] Fudge, *Christianity without the Cross*, p. 127.

[34] Gregory Boyd, *Oneness Pentecostals and the Trinity*, p. 136.

[35] Kidson, Interview.

[36] Cited in Fudge, *Christianity without the Cross*, p. 126. See also a similar Reformed view by another former UPCI minister and protégé of Sabin, Bernie Gillespie, website:

Those who interpret the composite of Acts 2:38 as the new birth view baptism as being an active agent in the removal of sin; hence the charge of baptismal regeneration. They develop baptismal themes that relate to remission of sins, cleansing, and holiness.

One theme for new birth Oneness writers besides the Name is water itself, especially as a cleansing agent in the remission of sins. As the laver in the Tabernacle of Moses was a symbol of purification, so is Christian baptism the antetype of cleansing from sin.[37] The separation and salvation that came to the Israelites at the crossing of the Red Sea are symbolized by the water.[38] Occasionally called "the water test," the test of true Christian obedience is water baptism in the name of Jesus.[39]

A second baptismal theme is spiritual circumcision. Interpreting baptism as new covenant circumcision brings together the ritual act of cleansing in water and the Name. A key passage for this connection is Col. 2:11-13, "In him also you were circumcised with a circumcision made without hands ...and you were buried with him in baptism." As circumcision is the mark of identity for Israel, a sign of holiness or cleansing from sin, and is associated with the invocation of the (male) child's name, so also is it with baptism. Haywood believes that Paul "unmistakably connects it with baptism of water and Spirit."[40] R.F. Tobin, Haywood's successor at Christ Temple in Indianapolis, clearly identifies baptism with the washing of cleansing: "Washing or baptism in water is without question essential to salvation and can in no wise be ignored." He then goes on to describe the burial in baptism as the "circumcision of Christ."[41] Ewart at one point describes baptism as

---

www.inchristalone.org/. Gillespie is pastor of Grace and Truth Community Church in Findlay, OH, and head of In Christ Alone! Ministries, the purpose of which is stated on the website: "It is the mission of In Christ Alone! Ministries (ICA!M) to declare the Gospel of Jesus Christ. It is the desire of this ministry to be a means whereby the Holy Spirit, through the Gospel of Christ, may create in the hearts of hearers the knowledge, conviction and assurance that Christ, out of sheer grace, has forgiven their sins, made them right with God, and granted them salvation. ICA! calls all Christians to a reawakening, which will inspire: 1.) A renewed vision of the biblical meaning of the Gospel of Jesus Christ; 2.) Those who do not trust in Christ to believe and be saved; 3.) All to offer praise which will give all glory to God alone."

[37] See Hobbs, *Whom Say Ye*, p. 94; also Isma Wells Erwin, *The Resurrection and The New Birth* (St. Louis, MO: Pentecostal Publishing House, 1954), p. 54.

[38] See Andrew Urshan, *Doctrine of The New Birth*, p. 34.

[39] *Ibid.*; see also Erwin, *Resurrection and New Birth*, p. 53.

[40] Hayood, *Birth of the Spirit*, p. 12.

[41] R.F. Tobin, *The Principles of the Doctrine of Christ* (Indianapolis, IN: Christ Temple, 1948), pp. 14, 15.

"true Christian circumcision," since in the Colossians passage the believer is identified with Christ in his death and burial.[42]

Haywood is the first major Oneness figure to interpret Acts 2:38 as
the new birth.[43] With Ewart and others, he follows the interpretation
of the popular Methodist commentator, Adam Clarke; that the birth of
water and Spirit in John 3:5 are parallel concepts for water and Spirit-
baptism in Acts 2:38. Of particular interest here is Haywood's teaching
on the efficacy of baptism in the remission of sins. There is some basis
to the claim that he was influenced significantly by the Campbellite
doctrine of baptismal regeneration.[44] There is a long tradition in UPCI
circles to distinguish between forgiveness and remission of sins, the
latter being effected by baptism. Forgiveness is God's juridical act of
pronouncing that one's sins are no longer charged against them. But
those sins are not actually removed until baptism. Bernard and others
recognize the linguistic weaknesses inherent in this distinction.[45]

Those who follow the evangelical-conversionist tradition understand baptism differently. Reeves, for instance, teaches that baptism is a
response to God's work of salvation by showing God that one intends
to leave off the past life and follow Christ: "This is the least that one
can do to show good faith to the true inward commitment. It is
downright disobedience to refuse." Yet baptism is more than a mere
sign to the world that one is a believer; it is an important "step of
faith" and an act of obedience.[46] In a later book, Reeves appears to add
to this slim baptismal theology an ecclesiological dimension, namely,
that forgiveness of sins is granted by Christ's work on the cross but the
double baptism in Acts 2:38 bestows adoption into the family of
God.[47]

It has been emphasized throughout this study that baptism is the
point at which the Name achieves its highest order in Oneness theol-

---

[42] Ewart, "Significance of Water Baptism," p. 12; see also Paterson, *Real Truth*, p. 6;
Kolenda, *For Remission*, pp. 59-62.

[43] See Chapter 9 above.

[44] This claim is made by former UPC minister, Daniel L. Scott, Jr., *Family Reunion and
Confession of Faith* (Nashville, TN: Global Christian Ministries, n.d.), cited in Fudge,
Christianity without the Cross, p. 121 n. 274.

[45] Bernard, *The New Birth, Series in Pentecostal Theology,* Volume 2 (Hazelwood, MO:
Word Aflame Press, 1984), pp. 141-45. For a fuller treatment of this teaching in the
UPCI, see Fudge, *Christianity without the Cross*, pp. 126-35.

[46] Reeves, *The Great Commission Re-Examined* (Granite City, IL: By the Author,
1970), pp. 26, 50.

[47] Reeves, *The Lost Sons of God* (Granite City, IL: Inspirational Tapes and Books,
1990), cited in Fudge, *Christianity without the Cross*, p. 82, fn. 41.

ogy. We have already noted (Chapter 12) that Jesus is the covenantal name of God *vis-à-vis* the so-called "titles" of Father, Son and Holy Spirit. It is precisely this hermeneutical distinction between name and titles that Oneness exegetes use to authenticate Matt. 28:19 and defend their Monarchian view of God and baptism in the name of the Lord Jesus Christ without creating an internal contradiction. Instead of the Matthean text being a hermeneutical problem, it is an important principle for establishing a theology of the Name in the New Testament.

Their argument leads in two directions. First, the use of the singular "name" in Matt. 28:19 is in itself a clue taken by Oneness theologians that what follows is not a formula but a commission. Reynolds points out that "'JESUS' is the 'NAME' (singular) of the Father, Son, and Holy Ghost. The terms, Father, Son, and the Holy Ghost, are titles and certainly are not names." To set one passage against the other as Trinitarians do shows that "they believe in a contradiction in Scripture."[48] Second, the direction taken by the Apostles warrants respecting that they knew what they were doing, and that they were faithfully following Jesus' command. Since (in Acts) they did not *repeat* the phrase in the Great Commission suggests that Matt. 28:19 is a command to be fulfilled, which is to use the one actual, proper name of Jesus. Paterson challenges the Trinitarians on this point: "Will anyone dare to say that the Apostles gave wrong instructions on the Day of Pentecost to 3,000 convicted souls?"[49] The conclusion to be drawn is that the baptismal *formula* to be used is in Acts, while Matt. 28:19 is the *commission* given by Jesus himself to baptize using his name.

There is often the appearance of inconsistency, or at least confusion, with regard to the complex name of Lord Jesus Christ. While the name of Jesus is the singular and proper name of God, the titles "Lord" and "Christ" are used variably in Acts to specify the divine identity of this person. As Ewart argues, the titles belong in the baptismal formula because "God hath made Him both Lord and Christ – Jehovah and Jehovah's Anointed."[50] Thus, the baptismal formula used by most Oneness Pentecostals includes the compound name, Lord Jesus Christ.[51]

It is increasingly clear that the Oneness practice of baptism in the name of Jesus is more compelling than its harmonizing hermeneutic. A

---

[48] Reynolds, *Truth*, pp. 44, 45; see also Andrew Urshan, *Almighty God*, p. 45.

[49] Paterson, *Real Truth*, p. 8; see also Andrew Urshan, *Almighty God*, p. 44.

[50] Ewart, *Name and Book*, p. 141.

[51] See *What We Believe*, p. 6; Vouga, *Gospel Message*, p. 18; Reeves, *Great Commission*, p. 36.

number of scholars conclude that early apostolic practice used some variation of the christological name. Lars Hartman, for instance, in examining the context of the baptismal phrase, "into the Name of Jesus," concludes that, "we can be quite certain that this baptism was given 'into the name of Jesus' or, at least, that it was referred to as a baptism 'into the name of Jesus.'" Given the early Jewish Christian context of the phrase, he further reasons that its practice in baptism carried convictions which were rooted in Semitic thought, yet "implied a rather 'high' christology."[52]

New Testament scholar, Larry Hurtado, in his study of early Christian devotion, likewise draws a connection between baptism and the use of the phrase "into the name of Jesus."[53] In an extensive discourse on Jesus Christ as the basis and goal of baptism, Karl Barth affirms – perhaps even prefers – the theological appropriateness of the phrase, "into Jesus Christ," by suggesting that the reason for its displacement by the obligatory Trinitarian formula was "for the sake of ecumenical peace even though its exegetical, dogmatic and theological necessity cannot be demonstrated."[54] Even Calvin saw no conflict between the two names invoked in baptism, the christocentric form being a sort of shorthand version of the full Trinitarian name. In his commentary on 1 Corinthians, he states: "When we wish to sum up in short compass the efficacy of baptism, we make mention of Christ alone; but when we are disposed to speak with greater minuteness, the name of the Father and that of the Spirit require to be expressly introduced."[55]

iii. Baptism of the Holy Spirit. The third act in the plan of salvation is the coming of the Holy Spirit. Most Pentecostal theology understands Spirit-baptism to be a second visitation of God to empower the Christian for ministry. It is an experience distinct from and subsequent to conversion, yet affirms the *indwelling* of the Spirit when one is born again. The *empowering* or anointing of the Spirit at the moment of Spirit-baptism is accompanied by speaking in tongues.[56]

---

[52] Lars Hartman, "Baptism 'Into the Name of Jesus' and Early Christology," *ST* 28 (1974), pp. 21, 43.

[53] Larry Hurtado, *One God, One Lord: Early Christian Devotion and Ancient Jewish Monotheism* (Philadelphia: Fortress, 1988), pp. 108-11.

[54] Karl Barth, *Church Dogmatics* IV/4 (trans. G.W. Bromiley; Edinburgh: T. & T. Clark, 1975-

77), p. 92.

[55] Cited in Bryan Spinks, "Calvin's Baptismal Theology and the Making of the Strasbourg and Genevan Baptismal Liturgies 1540 and 1542," *Scottish Journal of Theology* 48/1 (1995): 76-77.

[56] Frederick Dale Bruner, *A Theology of the Holy Spirit – The Pentecostal Experience and*

Oneness pneumatology in the new birth tradition, in contrast, places the experience of Spirit-baptism within the realm of soteriology, not beyond it. By its identification of Spirit-baptism with the birth of the Spirit, one does not have the indwelling Spirit until the experience of Spirit-baptism with speaking in tongues.

Oneness theology interprets John 3:5 through the filter of Pentecostal experience, arguing that "born" and "baptized" are "proven to be synonymous terms expressing the one and self-same thing."[57] Oneness pastor O.W. Williams takes this same stand that "the gift of the Holy Ghost, the baptism of the Holy Ghost, and the infilling of the Holy Ghost, are synonymous terms," and that Spirit-baptism with tongues is part of the plan for "full salvation" and, therefore, "necessary to salvation."[58]

Due in part to its emphasis on the evidential character of Spirit-baptism, Oneness theology treats the three acts in the plan of salvation experientially as a temporal sequence. The Spirit does not come in and through the water baptism, since the efficacy there lies primarily in the invocation of the name of Jesus. Rather, the birth or baptism of the Spirit *normally* follows water baptism, even if the delay is brief. In part, the promise of the Holy Spirit is theologically the culmination of a process in which prior conditions of repentance and baptism in Jesus' name have been fulfilled. Reeves points out that in Acts "in every case, the Holy Ghost was received after the people were baptized in water, with the exception of the Cornelius group."[59] Any alteration to the prescribed plan is a sovereign exception. Yet Oneness writers *theologically* view the three acts as part of one salvific event that may be experienced in rapid succession such as a worship or evangelistic service.

There are also lessons to be learned from the wider Pentecostal-charismatic debate on the issue of initiation or subsequence in the Spirit's coming. The tension largely revolves around the relationship between the theological and experiential dimensions of the Christian life, especially in the wake of the recent charismatic renewal. One strand of the discussion has been the debate over the exegetical legiti-

---

the New Testament Witness (Grand Rapids, MI: Eerdmans, 1970), pp. 59-62.

[57] Haywood, *Birth of the Spirit*, p. 5.

[58] O.W. Williams, *What Do You Think?* (Houston, TX: By the Author, n.d.), pp. 12, 17; see also Reeves, *The Holy Ghost With Tongues* (Granite City, IL: By the Author, 1966), p. 19.

[59] Reeves, *Holy Ghost*, p. 25.

macy of the Pentecostal doctrine that Spirit-baptism is a promised experience of empowerment subsequent to conversion.[60]

But the charismatic renewal has raised other issues, namely, the *lack* of experience among those who have been duly sacramentalized, and the *delayed* experience of those who have encountered the Spirit many years after their baptism. A number of theologians attempt to resolve the issue in a both-and manner. Charismatic theologian, Henry Lederle, believes that Spirit-baptism rightly belongs to Christian initiation and is part of the meaning of water baptism, but it is also an element in the ongoing charismatic dimension of the Christian life. This may be called "subsequence" but only in the sense that "the Christian life, also called the process of sanctification, is the ongoing development after one becomes a Christian."[61] Anglican charismatic John Gunstone makes a similar appeal, namely, that locating Spirit-baptism as part of Christian initiation does not foreclose on new outpourings and "surprises" of the Spirit: "Baptism in the Spirit is a fresh sending of the Spirit on one who has already received Christ through repentance, faith and water baptism."[62] He finds support for this integrative approach in Roman Catholic theologians such as the charismatic scholar Francis Sullivan, who believes that a biblical pneumatology embraces both theological and experiential elements:

> In my view, what people are receiving in the charismatic renewal is a real imparting of the Spirit, a new "outpouring of the Spirit" (the theological sense), which typically has effects that make them aware that the Spirit is working in a new way in their lives (the experiential sense).[63]

While Oneness soteriology bears some similarities to views that interpret Acts 2:38 as part of Christian initiation, it faces a similar challenge in its struggle to articulate a sound theological understanding of the *experiential* integrity in the Christian life of those who do not fit its theological mold – specifically those Christians outside its ranks.

---

[60] See above references to Dunn's *Baptism in the Holy Spirit*, and Turner's *Power from on High*.

[61] H.I. Lederle, *Treasures Old and New: Interpretations of "Spirit-Baptism" in the Charismatic Renewal Movement* (Peabody, MA: Hendrickson, 1988), p. 139.

[62] John Gunstone, *Pentecost Comes to Church: Sacraments and Spiritual Gifts* (London: Darton, Longman & Todd, 1994), p. 59.

[63] Cited in Gunstone, *Pentecost Comes to Church*, p. 60.

c. Non-Oneness Parallels

A small minority of Pentecostals, mostly Independent Trinitarians, baptize in the name of the Lord Jesus Christ. The most common interpretation for their practice echoes the explanation given by R.E. McAlister in his 1913 baptismal sermon at the Los Angeles camp meeting, in which he proposed that the name "Lord Jesus Christ" is the "counterpart of Father, Son and Holy Ghost," thereby making the baptismal pattern employed by the Apostles coherent.[64]

One of the oldest and most influential figures in this group is W.H. Offiler, whose name first appears in the New Issue circles in Los Angeles. He was baptized in Jesus' name by Glenn Cook but never embraced the Oneness doctrine of God.[65] However, he retained McAlister's original explanation of the christocentric baptismal formula and developed a mediating view of the Trinity. He left behind an active Independent work, Bethel Temple and Bible School in Seattle, Washington, which earned some notoriety as a result of its leadership in building the Indonesian Pentecostal movement begun in 1921.[66] In his work, *God and His Name,* Offiler affirms the doctrine of the Trinity but includes a section on the Name of God.[67] The triune Name is interpreted christocentrically to be "Lord Jesus Christ." Offiler even offers a harmonized formula to be used when administering water baptism: "I baptize thee in the NAME of the FATHER, and of the SON, and of the HOLY GHOST, the LORD-JESUS-CHRIST."[68]

A second example is Bethesda Missionary Temple in Detroit, Michigan. One of the early centers of the "Latter Rain" movement within Pentecostalism during the late 1940's, Bethesda Temple with its pastor, Mrs. Myrtle Beall, was affiliated with the Assemblies of God until the schism over the Latter Rain issue.[69] Following the schism, a

---

[64] Cited in Ewart, *Phenomenon,* p. 77.

[65] David Bernard, *A History of Christian Doctrine* – vol. III*, The Twentieth Century, A.D. 1900-2000* (Hazelwood, MO: Word Aflame, 1999), p. 109.

[66] Personal letter from the pastor of Bethel Temple, C. Joe McKnight, 5 Feb. 1974. Hollenweger incorrectly identifies this Indonesian work as a "Jesus Only" movement because of the practice of baptizing in the name of Jesus (*Pentecostals,* p. 71).

[67] W.H. Offiler, *God and His Name* (2nd ed.; Seattle, WA: By the Author, 1932).

[68] Offiler, *God and Name,* pp. 79, 94. As early as 1920, Offiler was declaring his opposition to the Oneness doctrine of God, but affirming a christocentric view of the Trinity. E.N. Bell cites an article written by Offiler, "The Godhead Bodily," which describes the Godhead as a "tri-unity" which "exists centrally in Jesus Christ"; see E.N. Bell, "The Godhead," *Pentecostal Evangel* (11 December 1920): 9.

[69] For a discussion of the Latter Rain Movement and the role played by Bethesda Temple, see D. William Faupel, "The Everlasting Gospel: The Significance of Eschatol-

distinctive doctrine of the Trinity emerged – the triune God has a revealed name, "Lord Jesus Christ," which is to be invoked in water baptism. The teaching is set forth in a book by Mrs. Beall's daughter, Patricia Beall Gruits, *Understanding God.* In it she teaches that baptism is to be administered in the name of the Lord Jesus Christ, as the singular "Name" of the Father, Son and Holy Spirit.[70] Though no acknowledgement is given to Offiler, the pastor of Offiler's church, C. Joe McKnight, alludes to some form of influence. He states that, as some of the ministers associated with Offiler's group joined the Latter Rain movement, "they certainly influenced the movement in some areas of doctrine."[71]

A third case is Ernest B. Gentile, pastor of Gospel Temple in San Jose, California, and president of Northern California Bible College. His teaching follows the identical pattern of including a doctrine of the name of God and baptism in the name of the Lord Jesus Christ that we observe in Offiler and Gruits. He oversees an Independent ministry, which bears the marks of influence by the Latter Rain movement. Gentile himself is a graduate of Offiler's school, Bethel Temple Bible School,[72] and author of a book outlining his distinctive doctrines, *God and His Word – A Catechism of Bible Doctrine.*[73] In the Preface he acknowledges his indebtedness to both Offiler and Gruits.[74] According to Gentile, his mediating teaching on the nature of the one-and-three in the Trinity has earned him praise from both Trinitarians and Oneness Pentecostals:

> I have had Oneness people say that we preach Oneness more strongly than their own churches. We have also had people say that we preach Threeness more strongly than the typical Trinity church. Our approach is to stick to the Bible terminology and concentrate more on enjoying and

ogy in the Development of Pentecostal Thought" (Ph.D. diss., University of Birmingham, 1989), pp. 394-518; Menzies, *Anointed to Serve,* pp. 322-25.

[70] Patricia Beall Gruits, *Understanding God* (rev. ed.; Detroit, MI: Whitaker, 1972), p. 364.

[71] C. Joe McKnight, personal letter, 5 February 1974.

[72] Ernest B. Gentile, personal letter, San Jose, CA, 6 November 1973. The "Statement of Faith" of the Bible School reveals Latter Rain distinctives such as personal, direct revelations, emphasis on prophecy, and the ministry of laying on of hands; see *Catalog, Northern California Bible College* (San Jose, CA: Privately published, n.d.), pp. 2, 4.

[73] Ernest B. Gentile, *God and His Word.*

[74] *Ibid.,* "Preface." For his teaching on baptism in the name of the Lord Jesus Christ, see p. 132.

experiencing God rather than interpreting something which most people cannot comprehend.[75]

It is this teaching that continues to hover as a compelling alternative on the outskirts of the orthodox Oneness movement.

A final example is a heterodox teaching by the late Lloyd L. Goodwin (d. 1996), former Independent Pentecostal pastor of Gospel Assembly Church in Des Moines, Iowa, and author of *Great Doctrines of the Bible*. In it he explicitly rejects the Oneness view of God as well as the Trinity, alternatively proposing without explanation that Jesus is not God but "the first act of God's creation." Like the others, he holds to a theology of the Name, teaching that "Jesus" is the family name of God and that baptism should therefore be administered according to Acts 2:38.[76] Similar to Oneness theology in general, there appears to be a pattern in which a doctrine of the name of God functions to compensate for an otherwise dangerously low or erroneous Christology.

3. The Name in the Church

Oneness soteriology is not an autonomous doctrine but is inseparably linked to the doctrine of the church and eventually to eschatology, all of which becomes the lens through which Oneness Pentecostals view the status of other Christians. Oneness ecclesiology functions as much to identify the state of those who are not in the church as those who are. The kingdom of God, Church, Bride of Christ, Body of Christ, are all synonyms in Oneness terminology for the same spiritual reality attained when the three acts in the salvation plan of Acts 2:38 are achieved.[77] Andrew Urshan is an exception in that he distinguishes between the kingdom of heaven and the kingdom of God. The former includes the wheat and tares, the good and bad whereas the kingdom of God is the realm where "nothing unrighteous or unclean can enter." Predictably, Trinitarian believers are consigned to the kingdom of heaven.[78]

For Oneness Pentecostals, the triple acts of Acts 2:38 constitute entry into the kingdom of God. The logic follows a series of textual cross-references. In addition to being a parallel text for Acts 2:38, John

---

[75] Ernest B. Gentile, personal letter, 6 November 1973.

[76] Lloyd L. Goodwin, *Great Doctrines of the Bible* (Des Moines, IA: Gospel Assembly Church, 1972), pp. 21, 32, 42, 51.

[77] See Haywood, *Birth of the Spirit*, p. 7.

[78] Andrew Urshan, "Twenty-Seven Questions and Answers on the New Birth," *Pentecostal Outlook* 12 (July 1943), p. 8.

3:5 is the necessary qualification for entry into the kingdom ("unless one is born of water and the Spirit, he cannot enter the kingdom of God"). Recalling Peter's confession at Caesarea Philippi that Jesus is the Christ, Jesus promised him the "keys to the kingdom" (Matt. 16:19), a mandate Peter fulfilled in his famous Pentecost sermon (Acts 2:38). As Urshan wrote early on, the keys that Jesus gave to Peter were the essentials of salvation summed up in Acts 2:38.[79] Hobbs also states the essence of this threefold message: "Christ gave the keys to the kingdom to Peter and gave him power to open His will and testament."[80]

The tantalizing and all too frequently hostile question arises – what status do Oneness Pentecostals accord Trinitarian Christians, Pentecostals and non-Pentecostals alike? A common response from the official UPCI writings is to remain agnostic on the question. They distinguish between the biblical doctrine of salvation as set forth in Acts 2:38 and the sovereign work of God. Bernard is representative: he acknowledges the biblical principles that God is sovereign, that believers are not to condemn others, and that God rewards sincere seekers after truth, especially if they walk in all the light they possess. But these give no warrant for speculation beyond the bounds of apostolic doctrine. So he concludes, "We can only leave unusual and hypothetical cases in God's hands."[81]

The dilemma in this reasoning of course is that it is difficult – some would say disingenuous – to insist upon this kind of theological silence in the presence of other Pentecostals with whom there is so much historical and doctrinal affinity, let alone the vast evangelical and Christian community. There are and have been from the earliest years efforts to take account of other Christians, even if the latter still find these attempts wanting. Reeves, for example, contrasts being in the church and having an "experience" of God: "To be in the Church Triumphant and to have some relationship to God are two different

---

[79] See Andrew Urshan, *Doctrine of the New Birth*, p. 25.

[80] Hobbs, *Whom Say Ye*, p. 113. For an expanded explanation, see Bernard, *The New Birth*, ch. 1. The doctrine of the Church in the Articles of Faith of the UPCI is minimalist, with only brief statements on healing, Holy Communion and foot washing; see Bernard *Understanding the Articles of Faith*, pp. 17-18. Bernard himself seems to have left this doctrine largely unattended in an otherwise wide range of topics addressed. See also Ralph Reynolds, *Cry of the Unborn: Understanding the Spiritual Birth Process* (Hood River, OR: Alpha Bible, 1991), ch. 3.

[81] Bernard, *Essentials of the New Birth* (Hazelwood, MO: Word Aflame, 1987), p. 37; also, *The New Birth*, ch. 12, pp. 304-24. See also J.L. Hall, *The United Pentecostal Church and the Evangelical Movement* (Hazelwood, MO: Word Aflame, 1990).

questions. Certainly many people have experienced varying degrees of blessings from God."[82] Elsewhere he teaches that one becomes a "true believer" by receiving "justification by faith."[83] Through this act of reconciliation we are no longer enemies of God, but we are His friends. "God first makes us His friends through reconciling us. It is on His friends that He confers the gift of the Holy Ghost."[84] That is, the Spirit will not enter an unreconciled and unjustified life.[85] In this initial stage one is a believer or friend of God, but is not yet indwelt by the Holy Spirit. Reeves is clear that the many wonderful experiences of God "must not be confused as the baptism of the Holy Ghost."[86]

A more positive distinction is found in such metaphors as the birth process and the "light" theory, popularized by Haywood and others. In the birth metaphor, for instance, Haywood makes the point that life begins at conception, not birth. Spiritually, this embryonic life is more than a nondescript experience of God; it is the beginning stage of full life in Christ. Trinitarian Christians and others are products of the Word, though not yet recipients of the Spirit: "Many may have been begotten by the Word but have never been born of the Spirit."[87] It is an error to assume that these believers are lost, as "many have been converted to God with a vital heart experience."[88] Appealing to the "light" theory, Haywood more confidently affirms that their final salvation is dependent upon their faithfulness to walk "in all the light that was given them while they lived."[89]

Andrew Urshan uses the same analogy, drawing the conclusion that those who have not yet been born again are "in the womb of the Church conceived." He compares their status with that of the Old Testament saints who were "saved by faith not receiving the promise

---

[82] Reeves, *Holy Ghost*, p. 39.

[83] Reeves, *Great Commission*, p. 60.

[84] Reeves, *Holy Ghost*, p. 42.

[85] This distinction echoes the older three-work Holiness teaching that the Spirit will not enter an unclean vessel; hence, the Spirit must first sanctify the life of the believer before coming in Spirit-baptism to empower.

[86] Reeves, *Holy Ghost*, p. 42.

[87] Haywood, *Birth of the Spirit*, p. 11.

[88] Haywood, "Editorial," *Christian Outlook* 2 (April 1924): 325.

[89] Haywood, *Birth of the Spirit*, p. 12. According to the late Morris Golder, Haywood's teaching is still observed within the black Oneness movement, especially the Pentecostal Assemblies of the World. It is likely due in large part to this positive approach that black Oneness groups and leaders fellowship and cooperate more readily with other Christians. Golder, Interview, Grace Apostolic Church, Indianapolis, IN, 22 May 1973.

of the Spirit."[90] Reynolds represents a recent attempt to revitalize this metaphor, recognizing that the silence within the Oneness fellowship has created a spirit of exclusivity and lack of charity toward others. An adherent of the new birth interpretation of Acts 2:38, Reynolds distinguishes Oneness believers from those who have experienced the "everlasting gospel," a difference between the cross and the Pentecostal fullness:

> The Bible does not leave us in ignorance concerning this matter. Such converts are born of the Word. They have been granted repentance and experienced the atoning power provided at Calvary. They are spiritually in the same condition as an unborn fetus. They need to be brought to birth.[91]

This distinction between Oneness believers and others is extended to eschatology. The general Oneness scheme builds on the inherited Dispensational doctrine of two resurrections. The first resurrection is the "Rapture" or secret "translation" of the Church from the world. The second resurrection occurs following the period of the Great Tribulation and Millennial reign prior to the Final Judgment. The first resurrection belongs to the Church, the "Bride of Christ,"[92] those who are "the anointed ones ...endowed and filled with the Holy Spirit."[93] Oneness pneumatology precludes the non-Oneness Pentecostals from the first resurrection. Since in much of Oneness theology the Holy Spirit does not indwell the believer until Spirit-baptism, non-Pentecostals are excluded from the resurrection promise in Rom. 8:11: "If the Spirit of him who raised Jesus from the dead dwells in you, he ...will give life to your mortal bodies also through his Spirit which dwells in you." Reynolds points out that eligibility for the first resurrection requires the mark of both the Name and the Spirit. According to Acts 15:14, God is going to "take out of them a people for his name," the invocation of which occurs in baptism. And according to Rom. 8:11, "it is the Holy Ghost who will quicken our bodies at the rapture."[94]

---

[90] Andrew Urshan, "Twenty-Seven Questions," pp. 8, 13.

[91] Reynolds, *Cry of the Unborn,* p. 100. While he expresses fear of weakening the Oneness message, he appears to be motivated to write the book to counter the extreme claims made by some: "I have heard the message weakened many times by the utterance of radical statements that could not be verified by the Scriptures," p. 9.

[92] Erwin, *Resurrection and New Birth,* p. 13.

[93] Andrew Urshan, "First and Second Resurrections," *Pentecostal Outlook* 10 (April 1941): 3.

[94] Reynolds, *Truth,* p. 101.

The second resurrection belongs to those who have not received "full salvation" according to Acts 2:38. Andrew Urshan describes this category as "the righteous men and women who lived a moral, righteous, and charitable life, believing in God before they passed away, without ever coming to the light of being born again according to Acts 2:38."[95] Haywood likewise identifies them as the righteous people of all ages. All Trinitarian Pentecostals and non-Pentecostals are grouped with non-Christians in the second resurrection:

> It is my candid opinion that all heathen, Israelites, Christian professors, who have never heard the true gospel of Christ, and those who die during the millennium, walking in the light of their times will be given eternal life at the last resurrection.[96]

Reynolds draws a further distinction in the eternal habitation: possessors of the fullness of Pentecost (Acts 2:38), "members of the church, the bride, the kingdom of God," will inherit the New Jerusalem. Believers of all ages, those whose names are "written in the Book of Life," will inhabit the new earth:

> Everyone that has not been born of the water and the Spirit or been baptized into the body of Christ and have become a member of the church, but whose names are recorded in the Book of Life by virtue of the atoning and efficacious work of the blood of the Lamb of God shed on Calvary's cross will be there.[97]

F.E. Curts, a Oneness teacher from an earlier generation, provides a third distinction, primarily to account for the experience of the Spirit in other Pentecostals. With the Old Testament Tabernacle as his blueprint, he identifies three classes of believers. The inner circle is the true New Testament Church following the Aaronic order, those who are obedient to the apostolic plan of salvation. The second group consists of the Trinitarian Pentecostals who have received Spirit-baptism but have not yet accepted the Oneness message – these follow the Levitical order. Since they have the quickening Spirit, they will be raptured in the first resurrection; and if alive during the Tribulation period, they will gain this order by their perseverance. Finally, there are the right-

---

[95] Andrew Urshan, "First and Second Resurrections," p. 3; see also Erwin, *Resurrection and New Birth*, p. 17.

[96] Haywood, "First and Second Resurrections," p. 4.

[97] Reynolds, *Cry of the Unborn*, pp. 118-120. Reynolds notes that this is also the eschatological view of the prominent Oneness teacher, S.G. Norris. For another concise outline of the eschatological events from a Oneness viewpoint, see Golder, *Principles*, pp. 20-24.

eous of the entire world who will receive the reward of eternal life – the Israelite tribes symbolize these.[98]

According to J.L. Hall, none of these eschatological views that distinguished between the first and second resurrections is officially endorsed by the UPCI, and they "have declined in influence in recent years."[99] While these views may have been exegetically and theologically deficient, they at least functioned to provide eschatological space for non-Oneness Christians. The present dilemma in official UPCI theology is that it provides no "place" theologically for other Christians, and maintains an attitude of silent agnosticism regarding their status.

So we see in Oneness theology a highly exclusive doctrine of salvation, the implications of which are unfolded in its doctrines of the church and last things. Admittedly, it inherits much of this eschatological compartmentalizing from its Pentecostal forebears, going back to Parham. But the lack of development beyond this schematizing, however, is an indicator more of theological isolation than theological acuity. For the present, however, some sort of inherited eschatological partitioning between the first and second resurrections at least softens an otherwise exclusive teaching.

4. The Name in Ministry

While the Oneness theology of the Name is concentrated in the core doctrines of God, Christ and salvation, it extends as well to the Christian life. The following themes illustrate the ways in which Oneness theologians understand the place of the name of Jesus in the Christian life.

a. The Name as Power

"Pentecost is power!" In this exclamation Ewart sums up the message of the early Pentecostal movement. But he directs much of the focus of this power onto the name of Jesus. More than any other Oneness figure, Ewart understands the phenomenon of "apostolic power" in terms of the name of Jesus, not just the outpouring of the Spirit. He is convinced that "what really happened at Pentecost was the declaration of a God-given charter to work miracles in the Name of the Lord Jesus Christ." He then sets this in stark contrast to the powerlessness of the church in our day, which lacks ministry in the name of Jesus. In-

---

[98] Curts, *Tabernacle*, pp. 33, 34, 36.
[99] Hall, *United Pentecostal Church*, p. 37.

stead of relying on customs and methods, "the early Church got the ear of the common people by a demonstration of the power in the Name of Jesus." For Ewart then, the name of Jesus was more than a doctrine for the early Christians – it was the key to their mission.[100]

b. The Name as Presence of the Ascended Lord

Ewart's explanation of the ascended and "absent" Lord who is present to the church in his Name, has eucharistic overtones. He states that the Name "actually took the place of the ascended Lord in outward manifestation."[101] This is not unlike the observation made by the Lukan scholar Ernst Haenchen: "While Jesus himself dwells in heaven until the Parousia, his name is present and active among us here and now; it performs miracles and is the channel of salvation." The name of Jesus is not merely a tool for the "magic conjurations of antiquity: it is God who acts when the name of Jesus is invoked."[102]

There is little reflection among Oneness theologians on the relationship between the power of the Name and the power of the Spirit. It is not unusual in popular theology for concepts to lack precision and meanings to become fluid. For example, at one point Ewart seems to collapse the function of the Name into Spirit-baptism. Having emphasized that the significance of Pentecost is the release of the name of Jesus to work miracles, he adds that this "is the meaning of the baptism in the Spirit."[103] Oscar Vouga, a former presbyter with UPCI, likewise makes little distinction. Miracles are being performed "through faith in the name of Jesus ...and with the anointing of the Holy Spirit and power."[104] Paterson comes as close as any drawing distinctions between the two. Like the others, he teaches that the name of the Holy Spirit is Jesus. The Spirit is sent in the name of Jesus (cf. John 14:26) and glorifies not himself but Jesus (cf. John 16:14-15).[105] Therefore, the indwelling of the Spirit is actually "Christ in you."[106] The Name then seems to function, like the sacraments, as the *outward* sign of identity or power while the Spirit of Christ or the Holy Spirit is the *inward* reality.

---

[100] Ewart, *Name and Book*, pp. 24, 31, 128.

[101] *Ibid.*, p. 26.

[102] Ernst Haenchen, *The Acts of the Apostles – A Commentary* (trans. Bernard Noble & Gerald Shinn; rev. trans. R. McL. Wilson; Philadelphia: Westminster, 1971), p. 92.

[103] Ewart, *Name and Book*, p. 33.

[104] Vouga, *Gospel Message*, p. 20.

[105] Paterson, *Real Truth*, p. 18.

[106] Col. 1:27; Paterson, *Real Truth*, p. 19.

c. The Name and Prayer

Ewart describes the name of Jesus as a legal power that makes prayer effective: "Jesus bequeaths to His disciples, and through them to all, the unique privilege of praying in His Name." It is a legal right, carrying with it "the power of attorney."[107] Thus the presence of Jesus is available in and through the legal agency of his Name bequeathed to the church. For this reason, as Haenchen observes, "Peter does not beg the exalted Jesus for healing, but releases the very power of healing through utterance of the name of Jesus."[108] As Jesus is present in the Spirit whom he dispenses to his followers, he is also present when he dispenses his Name.

d. The Name and Persecution

In the New Testament, the theme of persecution of Jesus' followers is probably attached more to his name than to the activity of the Spirit, since the name is intimately identified with the person himself. As Jesus is present in his name, those to whom his name has been bequeathed share in the same benefits and trials experienced by the one who originally bore that name. Ewart draws this conclusion:

> Wherever Jesus would have been glorified by His personal presence, that Name took His place. The same bitter hostility of the enemies of the truth was also hurled against the Name that was hurled against Jesus in the flesh.[109]

Oneness believers then are warned to expect harassment and persecution for upholding the name of Jesus.

Jesus' warning in Matt. 10:22 ("you will be hated by all for my name's sake") is in particular a source of consolation and encouragement for Oneness Pentecostals when they experience rejection or ridicule for their distinctive beliefs and practices, especially by other Christians. This identity as the persecuted minority for the sake of the name of Jesus runs through Oneness literature from the earliest years. Haywood asks: "Where are the people who are being hated for His name's sake? Is it not those who are being baptized in the name of Jesus?"[110]

---

[107] Ewart, *Name and Book*, p. 16, 17, 21. This theme of the legal right of the Christian to use the name of Jesus echoes the teaching on the giving of the Name in the atonement by Essek Kenyon, *The Wonderful Name of Jesus*; see Chapter 4 above.

[108] Haenchen, *Acts*, p. 200.

[109] Ewart, *Name and Book*, p. 26.

[110] Haywood, *Finest of the Wheat*, p. 32.

As a Oneness pioneer, Andrew Urshan seems to have given more attention than others to the theme of persecution for the Name. In one place he points out that, unlike persecution of Oneness Pentecostals, in other religious persecutions "none of these have suffered for the Name of Jesus." He describes the maltreatment of Oneness believers in his time as one of great intensity: "These One God people, or 'Jesus' name folks have and are now going through terrible misrepresentations, persecution, and fiery trials. It seems as if even God is pleased to afflict us."[111] He anticipates no abatement of the hostility, since one is to expect an intensification of hatred in the last days: "The day is coming upon us soon, when we shall be singled out and bitterly hated by all men for that worthy Name."[112]

Ewart likewise anticipates a deep-seated hostility to the Name by the world: "Men would love it enough to die for it; others would hate it with such an inveterate hatred that they would murder men for preaching it." He defines the opposition to Oneness Pentecostals as a form of persecution, calling scorn and mockery a "subtle form of persecution." Much persecution comes from other Christians themselves who deny the power of the name of Jesus and thereby ridicule the miracles that attend preaching and ministering in the name of Jesus. Ewart identifies the most harmful to be those cessationist evangelicals who are "'graciously' hostile or destructively 'favorable' to miracles performed in the Name of Jesus." They accept the miracles of the Bible but "dispensationalize or spiritualize or naturalize them" when applied to today.[113]

It is clear that much of the persecution these Oneness leaders have in mind is the ill treatment they experienced at the hand of their estranged mother, the Assemblies of God. Andrew Urshan states openly that the source of this persecution is "not by the nominal church members, but also by their very Pentecostal brethren."[114] Elsewhere he is even more specific:

> The General Council, which is a Pentecostal people's organization, are trying to close the doors of their assemblies and to prejudice the hearts of all the people of God against this glorious message ... by accusing us

---

[111] Andrew Urshan, *Life*, pp. 245, 246.
[112] Andrew Urshan, *Almighty God*, p. 56.
[113] Ewart, *Name and Book*, pp. 7, 61, 65.
[114] Andrew Urshan, *Life*, p. 245.

through their magazines of wrong doing, seeking to stain our God given character.[115]

Such statements characterize the bitterness of the schism in the early years. More than fifty years later, C.E. Hobbs's reminiscence of the 1916 Council of the Assemblies of God is laden with tones of persecution:

> Some two hundred men walked out of that conference, standing on the Word of God, and heard the echoes of those that chose not to. They stood every insult that the devil could manufacture, because they were willing to separate themselves for the Word of God.[116]

In the theme of persecution, Oneness leaders have defined their movement as the persecuted minority, drawing together materials from the New Testament and their own history of birth from the womb of rejection.

5. Summary

Oneness Pentecostals stand apart from the rest of the Pentecostal movement primarily in the conclusions they draw from their sectarian beliefs in the oneness of God and the revealed name in Jesus. The Oneness theology of the Name is most conspicuous in its soteriology, the core of which is expressed in its key text, Acts 2:38.

A couple of concluding notes are in order. One is that the biblical theme of the Name is evocative for many aspects of the Christian life, from prayer to persecution. As Jesus is the "Dispenser of the Spirit,"[117] so also is he the Giver of his Name. Not dissimilar to the Eucharist as the tangible and effective sign of the absent and ascended Jesus, Jesus is really present in his name. And as the epiclesis is the invocation of the Spirit over the bread and wine, the Spirit likewise infuses the Name when it is invoked in prayer or ministry. Because of the association of the Name with spiritual power in Acts, there is a significant relationship between the Name and the Holy Spirit in the life of the Christian. Roman Catholic scholar George MacRae points out that in

---

[115] Andrew Urshan, *Almighty God*, p. 71.

[116] Hobbs, *The Last Angel Message to God's People* (Lansing, IL: Lansing Apostolic Assembly, 1973), p. 10.

[117] Thomas Smail, *Reflected Glory – The Spirit in Christ and Christians* (Grand Rapids, MI: Eerdmans, 1975), p. 72.

Acts Christ is present among his people in four ways, two of which are through the Holy Spirit and by his Name.[118]

While Ewart at least attempts a rudimentary theology of the Name in terms of "Pentecostal power," few others give it attention. Recent concentration on producing and demonstrating a Oneness "ortho-doxy" in core doctrine and soteriology, or apologetically defending its doctrine, appears to have had the unintended consequence of neglect in terms of exploiting a Oneness theology of the Name for guidance in Christian living. Since New Testament followers of Jesus were known as the "people of the name" (Acts 15:14, 17), an incisive contempo-rary application of the Name would be useful as a rich counter-cultural metaphor for Christian identity in the world.

The second comment relates to Oneness soteriology and Acts 2:38. Arguably this text is a richer and more comprehensive paradigm for salvation than the more familiar text of John 3:16. Thomas Smail, for instance, considers the three elements in Acts 2:38 to be the New Testament essentials for initiation into Christ. These are the miracle of rebirth in which God acts by the Spirit, the experiential entry by faith and repentance into the fullness of Christ that results from the rebirth, and the sacramental act which proclaims and affirms our union with Christ. He calls for these elements to be treated in "their essential one-ness," not as isolated experiences, as has been done in much of the history of the Church.[119]

In his study of the Pentecostal theology of the Holy Spirit, F.D. Bruner similarly describes Acts 2:38 as a "comprehensive summary of the reception of Christian salvation." He sees the text primarily as a baptismal statement in which repentance and the Holy Spirit are in-separably drawn into the act of baptism. Similar to the Oneness teaching on repentance, he defines it as "the Spirit-enabled decision to be baptized." More sharply stated, "repentance is being baptized." The Holy Spirit is not an isolated experience but closely identified with the act of baptism: "Since the occurrence of Pentecost, Christian baptism becomes the locus of the Spirit's reception."[120] This means that repen-tance and reception of the Holy Spirit both occur in baptism.

Oneness theology would find much with which to agree in Bruner, especially the basic unity of the three elements as essentials in Christian

---

[118] George W. MacRae, "'Whom Heaven Must Receive until the Time' – Reflection on the Christology of Acts," *Interpretation – The Journal of Bible and Theology*, 27 (April 1973): 151-165.

[119] Smail, *Reflected Glory*, p. 89.

[120] Bruner, *Theology of the Holy Spirit*, pp. 166, 168.

initiation and the relation of faith to baptism. But the position of those Oneness theologians (not all Oneness representatives) who understand the coming of the Spirit exclusively in terms of Pentecostal Spirit-baptism is difficult to sustain scripturally and experientially. Scripturally, it is a faulty exegesis that restricts the common experience of the Holy Spirit promised to all believers to that which is directly connected with the requirement of speaking in tongues. Though the point needs to be argued elsewhere, there is simply insufficient evidence for the claim that all New Testament believers spoke in tongues, or without this gift were not indwelt by the Holy Spirit. Experientially, these Oneness Pentecostals are compelled by doctrinal constraint to deny the Spirit to the whole Christian community outside their movement, reducing them to secondary status in God's soteriological scheme. Such limiting categories are artificially imposed and overlook the broad scope of the Spirit's work in the New Testament church. It seems biblically untenable to conceive of a divine work of reconciliation and justification apart from the agency and infusion of the Spirit.

Oneness Pentecostals face doctrinal challenges that far outweigh those encountered by their Trinitarian Pentecostal counterparts in the Holiness and Reformed streams. Their initial protest in 1914 struck at the very core of Christian identity in both doctrine and praxis, leaving a gaping chasm between them and other Christians. The effect has been a theological and social marginalization from the mainstream Pentecostal and evangelical movements for nearly a century. Despite this, they have grown significantly at home and around the world. Their relationship with other Christians has been uneven but not non-existent. There are innumerable examples of cooperation and dialogue with other Christians. Less than a century is a short time to form a strong internal identity let alone to engage with the questions and sometimes hostile moves from detractors. That ecumenical engagement is happening at all is an encouragement. That it is happening *now* is an opportunity.

15

Whose Heresy? Whose Orthodoxy?

> None of the divisions of the movement of which I know, except the movement headed by Bro. Goss, holds much hope. I see more hope in Goss' division of the movement than in any of the others. There is one thing we will have to concede, and everyone does who is really intimate with their assemblies and with their preachers, and that is that they show more genuine spirituality than any other branch of the movement. The mere fact of their emphasis of Jesus, that the other divisions of the movement regard as extreme, has tended to bless them in that it has brought them into close touch with the Lord's life and Spirit.[1]
>
> – John G. Lake

For the uninformed outsider, Oneness Pentecostalism is a conundrum. Like other Pentecostal groups, it *should* be emphasizing the Spirit. But it speaks about Jesus and denies the Trinity. For its progenitor, the Assemblies of God, Oneness is a heretical aberration. But both approaches miss the point. For the outside observer, Oneness Pentecostalism is not just about Jesus, and Trinitarian Pentecostals are not just about the Spirit. Both are intensely christocentric and both experience God in a triadic way.[2] For the Trinitarian Pentecostal, the Oneness movement was conceived in [or born from] the same womb as they, just a little younger and slightly more rebellious.

It has been commonplace among Pentecostals and evangelicals to charge Oneness Pentecostals with heresy, and more recently even label them a cult.[3] But assassination by taxonomy is neither sufficient nor

---

[1] Personal letter by John G. Lake to Charles Parham, 24 March 1927.

[2] See Ralph Del Colle, "Oneness and Trinity: A Preliminary Proposal for Dialogue with Oneness Pentecostalism," *Journal of Pentecostal Theology* 10 (April 1997), pp. 85-110. Del Colle forcefully argues that a strong christocentric strain runs through much Catholic and Protestant spirituality and renewal movements, while holding faithfully to a Trinitarian faith.

[3] See especially E. Calvin Beisner, *"Jesus Only" Churches*, and Gregory A. Boyd, *Oneness Pentecostals and the Trinity*.

effective. We need to seek an alternative way that takes into account the more complex factors that constitute the movement.

1. Why Should We Take Oneness Pentecostalism Seriously?

New religious movements tend to proliferate at a great rate, especially during periods of social unrest and transition. Many remain small and are short-lived. They never gain the critical mass required to warrant serious social engagement. E.N. Bell and the Assemblies of God had hoped for, even prophesied, just such a fate for the New Issue: "We venture to predict it is now at high water-mark, and that the old issue so needless will dwindle down, as it always has."[4] We now know their prediction failed to materialize.

There are a number of reasons for the wider church to give attention to the Oneness movement at this point in its history. The first is demographic. When a movement attains a critical mass, its effect is registered within the larger social system. Responsible engagement with the new movement is essential in order to avoid the distorted reactions that come from ignorance and fear of the unfamiliar. It is the excessive reaction that socially produces persecution of minorities.

The present global strength of the Oneness trajectory is conservatively 14 million, and taking into account the un-researched groups, the figure could reach 15 to 20 million.[5] According to David Barrett's most recent global statistics for 2000, the total strength of denominational Pentecostals and charismatics outside mainline Christian traditions is approximately 360 million, including Oneness Pentecostals.[6] With the proliferation of new religious movements in the Western world within the past thirty years, evangelicals have given particular attention to identifying and classifying cults. What was a heresy fifty years ago is now often labeled a cult. Oneness Pentecostalism, particularly the United Pentecostal Church International, has not been spared the scrutiny. Whatever the intent, in a world fearful of brainwashing cults that snatch away children, to call any religious

---

[4] Bell, "Preliminary Statement," *Word and Witness* (June 12, 1915), p. 1.

[5] Talmadge French provides these figures in his study of the global Oneness movement, *Our God is One*, p. 17.

[6] David Barrett, "Global Statistics," *New International Dictionary of Pentecostal and Charismatic Movements*, p. 286. It is difficult to estimate the Oneness percentage of denominational Pentecostals, because Barrett classifies some of the large Oneness groups outside North America among the non-denominational Charismatics, e.g. three million in the True Jesus Church (China).

group a cult is emotive. If for only this reason, it is important that the Oneness movement receive fair and judicious treatment.

A second reason is that Oneness Pentecostalism is now generally regarded more favorably in academic circles. To begin with, statisticians have always included this third stream in their counting of Pentecostal heads. More importantly, as French points out, the approach tends to be more irenic than in the past.[7] Blumhofer, for instance, writes rather persuasively of the need to recognize the Oneness movement as part of the Pentecostal family:

> Although its doctrinal distinctives distanced it from the mainstream of classical Pentecostalism, from another perspective its adherents must be understood as participants in a valid expression of Pentecostal experience. And the doctrinal departure aside, if one admits the strong restorationist component at the heart of the definition of Pentecostalism, Oneness proponents were more zealously restorationist, more doggedly congregational, and more Christocentrically spiritual – in short, in some important ways more essentially Pentecostal than the mainstream.[8]

While organizational animosity still exists, especially within the white constituency, a conciliatory spirit is evident in such circles as the Society for Pentecostal Studies.[9] French concludes with this summary of the increasing influence of the movement:

> Oneness Pentecostalism has manifestly emerged as a movement in its own right, and a veritable "third force" among the diverse traditions which comprise worldwide Pentecostalism. Its prominence in every major discussion of Pentecostalism, its theological inclusion and involvement in world Pentecostalism, and its proliferating global presence and impact are increasingly evident.[10]

---

[7] To make this point, French surveys such recent studies as Blumhofer, *The Assemblies of God: A Chapter in the Story of American Pentecostalism*, Anderson, *Vision of the Disinherited*, Gill, *Towards a Contextualized Theology for the Third World*; Gerloff, *A Plea for British Black Theologies*; see French, "Introduction," *Our God Is One*, pp. 13-28.

[8] Blumhofer, *The Assemblies of God: A Chapter in the Story of American Pentecostalism*, vol. I, *To 1941* (Springfield, MO: Gospel Publishing House, 1989), pp. 237-38. See French, *Our God Is One*, p. 18.

[9] The Statement of Faith of the Society for Pentecostal Studies permits Oneness scholars to be full members. Dr. Manuel Gaxiola of Mexico, a Oneness leader in the indigenous Apostolic Church of the Faith in Christ Jesus, is a past president of the Society. The animosity is sharper between the Assemblies of God and the United Pentecostal Church International, probably due to the perpetuation of the memory of the 1916 expulsion. There is a history of greater cooperation between black Oneness and Trinitarian groups.

[10] Talmadge L. French, "Oneness Pentecostalism in Global Perspective: History, Theology, and Expansion of the Oneness Pentecostal Movement" (M.A. thesis, Wheaton

There are other reasons that become increasingly evident. One is the "spillover" factor: Oneness composers are producing music that has become popular in the wider Pentecostal and evangelical circles. This phenomenon is creating a cognitive dissonance among some Trinitarian Pentecostals who are told that the Oneness movement is a dangerous heresy, but they resonate spiritually with the music that flows from the same source. This dissonance is a signal that closer examination is warranted, as spiritual resonance with the other is an important resource for ecumenical dialogue.

Another factor in determining the right time for productive ecumenical encounter is the degree of institutional and theological maturity of the movement. Undoubtedly because of its isolation from the wider Pentecostal movement and fragmentation into small groups, the Oneness movement has lagged behind Trinitarian organizations. But that is changing as Oneness students are pursuing graduate programs and developing closer ties with the wider church. In 2001 the UPCI opened the first Oneness seminary, the Urshan Graduate School of Theology, which is currently pursuing accreditation.

2. Whose Heresy?

Heresy has become a weasel word over the last two centuries. It has been used to describe anything from a teaching that could get its propagator burned at the stake to the frivolous taunt against someone with a contrary opinion. Prior to the Pentecostal Revival, the term was used within the evangelical and Holiness circles to denounce variations within their own stream of faith. In the 1830's, the movement for social reform known as "Oberlin Perfectionism" was occasionally charged with theological heresy. The National Holiness Camp Meeting Association called the more radical "Third Blessing" wing of the Holiness movement, "The Third Blessing Heresy."[11] Since the established doctrine of a particular tradition was regarded as "biblical" and therefore revealed truth, any perceived deviation from it was classified as a heresy. With the advent of the Pentecostal movement, Holiness protesters were quick to label it too as heretical. When Durham burst on the scene at the end of the first decade of the Pentecostal Revival, it was the Holiness Pentecostals who declared the Finished Work teaching a heresy.[12]

College, 1998), p. 7.
[11] Faupel, *Everlasting Gospel*, pp. 65, 90.
[12] Small, "Theories and Traditions of Men Exploded Work of Holy Spirit – The Fin-

But the term was turned on its head in the Restorationist worldview. Instead of being a term of derision, it became a synonym for
pure biblical doctrine and practice *vis à vis* the creeds of an apostate
church. It was not that the creeds were in error, since most would
have agreed with them. But the antagonism was directed against a
near-apostate denominational church – "old Christendom" – whose
creeds were a contaminated means of binding people's beliefs to an
institution that served only to obstruct access to the pure Word of
God. Furthermore, when denominational leaders scorned the Pentecostals as heretics in the name of orthodoxy, this only reinforced the
latter's conviction that they were simply being "biblical." Anderson
locates this attitude within a wider movement of reaction to modernity, which spanned the period roughly from 1890 to 1925. The
mainline church with its creeds was rejected, because it was clearly
complicit in this downward spiral of modernity.[13]

The Finished Work teaching and the New Issue were regularly under attack for heresy. In 1912, R.E. McAlister reminded his readers
that the Finished Work advocates were being slandered as "latter day
heretics," but then gladly turned to Paul's speech in Acts 24:14 citing
Christianity as "the way which THEY CALL HERESY."[14] In the
same issue, Ewart wrote an article he boldly entitled "Defending
Heresies," in which he responded to the charge by outlining the standard Finished Work version of the Gospel: Spirit-baptism, healing,
baptism by immersion as identification with Christ, and the premillennial return of Christ. He then labeled as heresy all teachings that he
considered to be unbiblical, including Luther's support for infant baptism.[15] Haywood, after his conversion to the New Issue, was genuinely
puzzled that Trinitarian Pentecostals seemed afraid to challenge the
doctrine of the Trinity, especially when for him it diminished the centrality of Christ.[16] It is noteworthy that he did not regard the doctrine
of the Trinity to be a core Christian belief, as did the denominational
creed-based churches. At one time or another, a number of early
Oneness pioneers referred favorably to Sabellianism, especially its preference for the term "manifestations" to "persons" of the Godhead. But
the label likely appeared first as an accusation by the Trinitarians. And
as French observes, the effect of the charge of Sabellian heresy against

ished Work of Calvary," *Living Waters* 1/8 (March 1945), p. 1.
   [13] Anderson, *Vision of the Disinherited*, p. 225.
   [14] McAlister, "Confession of Faith," *Good Report* 1/3 (1912), p. 3.
   [15] Ewart, "Defending Heresies," *Good Report* 1/3 (1912), p. 12.
   [16] Haywood, "Trinitarianism," *Voice in the Wilderness* (Second Edition Special, n.d.), p. 3.

the New Issue "did little to thwart, but rather fueled, its expansion."[17] Indeed, the charge of heresy was a confirmation that the right people were persecuting it for the right reason – an apostate church fighting the Bride of Christ over creed and Bible!

In retrospect, it is clear that the early Pentecostals, including Oneness, employed the term heresy differently from its classical Christian usage. Also, the rhetorical tone in Oneness writings suggests that the effect was more polemical than substantial. And in their ready embrace of Sabellianism, it is apparent that the Oneness pioneers were not fully cognizant of the theological implications of Sabellian teaching, conclusions that they themselves would have rejected. As popular theologians, their immediate issues were paramount; they exploited the ideas of others for their own purposes.

The one exception in which these early Pentecostals turned to the historic church for help occurred immediately prior to the General Council meeting of 1916. Faced with this unexpected challenge to their doctrine of God, the Trinitarians were compelled to reach further into their history than either their Latter Rain or Restorationist paradigms were inclined to approve. The person most theologically equipped for the task was D.W. Kerr, a former minister with the Christian and Missionary Alliance. A shy but intelligent man, Kerr diligently researched issues relating to the doctrine of the Trinity. He spent many months prior to the meeting reading and taking copious notes on the doctrine and its attendant heresies. Brumback records an illuminating inside account of Kerr's activity during those months provided by Kerr's son-in-law: "Father Kerr was digging into the Word and reading Treffery on 'The Eternal Sonship' for months, as well as every other old book he could find which had any bearing on the subject."[18]

The importance of this observation is not that Kerr studied the subject, but that he resorted to the fourth-century debates and creeds of Christendom (though this may indicate that not all early Finished Work Pentecostals harbored strong antipathy toward the denominational church and its doctrinal traditions). What is significant is that, by finding a heretical label that seemed to fit the New Issue, the General Council in effect shifted the way in which the term "heresy" had been loosely applied and brought it more in line with the church's fourth-century use. It is likely, however, that Kerr was one of the few that

---

[17] French, "Oneness Pentecostalism in Global Perspective," p. 2.
[18] Cited in Brumback, *Suddenly from Heaven*, p. 205.

understood the theological significance of the traditional objections to Sabellianism. For most at the Council, a label was found which served its purpose.

For the Assemblies of God leadership, the historic label of Sabellianism has stuck and remains the reason for its refusal to fellowship or dialogue officially with Oneness Pentecostals. The concern for orthodoxy and fear of heresy increased as the Assemblies of God became increasingly influenced by evangelicals. This shift accelerated following World War II when the Assemblies of God officially became a member of the National Association of Evangelicals, and their superintendent, Thomas Zimmerman, became president.[19] As a result, Oneness Pentecostalism continued to be classified as an aberrant heresy without familial resemblance. While evangelical apologists are to be applauded for their concern to warn the faithful about heresies and cults, they frequently include Oneness Pentecostals alongside Mormons, Jehovah's Witnesses and Hare Krishna. The Christian Research Institute is a conservative evangelical organization that has for years maligned the Oneness movement as a heresy.

Two recent examples of evangelical apologetic against Oneness teaching will suffice. One is E. Calvin Beisner's *"Jesus Only" Churches*, a small book in the Zondervan series, *Guide to Cults and Religious Movements*.[20] It shares the series with books on such groups as Mormonism, Satanism, the Unification Church, Astrology, Witchcraft and Neo-Paganism. Beisner attempts an analysis and comparison with orthodox Trinitarian doctrine that, while accurate in its details, misses the historical and theological nuances that only a more thorough study would produce. As a result, this evangelical use of the orthodoxy-heresy taxonomy provides as easy classification with the heretics and cults. Of course this is the same template that allows Protestant evangelicals to charge the Roman Catholic Church with "cultish" characteristics.[21]

The second illustration is Gregory Boyd's book, *Oneness Pentecostals and the Trinity*. Drawing on the author's four-year sojourn in the United Pentecostal Church International, Boyd's otherwise commendable account of UPCI teaching takes on the tone of an exposé in his

---

[19] See William W. Menzies, *Anointed to Serve*, ch. 9.

[20] E. Calvin Beisner, *"Jesus Only" Churches*.

[21] This was a personal comment made to me by an evangelical student, who realized that it was a difficult theological task to charge Roman Catholicism with being a cult, but was ready to allude to its "cultish" practices and teachings. This attitude typifies the sort of familiar anti-Catholic rhetoric of a generation ago.

Introduction, "Confessions of an Ex-Oneness Pentecostal." Elsewhere he warns the unsuspecting faithful of the dangers of this movement: "In the past these views [e.g. Sabellianism] were always rejected by the orthodox church as dangerous heresies." Again, "the inconspicuousness and apparent harmlessness of this theological aberration renders it all the more dangerous."[22] He does not define what constitutes the danger, but its emotive intent is as unmistakable as it is unfortunate.

In the early Holiness and Pentecostal culture, heresy functioned more as a polemical term of derision for any doctrine that challenged the "orthodoxy" of a particular group, not a core doctrine of the Christian faith. With the crisis of 1916, the Assemblies leadership rediscovered ancient creedal orthodoxy and its usefulness in naming and expelling a modern version of a heresy. As Trinitarian Pentecostals closed ranks with the evangelicals, their resolve to maintain the ecclesiastical quarantine of the Oneness movement was strengthened and abetted by evangelical apologists whose mission was to identify and expose "dangerous" heresies. Oneness Pentecostals have continued to be a favorite target.

3. A Theological Method

Heresy, as understood historically by the church, is a much more serious matter than a family squabble among fellow Christians. The persecution and execution of heretics by the church is indeed an embarrassing chapter in Christian history, conduct that was often rationalized by the church's status as an arm of the state. But the early theological understanding still warrants consideration.

In his extensive study of heresy in Christian history, theologian Harold O.J. Brown describes both the nature and seriousness of this ecclesial act. Generally, heresy is born from one of two actions: either the premature hardening of, or an exaggerated attention to, some aspect of salvation history as revealed in Christ. It is not simply "false doctrine," but the person who bears witness to it "must be considered to have abandoned the faith." As an ecclesial matter, heresy is perceived to threaten the very existence of the church as it has historically understood itself. As Brown states, heresy "threatens to sink the ark, and thus make salvation impossible for everyone, not merely for the individual heretic."[23]

---

[22] Boyd, *Oneness Pentecostals and the Trinity*, pp. 9, 12.

[23] Harold O.J. Brown, *Heresies: Heresy and Orthodoxy in the History of the Church*, p. 2. Modern liberalism trivializes heresy by elevating deviating and innovative ideas a mark of

If heresy is indeed this serious, the term must be invoked sparingly and with great discernment. Not every naïve idea put forth constitutes a heresy. And reactionary movements may indeed resemble a heresy. Brown illustrates this in Fundamentalism: "In its preoccupation with a small number of doctrines, it resembles many of the classical heresies."[24] It is for this reason that we need to seek for Oneness Pentecostalism another classification that accounts for both *deviation* and *resemblance*.

The 19th-century theologian Friedrich Schleiermacher is helpful in this regard with his delineation between orthodoxy, heresy and heterodoxy. There is frequent confusion over a particular teaching, perhaps first appearing to be orthodox or charged as heretical, and in time revealed to be otherwise. In large part, what differentiates the heterodox from the heretical is its attitude to the historic faith, even if its actual teaching resembles heresy. Schleiermacher expresses this intention:

> Even if the heterodox cannot be definitely distinguished in content and expression from the heretical of older times, yet it must not be regarded as heretical, if only it seeks to make good its claim in connexion with the commonly accepted elements of our Church's system of doctrine.[25]

In our examination of the history and teaching of Oneness Pentecostalism, there is good reason to consider it as a heterodox expression of the faith, not heresy. It was born in the Pentecostal Revival and shares many other beliefs and practices with the wider movement. Elements of its teaching are borrowed from evangelical and early Pentecostal sources, and some are reinterpreted in novel ways. Some elements that are theologically vulnerable are compensated by other concepts, at least potentially. In addition to its doctrines of God and Christ, the central thematic of Acts 2:38 implies an ecclesial exclusivity that at best strains relationships with other Christians.

For all these difficulties, we must remember that its self-understanding was minted in the millennial-restorationist mold. While the millennial "Latter Rain" hermeneutic has waned, the movement is still fiercely restorationist. In contrast to mainline churches that set

---

theological creativity. Such influence disguises the threat and erodes the confidence in the Christian message.

[24] Brown, *Heresies*, p. 30.

[25] Friedrich Schleiermacher, *The Christian Faith*, vol. I (New York: Harper & Row, 1963), p. 110. I am indebted to Ralph Del Colle for bringing Schleiermacher's typology to my attention. Cf. his essay, "Oneness and Trinity," p. 99.

their compass by the creeds, Restorationists of all stripes reject them as creatures of an apostate church and proceed to construct their belief system from the Bible, as they interpret it. The exclusivity of Oneness Pentecostals, and their insistence upon re-baptism in the name of Jesus, cannot be properly understood outside this paradigm, an approach that is shared by many separatist Fundamentalist groups.

The familiar conservative/evangelical approach to doctrinally innovative groups is inadequate to assess the potential for affiliative identity with the broader Christian fellowship. This approach is generally definitional and propositional, and thereby gives little attention to either the practices of the community or the doctrinal system as a whole. A more useful direction is to explore doctrines as a form of grammar that guides the practices of a community of faith, an approach that has been developed by Lutheran theologian George Lindbeck. The following is an attempt to apply his taxonomy to Oneness doctrines.

In Lindbeck's system, doctrines function as *regulae fidei*, or rules that regulate the truth claims of a community. Though they may be stated in the form of propositions, those statements are understood to be, in the first place, a kind of grammar, or second-order doctrine, that carries no ontological freight. They function primarily to set boundaries of what may and may not be permitted, rather than to make constructive statements. As Lindbeck states, "Doctrines regulate truth claims by excluding some and permitting others, but the logic of their communally authoritative use hinders or prevents them from specifying positively what is to be affirmed."[26]

Lindbeck further refines this understanding of doctrine to be of a "cultural-linguistic" type.[27] Doctrine is a language of both the discursive and non-discursive sort that is necessarily expressed within a given cultural setting. It is not simply a cognitive proposition about some aspect of religion, but an identification of what is perceived to be "more important than anything else in the universe, and organizing all of life, including both behavior and beliefs, in relation to this." But this insight is not completely new. We have observed that Oneness Pentecostalism did not emerge *de novo* but was an adaptive expression of teachings that were already activated within the Evangelical-Pentecostal culture. This agrees with Lindbeck's insight that innovation

---

[26] George A. Lindbeck, *The Nature of Doctrine: Religion and Theology in a Postliberal Age* (Philadelphia: Westminster, 1984), p. 19.

[27] Lindbeck contrasts the cultural-linguistic type with the cognitive-propositional and experiential-expressive (symbolic) types, and their combinations.

does not arise from new experiences but "from the interactions of a cultural-linguistic system with changing situations."[28]

For Christians, doctrines are communal norms, the means by which this community seeks to remain faithful to the Christian story. As such, they attend to both the grammar or language and the way in which this Story is communicated and appropriated within the community. Since not all doctrinal beliefs are of equal importance in this task, Lindbeck develops a taxonomy to assist in distinguishing those doctrines that are essential from those that are not. It becomes particularly helpful as a grid to guide ecumenical conversation. The three primary axes that are used to assess doctrines are: unconditional-conditional, permanent-temporary, irreversible-reversible.[29]

A specific doctrine may be judged to be any combination of these three couplets, and may be more than one type, if viewed from different perspectives or by different religious groups. For instance, the traditional doctrine of the immortality of the soul is likely to be conditional, temporary, and reversible.

Lindbeck calls some doctrines "conditionally permanent," those beliefs that lack ecclesial consensus but are so deeply entrenched in the tradition that they are not likely to disappear. They are "reformable" in the sense that the doctrines remain, but the "particular conditions that prevail" are temporary and therefore reformable. That leaves room for ecumenical reconsiderations of a doctrine to be reviewed and restated in ways that meet the conditions of the new situation.

How does the church proceed in dialogue when the language or grammar of one group is significantly different from that of another, or may even sound like heresy?

Lindbeck turns to the christological incarnational principle that affirms the potential of the Christian faith to be adaptable to the forms of any culture without losing its distinctive content. As such, the task is to "state these doctrines in different terms that nevertheless have equivalent consequences."[30]

The task of discerning "equivalent consequences" is both difficult and delicate. It requires careful listening, observing the meanings of concepts within the group's culture and the ways they function in worship and practice, and discerning the inner logic of the doctrine as it functions within the group. Lindbeck applies his theory to the case of the doctrines of the Trinity and Christology as articulated in the

---

[28] Lindbeck, *Nature of Doctrine*, pp. 32-33, 39.

[29] *Ibid.*, pp. 85-87.

[30] Lindbeck, *Nature of Doctrine*, p. 93.

creeds of Nicea and Chalcedon. He offers three regulative principles that he discerns to be at work in the earliest Christian community, though only the first was specifically articulated. They are: (1) the "monotheistic principle" that there is only one God – the God of Abraham, Isaac, Jacob and Jesus; (2) the principle of "historical speci-ficity," that the stories of Jesus refer to a person who lived in a particular time and place in history, and (3) the principle of "Chris-tological maximalism," in which "every possible importance is to be ascribed to Jesus that is not inconsistent with the first rules."[31] The classical heresies were identified as such, because they were perceived as unable to meet all three criteria.

Lindbeck's understanding of the creeds, being creatures of the church, is that they are open to restatement. They are paradigms that are not to be replicated but "to be followed in the making of new formulations." He proceeds to make the bold claim that, on his read-ing, there "may be complete faithfulness to classical Trinitarianism and christology even when the imagery and language of Nicea and Chal-cedon have disappeared from the theology and ordinary worship, preaching, and devotion."[32] He does not recommend, however, that the creeds be rewritten simply to fit a new situation. For our purposes, Lindbeck's claim opens the possibility for fruitful ecumenical discus-sion with Oneness Pentecostals.

4. The Method Applied

Oneness Pentecostalism received the permanent stamp of heresy the day it was expelled from the Assemblies of God. Though the Trinitar-ian faction identified what they considered to be a number of "errors" taught by the New Issue leaders, it was Sabellianism that had the clear-est historical claim to being a heresy. D.W. Kerr, the composer of the Statement of Fundamental Truths, and J. Roswell Flower discovered the similarity. The label provided the Council with the imprimatur they needed to justify the expulsion. It remains the fundamental expla-nation by the Assemblies of God for their refusal to fellowship officially with the UPCI.[33]

---

[31] *Ibid.*, p. 94.

[32] *Ibid.*, p. 95.

[33] When the multiracial Pentecostal and Charismatic Churches of North America (PCCNA) was formed in 1994 in Memphis, a questioner from the floor asked about the possibility of Oneness churches also joining the fellowship. It is significant that the black leaders readily agreed it needed to happen, while the Assemblies of God representative

The increased visibility of Oneness Pentecostals through numerical growth and distribution of doctrinal literature has only served to confuse some and increase the tension for others. Aggressive evangelistic strategies combined with the dominant teaching by many in the UPCI that Acts 2:38 is the new birth has intensified the work of evangelical apologists, who often charge that Oneness Pentecostals are not just heretics but now qualify as a cult. The result exacerbates rather than ameliorates the tension between Oneness Pentecostals and their Trinitarian counterparts.

A number of observations can be made. First, Oneness theology is still in its infancy and has yet to address a number of lacunae in its doctrinal system.[34] Furthermore, it still views its teachings as "apostolic truth" or first order doctrine, which makes it difficult to engage in critical theological dialogue. At the same time, as we have already observed, Oneness Pentecostalism was born in and embodies the spirituality and much of the theology of the wider Pentecostal tradition. Rather than defining the Oneness movement simply by identifying some aspect of its teaching with a classical heresy, it is more helpful to locate it first and foremost within its more common cultural context of Pentecostalism.

Worship is an appropriate point of commonality between Oneness and Trinitarian not simply because it is Pentecostal, but because, as Lindbeck points out, doctrine is embedded in the worship and practices of the community. Del Colle reminds us that the term "orthodoxy" means literally "right worship," and therefore considers "the doxological expression of the People of God to be significant in the evaluation of doctrine."[35] The distinctive and common element in Pentecostalism is the experience of Spirit-baptism, an encounter that for both Oneness and Trinitarians yields an intensification of christocentric piety. As we observed, christocentric piety has been common in the Pietist and evangelical traditions, in ways that are not antithetical to their Trinitarian confession. Indeed, there is a profoundly Trinitarian interplay between the Spirit and Jesus in the Pentecostal experience of God. As Del Colle states:

---

resisted the suggestion.

[34] An appeal for "theological space" is made by Dr. Manuel Gaxiola, Oneness scholar and bishop in the Mexican Oneness church, *Iglesia Apostólica de la Fe en Christo Jesús,* since the Oneness movement is still in its infancy and its theological self-understanding is still in the process of being formulated; see Gill, *Toward a Contextualized Theology for the Third World*, p. 233.

[35] Del Colle, "Oneness and Trinity," p. 86.

The intensified awareness of the glory of God in the face of Christ Jesus (2 Cor. 4:6) is a pneumatologically generated consciousness, a ministry of the Spirit (2 Cor. 3:8) even as the Spirit inspires the confession of Jesus' Lordship (1 Cor. 12:3).[36]

This common christocentric piety was expressed, as we observed, among late 19th-century evangelicals who were engaging in a study of the names and titles of God in the Old Testament to demonstrate the unity or oneness of Christ with God, not the distinctions between them. Del Colle makes the illuminating point that historically the church resolved the unity or equality of Christ with God prior to its resolution of the distinctions within the Godhead. All delineations of the triadic distinctions and Christ's dual nature were "subordinate to the doxological recognition that the Godhead is in Jesus." This strand of piety produces a "pronounced christocentrism" that has always persisted within both Catholic and Protestant traditions.[37] In sum, the intensified christocentric piety of Oneness believers is an integral element in a long Catholic and Protestant tradition – one that is triadic and, with other Pentecostals, generated by the experience of Spirit-baptism. This underlines the point that Oneness Pentecostalism is sufficiently bound up with the Pentecostal-charismatic experience to subvert any serious effort to impose a taxonomy that would mark it out as heresy.

But with the expulsion of the New Issue from the Assemblies of God in 1916, a distinctive communal trajectory emerged, one with its own grammar and practices. Whereas the Pentecostal heritage engendered commonalities, the Oneness anomaly produced dissonance and dissimilarity. The particularities of the Oneness teaching on God, Christ and salvation are discontinuous with core beliefs of historic Christianity and thereby create an ecumenical challenge. Because there is every indication that Oneness Pentecostalism will continue to be a significant religious and social force, it is an object of ecumenical interest.

Following Lindbeck's taxonomy of beliefs, we propose that Oneness Pentecostalism fits best according to the type, "conditionally permanent." This category applies to those beliefs that lack ecclesial consensus (i.e., conditional), but are sufficiently rooted in a tradition to be unlikely to disappear (i.e., permanent). Oneness Pentecostalism is by now a well-established tradition, with its rejection of the creedal doctrine of the Trinity and insistence upon re-baptism being firmly

[36] *Ibid.*, p. 93.
[37] *Ibid.*, p. 92.

established for the foreseeable future. The grammar and terminology of its doctrines are at odds with the church's tradition. Therefore, the way forward is to engage in the hard work of seeking what Lindbeck calls "equivalent consequences."

As mentioned above, Lindbeck cautions that the grammar may initially be unrecognizable by Nicene or Chalcedonian formulations, and may even resemble a classical heresy. So to move the ecumenical project forward, we refer the Oneness doctrine to the three regulative principles that have guided doctrinal formulations from the beginning. The first principle, that there is only one God, is so deeply entrenched in Oneness doctrine as to be indisputable. Second, both Oneness and Trinitarian Pentecostals readily affirm the principle of "historical specificity" – that Jesus was a person who lived in a particular time and place. The third principle, "Christological maximalism," calls for ascribing "every possible importance" to Jesus that does not negate the first two rules. In the language of the creed, it is a declaration that Jesus Christ is *fully* God and *fully* human. It is with this third principle that Oneness doctrine faces its most rigorous test. We now examine four areas in light of this principle: the nature of the Trinity, the eternal Sonship, the name of Jesus, and salvation according to Acts 2:38. We will keep in mind two questions: What is the doctrine intending to oppose? And what formulation can be changed without losing the illuminative center.

a. The Nature of the Trinity

In 1916, Frank Ewart wrote that his original insight into the proper name to be invoked in baptism had evolved into an affirmation of the radical oneness of God. Certainly by that date the New Issue was being charged with Sabellianism. It is not clear whether Ewart initiated the term "manifestation" as a substitute for the "persons" in the Trinity, or appropriated it from the literature on Sabellianism. Three of the doctrinal pioneers (Ewart, Haywood, and Small) wrote approvingly of Sabellianism as being more in keeping with the Scripture than the church's creedal language, referring to 1 Tim. 3:16, "God was manifested in the flesh" (KJV). Their reasoning – "manifestations" more than "persons" preserves the oneness of God in His being and the full christocentric revelation of the one God.

While many christocentric Trinitarians would affirm the emphasis on the centrality of Christ that Oneness formulators were attempting to preserve, the latter were unaware of the implications of the term as it had been hammered out in the early centuries. Though the manifestations in Oneness thought appear simultaneously, this does not preserve the doctrine from the inherent weakness implied in the term "manifestation." First, manifestation does not imply that the initiator is constitutively present. That is, God is hidden behind, not in, the physical manifestation, and in effect does not ontologically inhabit the phenomenal appearance. There is no real incarnation in a manifestation. Practically, this means that one can never be certain that the God who appears in one manifestation is the *real* God, or that the God who appears *now* is the same God that appeared in the first century. Further, the God behind the masks is fundamentally impersonal.[38] Second, the number of manifestations is not limited to the biblical triad. Sabellianism ultimately dismisses the exclusive revelation of Father, Son and Holy Spirit, as they are revealed in the story of Jesus.

Oneness teaching holds tenaciously to the term, supposedly for the choice of biblical vocabulary and protection of the monarchy of God. But the theological lacunae are many. Admittedly, Trinitarians who have been dissatisfied with the term "persons" for similar reasons have found it difficult to find a substitute that connotes a personal God without intimating an implicit tritheism. Barth's "modes of existence" is adequate for theological discourse but fails miserably in liturgical use. Ironically, the frequent reference to "Father, Son and Holy Spirit" in Oneness confessional statements suggests that Oneness theologians implicitly understand that the biblical triad is distinctive and exclusive of all other manifestations. Nor would they support the conclusions implied in Sabellianism. Del Colle, reflecting the long theological traditon of Trinitarian thought, recommends that "persons" be interpreted as relations rather than as individual substances. This simply means that, while using personalist language, each is defined negatively by who they are not. Del Colle calls this "the inseparable non-identity of the Father, Son, and Holy Spirit."[39] When we speak of the Son, we mean that he is neither the Father nor the Spirit, and so on.

One might appropriately ask what is served in Oneness doctrine by resisting the affirmation of eternal distinctions, so long as the core confession of the full revelation of God in Jesus Christ is preserved. This seems to be what early Oneness theologians were seeking when they published selections from the writings of the Presbyterian J. Monro Gibson, a christocentric Trinitarian. Oneness theologians could ad-

---

[38] See C. FitzSimons Allison, *The Cruelty of Heresy: An Affirmation of Christian Orthodoxy* (Harrisburg, PA: Morehouse, 1994), p. 76. Urshan rejected the Sabellian label for this same reason, that in the end it posited an impersonal deity.

[39] Del Colle, "Oneness and Trinity," p. 100.

vance an ecumenical conversation by either substituting a more adequate term for "manifestation," or explicating the term in such a way
that a full incarnation is clearly understood. Neither alternative would
dismantle the intrinsic structure of Oneness doctrine.

b. The Sonship of Jesus

In Oneness doctrine, the purpose for limiting the sonship of Jesus to
his humanity is to preserve the monarchy of God. A pre-existent or
eternal Son would require belief in some form of distinction within
the Godhead, which in turn would threaten the christocentric revelation of God. The divine nature in Jesus is the Father, not the eternal
Son. Some Oneness theologians (e.g. Kenneth Reeves) allow for the
pre-existent Word, since it is understood as the expression of the mind
of God, a "personification" rather than a hypostatically distinct "person."

The historical Oneness denial of the orthodox teaching of the Eternal Son was based upon a misunderstanding of its theological meaning.
By the fourth century the church was interpreting generation as an
eternal relationship, not a temporal begetting.

It is noteworthy that all the pioneer Oneness theologians approvingly cited the Methodist Bible commentator, Adam Clarke, in his
rejection of the eternal sonship of Christ, a conclusion that he based
upon the same misunderstanding. He wrote that the Word was pre-
existent, but the Son was begotten in Mary. Our study has provided
credible evidence that this and similar key elements in Oneness doctrine
were transplants from Trinitarian or classical sources: Sabellianism,
Adam Clarke and J. Monro Gibson. These provided pivotal concepts
that helped Oneness doctrinal architects construct the inner logic
needed for the overall coherence of their belief system.

But the rejection of the eternal sonship created another dilemma,
namely, that of the relationship of the divine and human natures in
Christ. Oneness theologians, like some Trinitarian writers before
them, were in effect Nestorians who separated the two natures and
assigned various acts of Jesus to the appropriate nature. This separation
was also useful in explaining Jesus' dereliction on the cross as an actual
abandonment, though temporary, by God. That is, there is in effect no
permanent incarnation, only a temporary arrangement in which the
deity can leave the body at will. Admittedly, it occurred only once.
But that it occurred at all reveals the provisional nature of the union.

Oneness theologian David Bernard (who may have discerned this
weakness) has proposed a theologically sounder understanding of the

union of the two natures than the general teaching of his predecessors. He declared that the union of the natures in Christ is "a permanent, inseparable, essential union" – a statement that by itself affirms the Christology of Chalcedon.[40] This doctrinal "adjustment" illustrates Lindbeck's "conditional" category of doctrine in which a religious community may develop its belief system in a way that compensates for an inherited weakness or accommodates its ecumenical allies. Undoubtedly in this case, the former was the motivating force.

A topic for continued dialogue is the nature of the incarnation and the relationship between the Father and the Son in the human person. Trinitarian theology seeks to ensure that in the divine mystery God enters fully the human condition without ceasing to be God. To paraphrase Athanasius, that which needs redeeming must be "assumed." The doctrine of the eternal sonship is intended to preserve that christological truth of the incarnation. Del Colle advances the dialogue on this issue by proposing a Spirit-christology that may find acceptance by both Oneness and Trinitarian theologians. Jesus, in his birth and ministry, depends upon the agency of the Spirit, but in a way that affirms both his deity and humanity. Del Colle sums up this approach: "The divine Son is manifested precisely as a human being whose *human* acts are those of the divine Son *incarnate* because the Holy Spirit mediates Jesus' relation to the Father."[41]

c. The Name of Jesus

A unique but contentious doctrine of the Name emerged quickly as the theological rationale for baptizing in the name of the Lord Jesus Christ. Parham and Durham had already provided the foundation for it in the theological concept of full *identification* with Christ, Parham being the one who had accordingly shifted briefly to the christocentric name to be invoked in baptism.

But it was a study of the names and titles of God in the Bible that provided Ewart with the full theological defense for the practice of re-baptism. Ewart's enthusiasm for William Phillips Hall's *Remarkable Biblical Discovery* suggests that Hall may well have provided the seminal document for Ewart's own ideas on the name of God. Hall published his first book in 1913, *What's in a Name?*[42] While Hall's "discovery"

---

[40] David Bernard, "Oneness Christology," in *Symposium on Oneness Pentecostalism 1986* (St. Louis, MO: United Pentecostal Church International, 1986), p. 130; cited in Del Colle, "Oneness and Trinity," p. 106.

[41] Del Colle, "Oneness and Trinity," p. 97.

[42] William Phillips Hall, *What is "The Name"? Or "The Mystery of God" Revealed*

was that "Lord" is the revealed name for both Yahweh and Jesus, Ewart concluded that "Jesus" is the revealed name of God for the New Covenant period. This distinctive understanding of the Name produced a crucial shift in Oneness baptismal theology, from invoking the Name as one element in the whole act of identifying with Christ's death, burial and resurrection in baptism to the Name becoming the singularly effective agent in the act of identification. That is, baptism in the name of Jesus was not an act that signifies a fuller identification with Christ, but the only valid form of baptism, since the trinitarian formula was considered to be merely a title of relationship or function. The original christocentric insight impelling early evangelicals – Parham, Durham and R.E. McAlister (his baptismal sermon) – was reduced to a kind of *nomeno*-centrism in which the invoked Name becomes the exclusive effective element in the baptismal act.

The theology of the Name in Oneness Pentecostalism is unique in a number of ways. Ewart appears to be the one who concluded that the name "Jesus" denotes deity rather than the human person. Its singularity also led Ewart to reject the traditional doctrine of the Trinity in favor of the radical monarchy of God. Third, the application of the Name in baptism shifts its role beyond doxology to fundamental doctrine. Finally, the Name is the cohering center for the Oneness theological system.

There is within Scripture potential for developing a theology of the Name. As Emil Brunner demonstrates, the purpose of the revelation of the Name of God is to establish the *particularity* of the Christian revelation, namely, that the only God we know is the God who revealed Himself to Abraham, Isaac, Jacob and entered history in the person of Jesus. To identify with this God means, among other things, taking on God's Name. A baptismal theology would be one appropriate trajectory in a theology of the Name. In addition, since taking on the name of another implies becoming a member of a family, referencing the Name in baptism denotes an identity in an ecclesial family in which God is experienced as "Abba"-Father and fellow believers are "brothers and sisters." A theology of the Name can therefore help us appropriate an important aspect of the Pauline understanding of the Church as the family of God.[43]

(Greenwich, CT: By the Author, 1913). He published a second book on the theme of the Name seven years later, *Calling upon the Name of the Lord* (Cos Cob, CT: Christ Witness, 1920).

[43] For an excellent study of Paul's notion of the church in terms of the metaphor of family, see Robert Banks, *Paul's Idea of Community* (rev. ed.; Peabody, MA: Hendrickson

But there are particular weaknesses in the Oneness theology of the Name in its present configuration, only two of which we will mention briefly. One is the indefensible exegesis of Matt. 28:19, in which "Father, Son and Holy Spirit" are reduced to titles of divine function in salvation history, and the "name" of each is claimed to be "Jesus," the name to be invoked in baptism according to Acts 2:38. This strained interpretation, driven by the need to harmonize texts, overlooks the more compelling view that the Matthean formula is a compound divine name.

Second, while there is some indication of a tradition of the name of Jesus in the earliest Jewish Christian materials in the New Testament, this tradition apparently gave way to other christological expressions, or it was at least limited to certain Christian communities.[44] For our purposes, it is significant that any waning or localization was evident within the canonical text itself. This is a problem for Oneness exegetes who are committed to the authoritative biblical text and dismiss only post-canonical sources. In other words, what authority does a biblical perspective carry, if there is evidence that it was not universally believed or practiced within the apostolic church? Even if we can identify a christological strand of the name of Jesus, it is undoubtedly not the dominant tradition, and the apostolic church did not consider it to be so, otherwise it would have been universalized. Our critique of Oneness Pentecostalism is that it has taken a legitimate but provisional theme from Apostolic Christianity and made it the non-negotiable center.

d. Salvation and Acts 2:38

The choice of Acts 2:38 as the pattern for full salvation, or preferably Christian initiation, is a rich and complex one. First, it incorporates the various elements in the act of becoming a Christian – faith, baptism, and reception of the Spirit. It involves God, the individual and the Christian community – the penitent confesses sins, the Christian community baptizes, and the Spirit comes. The threefold action is also clearly Trinitarian – one turns to *God* in repentance, identifies with *Christ* in baptism, and receives the gift of the *Spirit*. This last observation leads to the conclusion that Oneness Pentecostals, while adhering to the radical oneness of God, are Trinitarian in their Christian experience. In addition, those Oneness representatives who teach Acts 2:38

Publishers, 1994).

[44] For a brief treatment of the name of Jesus in the New Testament, see Longenecker, *Christology of Early Jewish Christianity*, p. 46.

as the new birth share common ground with such scholars as James Dunn and Max Turner, who point out that all three elements in Acts 2:38 are initiatory for the Christian life.[45]

Oneness Pentecostals, however, have blended evangelical exegesis and Pentecostal experience in a way that has produced a highly exclusive practice, even of other Pentecostals. They have done this by (1) requiring re-baptism in the name of Jesus for all other Christians, and (2) interpreting the "gift of the Spirit" as Pentecostal Spirit-baptism. While they (or Durham before them) may be applauded for emphasizing the importance of baptism, the richness of the earlier theology of identification with Christ has been lost in their shift to the Name as the only active agent in the baptismal act.

Furthermore, the recent trend in the UPCI (less so in the black Oneness churches, which still adhere closely to Haywood's teachings) is to suppress the earlier speculations about the destiny of those not "born again" according to Acts 2:38. Though this exegesis of correlating John 3:5 with Acts 2:38 was flawed, the early teachers at least attempted to acknowledge the presence of other Christians. Those who interpret Acts 2:38 as full identification with Christ appear to have more room for embracing other Christians.

Even Haywood and Urshan, who taught Acts 2:38 as the new birth, concluded that life begins at conception, not birth. This permitted them to accept the experience of other Christians, even if it was not the fullness of God's purpose for the church. For Haywood at least, the teaching of the new birth was located within the broader pattern of "full" salvation.

The exclusive Oneness praxis of Acts 2:38 continues to be the greatest stumbling block for other Christians, causing confusion and often offense. In the interest of unity, our task is not to strive to dismantle the movement but to explore possible future developments that accomplish two goals: achieve the degree of unity wherein Oneness and Trinitarian Christians can confess each others as "full" brothers and sisters in Christ, and do so in a way in which Oneness Pentecostals can still recognize themselves as a distinctive but genuine presence within the Christian family.

---

[45] I recognize that the debate continues between certain Pentecostal scholars such as Robert Menzies and evangelical scholars, over whether or not reference to the Spirit in Acts is soteriological or prophetic. It is beyond the scope of this study to address the issue, other than to indicate that the Oneness teaching finds itself in harmony with many evangelicals in its view that Spirit-baptism is part of Christian initiation.

We offer three suggestions. One is that the way forward may be the way back: there is theological and ecumenical potential for developing a baptismal theology rooted in Durham's teaching on the identification with Christ. Second, while Oneness Pentecostals still insist on rebaptizing all other already-baptized Christians, a future Oneness baptismal theology might draw the distinction between that which is necessary for salvation and that which is a gift of grace to the wider church. The practice in some Baptist traditions currently follows this theological line of development: immersion of adult believers is a practice that Baptists believe needs to be recovered and shared with a wider post-Christendom church, but it is not required of one who was already baptized as an infant. This was also the guideline agreed upon at the Third General Council meeting in 1915: each side was to limit its baptismal practice to new converts or those desiring baptism in the name of Jesus to satisfy their conscience.

A third possible direction is suggested in the recent work by Roman Catholic scholars, Kilian McDonnell and George Montague, *Christian Initiation and Baptism in the Holy Spirit: Evidence from the First Eight Centuries*.[46] Their conclusion is that the early church expected the manifestation of the Spirit to accompany baptism. All Pentecostals applaud this expectation. But Trinitarian Pentecostals qualify it by privileging speaking in tongues as *the* manifestation to be expected. Oneness Pentecostals concur with the authors that this pneumatic manifestation is part of Christian initiation, not subsequent to it. But they qualify it by both the baptismal formula and the requirement of speaking in tongues. For our purpose, McDonnell and Montague have brought to our attention the importance of the experiential dimension or "spiritual manifestations" in Christian initiation, so neglected in subsequent centuries. But they wisely do not formulate a doctrine of requirement. Understandably, this approach is less definitive than what Pentecostals traditionally expect in the "crisis" experience of Sprit-baptism. But it is a particular challenge to those Oneness believers who teach that one has not received the Spirit at all prior to Spirit-baptism. Our proposal is that the experiential aspect of faith is to be desired and sought, but it is difficult to legislate doctrinally, and inappropriate to marginalize those who do not conform to a prescribed pattern. The confessional statements in most Pentecostal assemblies recognize this

---

[46] Kilian McDonnell and George T. Montague, *Christian Initiation and Baptism in the Holy Spirit: Evidence from the First Eight Centuries* (Collegeville, MN: The Liturgical Press, 1991).

by permitting full membership to those who have not yet received but are diligently seeking to be baptized in the Spirit.

5. Summary

In conclusion, Oneness Pentecostals conform most closely to Lindback's "conditionally permanent" presence in the Christian family. Instead of dwindling, they are projected to share in the numerical bounty of the growing Pentecostal movement in the 21st century. If Lindbeck is correct, it means that Oneness Pentecostals will be part of the Christian landscape for generations to come. Our common task in the future will be to listen carefully, seek "equivalent consequences," and encourage Oneness Pentecostals to develop their theology and practice, in the hope that a continuing mutual encounter will bear the fruit of oneness in that wider family called Christian.

16

Conclusion

Oneness Pentecostalism was born in the infancy of a religious movement that within a century would be a recognizable tradition and force
for shaping global Christianity in the 21st century. But a hundred years
in the future was unthinkable. Like other Pentecostals, the Oneness
movement understood itself to be the restoration of apostolic Christianity that would appear in history immediately prior to the return of
Christ. It carved out its identity with the twin resources of the Bible
and a Spirit-guided hermeneutic of revelation, the divinely appointed
authorities for restoring apostolic doctrine and practice. An otherwise
conventional baptismal sermon in 1913 was heralded as the moment of
supernatural visitation whereby the name of God, lost for centuries in
the rubble of a corrupt church, was liberated to restore to the church
the full recognition and power of Jesus.

This "new thing" came as a surprise: the converts believed it came
"suddenly from heaven,"[1] while onlookers speculated otherwise – the
fanciful imaginations of its promoters, or the pool of fourth-century
heretics. But they failed to look on their own historical doorstep. The
New Issue did not descend from on high but emerged within the religious currents that had recently preceded it. A radically christocentric
doctrine and baptismal practice were ignited under the right conditions for conflagration: a spirituality that contended for the supremacy
of Jesus in all things, and a concern that this cornerstone of faith was
being undermined by liberal sceptics on one hand and a string of spiritual experiences on the other. They inherited the first condition from
the Holiness and evangelical streams in the late 19th century. The
other came from the first schismatic movement in Pentecostalism,

---

[1] See Acts 2:2, "And suddenly there came a sound from heaven as of a rushing mighty
wind, and it filled all the house where they were sitting." This is the inspiration for the
title of the book by Carl Brumback, *Suddenly from Heaven – A History of the Assemblies of
God* (Springfield, MO: Gospel Publishing House, 1961).

launched by William Durham, a spiritual mentor to their pioneering leaders.

The Jesus-centered faith of a previous generation, especially in the Keswick Holiness movement, had bound its doctrine of Christ closely to the devotional life and practical concern for evangelism and mission. Both were perceived to be under threat from the corrosive effects of Unitarianism and modernist theology. One particular response was to defend the "full" and "supreme" deity of Christ, which its representative Bible teachers did by embarking on a study of the names and titles of God in the Old Testament to show that Jesus fulfilled all the attributes of Yahweh. The primary goal was to demonstrate that Jesus was completely *one* with Yahweh. Theological questions of the distinction between the persons in the Godhead were far from their mind and seemed of little consequence for their mission. One important conclusion by some was that the "Name" was carried into the New Covenant, as "Lord" or "Jesus."

In 1910, William Durham touched off a chain reaction in the early Pentecostal Revival with his teaching on the Finished Work of Calvary, a christocentric "correction" to the perceived overemphasis in the Wesleyan Holiness movement on sanctification as a second work of grace and an excessive seeking for prescribed spiritual crisis experiences. The implication of the doctrine, shaped largely along the lines of Keswickian theology, was a call to be fully "identified with Christ." Durham was soon convinced that water baptism was an important element in this identification, the key text being Rom. 6:4. A parallel passage – Acts 2:38 – soon became the text of choice for the masthead of Durham's magazine, *The Pentecostal Testimony*.

The New Issue was born in 1914 within the fledgling fellowship of the Assemblies of God – just three days after the organization's first meeting. Following two years of tension and conflict, one-fifth of that fellowship was excommunicated on the charge of heresy. The movement reappeared in organizational form within months but did not capture its final pioneer theologian, Andrew Urshan, until he defected to its ranks in 1919. While the Assemblies of God had begun to stabilize by 1920, the Oneness organization – the Pentecostal Assemblies of the World – continued in a state of turmoil and fragmentation for two more decades.

Some of the instability was for good reason. Unlike most denominations that had long since succumbed to racial segregation, the PAW valiantly fought to maintain its interracial identity. But by 1924 the battle was lost. Further organizational fragmentation continued for more than a decade, but was matched by restlessness for unity. While a major interracial merger was achieved in 1932, the experiment collapsed in pain and bitterness five years later. Two large white groups continued to pursue unity until they successfully accomplished a merger in 1945. But the vision for a fully interracial body finally succumbed to fraternal associationalism, and remains today a vision to be realized.

The New Issue had begun simply enough with a baptismal formula, but mushroomed into a distinctive and somewhat coherent doctrine within five years. No one architect can claim responsibility for the overall belief system. A number of key elements in the doctrine are reconstructed fragments of ideas from Trinitarian forebears such as Methodist commentator Adam Clarke, Presbyterian J. Monro Gibson, and Bible Society President William Phillips Hall – not to mention a fourth-century heretic whose term "manifestation" to describe the Trinity made more sense to these first Oneness theologians than the confusing term "person."

As the eschatological expectation of the Last Days restoration of apostolic truth faded, the primary vision for the Oneness movement shifted to its Primitivist aspirations. The Oneness appeal, like that of the wider Pentecostal movement, is that it is biblical – more than that, a replication of apostolic doctrine and practice. Theologically, its recurring themes are the oneness of God and baptism in the name of Jesus, but its cohering idea is the Name. Its core doctrinal formulations have remained relatively unchanged since the beginning, sometimes appearing to be frozen in time. Also present from the beginning are the antagonists who have never wearied of letting the world know the dangers of this "heresy" or "cult."

The challenge for the future is hidden in its name and its inheritance: oneness. The earliest appeal to oneness in 1910 was that the Pentecostal movement be united. A decade later that appeal was applied sharply to racial unity. By 1930 it became a descriptor for the movement. Throughout its history, lack of oneness with fellow Pentecostals and other Christians has been enigmatic: for some a mark of doctrinal purity, for others a sign of sin.

The future for Oneness Pentecostals is located within this heritage. If, as they believe, a name embodies the character of the ones who bear it, then oneness is still a vision to be realized. The future will depend upon that restlessness of spirit for oneness, which will not be satisfied until it is fulfilled. This task is surely not theirs alone to bear.

Bibliography

Allchin, A.M. & H.A. Hodges. *A Rapture of Praise – Hymns of John and Charles Wesley*. London: Hodder & Stoughton, 1966.

Anderson, Ray S. *Ministry on the Fireline: A Practical Theology for an Empowered Church*. Downer's Grove, IL: InterVarsity Press, 1993.

Anderson, Robert Mapes. *Vision of the Disinherited: The Making of American Pentecostalism*. New York: Oxford University Press, 1979.

Apostolic Ministerial Alliance, Inc., Preamble, Constitution, and By-Laws of. Tipton, IN, 1937.

Apostolic Ministers Fellowship. By the Organization, n.d.

Armstrong, Edward. "Sane and Insane Practices," *Weekly Evangel* 98 (10 July 1915): 1.

Arthur, William. *The Tongue of Fire: or, The True Power of Christianity* (New York: Harper & Brothers, 1856).

Back cover, *Pentecostal Herald* 44 (March 1969).

Bainbridge, Harriette B. "Jesus Only." *Christian Alliance and Foreign Missionary Weekly* 14 (1 May 1895): 275.

Bauckham, Richard. *God Crucified: Monotheism and Christology in the New Testament*. Grand Rapids, MI: Eerdmans, 1998.

Beasley-Murray, G.R. *Baptism in the New Testament*. Grand Rapids, MI: Eerdmans, 1962.

Becton, Cleveland. United Pentecostal Church International, Hazelwood, MO: Interview, 15 June 1973.

Beisner, E. Calvin. *"Jesus Only" Churches*. Grand Rapids, MI: Zondervan, 1998.

Bell, E.N. "The 'Acts' on Baptism in Christ's Name Only," *Weekly Evangel* 94 (12 June 1915): 1-3.

___. "Andrew Urshan's New Stand," *Christian Evangel* 284 and 285 (19 April 1919): 9.

——. "Bro. Bell on the Trinity," *Weekly Evangel* 114 (6 November 1915): 1.

——. "Davis City Camp-Meeting Report," *Weekly Evangel* 105 (28 August 1915): 2.

——. "Editorial Explanation on Preliminary Statement," *Word and Witness* 12 (June 1915): 1.

——. "Editorial," *Weekly Evangel* 86 (17 April 1915): 2.

——. "Editorial," *Word and Witness* 12 (June 1915): 1.

——. "The Great Battle for the Truth, *Christian Evangel* 300 and 301 (9 August 1919): 1-2.

——. "The Great Outlook," *Weekly Evangel* 92 (29 May 1915): 3.

——. "'Meat in Due Season' Corrected," *Word and Witness* 12 (October 1915): 4.

——. "Personal Statement," *Weekly Evangel* 108 (18 September 1915): 2.

——. "Personal Statement," *Word and Witness* 12 (October 1915): 4.

——. "Questions and Answers," *Weekly Evangel* 177 (17 February 1917): 9.

——. "Questions and Answers," *Weekly Evangel* 200 (28 July 1917): 9.

——. "Questions and Answers," *Weekly Evangel* 213 (3 November 1917): 9.

——. "Scriptural Varieties on Baptismal Formula," *Weekly Evangel* 97 (3 July 1915): 1, 3.

——. "There is Safety in Counsel," *Weekly Evangel* 108 (18 September 1915): 1.

——. "There is Safety in Counsel," *Word and Witness* 12 (October 1915): 1.

——. "The Sad New Issue, "*Word and Witness* 12 (June 1915): 2-3.

——. "The Urshan Trouble, "*Christian Evangel* 288 and 289 (17 May 1919): 6-7.

——. "To Act in the Name of Another," *Word and Witness* 11 (May 1915): 2-3.

——. *Who Is Jesus Christ?* reprint ed. Houston, TX: Herald Publishing House, n.d.

——. "Who is Jesus Christ?" *Weekly Evangel* 103 (14 August 1915): 1.

——. "Who is Jesus Christ? " *Word and Witness* 12 (September 1915): 5.

Berkouwer, G.C. *The Person of Christ*. Trans. John Vriend. *Studies in Dogmatics*. Grand Rapids, MI: Eerdmans, 1955.

Bernard, David K. *Essentials in Holiness*. Hazelwood, MO: Word Aflame Press, 1989.

——. *Essentials in the New Birth*. Hazelwood, MO: Word Aflame Press, 1987.

——. *God's Infallible Word*. Hazelwood, MO: Word Aflame Press, 1992.

——. *A History of Christian Doctrine* – vol. III, *The Twentieth Century, A.D. 1900-2000*. Hazelwood, MO: Word Aflame Press, 1999.

——. *In the Name of Jesus*. Hazelwood, MO: Word Aflame Press, 1992.

——. *The Message of Romans*. Hazelwood, MO: Word Aflame Press, 1987.

——. *The New Birth*. Series in Pentecostal Theology, vol. II. Hazelwood, MO: Word Aflame Press, 1984.

——. *The Oneness of God*. Series in Pentecostal Theology, vol. I. Hazelwood, MO: Word Aflame Press, 1983.

——. *The Oneness View of Jesus Christ*. Hazelwood, MO: Word Aflame Press, 1994.

——. *Oneness and Trinity, A.D. 100-300: The Doctrine of God in Ancient Christian Writings*. Hazelwood, MO: Word Aflame Press, 1992.

——. *The Trinitarian Controversy in the Fourth Century*. Hazelwood, MO: Word Aflame Press, 1993.

——. *Understanding the Articles of Faith: An Examination of United Pentecostal Beliefs*. Hazelwood, MO: Word Aflame Press, 1998.

Bethune-Baker, J.F. *An Introduction to the Early History of Christian Doctrine*. London: Methuen, 1954.

"Bible Scholarship and the Deity of Christ," *Sunday School Times* 52 (25 December 1910): 635.

Bjornstad, James & Bjorck, Walter. *Jesus Only: A Modalistic Interpretation*. Wayne, NJ: Christian Research Institute, 1970.

Bloesch, Donald G. *The Evangelical Renaissance*. Grand Rapids, MI: Eerdmans, 1973.

Bloom, Anthony. *Beginning to Pray*. New York: Paulist Press, 1970.

Blumhofer, Edith. *Restoring the Faith: The Assemblies of God, Pentecostalism, and American Culture*. Urbana, IL: University of Illinois Press, 1993.

Bousset, Wilhelm. *Kyrios Christos – A History of the Belief in Christ from the Beginning of Christianity to Irenaeus*, 5th ed. Trans. John E. Steely. New York: Abingdon, 1970.

Boyd, Gregory A. *Oneness Pentecostalism and the Trinity*. Grand Rapids, MI: Baker Book House, 1992.

Branham, William M., *Conduct, Order, Doctrine of the Church*. Jeffersonville, IN: Spoken Word Publications, 1973.

——. *Questions and Answers*. Jeffersonville, IN: Spoken Word Publications, 1961.

——. *The Spoken Word*. Jeffersonville, IN: Spoken Word Publications, 1972.

——. *The Spoken Word*, Vol. 3 No. 13, *Marriage and Divorce*. Jeffersonville, IN: Spoken Word Publications, 1965.

——. *The Spoken Word*, Vol. 6 No. 10, *The Uniting Time and Sign*. Jeffersonville, IN: Spoken Word Publications, 1963.

Bridegroom Songs, The. Indianapolis, IN: Christ Temple Bookstore, n.d.

Brown, Dale, "The Wesleyan Revival from a Pietist Perspective," *Wesleyan Theological Journal* 24/1 (Spring 1989): 6-16.

——. *Understanding Pietism*. Grand Rapids, MI: Eerdmans, 1978.

Brown, Harold O.J. *Heresies: Heresy and Orthodoxy in the History of the Church*. Peabody, MA: Hendrickson, 1988.

Bruce, Dickson D., Jr. "And They All Sang Hallelujah: Plain-Folk Camp-Meeting Religion, 1800-1845" (Ph.D. diss., University of Pennsylvania, 1971).

Brumback, Carl, *God in Three Persons*. Cleveland, TN: Pathway Press, 1959.

——. *Suddenly from Heaven – A History of the Assemblies of God*. Springfield, MO: Gospel Publishing House, 1961.

Bruner, Frederick Dale. *A Theology of the Holy Spirit – The Pentecostal Experience and the New Testament Witness*. Grand Rapids, MI: Eerdmans, 1970.

Brunner, Emil. *Dogmatics*, vol. I, *The Christian Doctrine of God*. Trans. Olive Wyon. Philadelphia: Westminster, 1950.

Bundy, David. "European Pietist Roots of Pentecostalism." Eds. Stanley M. Burgess & Gary McGee. *New International Dictionary of Pentecostal and Charismatic Movements*. Grand Rapids, MI: Zondervan, 2002.

——. "Documenting 'Oneness' Pentecostalism: A Case Study in the Ethical Dilemmas Posed by the Creation of Documentation," *Summary of Proceedings, Fifty-third Annual Conference of the American Theological Library Association, June 9-12, 1999*. Ed. Margret Tacke Collins.

——. "G.T. Haywood: Religion for Urban Realities." Ed. James R. Goff Jr. & Grant Wacker. *Portraits of a Generation: Early Pentecostal Leaders* (Fayetteville, AR: The University of Arkansas Press, 2002), pp. 237-53.

Cagle, Odell. *Echoes of the Past*. Oneness Pentecostal Pioneer Series. Stockton, CA: Apostolic Press, 1972.

Campbell, Alexander. *The Christian System in Reference to the Union of Christians, and a Restoration of Primitive Christianity, As Plead in the Current Reformation*. Nashville, TN: Gospel Advocate, 1956.

Catalog, Northern California Bible College. San Jose, CA: By the Author, n.d.

Chalfant, William B. *Ancient Champions of Oneness*. Hazelwood, MO: Word Aflame Press, 1979.

Chappell, F.L. "Hear Ye! Hear Ye!" *Witness of God* (n.d.): 2-6.

Chappell, Paul G. "The Divine Healing Movement in America" (Ph.D. diss., Drew University, 1983).

Clanton, Arthur L. *United We Stand – A History of Oneness Organizations* (Hazelwood, MO: Pentecostal Publishing House, 1970.

Child, Brevard, "The Search for Biblical Authority Today," *Andover Newton Theological Journal* (1978): 202.

Collins, David. Telephone Interview from Detroit, Michigan, 1 September 1974.

Collins, Kenneth, "John Wesley's Critical Appropriation of Early German Pietism," *Wesleyan Theological Journal* 27/1 & 2 (Spring-Fall 1997): 57-92.

——. "John Wesley's Doctrine of the New Birth," *Wesleyan Theological Journal* 32/1 (Spring 1997): 53-68.

Combined Minutes of the General Council of the Assemblies of God, April 2-12, November 15-29, 1914. St. Louis, MO: Gospel Publishing House, 1915.

Congar, Yves. *The Mystery of the Temple; Or, The Manner of God's Presence to His Creatures from Genesis to the Apocalypse*. Trans. Reginald F. Trevett. New York: Newman, 1962.

"Consolidation of Emmanuel's Church in Jesus Christ and Pentecostal Ministerial Alliance at Present Impossible," *Pentecostal Witness* 3 (1 December 1926): 3.

"Controversy Discouraged," *Weekly Evangel* 108 (18 September 1915): 2.

"Controversy Discouraged," *Word and Witness* 12 (October 1915): 4.

Cragg, Gerald R. *The Church and the Age of Reason, 1648-1789*. Baltimore, MD: Penguin Books, 1960.

Crayne, Richard, *Pentecostal Handbook*. 1030 W. 4th North Street, Morristown, TN: By the Author, 1963.

Cullmann, Oscar. *The Christology of the New Testament*, rev. ed. Trans. Shirley C. Guthrie & Charles A.M. Hall. Philadelphia: Westminster, 1963.

Curts, F.E. *The Tabernacle in the Wilderness*, St. Louis, MO: Pentecostal Publishing House, n.d.

Dalcour, Edward L. *A Definitive Look at Oneness Theology: Defending the Tri-Unity of God*. New York: University Press of America, 2005.

Daniélou, Jean & André Chouraqui. *The Jews-Views and Counterviews – A Dialogue between Jean Daniélou and André Chouraqui*. New York: Newman, 1967.

Daniélou, Jean. *The Development of Christian Doctrine before the Council of Nicaea*, vol. I: *The Theology of Jewish Christianity*. Ed. & trans. John A. Baker. London: Darton, Longman & Todd, 1964.

Davies, Horton. *The Challenge of the Sects*. Philadelphia, PA: Westminster, 1961.

Dayton, Donald W. "Asa Mahan and the Development of American Holiness Theology," *Wesleyan Theological Journal* 9 (Spring 1974): 60-69.

——. *Discovering an Evangelical Heritage*. New York: Harper & Row, 1976.

——. "The Evolution of Pentecostalism," *The Covenant Quarterly* 32 (August 1974): 28-40.

——. "From 'Christian Perfection' to the 'Baptism of the Holy Ghost,'" *Aspects of Pentecostal-Charismatic Origins.* Ed. Vinson Synan. Plainfield, NJ: Logos International, 1975.

——. "Presidential Address: The Wesleyan Option for the Poor," *Wesleyan Theological Journal* 26/1 (Spring 1991): 7-16.

——. *Theological Roots of Pentecostalism.* Grand Rapids, MI: Zondervan, 1987.

——. "Theological Roots of Pentecostalism." Unpublished Paper to American Academy of Religion Annual Meeting on "Free Church Studies" in Washington, D.C. 26 October 1974. (Mimeographed)

Dayton, Donald & Robert K. Johnston, eds. *The Variety of American Evangelicalism.*

Downers Grove, IL: InterVarsity Press, 1991.

Dearing, John H. *Bible Study Notes.* Typescript, n.d.

——. Three Views of the Godhead. Bangor, ME: By the author, *c.* 1937.

Del Colle, Ralph. *Christ and the Spirit: Spirit-christology in Trinitarian Perspective.* New York: Oxford University Press, 1994.

——. "Oneness and Trinity: A Preliminary Proposal for Dialogue with Oneness Pentecostalism," *Journal of Pentecostal Theology* 10 (April 1997): 85-110.

Dieter, Melvin E. *The Holiness Revival of the Nineteenth Century,* Studies in Evangelicalism, 1. 2nd ed. Lanham, MD: Scarecrow, 1996.

——. "Wesleyan-Holiness Aspects of Pentecostal Origins." *Aspects of Pentecostal-Charismatic Origins.* Ed. Vinson Synan. Plainfield, NJ: Logos International, 1975.

Dillenberger, John, ed. *Martin Luther – Selections From His Writings.* Garden City, NY: Doubleday, 1961.

Directory of Sabbath-Observing Groups, 9th ed. Fairview, OK: Bible Sabbath Association, 2001.

Discipline Book of the Church of Our Lord Jesus Christ of the Apostolic Faith, Inc., The. rev. ed. New York: By the Organization, 1969.

Dix, Dom Gregory. *Jew and Greek – A Study in the Primitive Church.* London: Dacre, 1953.

Dodd, C.H. *The Interpretation of the Fourth Gospel.* Cambridge: Cambridge University Press, 1953.

Dugas, Paul D., ed. & comp. *The Life and Writings of Elder G.T. Haywood,* Oneness Pentecostal Pioneer Series. Stockton, CA: W.A.B.C. Apostolic Press, 1968.

Dunn, J.D.G. *Baptism in the Holy Spirit: A Re-Examination of the New Testament Teaching on the Gift of the Holy Spirit in Relation to Pentecostalism Today.* Philadelphia: Westminster, 1970.

Duprau, Lura F. *Babylon – Ancient and Modern.* Portland, OR: Apostolic Book Publishers, n.d.

Durasoff, Steve. *The Russian Protestants – Evangelicals in the Soviet Union, 1944-1964.* Rutherford, NJ: Fairleigh Dickinson University Press, 1969.

Durham, William H. "An Open Letter to My Brother Ministers," *Pentecostal Testimony* II/3 (July 1912): 14.

——. "A Word to Correspondents," *Pentecostal Testimony* II/1 (January 1912): 15-16.

——. "False Doctrines," *Articles Written by Pastor W.H. Durham, Taken from Pentecostal Testimony* (Springfield, MO: Assemblies of God Archives, n.d.): 43.

——. "Identification with Christ," *Articles Written by Pastor W.H. Durham, Taken from Pentecostal Testimony* (Springfield, MO: Assemblies of God Archives, n.d.): 27-30.

——. "Personal Testimony of Pastor Durham," *Pentecostal Testimony* II/3 (July 1912): 3.

——. "Sanctification – Is It a Definite, Second, Instantaneous Work of Grace?" *Articles Written by Pastor W.H. Durham, Taken From Pentecostal Testimony* (Springfield, MO: Assemblies of God Archives, n.d.): 15-16.

——. "Sanctification – The Bible Does Not Teach That It Is a Second Definite Work of Grace," *Articles Written by Pastor W.H. Durham, Taken from Pentecostal Testimony* (Springfield, MO: Assemblies of God Archives, n.d.): 1.

——. "Some Other Phases of Sanctification, *Pentecostal Testimony* II/3 (July 1912): 10.

——. "The Finished Work of Calvary – Identification with Jesus Christ Saves and Sanctifies," *Pentecostal Testimony* II/1 (January 1912): 1.

——. "The Finished Work of Calvary – It Makes Plain the Great Work of Redemption," *Pentecostal Testimony* II/3 (June 1912): 6.

——. "The Great Battle of Nineteen Eleven," *Pentecostal Testimony* II/1 (January 1912): 7.

——. "The Great Need of the Hour," *Pentecostal Testimony* II/1 (January 1912): 10.

——. "The Two Great Experiences or Gifts," *Articles Written by Pastor W.H. Durham, Taken from Pentecostal Testimony* (Springfield, MO: Assemblies of God Archives, n.d.): 4.

——. "The Winnipeg Convention," *Pentecostal Testimony* II/1 (January 1912): 11-12.

"Editorial – The Mystery of God," *Weekly Evangel* 140 (20 May 1916): 1.

"Editorial," *Weekly Evangel* 113 (30 October 1915): 2.

Erwin, Isma Wells. *The Resurrection and the New Birth*. St. Louis, MO: Pentecostal Publishing House, 1954.

Ewart, Frank J. "Cyrus: A Type of the Man-Child," *End Time Witnesses* (n.d.).

——. *The Creedless Christ* (Privately published, n.d.).

——. "Defending Heresies," *The Good Report* 1/3 (1912): 12.

——. "The Einstein Theory," *Apostolic Herald* 17/9 (September 1942): 2.

——. *Jesus – the Man and Mystery*. Nashville, TN: Baird-Ward, 1941.

——. "The Last Theophany," *Pentecostal Herald* 21/1 (January 1946): 4.

——. "Least Yet Best Known Man," *Apostolic Herald* 17/6 (June 1942): 12.

——. "Like Precious Faith," *Apostolic Herald* 17/8 (August 1942): 7.

——. "The Mystery of Jesus," *Apostolic Herald* 16/3 (March 1941): 1.

——. *The Name and the Book*. Chicago, IL: Daniel Ryerson, 1936.

——. "The Oneness of God," *Apostolic Herald* 19/1 (January 1944): 3.

——. *The Phenomenon of Pentecost – A History of the "Latter Rain"*. St. Louis, MO: Pentecostal Publishing House, 1947.

——. *The Revelation of Jesus Christ*. St. Louis, MO: Pentecostal Publishing House, n.d.

——. "The Significance of Water Baptism," *Apostolic Herald* 16/1 (January 1941): 12.

——. "Statement of My Faith," *Apostolic Herald* 15/2 (February 1940): 5.

——. "Who Is the Man Child?" *End Time Witnesses* (n.d.).

——. "Word Studies in the Bible," *Apostolic Herald* 15/9 (September 1940): 2.

Excerpts from the Life of the Rt. Rev. W.T. Phillips and Fundamentals of the Apostolic Overcoming Holy Church of God, Inc. Mobile, AL: A.D.H. Church Publishing House, n.d.

Facts about the United Pentecostal Church International. Hazelwood, MO: Pentecostal Publishing House, n.d.

Farkas, Thomas. "Durham's 'Finished Work of Calvary' Teaching and Traditional Doctrines of Sanctification" (Ph.D. diss., Southern Baptist Theological Seminary, 1993).

Faupel, D. William. *The Everlasting Gospel: The Significance of Eschatology in the Development of Pentecostal Thought.* Sheffield: Sheffield Academic Press, 1996; repr. Blandford: Deo, 2007.

Fauss, Oliver F. *Baptism in God's Plan.* Hazelwood, MO: Pentecostal Publishing House, 1955.

——. *Buy the Truth, and Sell It Not.* St. Louis, MO: Pentecostal Publishing House, 1965.

——. "Letter from P.M.A.," *Pentecostal Witness* 3 (1 January 1927): 1-2.

Finney, Charles G. *Lectures on Revivals of Religion.* Boston: John P. Jewett, 1856.

——. *Sermons on the Way to Salvation.* Oberlin: Edward J. Goodrich, 1891.

——. *Skeletons of a Course of Theological Lectures*, vol. I. Oberlin: James Steel, 1840.

Fitch, Theodore. *Do You Know Who Died On Calvary?* Council Bluffs, IA: By the Author, n.d.

——. *God the Father Is Omnipresent Spirit.* Council Bluffs, IA: By the Author, n.d.

——. *Jesus Pre-existed As Lord.* Council Bluffs, IA: By the Author, n.d.

——. *Jesus – The Name That Is Above Every Name.* Council Bluffs, IA: By the Author, n.d.

——. *Lovely Titles of Jesus.* Council Bluffs, IA: By the Author, n.d.

——. *Pray to the Man Jesus: He Is Our Heavenly Father,* Council Bluffs, IA: By the Author, n.d.

——. *The Beauty and Majesty of the Man Jesus.* Council Bluffs, IA: By the Author, n.d.

Flower, J. Roswell. "Editorial," *Weekly Evangel* 95 (19 June 1915): 2.

——. "Great Victory in Fellowship," *Weekly Evangel* III (16 October 1915): 1-2.

——. "History of the Assemblies of God," Lecture Notes, Springfield, MO, 1949. (Mimeographed)

——. "Mis-Statement Corrected," *Weekly Evangel* 99 (17 July 1915): 2.

Flynn, David M. "The Debate between Oneness Pentecostalism and Its Trinitarian Opponents" (M.Th. thesis, Brunel University, 1998).

Foster, Fred J. *"Think It Not Strange" – A History of the Oneness Movement.* St. Louis, MO: Pentecostal Publishing House, 1965.

French, Talmadge L. "Oneness Pentecostalism in Global Perspective: History, Theology, and Expansion of the Oneness Pentecostal Movement" (M.A. thesis, Wheaton College, 1998).

——. *Our God is One: The Story of the Oneness Pentecostals.* Indianapolis, IN: Voice and Vision Publications, 1999.

Frodsham, Stanley. Personal letter to Robert Cunningham, 20 July 1963.

Fudge, Thomas A. *Christianity without the Cross: A History of Salvation in Oneness Pentecostalism.* Parkland, FL: Universal Publishers, 2003.

——. "Did E.N. Bell Convert to the New Issue?" *Journal of Pentecostal Theology* 18 (April 2001): 122-40

Gaebelein, Arno C. ed. *Christ and Glory – Addresses Delivered at the New York Prophetic Conference, Carnegie Hall, November 25-28, 1918.* New York: Publication Office "Our Hope," 1919.

——. *The Christ We Know – Mediations on and Glory of Our Lord Jesus Christ.* New York: Publication Office "Our Hope," 1927.

——. *The Church in the House.* New York: Publication Office "Our Hope," n.d.

——. *The Hope of the Ages – The Messianic Hope in Revelation, in History and in Realization.* New York: Publication Office "Our Hope," 1938.

——. *Listen – God Speaks.* New York: Publication Office "Our Hope," 1936.

——. *The Lord of Glory – Meditations on the Person, the Work and Glory of Our Lord Jesus Christ.* New York: Publication Office "Our Hope." 1910.

"General Council Meets in St. Louis," *Weekly Evangel* 106 (September 4, 1915): 1.

General Council Minutes of the Assemblies of God, 1915. Springfield, MO: Gospel Publishing House, 1916.

General Council of the Assemblies of God, Minutes, 1914-1969. Springfield, MO: Gospel Publishing House.

"General Joint Convention Report," *Pentecostal Witness* 4 (1 December 1927): 8.

Gentile, Ernest B. *God and His Word – A Catechism of Bible Doctrine,* rev. ed. Hong Kong: Asian Outreach, 1971.

——. Personal Letter, 6 November 1973.

Gerloff, Roswith I.H. *A Plea for British Black Theologies: The Black Church Movement in Britain in Its Transatlantic Cultural and Theological Interaction with Special Reference to the Pentecostal Oneness (Apostolic) and Sabbatarian Movements* (New York: Peter Lang, 1992).

Gezahagne, Teklemariam. *Bible Writers' Theology.* Arkansas: Ozark Mountain, 1999.

Gibson, John Monro. *Christianity According to Christ,* 2nd ed. Nisbet's Theological Library. London: James Nisbet, 1889.

——. *The Gospel of Matthew.* The Expositor's Bible, 15. New York: A.C. Armstrong, 1902-1908.

——. *The Inspiration and Authority of Holy Scripture.* New York: Fleming H. Revell, n.d.

——. Reprinted as "The Mystery of the Father, Son, and Holy Spirit," *Pentecostal Herald* 28 (December 1953): 5.

Gill, Kenneth D. *Toward a Contextualized Theology for the Third World: The Emergence and Development of Jesus' Name Pentecostalism in Mexico.* Studies in the Intercultural History of Christianity, 90. New York: Peter Lang, 1994.

Gillespie, Bernie L. Website: http://www.inchristalone.org/. Accessed 25 August 2004.

Goff, James R., Jr. & Grant Wacker, eds. *Portraits of a Generation: Early Pentecostal Leaders*. Fayetteville, AR: The University of Arkansas Press, 2002.

Goff, James R., Jr. *Fields White unto Harvest: Charles F. Parham and the Missionary Origins of Pentecostalism*. Fayetteville, AR: The University of Arkansas Press, 1988.

Golder, Morris E. *History of the Pentecostal Assemblies of the World*, Indianapolis, IN: By the Author, 1973.

——. *"The Principles of Our Doctrine"*. Cincinnati, OH: Apostolic Light, n.d.

——. Interview, Grace Apostolic Church, Indianapolis, IN, 22 May 1973.

——. Interview, Grace Apostolic Church, Indianapolis, IN, 18 May 1974.

Goodwin, Lloyd L. *Great Doctrines of the Bible*. Des Moines, IA: Gospel Assembly Church, 1972.

Gordon, A.J. "The Canceled Check," *The Watchword* 2 (January 1880): 66-67.

——. "Finding Her Title-Deed," *The Watchword* 1 (August 1879): 204.

——. *In Christ*. Boston: Howard Gannett, 1883.

Goss, Ethel E. *The Winds of God – The Story of the Earl Pentecostal Days (1901-1914)*. New York: Comet, 1958.

Goss, Howard. "Godhead," *Pentecostal Herald* 23 (December 1948): 7.

Gray, David. Phone Interview, 9 February 1996.

Gracious Gospel, Book One. Portland, OR: Gilbert Christian Assembly, n.d.

Gruits, Patricia B. *Understanding God*, rev. ed. Detroit, MI: Evangel, 1972.

Haenchen, Ernst. *The Acts of the Apostles – A Commentary*. Trans. R. McL. Wilson. Philadelphia: Westminster, 1971.

Hall, William Phillips. *Calling upon the Name of the Lord*. Cos Cob, CT: Christ Witness, 1920.

——. *Remarkable Biblical Discovery Or "The Name" of God According to the Scriptures*, 3rd ed. New York: American Tract Society, 1931.

——. *Remarkable Biblical Discovery*, abridged. St. Louis, MO: Pentecostal Publishing House, 1951.

——. *What is "The Name"? OR "The Mystery of God" Revealed*. Greenwich, CT: By the Author, 1913.

Hanby, S.R. *The Apostles' Doctrine*. Hazelwood, MO: Pentecostal Publishing House, n.d.

Harnack, Adolf. *History of Dogma*, 3rd ed. Vol. I. Trans. Neil Buchanan. New York: Dover, 1961.

Harrison, Everett F., ed. *Baker's Dictionary of the of the Bible*, 3rd ed. Grand Rapids, MI: Baker Book House, 1966.

"Have You Been Baptized in the Name of Jesus Christ?" *The Victorious Gospel* (Early Spring 1915): 4-5.

Haywood, G.T. "An Open Letter," *Christian Outlook* (October 1923): 208.

——. *Before the Foundation of the World*. Indianapolis, IN: Christ Temple, 1923.

——. *The Bridegroom Songs*. Indianapolis, IN: Christ Temple Bookstore, n.d.

——. "Dangers of Denying the Father," *Voice in the Wilderness* 2 (13 November 1922): 5; *Pentecostal Outlook* (April 1932): 3.

——. *Divine Names and Titles of Jehovah*. Indianapolis, IN: Christ Temple, n.d.

——. "Division Coming?" *Christian Outlook* 2 (June 1924): 374.

——. "Editorial," *Christian Outlook* 2 (April 1924): 325.

——. "Editorial," *Christian Outlook* 2 (September 1924): 441.

——. "Entering by the Door," *Voice in the Wilderness* 19 (n.d., ca. 1917): 2.

——. *Ezekiel's Vision.* Indianapolis, IN: Christ Temple, n.d.

——. "First and Second Resurrections," *Christian Outlook* 1 (April 1923): 4.

——. "New Organizations," *Christian Outlook* 2 (October 1924): 466.

——. "One Convention," *Christian Outlook* 2 (August 1924): 418.

——. *The Birth of the Spirit and the Mystery of the Godhead.* Indianapolis, IN: The Voice in the Wilderness, n.d.

——. "The Fatherhood of God in Christ," *Christian Outlook* 2 (June 1924): 385.

——. *The Finest of the Wheat.* Indianapolis, IN: Christ Temple, n.d.

——. *The Marriage and Divorce Question in the Church.* Indianapolis, IN: Christ Temple, n.d.

——. *The Old and New Tabernacle Compared.* Indianapolis, IN: The Voice in the Wilderness, n.d.

——. *The Resurrection of the Dead.* Indianapolis, IN: Christ Temple, n.d.

——. *The Victim of the Flaming Sword.* Indianapolis, IN: Christ Temple, n.d.

——. "The Word of God," *Voice in the Wilderness* (n.d., ca. 1918).

——. "To Our Brethren of Color," *Christian Outlook* 4 (January 1926): 3.

——. "United Methodism – North and South," *Christian Outlook* 2 (November 1924): 481.

——. "Unity," *Christian Outlook* 3 (July 1925): 124.

Hedding, Elijah. *The Substance of a Sermon Delivered in Bath (Maine), July 4, 1822.* Boston: Lincoln & Edmands, n.d.

Hexham, Irving & Karla Poewe. *New Religions as Global Cultures: Making the Human Sacred.* Boulder, CO: Westview, 1997.

Hibbard, J.C. *The Godhead Made Plain.* Dallas, TX: The Gospel Lighthouse Church, 1961.

Hobbs, C.E. *The Last Angel Message to God's People.* Lansing, IL: Lansing Apostolic Church, 1973.

——. *The Love of God.* Lansing, IL: Lansing Apostolic Church, 1973.

——. *Whom Say Ye That I Am?* Lansing, IL: Lansing Apostolic Church, 1971.

Hodgson, Leonard. *The Doctrine of the Trinity.* New York: Charles Scribner's Sons, 1944.

Hollenweger, Walter J. *The Pentecostals – The Charismatic Movement in the Churches.* Trans. R.A. Wilson. Minneapolis, MN: Augsburg, 1972.

Holliday, Robert K. *Tests of Faith.* Oak Hill, WV: The Fayette Tribune, 1966.

Hoover, Mario G. "Origin and Structural Development of the Assemblies of God" (M.A. thesis, Southwest Missouri State College, 1968).

Hopkins, Evan H. "Our Lord's Names and Their Message," *The Keswick Week, 1911.* Ed. Evan H. Hopkins. London: Marshall Brothers, 1911.

Horton, Wade. *The Trinitarian Concept of God.* Cleveland, TN: Pathway, 1964.

Howell, Joseph H. "The People of the Name: Oneness Pentecostalism in the United States" (Ph.D. diss., Florida State University, 1985).

Hunter, Harold D. "The Resurgence of Spirit Christology," *EPTA Bulletin: The Journal of the European Pentecostal Theological Association* 11/1 & 2 (1992): 50-57.

——. *Spirit Baptism: A Pentecostal Alternative.* Lanham, MD: University Press of America, 1983.

Hutchinson, Cyril. Personal Letter, 8 January 1974.

"Important Announcement by Request of the Credential Committee, *Weekly Evangel* 145 (24 June 1916): 8.

"In Doctrines," *Christian Evangel* 52 (1 August 1914): 2.

Jacob, Edmond. *Theology of the Old Testament*. Trans. A.W. Heathcote & P.J. Allcock. New York: Harper & Row, 1958.

Jacobsen, Douglas. *Thinking in the Spirit: Theologies of the Early Pentecostal Movement*. Indianapolis, IN: Indiana University Press, 2003.

Jensen, G.K. *When God Became Flesh*. New Westminster, Canada: Plowright Printing Co., Ltd., n.d.

Johnson, S.C. *Is Jesus Christ the Son of God Now?* Philadelphia, PA: By the Author, n.d.

Jones, Charles E. *A Guide to the Study of the Pentecostal Movement*. 2 vols. Metuchen, NJ: Scarecrow, 1983.

Jones, Mrs. Sam P. *The Life and Sayings of Sam P. Jones*. Atlanta, GA: Franklin-Turner, 1907.

Kaufman, Gordon D. *Systematic Theology: A Historicist Perspective*. New York: Charles Scribner's Sons, 1968.

Kelly, J.N.D. *Early Christian Doctrines*. 2nd ed. New York: Harper & Row, 1960.

Kelly, Vonelle. Unpublished paper, "The UPCI and 'Divine Flesh.'" n.d.

Kenyon, Essek W. *The Father and His Family*. Spencer, MA: Reality Press, 1916.

——. *The Two Kinds of Faith: Truth's Secret Revealed*. 4th ed. Seattle, WA: Kenyon's Gospel Publishing Society, 1942.

——. *The Two Kinds of Knowledge,* 18th ed. Lynnwood, WA: Kenyon's Gospel Publishing Society, 1966; originally published in 1938.

——. *The Two Kinds of Life: The Biological Miracle of the Age*. Seattle, WA: Kenyon's Gospel Publishing House, 1943.

——. *The Wonderful Name of Jesus*. Los Angeles: West Coast, 1927.

Kevan, Ernest F. "Dispensation," *Baker's Dictionary of the Bible*. 3rd ed. Everett F. Harrison, ed. Grand Rapids, MI: Baker Book House, 1966, p. 167.

——. "Millennium," *Baker's Dictionary of the Bible*. 3rd ed. Everett F. Harrison, ed. Grand Rapids, MI: Baker Book House, 1966, p. 353.

Kidson, Loy E. *Do All Speak With Tongues?* Houston, TX: By the Author, 1971.

Kidson, W.E. 1312 North Sixty-Seventh St., Houston, TX. Interview, 6 July 1973.

——. *In the Service of the King – Autobiography of W.E. Kidson*. Houston, TX: By the author, n.d.

——. "Minutes of the Conference," *Apostolic Herald* 6 (November 1931): 5-7.

——. "The Eighth Annual Conference," *Apostolic Herald* 8 (February 1933): 4.

——. "The Pentecostal Ministerial Alliance, Inc.," *Apostolic Herald* 2 (January 1927): 3.

Kilgore, Claude P. "Letter," *Apostolic Herald* 5 (March 1930): 9.

Kittel, G. & G. Friedrich, eds. *Theological Dictionary of the New Testament,* 10 vols. (ET; Grand Rapids, MI: Eerdmans, 1964-1976).

Knapp, M.W. ed. *Jesus Only – A Full Salvation Year Book*. Cincinnati, OH: M.W. Knapp, Publisher of Salvation Literature, n.d.

Kolenda, E.J. *For Remission-The Purpose of Calvary*. South Bend, IN: Apostolic Publishing Association, 1960.

Lampe, G.W.H. *The Seal of the Spirit*. New York: Longmans, Green & Co., 1951.

Larden, Robert A. *Our Apostolic Heritage – An Official History of the Apostolic Church of Pentecost, Inc*. Calgary, Canada: Kyle Printing and Stationery Ltd., 1971.

Lawrence, B.F. "'Meat in Due Season' Corrected," *Weekly Evangel* 202 (11 August 1917): 9.

Lederle, H.I. *Treasures Old and New: Interpretations of "Spirit-Baptism" in the Charismatic Renewal Movement*. Peabody, MA: Hendrickson, 1988.

Lewis, M.E. "Jesus Only," *Christian and Missionary Alliance* 20 (19 January 1898): 63.

Lie, Geir, "E.W. Kenyon: "Sektstifter eller kristen lederskikkelse? En historisk undersøkelse av Kentons teologi med særlig henblikk på dens historiske røtter og innflytelsen på samtid og ettertid" (M.A. thesis, Free Faculty of Theology, Oslo, Norway, 1994). (English translation: "E.W. Kenyon: Cult Founder or Evangelical Minister?")

——. Personal Correspondence, 15 September 2002.

Lindquist, F.J. *The Truth about the Trinity and Baptism in Jesus' Name Only*. Minneapolis, MN: Northern Gospel Publishing House, 1961.

Longenecker, Richard N. *The Christology of Early Jewish Christianity*. Studies in Biblical Theology, 17. Naperville, IL: Alex R. Allenson, 1970.

MacRae, George. "Whom Heaven Must Receive until the Time – Reflection on the Christology of Acts," *Interpretation: The Journal of Bible and Theology* 27 (April 1973): 151-165.

McClain, S.C. *Student's Handbook of Facts in Church History*. St. Louis, MO: Pentecostal Publishing House, 1948.

McConnell, Daniel Ray. *A Different Gospel: A Historical and Biblical Analysis of the Modern Faith Movement*. Peabody, MA: Hendrickson, 1988.

McKnight, C. Joe. Personal Letter, 5 February 1973.

McLoughlin, William G., Jr. *Billy Sunday Was His Real Name*. Chicago: University of Chicago Press, 1955.

Magee, Gordon. *Is Jesus in the Godhead or Is the Godhead in Jesus*. Pasadena, TX: By the Author, n.d.

Mahan, Asa. *Out of Darkness into Light; or, The Hidden Life Made Manifest*. New ed. London: Charles H. Kelly, 1874.

Manual – United Pentecostal Church International. Hazelwood, MO: Pentecostal Publishing House, 1974.

Menzies, William W. *Anointed to Serve – The Story of the Assemblies of God*. Springfield, MO: Gospel Publishing House, 1971.

——. Evangel College, Springfield, MO: Interview, 20 June 1973.

——. "The Non-Wesleyan Origins of the Pentecostal Movement," *Aspects of Pentecostal-Charismatic Origins*. Ed. Vinson Synan. Plainfield, NJ: Logos International, 1975.

Miller, Albert G. "Pentecostalism as a Social Movement: Beyond the Theory of Deprivation," *Journal of Pentecostal Theology* 9 (October, 1996), pp. 97-114.

Miller, John. *Is God a Trinity?* 3rd ed. Princeton, NJ: By the Author, 1922.

——. *Questions Awakened by the Bible. I. Are Souls Immortal? II. Was Christ in Adam? III. Is God a Trinity?* 2nd ed. Philadelphia: J.B. Lippincott, 1877.

Miller, Luke. *A Review of the "Jesus Only" Doctrine.* Austin, TX: Firm Foundation, 1959.

Miller, Perry. *Errand into the Wilderness.* New York: Harper & Row, 1956.

Minute Book and Ministerial Record of the General Assembly of the Apostolic Assemblies. By the Organization, n.d.

Minute Book 1919 (1907-1919 – Pentecostal Assemblies of the World. By the Organization, n.d.

Minute Book of the Pentecostal Assemblies of the World, 1922-1923. By the Organization, n.d.

Minute Book of the Pentecostal Assemblies of the World, 1924. By the Organization, n.d.

Minute Book of the Pentecostal Assemblies of the World, 1925-1930. By the Organization, n.d.

Minutes of the General Council of the Assemblies of God, 1914. By the Organization, n.d.

Miyakawa, T. Scott. *Protestants and Pioneers – Individualism and Conformity on the American Frontier.* Chicago: The University of Chicago Press, 1964.

Moody, Dale. "Shekinah," *The Interpreter's Dictionary of the Bible,* vol. IV. George A. Buttrick, ed. Nashville: Abingdon, 1962, pp. 317-319.

Needham, George C. "The Name Jesus – A Bible Reading," *The Watchword* 4 (January 1882): 92.

Nelson, Douglas. "For Such a Time as This: The Story of William J. Seymour and the Azusa Street Revival" (Ph.D. diss., University of Birmingham, 1981).

Nichol, John T. *The Pentecostals – The Story of the Growth and Development of a Vital New Christian Church.* rev. ed. Plainfield, NJ: Logos International, 1971.

Niebuhr, H. Richard. "The Doctrine of the Trinity and the Unity of the Church," *Theology Today* 3 (October 1946): 371-84.

——. *The Kingdom of God in America.* New York: Harper & Row, 1959.

Nienkirchen, Charles W. *A.B. Simpson and the Pentecostal Movement: A Study in Continuity, Crisis, and Change.* Peabody, MA: Hendrickson, 1992.

Niles, D. Preman. "The Name of God in Israel's Worship – The Importance of the Name Yahweh" (Ph.D. diss., Princeton Theological Seminary, 1974).

Norris, David S. "No Other Name: A Socio-Historical Approach to the Argument of Luke-Acts (Pierre Bourdieu)" (Ph.D. diss., Temple University, 2000).

Norris, S.G. *The Mighty God in Christ.* St. Paul, MN: Apostolic Bible Institute, n.d.

Offiler, W.H. *God, and His Name.* 2nd ed. Seattle, WA: By the Author, 1932.

O'Malley, J. Steven. "Pietistic Influence on John Wesley: Wesley and Gerhard Tersteegen, *Wesleyan Theological Journal* 13/2 (Fall 1996): 48-70.

Ooton, L.R. *Concerning the Times and Seasons.* Tipton, IN: By the Author, 1969.

——. *Dimensions and Glory of Heavenly Jerusalem*. Tipton, IN: By the Author, 1966.

——. *God's Time Piece*. Tipton, IN: By the Author, 1967.

——. *Sermons from the Sermon on the Mount*. Tipton, IN: By the Author, 1970.

——. *The Sower the Seed and the Soil*. Tipton, IN: By the Author, 1973.

——. Interview, Tipton, IN, 17 May 1974.

——. *Truth in Love Songs*. Tipton, IN: By the Author, 1965.

——. *What Is Time?* Tipton, IN: By the Author, 1970.

——. "Our Organization," *Pentecostal Outlook* 1 (April 1932): 4.

Opperman, D.C.O. "Brother Bell Is on Both Sides of Fence," *The Blessed Truth* 4/18 (1 October 1919): 1-2.

Outler, Albert, Ed. *John Wesley*. New York: Oxford University Press, 1964.

Paddock, Ross P. Apostolic World Christian Fellowship Conference at Apostolic Temple, South Bend, IN: Interview, 16 May 1974.

Palmer, Phoebe. *Promise of the Father, or, A Neglected Specialty of the Last Days*. Boston: Henry V. Degen, 1885.

Parham, Charles F. *A Voice Crying in the Wilderness*. Reprinted in *The Sermons of Charles F. Parham*. Ed. Donald Dayton. New York: Garland, 1985.

Paterson, John. *God in Christ Jesus*. Montreal, Canada: By the Author, 1964.

——. *The Real Truth about Baptism in Jesus' Name*. Hazelwood, MO: Pentecostal Publishing House, 1953.

Payne, J.T. *What Manner of Man Is This*. Covington, GA: By the Author, n.d.

Peck, George B. "In His Name," *The Christian Alliance and Foreign Missionary Weekly*. 15 (14 August 1895): 102-03.

Pederson, John. *Israel – Its Life and Culture*. 2 vols. London: Oxford University Press for Geoffrey Cumberlege, 1926.

Pentecostal Churches of the Apostolic Faith Association, Inc. – Ministerial Record, Codified Rules and Minutes, 1957-1958. Indianapolis, IN: Christ Temple, 1959.

Pierson, A.T. "Jesus-Christ-Lord," *The Keswick Week, 1909*. Ed. Evan H. Hopkins. London: Marshall Brothers, 1909.

Pinson, M.M. "What Think Ye of Christ? Whose Son Is He? Matt. 22:42," *Weekly Evangel* 116 (20 November 1915): 3.

Pittenger, Norman. Ed. *Christ for Us Today*. London: SCM Press, 1968.

Podaras, William N. *The Mystery of God*. Gastonia, NC: Tabernacle of God, n.d.

——. *What Is the Bible Evidence of Receiving the Holy Ghost*. Gastonia, NC: Tabernacle of God, n.d.

Pugh, J.T. *For Preachers Only*. Hazelwood, MO: Pentecostal Publishing House, 1971.

——. *How to Receive the Holy Ghost*. St. Louis, MO: Pentecostal Publishing House, 1969.

Ramsey, Arthur Michael. *The Glory of God and the Transfiguration of Christ*. New York: Longmans, Green & Co., 1949.

Rattenbury, J. Ernest. *The Evangelical Doctrines of Churches Wesley's Hymns*, London: Epworth, 1942.

Read, R.R. *Water Baptism – The Formula and Its Meaning*. Christchurch, NZ: Assemblies of God Bookroom, n.d.

Reasoner, Victor Paul. "The American Holiness Movement's Paradigm Shift concerning Pentecost," *Wesleyan Theological Journal* 31/2 (Fall 1996): 132-46.

Reed, David A. "Aspects of the Origins of Oneness Pentecostalism," in Vinson Synan, ed. *Aspects of Pentecostal-Charismatic Origins*. Plainfield, NJ: Logos International, 1975.

——. "Oneness Pentecostalism," in Stanley M. Burgess, ed., *The New International Dictionary of Pentecostal and Charismatic Movements* (rev. ed.; Grand Rapids, MI: Zondervan, 2002), pp. 936-944.

——. "Oneness Pentecostalism: Problems and Possibilities for Pentecostal Theology," *Journal of Pentecostal Theology* 11 (October 1997): 73-93

——. "Origins and Development of the Theology of Oneness Pentecostalism in the United States" (Ph.D. diss., Boston University, 1978).

——. "Origins and Development of the Theology of Oneness Pentecostalism in the United States," *Pneuma* 1/1 (Spring 1979): 31-37.

——. "The 'New Issue' of 1914: New Revelation or Historical Development?" (Paper presented at the twenty-third annual meeting of the Society for Pentecostal Studies, Wheaton, IL, November 11, 1994).

Reeves, Kenneth V. *The Godhead*. Granite City, IL: By the Author, 1971.

——. *The Great Commission Re-Examined*. Granite City, IL: By the Author, 1970.

——. United Pentecostal Church, International, Hazelwood, MO: Interview, 12 June 1973.

Restoration of Original Name New Testament. Junction City, OR: Missionary Dispensary Bible Research, 1968.

Reynolds, Ralph V. *Cry of the Unborn: Understanding the Spiritual Birth Process*. Hood River, OR: Alpha Bible, 1991.

——. *Truth Shall Triumph – A Study of Pentecostal Doctrines*. St. Louis, MO: Pentecostal Publishing House, 1965.

Richardson, Cyril C. *The Doctrine of the Trinity*. New York: Abingdon, 1958.

Rider, James Donald. "The Theology of the 'Jesus Only' Movement" (Th.D. diss., Dallas Theological Seminary, 1956).

Riss, R.M. "Kenyon, Essek William," in Stanley M. Burgess, ed., *The New International Dictionary of Pentecostal and Charismatic Movements* (rev. ed. Grand Rapids, MI: Zondervan, 2002), pp. 819-20.

Robinson, F.A. ed. *Mother Whittemore's Records of Modern Miracles*. Toronto, Canada: Missions of Biblical Education, n.d.

Robinson, James M. & John B. Cobb, eds. *Theology as History*, vol. III of *New Frontiers in Theology*. New York: Harper & Row, 1967.

Rowe, G.B. *Reincarnation of Adam as Jesus Christ, Or Adam, Then and Now*. South Bend, IN: Apostolic Publishing Association, n.d.

Sabin, Robert. Apostolic Bible Institute, St. Paul, MN: Interview, 20 May 1974.

——. Oneness-Trinitarian Debate with James White, 1999. http://www.aomin.org/BriefHistoryAO.html.

Sandall, Robert. *The History of the Salvation Army*, vol. I, *1865-1878*. London: Thomas Nelson, 1947.

Sandeen, Ernest R. *The Roots of Fundamentalism – British and American Millenarianism – 1800-1930*. Chicago, IL: University of Chicago Press, 1970.

Sawyer, Thomas J. *Who Is Our God? The Son or the Father? A Review of Rev. Henry Ward Beecher*. New York: Thatcher & Hutchinson, 1859.

Schoeps, Hans-Joachim. *Jewish Christianity – Factional Disputes in the Early Church*. Trans. Douglas R.A. Hare. Philadelphia: Fortress, 1969.

Sellers, R.V. *Two Ancient Christologies – A Study in the Schools of Alexandria and Antioch in the Early History of Christian Doctrine*. London: SPCK, 1940.

Seymour, William J. "Fire Falling at Hermon," *The Apostolic Faith* 1/1 (September 1906): 3.

Simmons, Dale H., "'I Love You but I Just Can't Marry You': E.W. Kenyon and the Pentecostal Movement." Paper presented at the Twenty-fifth Annual Meeting of the Society for Pentecostal Studies, Toronto, March 9, 1996.

——. *E.W. Kenyon and the Post-Bellum Pursuit of Peace, Power and Plenty*. Metuchen, NJ: Scarecrow, 1996.

Simpson, A.B. *The Gospel of Matthew*. Christ in the Bible, 13 & 14. Harrisburg, PA: Christian Publications, n.d.

——. *The Christ of the Forty Days*. New York: Christian Alliance, n.d.

——. *Echoes of the New Creation*. New York: Christian Alliance, 1903.

——. *The Four-Fold Gospel*. New York: Christian Alliance, 1890.

——. *The Holy Spirit or Power from on High*. 2 vols. Harrisburg, PA: Christian Publications, n.d.

——. *In Heavenly Places*. New York: Christian Alliance, 1892.

——. *The Names of Jesus*. New York: Christian Alliance, 1892.

——. *Songs of the Spirit*. New York: Christian Alliance, 1920.

——. *Wholly Sanctified*. Harrisburg, PA: Christian Publications, 1925.

Smail, Thomas A. *Reflected Glory – The Spirit in Christ and Christians*. Grand Rapids, MI: Eerdmans, 1975.

Small, Franklin. *A Synopsis of the Name and Deity of Christ*. Winnipeg, Canada: Zion Apostolic Church, n.d.

——. *Living Waters – A Sure Guide for Your Faith*. Winnipeg, Canada: Columbia Press, Ltd., n.d.

——. "Theological World Faces Reconstruction," *Living Waters* 1 (January 1930): 3-5.

——. *Zion Church Question Box – Christ's Son-ship and Godlikeness Contrasted*. Winnipeg, Canada: Zion Apostolic Church, n.d.

Smith, Francis. Telephone Interview from Akron, OH, 1 October 1977.

Smith, F.L. *What Every Saint Should Know*. East Orange, NJ: Lutho, n.d.

Smith, Hannah Whitall. *The Christian's Secret of a Happy Life*. new and enl. ed. New York: Fleming H. Revell, 1888.

Smith, H. Sheldon, Robert T. Handy, & Lefferts A. Loetscher. *American Christianity: A Historical Interpretation with Representative Documents*, vol. II: *1820-1960*. New York: Charles Scribner's Sons, 1963.

Smith, Taylor. "The Name above Every Name," *The Keswick Week, 1920*. Ed. Evan H. Hopkins (London: Marshall Brothers, 1920): 23.

Smith, Timothy. *Revivalism and Social Reform in Mid-Nineteenth-Century America*. New York: Abingdon, 1957.

Solbrekken, Max. *What the Bible Teaches about Water Baptism*. White Rock, BC, Canada: Solbrekkan Evangelistic Association, 1968.

Spener, Philip Jacob. *Pia Desideria.* Trans. & ed. Theodore G. Tappert. Seminar Editions, Gen. Ed. Theodore G. Tappert. Philadelphia: Fortress, 1964.

Spinks, Bryan. "Calvin's Baptismal Theology and the Making of the Strasbourg and Genevan Baptismal Liturgies 1540 and 1542," *Scottish Journal of Theology* 48/1 (1995): 55-78.

Springfield, Melvin R. *Jesus the Almighty.* 2nd ed. Portland, OR: Parry Mail Advertising Service, 1972.

Stairs, Philip D. "The Problem of the Formula Used with Water Baptism" (M.A. thesis, Winona Lake School of Theology, 1968).

Stark, Rodney & William Sims Bainbridge, "Of Churches, Sects, and Cults: Preliminary Concepts for a Theory of Religious Movements," *Journal for the Scientific Study of Religion* 18/2 (1979): 117-131.

Stevenson, Herbert F. ed. *Keswick's Authentic Voices – Sixty-Five Dynamic Addresses Delivered at the Keswick Convention, 1875-1957.* Grand Rapids, MI: Zondervan, 1959.

Stoeffler F. Ernest. *German Pietism during the Eighteenth Century.* Leiden: E.J. Brill, 1973.

——. *The Rise of Evangelical Pietism.* Studies in the History of Religions, 9. Leiden: E.J. Brill, 1965.

Stokes, G.T. *The Acts of the Apostles.* The Expositor's Bible, 17. New York: A.C. Armstrong, 1902-1908.

Streitferdt, Thomas. *The Word Became Flesh.* Orange, NJ: Lutho, 1961.

Strickland, William C. "The Meaning of the Name of God in Biblical Theology" (Th.D. diss., Southern Bapist Theological Seminary, 1953).

Stroud, G.C. "By Way of Explanation Concerning the-Movement Formulated at Houston, Texas," *Pentecostal Witness* 2 (1 February 1926): 1-2.

Sunday School Times, The 52 (5 March 1910): 118.

Sweet, William Warren. *Revivalism in America: Its Origin, Growth and Decline.* New York: Scribner's, 1944.

Symposium on Oneness Pentecostalism, 1988 and 1990. Hazelwood, MO: Word Aflame Press, 1990.

Synan, Vinson. ed. *Aspects of Pentecostal-Charismatic Origins.* Plainfield, NJ: Logos International, 1975.

——. "The Classical Pentecostals," *New Covenant* 2 (May 1973): 7-10, 27.

——. *The Holiness-Pentecostal Tradition: Charismatic Movements in the Twentieth Century.* Grand Rapids, MI: Eerdmans, 1971, 1997.

Taylor, John V. *The Go-Between God – The Holy Spirit and the Christian Mission.* Philadelphia: Fortress, 1973.

"The Holy Ghost a Person," *Weekly Evangel* 117 (27 November 1915): 2.

"The Missionary Meeting," *The Keswick Week, 1895.* Evan H. Hopkins, ed. London: Marshall Brothers, 1895.

"The St. Louis Conference," *Pentecostal Outlook* 10 (January 1932): 2-3, 14.

Tinney, James S. "The Significance of Race in the Rise and Development of the Apostolic Pentecostal Movement." Paper delivered at the First Pentecostal Symposium on Aspects of the Oneness Pentecostal Movement, Harvard Divinity School (July 1994).

Tobin, R.F. *The Principles of the Doctrine of Christ.* Indianapolis, IN: Christ Temple, 1948.

Torrey, Reuben A. *The Baptism with the Holy Spirit*. Minneapolis, MN: Bethany
Fellowship, n.d.

——. *What the Bible Teaches*. New York: Fleming H. Revell, 1898.

"Unconventional Religious Sects Still Active in Appalachia," *The Providence
Journal* (19 August 1973), sec. B, p. 7.

"Unity Conference," *Pentecostal Witness* 7 (September 1931): 13.

Urshan, Andrew D. *The Almighty God in the Lord Jesus Christ*. Los Angeles: By
the Author, 1919; reprint ed. Portland, OR: Apostolic Book Corner, n.d.

——. *Apostolic Faith Doctrine of the New Birth*. By the Author, n.d.; reprint ed.
Portland, OR: Apostolic Book Corner, n.d.

——. "Confession of Faith," *Weekly Evangel* 236 and 237 (20 April 1918): 13.

——. *The Doctrine of the New Birth or the Perfect Way to Eternal Life*. Cochrane,
WI: Witness of God, 1921.

——. "Editorial," *Witness of God* 2 (July 1921): 1-2.

——. "First and Second Resurrections," *Pentecostal Outlook* 10 (April 1941): 3,
12.

——. "The Blessed Three-ness of the Godhead Slightly Revealed in Nature and
Perfectly Demonstrated and Proved in the Person and Name of Our Lord
Jesus Christ," *Witness of God* 4 (July 1923): 2-4.

——. "The Blessed Trinity of God Revealed in Nature and Demonstrated or
Personified in Jesus Christ Our Lord," *Pentecostal Witness* 3 (1 July 1927):
2-3.

——. "The Divinity of Jesus Christ, Or the Absolute Deity of the Son of God
according to the Old and New Testament" *Pentecostal Witness* 3 (1 April
1927): 2.

——. "The Doctrine of the Trinity and the Divinity of Jesus Christ," *Pentecostal
Witness* 3 (December 1926): 1-2.

——. "The Holy Spirit's Relationship," *Pentecostal Herald* 38 (December 1963):
3.

——. *The Life Story of Andrew Bar David Urshan: An Autobiography*. Oneness
Pentecostal Pioneer Series. Stockton, CA: WABC Press, 1967.

——. "The Name of God," *Pentecostal Outlook* 9 (January 1940): 4-5, 13.

——. "The New Birth and the Kingdom of God," *Witness of God* 2 (September
1921): 1.

——. "The New Light or the More Light," *Witness of God* 1 (September 1920):
2.

——. "The Sevenfold Deity of Christ and the Divine Seven," *Witness of God* 1
(June 1920): 1-14.

——. "The Trinity," *Witness of God* 1 (May-June 1920): 12.

——. "Twenty-Seven Questions and Answers on the New Birth," *Pentecostal
Outlook* 12 (August 1943): 8-11, 13.

——. "Why I Was Baptized in the Name, Lord Jesus Christ" *The Voice of Calvary
Tabernacle* 13 (April 1957): 9-13.

Urshan, Nathaniel A. *Calvary Tabernacle*. Indianapolis, IN: Interview, 23 May
1973.

——. *Consider Him – David's Son and David's Lord*. St. Louis, MO: Pentecostal
Publishing House, n.d.

——. *These Men Are Not Drunk!* St. Louis, MO: Pentecostal Publishing House, n.d.

Vouga, Oscar, *Our Gospel Message*. St. Louis, MO: Pentecostal Publishing House, n.d.

Wacker, Grant *Heaven Below: Early Pentecostals and American Culture*. Cambridge, MA: Harvard University Press, 2001.

——. "The Functions of Faith in Primitive Pentecostalism," *Harvard Theological Review* 77/3-4 (July/October, 1984): 353-75

——. "Playing for Keeps: The Primitivist Impulse in Early Pentecostalism," in R.T. Hughes, ed. *The American Quest for the Primitive Church*. Urbana, IL: University of Illinois Press, 1988, pp. 196-219.

Walkem, Charles W. *The Jesus Only Theory – A Brief Analysis of the Trinity*. Los Angeles: The Church Press, n.d.

Ward, Helen M. *The Truth about the Godhead*. Detroit, MI: Halo, 1968.

Watson, Philip S., ed. *The Message of the Wesleys – A Reader of Instruction and Devotion*. New York: Macmillan, 1964.

Webb-Peploe, Prebendary. "Jesus Christ, Lord," *The Keswick Week, 1910*. Ed. Evan H. Hopkins. London: Marshall Brothers, 1910.

Weborg, C. John. "Pietism: Theology in Service of Living toward God," Donald W. Dayton & Robert K. Johnston, eds. *The Variety of American Evangelicalism*. Downers Grove, IL: InterVarsity Press, 1991, pp. 161-83.

Weeks, Robert D. *Jehovah-Jesus: The Oneness of God; The True Trinity*. New York: Dodd, Mead & Co., 1876.

——. *Jehovah-Jesus – The Supreme God: Son of God, Son of Man*. Ed. C. Haskell Yadon. Twin Falls, ID: By the Editor, 1952.

Welch, Claude. *In This Name – The Doctrine of the Trinity in Contemporary Theology*. New York: Charles Scribner's Sons, 1952.

——. *Protestant Thought in the 19th Century*, vol. I, *1700-1870*. New Haven, CT: Yale University Press, 1972.

Wesley, John. "The Almost Christian," *The Bicentennial Edition of the Works of John Wesley*. Vol. I. Albert Outler, ed. Nashville: Abingdon, 1984.

Whale, J.S. *Christian Doctrine*. Cambridge: Cambridge University Press, 1963.

What We Believe and Teach – Articles of Faith of the United Pentecostal Church. St. Louis, MO: Pentecostal Publishing House, n.d.

Wigle, E. *Prevailing Prayer or The Secret of Soul Winning*. Grand Rapids, MI: Stanton Printing Co., 1891.

Williams, J. Rodman. Episcopal Charismatic Conference, Dallas, TX: Interview, 2 February 1973.

Williams, O.W. *What Do You Think?* Houston, TX: By the Author, n.d.

Williams, Smallwood E. *Significant Sermons*. Washington D.C.: The Bible Way Church, 1970.

Wilson, Bryan R. *Sects and Society – A Sociological Study of the Elim Tabernacle, Christian Science, and Christadelphianism*. Berkeley, CA: University of California Press, 1961.

Wilson, George. "The Alpha and the Omega of the Blessed Life," *The Keswick Week, 1898*. Ed. Evan H. Hopkins (London: Marshall Brothers, 1898): 122.

Wings of Life. Texarkana, TX: Privately Published, n.d.

Winters, Elvira. Telephone Interview, 9 February 1996.

Witherspoon, W.T. "Official Board Meeting," *Pentecostal Outlook* 1 (April 1932): 12.

Womack, David A. *The Wellsprings of the Pentecostal Movement*. Springfield, MO: Gospel Publishing House, 1968.

"Wonderful Miracles Wrought in Jesus' Name," *The Latter Rain Evangel* (July 1913): 2-4.

Woo, Thomas Matthew. "The Phrase 'In Jesus' Name As Used in Acts in Relation to the Old Testament Background and New Testament Usage" (M.Th. thesis, Southern Baptist Theological Seminary, 1954).

Yong, Amos. "Oneness and Trinity: The Theological and Ecumenical Implications of Creation *Ex Nihilo* for an Intra-Pentecostal Dispute," *Pneuma* 19/1 (1997): 81-107.

Young, Elzie. Apostolic World Christian Fellowship Conference at Apostolic Temple, South Bend, IN: Interview, 15 May 1974.

Zimmerman, Thomas F. Assemblies of God Headquarters, Springfield, MO: Interview, 22 June 1973.

Zinzendorf, Nicholaus Ludwig Count von. *Nine Public Lectures on Important Subjects in Religion*. Trans. & ed. George W. Forell. Iowa City, IA: University of Iowa Press, 1973.

Index of Authors and Names

Aberhart, William 66
Akers, E.F. 216
Allchin, A.M. 15
Allison, C. FitzSimons 353
Anderson, Ray S. 33, 34
Anderson, Robert Mapes 77,
    78, 80, 83, 97, 98, 110,
    113, 118, 122, 124, 209,
    211, 340, 342
Argue, A.H. 85, 94, 189
Armstrong, Edward 171
Astor, John Jacob 64
Aulén, Gustaf 33
Bainbridge, Harriette B. 41
Bainbridge, William S. 9, 108
Banks, Robert 356
Barnes, Mother Mary 145
Barrett, David 339
Barrett, T.B. 81
Bartleman, Frank 109, 127
Barth, Karl 321, 353
Bassett, Paul Merritt 25, 118
Bauckham, Richard 236, 240,
    253
Baxter, Richard 15
Beal, Myrtle 324
Beasley-Murray, G.R. 314,
    315
Becton, Cleveland M. 292
Beecher, Henry Ward 34, 36

Beisner, E. Calvin 230, 314,
    338, 344
Bell, E.N. 85, 95, 96, 143,
    144, 146-49, 186, 209-11,
    324, 339,
Bengal, John Albert 20
Bernard, David K. 191, 247,
    251, 252, 254, 262, 264,
    269, 271, 275, 276, 289,
    293, 299-301, 311, 314-
    16, 319, 324, 327, 332,
    354, 355
Bethune-Baker, J.F. 266
Bietenhard, Hans 239, 308
Bjorch,Walter 265
Bjornstad, James 265
Bloesch, Donald G. 11
Bloom, Anthony 39
Blumhardt, Christoph 12
Blumhardt, Johann 12
Blumhofer, Edith 77, 78, 84,
    95, 97, 100, 340
Boardman, William 121
Booth-Clibborn, William 110,
    131-33, 212
Bousset, Wilhelm 239, 243
Bowald, Mark xi
Boyd, Gregory 5, 230, 317,
    338, 344, 345
Branham, William (Branha-
    mites) 222

Brickey, J.C. 143, 144, 156
Brown, Dale 10, 11, 13, 20,
    25, 202
Brown, E. Kent x
Brown, Harold O.J. 266, 267,
    269, 345, 346
Brown, William Adams 51
Bruce, Dickson D. 35
Brumback, Carl 1, 67, 96,
    139, 142, 145, 146, 151,
    157, 162, 163, 164, 169,
    170-72, 201, 261, 265,
    304, 343, 361
Bruner, Frederick Dale 321,
    336
Brunner, Emil 236, 242, 247,
    250, 281, 305, 306, 356
Bundy, David x, 5, 11, 20
Bunyan, John 15
Burgess, Stanley M. 11, 102,
    232
Burr, Murray 220
Caird, G.B. 253, 285
Calvin, John (Calvinist) 25,
    52, 71, 321
Campbell, Alexander (Camp-
    bellite) 71, 319
Carmichael, Miss Wilson 40
Chapman, Mark D. 270
Chappell, Frederick L. 46,
    248
Chappell, Paul G. 121
Childs, Brevard 236
Chouraqui, André 241
Clanton, Arthur L. x, 1, 139,
    140, 151, 152, 208, 209,
    212-19
Clarke, Adam 186, 195, 198,
    318, 354, 363
Clarke, William Newton 52
Clayton, Allen 94, 98, 106

Clement 304
Collins, A.P. 159
Collins, David 291
Collins, Kenneth 11, 13, 27,
    28
Collins, Margaret Tacke 5
Congar, Yves 241
Cook, Glenn A. 110, 117,
    118, 123, 126, 142, 143,
    145, 148, 168, 324
Cragg, Gerald R. 10, 28
Crawford, Florence 86, 96,
    138
Crayne, Richard 222
Crouch, A.F. 172
Cullmann, Oscar 306
Cunningham, Robert x, 164
Curts, F.E. 283, 330
Daniélou, Jean 233, 235, 236,
    239-41, 243, 244, 292
Darby, J. Nelson 42, 102
Davies, Horton 72
Davis, Carro 172
Davis, T.C. 212
Dawson, Collins x
Dayton, Donald x, 3, 9, 11,
    18, 20, 22, 24, 25, 29, 30,
    32, 38, 42, 68, 77, 78, 98,
    112, 115, 120, 130, 133
Dearing, John H. ix, 310
Del Colle, Ralph x, 231, 272,
    305, 338, 346, 350, 351,
    353, 355
Denny, Frank 138, 139
Dieter, Melvin 18, 19, 29
Dillenberger, John 65
Dix, Dom Gregory 236
Dodd, C.H. 235
Dowie, Alexander 79, 85, 95
Dugas, Paul D. 145

Dunn, James D.G. 312, 313, 322

Durham, Bessie Mae 100

Durham, William H. 2-4, 28, 77, 79, 83-107

Edwards, Jonathan 17

Ewart, Frank J. 1-3, 23, 32, 34, 57, 58, 62, 63, 66, 67, 83, 96, 97, 104, 105, 110, 117, 118, 122, 123, 126-28, 131, 133, 136, 138-46, 148, 150, 155-57, 160, 164, 168, 169, 173, 175, 176, 178-80, 185, 189, 190-92, 196, 197, 202, 204, 205, 208, 209, 211, 219, 229, 247-52, 254-56, 258, 262, 267, 275-78, 280-82, 284, 286, 287, 296, 298, 299, 302, 309, 315, 316, 318, 320, 323, 331-35, 342, 352, 355, 356

Farrow, George 167

Farrow, Lucy 80

Faupel, D. William x, 3, 18, 77, 78, 83-85, 87, 94-100, 106, 109, 110, 112-16, 118, 119, 121, 129, 132, 134, 136-38, 324, 341

Fauss, Oliver F. 151, 153-55, 164, 170, 174-77, 179, 185, 188, 215, 309, 311

Fénelon, François 25

Finney, Charles G. 18, 25, 29, 35, 50, 64

Fisher, Elmer 95, 142, 143

Fitch, Theodore 258, 259, 263, 275, 283, 285, 289, 294, 301, 304

Fletcher, John 29

Flower, J. Roswell 95, 139, 145, 148, 151, 157, 158, 159, 161, 163, 169, 349

Forell, George W. 14

Foster, Fred J. 67, 139, 144, 145, 172, 173, 208, 209, 212, 214

Fox-Parham, Mrs. Charles 116

Francke, August H. 12, 13

Frazee, J.J. 96

French, Talmadge L. 146, 219, 221, 339, 340, 342, 343

Frodsham, Stanley H. 137, 163, 164

Fudge, Thomas 5, 151, 201, 218-21, 247, 311, 317, 319

Gaebelein, Arno C. 41, 42, 46-48, 55, 56, 59, 60, 61, 63, 73

Gaxiola, Manuel x, 340, 350

Gentile, Ernest B. 278, 325

Gerloff, Roswith I.H. x, 4, 6, 82, 340

Gezahagne, Teklemariam 292, 293

Gibson, John Monro 36, 37, 46-51, 54-56, 58, 61, 153, 181, 187, 210, 353-54, 363

Gill, Jeffrey x

Gill, Kenneth x, 4, 227, 229, 231, 340, 350

Gillespie, Bernie x, 317

Golder, Morris E. x, 145, 208, 209, 211-13, 216, 217, 254, 259, 264, 282, 283, 290, 294, 328, 330

Goodwin, Lloyd L. 325, 326

Gordon, A.J. 42, 46, 60, 64, 73, 248

Gordon, George A. 51

Goss, Ethel E. 94

Goss, Howard A. ix, 67, 94, 95, 97, 116, 144, 149, 156, 162, 164, 170, 171, 176-77, 207, 212, 217, 220, 260, 338

Gray, David 168, 191, 197

Grimes, Samuel 216

Grimes, Mrs. S.K. 246

Gruits, Patricia Beall 278, 324, 325

Gunstone, John 323

Gunton, Colin 270

Guyon, Madame 25

Haenchen, Ernst 332

Hall, J.L. 210, 311, 314, 327, 330,

Hall, William Phillips 2, 45-46, 57-58, 62, 66, 67, 73, 178, 193, 196, 277-78, 355, 363

Hancock, S.N. 217, 290-91

Hanby, S.R. 294

Handy, Robert 51

Hardy, Clarence 190

Harford-Battersby, Canon 38

Harnack, Adolf 243

Harrison, Everett F. 42

Hartman, Lars 320, 321

Haywood, Garfield T. 3-5, 9, 96, 110, 111, 119, 126-28, 131, 133, 142, 145, 147, 159, 164, 168, 169, 175, 177, 179, 182, 186-89, 195, 197-205, 208, 209, 211-13, 217, 219, 221, 228, 229, 248, 250, 251, 254, 258, 260, 265,

274, 276, 283, 286, 287-90, 301, 308, 316, 317-19, 322, 326, 328-30, 333, 342, 352, 358

Hedding, Elijah 37, 47, 60, 294

Hexham, Irving 9

Hippolytus 304

Hobbs, Clifford E. 254, 257, 259, 275, 282, 283, 285-88, 297, 301, 304, 318, 326, 327, 334

Hodges, H.A. 15

Hodgson, Leonard 259, 270

Hogman, Jaeko 9

Hollenweger, Walter J. 36, 53, 175, 324

Holliday, Robert K. 222

Hopkins, Evan H. 38, 40, 46, 59, 61

Howell, Joseph 82

Hunter, Harold D. x, 26, 222, 305

Huntington, Frederic D. 51

Hurtado, Larry 321

Hutchinson, Cyril 34, 66

Ignatius 304

Iverson, Emil L. 103

Jacques, Earl ix

Jacob, Edmond 247

Jacobsen, Douglas 5, 9, 12, 77, 103, 104, 108, 120

Jamieson, S.A. 163

Jensen, G.K. 257, 301

Johnson, Benton 108

Johnson, S.C. 301, 302

Johnston, Robert K. 9, 25

Jones, Charles E. x, 6

Jones, James W. x

Jones, Sam P. 20, 21

Kaufman, Gordon D. 270, 271
Kelly, Vonelle 292, 293
Kelly, J.N.D. 237, 253, 265, 266, 303, 304
Kenyon, Essek W. 21, 22, 24, 28, 32, 41, 45, 46, 50, 57, 59, 60, 65, 66, 68, 77, 100-05, 119, 134, 195, 201, 332
Kerr, D.W. 83, 111, 163, 343, 349
Kevan, Ernest F. 42, 71
Kidson, W.E. x, 213-15, 218, 220, 229, 297, 317
Kilgore, Claude P. 214
Killam, Gil 230
King, J.H. 77
King, "Sister" 127
Kittel, Gerhard 239, 308
Kolenda, E.J. 277, 318
Knapp, Martin Wells 41, 80
Krebs, Stanley L. 187
LeFleur, R.L. 176
Lake, John G. 338
Lampe, G.W.H. 244, 309
Larden, Robert A. 23, 63, 138, 139, 143-45, 147, 170, 172, 211
Lawrence, B.F. 201
Lawson, R.C. 217
Lederle, H.I. 323
Leonard, T.K. 163
Lewis, A.W. 216
Lie, Geir x, 101, 102, 105
Lindbeck, George 347-52, 355, 361
Lindquist, F.J. 261
Longenecker, Richard 233, 234, 238-40, 357
Lum, N. Clara 86

Luther, Martin 11, 65
Ma, Wonsuk x
Macchia, Frank x, 12
MacRae, George 335
MacRobert, Ian 86
Magee, Gordon x, 260, 262, 264, 281, 282, 284-88, 293, 294, 296-99, 301
Mahan, Asa 18, 30, 42, 50
Marsden, George M. 18, 34, 37, 114
Mason, C.H. 97, 190
McAlister, Robert E. 1, 3, 94-96, 104, 105, 110, 126, 138, 139, 140-42, 144, 147, 148, 168, 170, 174, 175, 177, 310, 323, 324, 342, 356
McClain, S.C. 173, 189
McConnell, Daniel Ray 102
McDonnell, Kilian 359
McGee, Gary 11, 233
McLoughlin, William 35
McKnight, C. Joe 324, 325
McPherson, Aimee Semple 38, 39, 85
Menzies, Robert 312, 358
Menzies, William x, 30, 31, 37, 38, 42, 142, 158, 159, 163, 265, 324, 344
Miller, Albert 108, 109
Miller, John 47, 48, 52, 54, 159
Miller, Luke 262
Miller, Perry 60, 66, 70, 71, 77
Miyakawa, T. Scott 17
Montague, George 359
Moody, Dale 237, 238, 241
Moody, D.L. 30
Moody, W.E. 128

Moore, Jennie Evans 86
Morgan, G.L. 84, 100
Morgan, John 29
Morse, Harry 140
Murray, Andrew 64, 220
Myland, D. Wesley 78, 119
Needham, George C. 61
Nelson, Douglas J. 80, 86, 98,
     164
Nelson, J. Robert ix
Nichols, John T. 39
Niebuhr, H. Richard 18, 19,
     35, 36, 71, 153, 171
Nienkirchen, Charles W. 63
Niles, D. Preman 235
Norris, David S. 235
Norris, S.G. x, 218, 254, 259,
     260, 282-85, 287, 295,
     299, 302, 330
Offiler, W.H. 230, 278, 324,
     325
O'Malley, J. Steven 40
Ooton, L.R. x, 217, 218, 228,
     275, 294
Opperman, D.C.O. 164, 207,
     208
Outler, Albert 15, 16, 26
Ozman, Agnez N. 80
Paddock, Ross P. 218
Palmer, Phoebe 21, 37, 79,
     115, 121-23, 129, 130-32,
     134, 136, 192
Pannenberg, Wolfhart 252
Parham, Charles 22, 67, 68,
     79, 80, 81, 85, 86, 92, 95,
     105, 114-16, 120-27, 130,
     131, 133, 134, 144, 149,
     171, 172, 197, 331, 338,
     355, 356
Parker, Theodore 34

Paterson, John 36, 250, 255,
     257, 259, 262, 267-69,
     275-77, 282, 285-87,
     293-95, 297, 298, 300,
     301, 304, 315, 316, 318,
     320, 332
Peck, George B. 63, 64, 65
Pedersen, John 61
Perkins, William 15
Pethrus, Lewi 108
Pickard, Patricia x
Pierson, A.T. 46
Pinson, M.M. 95, 137, 162
Poewe, Karla 9
Prestige, G.L. 266
Pridgeon, Charles H. 197
Pryor, Hattie E. 184
Pugh, J.T. 315
Rader, Paul 218
Rahner, Karl 247, 270
Ramsey, Michael 237, 238,
     242, 283
Rattenbury, J. Ernest 16
Raudzsus, Juanita x
Reasoner, Victor 28, 29
Reed, David A. 102, 227, 232
Reeves, Kenneth x, 253-56,
     258-60, 262, 264, 267,
     268, 275, 276, 282, 283,
     285, 286, 293-95, 297,
     302, 319, 320, 322, 327,
     328, 354
Reynolds, Ralph 254, 262,
     276, 284, 287, 294, 304,
     308, 310, 312, 313, 315,
     316, 320, 327-30
Richardson, Cyril C. 272
Rider, James D. 4
Riss, R.M. 102, 104
Ritschl, Albrecht 11
Robeck, Cecil M. 140

Roberts, L.V. 145, 150, 157, 164
Roberts, Mark x
Robinson, F.A. 41, 252
Rogers, H.G. 150, 156, 164, 207
Rowe, David 207
Rowe, G.B. 291, 292
Rowe, William G. x,
Rowe, Worthy 207
Ruotsalainen, Paavo 9
Sabellius (Sabellian, Sabellianism) 180, 182, 230, 247, 265-68, 342-45, 349, 352-54
Sabin, Robert x, 52, 317
Sandall, Robert 40, 41
Sandeen, Ernest R. 37
Sandford, Frank W. 116
Sawyer, Thomas J. 34
Schaepe, John G. 1, 139, 140, 141
Schleiermacher, Friedrich 231, 346
Schoeps, Hans-Joachim 236, 241-43
Scofield, C.I. 24, 42
Scott, Jr, Daniel L. 319
Scott, H.O. 199
Scott, R.J. 137, 138
Seitz, Christopher 305
Sellers, R.V. 242
Seymour, William J. 22, 23, 79, 80, 81, 85, 86, 95, 96, 130, 131, 138
Shelton, S. McDowell 302
Sibbes, Richard 15
Simmons, Dale H. 21, 22, 24, 77, 84, 101-05, 119, 134
Simpson, Albert B. 30, 31, 38, 39, 41, 42, 44, 46, 48, 50,

56, 57, 59, 60, 62, 63, 65, 77, 79
Smail, Thomas 335, 336
Small, Franklin 3, 23, 36, 37, 40, 63, 94, 106, 143, 144, 147, 168-70, 173, 174, 178-82, 185, 187, 188, 190, 191, 193-97, 199, 208, 211, 212, 218, 219, 230, 262, 273, 277, 280, 341, 352
Smith, Hannah Whitall 40
Smith, Mabel 84
Smith, Francis 221
Smith, Taylor 61, 62
Smith, Timothy 11, 51
Spener, Philip Jacob 12, 13
Spinks, Bryan 321
Spittler, Russell ix, 2
Springfield, Melvin R. 254, 256, 257, 262, 275, 286, 287, 294, 295, 297, 299
Spurgeon, Charles 62
Stairs, Philip D. x, 243
Stark, Rodney 9, 108
Stevenson, Herbert F. 38
Stoeffler, F. Ernest 10, 11, 12, 13
Straton, Roach 194
Streitferdt, Thomas 254, 264, 265, 268, 269, 282, 295, 297, 299, 301
Strickland, William C. 235
Stroud, G.C. 214
Studd, George 148
Sullivan, Francis 323
Sunday, Billy 20, 35
Suurmond, Jean-Jacques 81, 82
Sweet, William Warren 18, 34
Sykes, Dr. 1, 138, 139

Synan, Vinson ix, 2, 29, 37, 39, 78, 80, 81, 86, 102, 142, 145, 209, 211, 213, 232

Taylor, Ken x, 61, 62

Terry, Neely 80

Tersteegen, Gerhard 39, 40

Tertullian 265, 266, 304

Thomas, J. Christopher xi

Thorsen, Donald A.D. 17

Tinney, James S. x, 82

Tobin, R.F. 318

Tomlinson, A.J. 124

Torrance, James 270

Torrey, Reuben A. 30, 49, 50, 64, 127

Turner, Max 312, 313, 322, 358

Tyson, James A. 83, 96

Tyson, James L. 212, 213

Urshan, Andrew D. 3, 5, 6, 46, 67, 83, 85, 144, 168, 169-71, 175-82, 185-87, 189-91, 195, 197, 198, 201-05, 209-11, 213, 218, 228, 248, 250, 251, 255, 258, 259, 261-64, 267, 273, 276, 280, 282, 284, 288, 289, 295, 299, 315, 316, 318, 320, 326, 328, 329, 333, 334, 353, 358, 362

Urshan, Nathaniel A. x, 53, 248, 259, 260, 262, 264, 280, 285, 287, 288, 290, 301

Van Deusen-Hunsinger, Deborah 227

Vouga, Oscar 254, 258, 320, 332

Wacker, Grant x, 5, 20, 21, 78, 84, 113, 119, 130, 141

Walkem, Charles W. 262

Watson, George D. 118

Watson, Philip S. 16

Weborg, C. John 9, 11, 13

Webster, John 227

Weeks, Robert D. 47, 52-54, 73, 289, 290

Welch, J.W. 147, 162

Welch, Claude 15, 32, 43, 270

Wesley, Charles 16

Wesley, John 10, 11, 13

Westfield, Winifred 118, 131

Whale, J.S. 266

White, Charles E. 121, 129, 130, 132, 134, 146

Whitmore, Bessie Mae 84

Wigle, Evangelist 64

Williams, J. Rodman 66

Williams, O.W. 322

Williams, Smallwood E. x

Wilson, Bryan 9

Wilson, George 38

Winters, Elvira 141, 191, 197

Witrherspoon, A.W. 191

Witherspoon, W.T. 191, 216, 218, 310-12

Woodworth-Etter, Maria 109, 137, 139

Womack, David A. 173

Yadon, C. Haskell 53, 73, 220, 289, 290, 304

Yong, Amos x, 272

Young, Elzie 291

Zinzendorf, Nicholaus L. 12, 14, 31

Zimmerli, Walter 252

Zimmerman, Thomas F. 189, 344

Index of Biblical References

OLD TESTAMENT

Genesis
1:1   286
1:26   181, 261
3:22   261

Exodus
3:13-15   248
3:14   47, 58, 252
33:17-18   238
33:18-19   247
40:34   237
10:35-36   237

Deuteronomy
6:4   236, 252, 280
12:5   11, 21 238

1 Kings
8:27-29   237

Psalms
54:1   244

Isaiah
9:6   286
28:16   56

Jeremiah
31:22   138, 147

Zechariah
14:9   251

NEW TESTAMENT

Matthew
1:21   239, 175, 275, 276
1:23   55
1:21-25   239
10:22   333
16:19   326
26: 61-65   241
27:46   298
28:19   243, 249, 276,
            277, 281, 306

Luke
18:38   39

John
1:1   286
1:14   241, 282
3:5   191, 195, 198,
            199, 310, 312, 319, 322,
            326, 358
3:16   313, 336
4:24   254
5:43   275, 276
14:10   282
14:13-14   239
15:16   239

16:23, 26   239
14:26   276, 332
14:28   293
16:14–15   322
17:5   286
17:17, 21, 22   229

Acts
2:2   361
2:21   239
2:38   ix, 2, 3, 5, 63, 65,
   66, 78, 92, 113, 121, 122,
   123, 126, 127, 128, 131,
   132, 133, 123, 135, 139,
   143, 144, 150, 154, 168,
   169, 174, 175, 183, 188,
   189, 190, 191, 192, 193,
   194, 195, 196, 197, 198,
   199, 200, 201, 202, 203,
   205, 210, 214, 218, 219,
   220, 223, 229, 248, 277,
   309, 310, 311, 312, 313,
   317, 318, 319, 323, 326,
   329, 330, 335, 336, 346,
   350, 352, 357, 358, 362
4:7   244
4:12   276, 308, 327, 328
4:18   204
5:28   204, 244
8:35   42
9:20   42
15:14   329, 335
15:17   335
17:18   42
24:14   342

Romans
6:4   90, 92, 124, 201,
   309, 310, 362
6:4–6   90
8:11   329

10:12   239

1 Corinthians
12:3   351
15:28   300, 302, 303

2 Corinthians
3:8   351
4:6   284, 351
4:10   283

Ephesians
4:3   83
4:5   188
4:13   83

Philippians
2:7   283
2:9–11   154, 239, 276,
   306

Colossians
1:15   255
1:19   241, 281
1:27   332
2:8–9   47
2:9   48, 58, 154, 185,
   205, 241, 260, 268, 280,
   281, 282
2:11–13   318
3:17   190, 211, 315

1 Thessalonians
5:24   315

1 Timothy
2:5   294
3:16   260, 283, 352

Hebrews
1:3   283, 284

1:4   275, 278
1:4–5   306
10:5   59

1 John
2:22   187

Revelation
1:9   42, 177
1:11   185
9:12   42, 56
12:17   42
13:8   286
19:10   42
20:4   42, 71

Journal of Pentecostal Theology
Supplement Series

1. Steven J. Land, *Pentecostal Spirituality: A Passion for the Kingdom*. ISBN 1 85075 442 X.
2. Cheryl Bridges Johns, *Pentecostal Formation: A Pedagogy among the Oppressed*. ISBN 1 85075 438 1.
3. ** Jon Ruthven, *On the Cessation of the Charismata: The Protestant Polemic on Miracles*. ISBN 1 85075 405 5. ** Out of print. NEW EDITION: see no. 33.
4. Harold D. Hunter & Peter D. Hocken (eds.), *All Together in One Place: Theological Papers from the Brighton Conference on World Evangelization*. ISBN 1 85075 406 3.
5. Mark Wilson (ed.), *Spirit and Renewal: Essays in Honor of J. Rodman Williams*. ISBN 1 85075 471 3.
6. Robert P. Menzies, *Empowered for Witness: The Spirit in Luke-Acts*. ISBN 1 85075 721 6.
7. Stephen E. Parker, *Led by the Spirit: Toward a Practical Theology of Pentecostal Discernment and Decision Making*. ISBN 1 85075 746 1.
8. Larry R. McQueen, *Joel and the Spirit: The Cry of a Prophetic Hermeneutic*. ISBN 1 85075 736 4.
9. Max Turner, *Power from on High: The Spirit in Israel's Restoration and Witness in Luke-Acts*. ISBN 1 85075 756 9.
10. ** D. William Faupel, *The Everlasting Gospel: The Significance of Eschatology in the Development of Pentecostal Thought*. ISBN 1 85075 761 5. ** REPRINT by DEO
11. Wonsuk Ma & Robert P. Menzies, *Pentecostalism in Context: Essays in Honor of William W. Menzies*. ISBN 1 85075 803 4.
12. John Michael Penny, *The Missionary Emphasis of Lukan Pneumatology*. ISBN 1 85075 800 X.
13. John Christopher Thomas, *The Devil, Disease, and Deliverance: Origins of Illness in New Testament Thought*. ISBN 1 85075 869 7.
14. Samuel Solivan, *The Spirit, Pathos and Liberation: Toward an Hispanic Pentecostal Theology*. ISBN 1 85075 942 1.
15. Allan H. Anderson & Walter J. Hollenweger, *Pentecostals after a Century: Global Perspectives on a Movement in Transition*. ISBN 1 84127 006 7.
16. Roger Stronstad, *The Prophethood of All Believers: A Study in Luke's Charismatic Theology*. ISBN 1 84127 005 9.
17. Daniel E. Albrecht, *Rites in the Spirit: A Ritual Approach to Pentecostal/Charismatic Spirituality*. ISBN 1 84127 017 2.
18. Blaine Charette, *Restoring Presence: The Spirit in Matthew's Gospel*. ISBN 1 84127 059 8.
19. Matthias Wenk, *Community Forming Power: The Socio-Ethical Role of the Spirit in Luke-Acts*. ISBN 1 84127 125 X.

20. Amos Yong, *Discerning the Spirit(s): A Pentecostal-Charismatic Contribution to Christian Theology of Religions*. ISBN 1 84127 133 0.

21. Simon Chan, *Pentecostal Theology and the Christian Spiritual Tradition*. ISBN 1 84127 144 6.

22. Gerald Hovenden, *Speaking in Tongues: The New Testament Evidence in Context*. ISBN 1 84127 307 6.

23. Lynne Price, *Theology out of Place: A Theological Biography of Walter J. Hollenweger*. ISBN 0 82646 028 3.

24. Wonsuk Ma & Robert P. Menzies, *The Spirit and Spirituality: Essays in Honour of Russell P. Spittler*. ISBN 0 56708 167 2.

25. Peter Althouse, *Spirit of the Last Days: Pentecostal Eschatology in Conversation with Jürgen Moltmann*. ISBN 0 82647 162 5.

26. Martin William Mittelstadt, *The Spirit and Suffering in Luke-Acts: Implications for a Pentecostal Pneumatology*. ISBN 0 82647 164 1.

27. S. David Moore, *The Shepherding Movement: Controversy and Charismatic Ecclesiology*. ISBN 0 82647 160 9.

28. Kenneth J. Archer, *A Pentecostal Hermeneutic for the Twenty-First Century: Spirit, Scripture and Community*. ISBN 0 56708 367 5.

Volumes 1-28 were originally published by Sheffield Academic Press/Continuum. Subsequent titles are published by Deo Publishing under ISSN 0966 7393:

29. Kimberly Ervin Alexander, *Pentecostal Healing: Models in Theology and Practice*. ISBN 90 5854 031 6 / 978 90 5854 031 7.

30. Robby Waddell, *The Spirit of the Book of Revelation*. ISBN 90 5854 030 8 / 978 90 5854 030 0.

31. David Reed, *"In Jesus' Name": The History and Beliefs of Oneness Pentecostals*. ISBN 978 1 905679 01 0.

32. Lee Roy Martin, *The Unheard Voice of God. A Pentecostal Hearing of the Book of Judges*. ISBN 978 1 905679 07 2.

33. Jon Ruthven, *On the Cessation of the Charismata: The Protestant Polemic on Post-biblical Miracles*. Revised edition of no. 3. ISBN 978 1 905679 04 1.

34. Okopu Onyinah, *Pentecostal Exorcism: Witchcraft and Demonology in Africa*. ISBN 978 1 905679 06 5.

Pentecostal Commentary series titles are now also published by *Deo Publishing*.

Also published by Deo Publishing:
John Christopher Thomas, *The Spirit of the New Testament*. ISBN 90 5854 029 4 / 978 905854 29 4.